Hadley Hicks was legendary. Our lives intersected at Prescott High School....my admiration has matured into friendship with a devoutly religious man, an educator, motivator and coach; a man who is an ultimate practical joker. Hadley's love and enthusiasm for youth was contagious

Les Fenderson,
Teacher,
Prescott High, 1963-2007

A wise man once said, "Success in life is founded in relationships." I believe the readers will learn from Hadley Hicks as he shares from his 30 years of relationships in education. This book will be a valuable resource and inspiration.

Bob Young,
NAIA Coach of the Year, 1996

I am not surprised that Hadley Hicks wrote a book about his career in teaching-coaching. He approaches every situation with honesty, integrity, and a keen sense of humor. This book is a great guide for teaching, coaching and finding faith. Read on, you won't be disappointed.

Larry Gray,
Counselor,
Principal

So You Wanna Be a Legend.
So Did I.

The Reflections of a Teacher-Coach.
A Search for Significance.

Hadley Hicks

WestBow
PRESS

Copyright © 2010 Hadley Hicks

All rights reserved. No part of this book may be used or reproduced by any means, graphic, electronic, or mechanical, including photocopying, recording, taping or by any information storage retrieval system without the written permission of the publisher except in the case of brief quotations embodied in critical articles and reviews.

WestBow Press books may be ordered through booksellers or by contacting:

WestBow Press
A Division of Thomas Nelson
1663 Liberty Drive
Bloomington, IN 47403
www.westbowpress.com
1-(866) 928-1240

Because of the dynamic nature of the Internet, any Web addresses or links contained in this book may have changed since publication and may no longer be valid. The views expressed in this work are solely those of the author and do not necessarily reflect the views of the publisher, and the publisher hereby disclaims any responsibility for them.

ISBN: 978-1-4497-0231-1 (sc)
ISBN: 978-1-4497-0232-8 (e)

Library of Congress Control Number: 2010929969

Printed in the United States of America

WestBow Press rev. date: 8/31/2010

Contents

Dedication		vii
Preface		ix
Introduction		xi
PART ONE		**1**
Chapter 1	The Stuff Legends Are Made Of	3
Chapter 2	The University of Arizona	10
Chapter 3	My Pride Restored at Ft. Ord	31
Chapter 4	Arizona State *Sun Devils*	57
Chapter 5	Carmel High School	114
Chapter 6	Prescott High School	177
PART TWO		**199**
Chapter 7	Flagstaff High School	201
Chapter 8	The Death of The Legend	232
Chapter 9	I Messed Up !	249
Chapter 10	God Hates Divorce	261
Chapter 11	Sioux Falls College	277
Chapter 12	Sterling College	283
Chapter 13	Significance Found	332
Epilogue		347
My Thanks To......		353

DEDICATION

To my precious wife, Nancy, whose passionate intensity for our Lord Jesus Christ is a daily inspiration to me and our wonderful family.

To my Legacy:

Daughter Susie McDonald and her husband Dennis and their children
    Jason and his wife Camille
    Megan

Son Mike Hicks, with the Lord, and his wife Jean and their children
    Michael
    Taylor

Son Steve Hicks and his wife Lori and their children
    Joanna Street and her husband Keifer
    Luke Hicks and his wife Brianna and their son
    Nolan
    Elizabeth

Daughter Kristin Randolph and her husband Scott and their children
    Harrison
    Addie
    Jolie
    Quentin

Son Anthony Stecker and his wife Mieka and their children
    Annika
    Adrie
    Dylan
    Ethan
    Bennett

May this book be a testimony to my children forever.
Joshua 4:4-7

Preface

May the favor of our Lord our God rest upon us; establish the work of our hands for us-yes, establish the work of our hands.
Psalm 90:17

Bisbee, Arizona, July, 1952

I graduated from Bisbee High School in May of 1952 with what one might call celebrity status. I was the featured speaker at both the Arizona Boys' State and Arizona Girls' State opening ceremonies. I was invited to more civic club luncheons than I could work into my busy schedule. Sadly, I could not attend them all. It was at those men only affairs where I got my biggest ego strokes. The one I recall so vividly and enjoyed the most was when the master of ceremonies introduced me as, "Already a young man who has become a legend in Arizona.... Hadley Hicks!".

"*Hadley Hicks.....legend.*" I kind of liked that. It had a ring to it.

This is a book of memories.

The teammates, coaches, students, parents, teachers, and school administrators mentioned are real people. The experiences, events and my opinions associated with these people are based upon facts. Exact names, dates, and games may be a little hazy; by and large I stay in the ball park.

I was employed by five educational systems spanning 30 years; give or take a few years for various other ventures. For brevity's sake I highlight only a few key years and events.

The lessons learned and to be learned are some times obvious; some times not so obvious.

I have taken author privilege when a story involves dialogue. People and events mentioned in the author's first book, The B Shines Brighter: The Bisbee High School

Legacy are referenced by a (B). There is a God-thread woven throughout both books. Scripture references are The New King James Version.

My prayer is that this book will joggle the memories of some old timers out there who have devoted their lives to teaching-coaching our youth. Perhaps the book will encourage others who are currently swimming up-stream in our public education system. Most of all I pray that God will touch the readers as He did me. Teaching-coaching is a most rewarding profession. When done for Him, it reaps an Eternal reward.

INTRODUCTION

*For they loved the praise of men
more than the praise of God.
John 12:43*

BISBEE HIGH SCHOOL, BISBEE, ARIZONA
1948-1952

Miss Woundy, my Bisbee High School Senior English teacher, had a way about her that could make a cocky guy like me pause and ponder. I entered her class that first day of my Senior year in September of 1951 having heard a lot about Miss Woundy's strict, yet fair treatment of each student. I had been advised to sit in the first row; as close to her desk as possible. She usually paid more attention to the dunderheads who sat in the back of class. Kathy Phillips had saved me a seat next to her in the front row near Miss Woundy's desk.

As I strutted into class, Miss Woundy greeted me with, "Well, Hadley, it will be wonderful having the star with us this year. Welcome". I knew from that greeting that Miss Woundy knew. She knew I was the star.

My high school major was Eligibility. I worked hard at staying eligible for participation in sports. It would be no sweat staying eligible in Woundy's class. She knew.

As I left class that first day, Miss Woundy stopped me and said, "By the way, Hadley, do you know how Webster's Dictionary defines 'a star'? A star, according to the dictionary, is '..a self contained mass of gas.' Have a good day, Hadley." (B)

From 1948 to 1952 I had become the most well known high school athlete in the state of Arizona. I was an outstanding athlete, lettering in 15 out of a possible 16 varsity sports at Bisbee High School, a Class B school of 500 students.

I missed out on lettering in varsity basketball my freshman year through no fault of my own. I had flunked the first semester of freshman English and was therefore ineligible for basketball that winter.

Miss Shreve, freshman English teacher, had a thing about cool freshmen athletes. She expected them to attend all her classes, pay attention, and turn in work on time. She was most unreasonable.

In June 1951, I was elected Governor of Arizona Boys' State. I say this with all the modesty I can muster: I was fast becoming a legend. My high school football jersey, #20, was retired by Bisbee High School at the end of the 1951 football season.

I had grandiose aspirations for my future based upon my high school achievements and a well ingrained exalted self-concept. I was going to continue my stellar exploits on into college, then into the professional ranks of football or baseball.

In the meantime I would just be content to excel in football and baseball at the University of Arizona. I would likely be a four year starter for *The Wildcats* in both football and baseball; possibly I would letter in track as well.

After that I would consider my options. Would it be professional football or professional baseball? When my professional career was over, I would come back to my beloved Arizona with a wife and children. I would coach a few years on the high school level before becoming *the* head coach at The University of Arizona in either football or baseball; depending, of course, on which position was available at that time.

My beloved University of Arizona would find a spot for the legend somewhere.

The Legend
1951-1974

PART ONE

1948-1979

For He has made everything beautiful in its time.
Also He has put eternity in their hearts, except that
no one can find out the works that God
does from beginning to end.
Ecclesiastes 3:11

CHAPTER ONE

The Stuff Legends Are Made Of
1948-1952

Therefore, let him who thinks he stands take heed lest he fall.
1 Cor. 10:12

BISBEE, ARIZONA, MAY, 1952

The Warren Ball Park! (B) What a great place to hold graduation ceremonies! You talk about "A Field of Dreams". For most of us in the Bisbee High School Graduating Class of 1952, graduation on the green diamond of the Warren Ball Park rekindled memories and dreams that were as varied as those who harbored those memories and dreams.

For many of us, and for me personally, the memories went as far back as the early 1940's. Billy Martin and Clint Courtney (B), both destined to become Major League baseball players, were among my childhood idols. They played on this same diamond when they were rookies in the Arizona-Texas Minor League.(B) My dreams of playing major league baseball materialized about that time as well. As I grew older, my heroes were the Bisbee High *Pumas* who called the Warren Ball Park their home.

For the past six years I had played center field in this ball park; two years for The Bisbee American Legion team, then, four years for the Bisbee High *Pumas*. I played well enough to get looks from several major league scouts. The New York *Yankees* and the Chicago *Cubs* were the two teams who took the most interest. They both made attractive offers.

However, football was much more glamorous than baseball. I had made a reputation for myself throughout Arizona. One could even say my name was known nation wide as I had been selected on *The Wigwam Wisemen's High School All America Football Team* of 1951. My picture and the pictures of the others selected were prominently displayed on a full page in the February 13, 1952 issue of *SPORTING NEWS*. In fact, my picture was just to the left of the great Bart Starr of Green Bay *Packer* fame; he was the quarterback on that high school All America team. I was in good company.

I might mention, in all humility, that I was also selected on <u>High School Coach Magazine's</u> 1951 All America track team as one of the leading broad jumpers in the nation. My best jump was 23'5". I even practiced broad jumping a time or two after baseball practice. The broad jump-high jump pit that Coach Fuzzy Warren had dug was against the fence along the left field line of The Warren Ball Park.

Football was my game. I was indeed a legend in my own mind and in my own time. At that juncture, I was the all-time leading Arizona high school ground gainer with 4,440 total yards gained from scrimmage. I had scored 44 touchdowns. I had a number of touchdowns called back. The 4,440 yards were gained in three years as a running back and eight games per year.

In my freshman year I was the *Puma's* starting quarterback. I did gain one yard and a touchdown on a quarterback sneak my freshman year against Mesa High. I don't know if that yard is included in my over-all total.

All said, my football credentials were impressive; impressive enough to get scholarship offers from Notre Dame, Southern California, Tulane, The University of Colorado (which offered to pay for my wardrobe while I was a student there), Arizona State College (now Arizona State University) and The University of Arizona. I was indeed the stuff of which legends were made!

Though I could not verbalize my feelings as I marched across the Warren Ball Park infield to get seated for the graduation ceremony, I had tears in my eyes. This was the end of four great years for me.

I was the reigning Governor of The 1951 Arizona Boys' State; elected to that prestigious position the summer before. I was to swear in the 1952 Governor a few weeks after graduation. I was eagerly looking forward to that honor.

It was a long held tradition for the reigning Governor of Arizona Boys' State to give a speech to the Arizona Girls' Staters who held their conference at The University of Arizona in Tucson. I looked forward to gracing the Arizona Girls' Staters with my presence.

The reigning Governor of Arizona Girls' State would then honor the Boys' Staters with her presence at Arizona State College, Flagstaff, Arizona.

I hoped to begin another tradition. I planned to have a date with the Arizona Girls' State Governor when she came to Flagstaff for her visit with The Arizona Boys' Staters. Why not? After all, I was The Arizona Boys' State reigning Governor. And, Arizona Girls' State Governors were always very cute.

The second honor I was to receive that summer was an invitation to play in the Arizona High School All-Star Football Game. The All-Star game was held each summer in Flagstaff on the Arizona State College campus. I had turned down an invitation to play in the National High School All-Star Game in Montgomery, Alabama because as I reasoned, I planned to play football at The University of Arizona.

Since I was the biggest name in Arizona sports, I felt I owed it to my friends and the people of Arizona to play my last high school game in-state.

The graduation ceremony was finally over. I don't remember what the main speaker for the evening had to say. His name was Dr. O.K. Garrettson, Dean of the University of Arizona Education Department. I do remember that his speech was something about "The only security in the world is found in...". I paid little attention as I knew my security was in my athletic ability.

So You Wanna Be a Legend. So Did I.

I don't even remember what our two designated class brains, Salutatorian Bill Bonham and Valedictorian Dolly Belle Adams, had to say. I do remember a twinge of envy and resentment as they spoke; heck, I was the legend. I should have been either valedictorian or salutatorian. Our Bisbee High School Adiministration just placed too much emphasis on grade point average.

The speeches and music were finally over; now the fun begins! As we marched off the field to the traditional strains of *Pomp and Circumstance* my thoughts were on the uncontested, congratulatory kissing which was about to take place as we turned in our graduation gowns; we had to say "good bye" to many of our classmates.

Then, it was on to The Ft. Apache Drive-Inn Movie Theater where our after-graduation party took place. The parents of class mate Alexandra Diamos owned the drive-in. They graciously opened the concession area for an on-the-house food feast and dance.

My date for the after graduation party was Mary Louise Stensrud. She had been my steady and very best friend for the past four years. Mary Louise graduated the year before and had gone on to college at Arizona State College in Tempe, Arizona.

She attended the graduation ceremony that evening; obviously she was not with me when all the kissing of female class mates took place.

Needless to say, she was a bit miffed when I showed up with lipstick all over my face. What did she expect? I was the legend and had just graduated. It would not have been fair to the girls in my graduating class for me to refuse their advances. This "steady" business could only go so far.

We did not start off our date that evening on the best of terms. I took her home early and returned to the party. She wasn't having fun anyway and I was. Our relationship seemed to go down hill from that point on.

A few days later I was on my way to Tucson to give some words of wisdom to the girls attending Girl's State. There I met Sylvia Sanders, the reigning Governor of Girl's State. I was not disappointed. She was a cutie! After my speech, Sylvia and I agreed to a dinner date when she came up to Flagstaff the following week to address The Boy's Staters. The legend was moving fast!

I spent the next week in Flagstaff where I accepted the accolades of the 1952 Boy's Staters. The main questions from most of them were, "Are you going to play football and baseball at the University of Arizona? What are you going to major in?" My reply was a modest, "Well, I have a football scholarship, but I am sure baseball coach Frank Sancet wants me to play baseball as well. My college major is going to be History with a Physical Education minor."

On the first day of Boy's State at Arizona State College in Flagstaff, Sylvia Sanders, Girl's State Governor, arrived with three chaperones. I was not the least bit intimidated. I met Sylvia when she and the three ladies checked into the women's dormitory. I reminded her of our date.

The head chaperone, probably not at all well versed on my credentials, made a point of letting me know that Sylvia had an 8:00 pm appointment at the Boy's State opening assembly. Plus, she was adamant that Sylvia was not going anywhere after the assembly.

Being the charming person that I was, I talked the lady into letting me take Sylvia to dinner before the assembly. I promised to have her back in plenty of time for her scheduled appearance. It was then 5:00 pm. The head chaperone told Sylvia that she could go to dinner with me, but we had to go to a restaurant within walking distance of the Arizona State College campus. Sylvia was not to get in a car with me. Not exactly the kind of date I envisioned.

That date would prove to be one of the most embarrassing and humiliating events of my life!

Sylvia went to her room, freshened up, put on her best dress, and met me back in the lobby of the dorm. It was 6:00 pm. We walked to the nearest restaurant which was *The Golden Drumstick,* a very nice, upscale pre-*Kentucky Fried* place. It looked pretty swank when we walked in. The waiter showed us to a quaint, small table for two situated in the middle of a packed room. It was a perfect setting. People all around me. Most of them, I was certain, knew who I was. Being very much a gentleman, I pulled out the chair for Sylvia. I could just hear all the ladies thinking, *"...and he is such a gentleman, too.."*

Both Sylvia and I were dressed very elegantly. I had on a nice gray two piece suit complete with white shirt and a flashy tie. Sylvia was very lovely in a beautiful white dress. We both ordered a chicken dinner complete with salad and fries. Our conversation was very mature. I had asked her if she knew much about football. She said,"No", so I proceeded to review my gridiron accomplishments. She was completely in the dark about all of it. Her only comment was, "My, I didn't know you were so famous."

By that time, our meals were placed in front of us and we began to eat. Being a french fry connoisseur, I asked the waiter for a bottle of ketchup. The bottle he brought was a new, un-opened one. Knowing that it was probably uncouth to stick a knife up the neck of the bottle to get the flow started, I began to bang on the bottom of the bottle. Unfortunately the bottle was pointed directly in Sylvia's direction. When the bright red ketchup was pounded loose, it came forth with a vigorous *gush;* not only splattering all over my dish, but all over the front of Sylvia's lovely white dress as well!! How embarrassing! An audible gasp went up from the several tables near us. For the first time in my life, I hoped nobody knew that I was Hadley Hicks, All American!

Several kind patrons offered Sylvia napkins to wipe the mess off her dress. A waiter brought her a wet towel. Nothing helped. Her dress had a very noticeable red blob which extended from her waist up to her neck. And, she had a speech to deliver in less than an hour and a half!

Through it all, Sylvia showed that she was a "class" young lady. She was very poised and gracious. I was near tears humiliated almost beyond endurance. Before we could finish our meal, Sylvia informed me that we had better be leaving so she could change her dress before her scheduled speech. I was more than glad to leave. We prepared to leave in such a hurry that Sylvia had to inform me that I had not picked up the bill nor had I left a tip. I had a couple of quarters in my pocket. I left one for a tip, paid the bill and got out of there!

So You Wanna Be a Legend. So Did I.

We got back to the dorm in time for Sylvia to get re-dressed and make it to the assembly a few minutes before 8:00 pm. She gave an excellent speech.

After her speech, I met her at the dorm and apologized again for ruining her white dress. Sylvia, of course, was most kind and accepted my apology. She even said she was looking forward to seeing me at The University of Arizona in September. She said something about hoping I would make the rugby team. She had no clue.

The rest of that summer of 1952 flew by! As out-going Governor of Arizona Boys' State, I was obligated to speak at several civic organizations' state meetings. I enjoyed those as the folks were always most generous with their praises of my accomplishments. I never seemed to tire of people telling me how great I was. Through it all, I maintained my outward facade of humility.

I was very excited about playing in the Arizona All-Star Football Game. Bill Monahan, my Bisbee High *Puma* teammate, was also chosen to play in the All-Star Game. Bill was an offensive guard; a great blocker. He was the one mostly responsible for my 44 touchdowns.

We felt good about the team we would be on. Each year the two teams were comprised of players selected from the larger Arizona high schools, the Class A All-Stars; pitted against players from the smaller schools, the Class B All-Stars.

Our coaches were Coach Vern Braasch from Class A West Phoenix High School and Coach Jason "Red" Greer from Class A Tucson High School. Both were outstanding coaches. I always felt however that Class B coaches should have been coaching us; the Class B All Stars.

The All-Star selection committee had a stupid rule that had Class A coaches coaching the Class B team and Class B coaches coaching the Class A team.

The Class B coaches coaching the Class A team that year were newly appointed Bisbee High Coach Max Spilsbury (B) and Flagstaff High Coach Roy Smith.

Another very stupid rule was in effect. Each year the two teams, the Class A team and the Class B team, were required to alternate the offensive formations they were required to use. One team would use the basic T formation while the other team would use the not so basic single wing formation. Guess which team was designated to use the single wing that year? Yep, the Class B team!

Had we been able to use the T formation in that All-Star game, I really believe we could have held our own with the big guys. As it was, we got beat 19-0.

I did not come anywhere near gaining 100 yards; nor did I score a touchdown. But, I had an excuse. We were using the stupid single wing!

I felt I had let a lot of people down.

The most exciting part of the whole evening was in the locker room before the game when our coaches announced that my Bisbee High teammate Bill Monahan and I were elected by the team to be the team captains for the game. That was a great thrill for both of us.

My last high school football game was a complete failure. My only consolation was that I did not believe that Coach Warren Woodson at The University of Arizona used the stupid single wing! The legend was moving on.

An Early Seed

One event occurred about mid-week of the All-Star Game week that seemed most insignificant at the time. Yet, years later, approximately twenty-two years later, God harvested a fruit which had been slowly maturing from a seed which He planted that day in Flagstaff, Arizona.

Bill Monahan and I were dormitory room mates the week of the All Star Football Game. One morning I woke early. Looking down from the top bunk, I saw Bill on his knees, praying. I didn't think too much of it at the time.

Bill and I attended St. Patrick's Catholic Grade School (B) together for a couple of years. Though I was not Catholic, my parents on the advice of doctors sent me to the smallest school in Bisbee, Saint Patrick's Grade School. It was thought that I had tuberculosis and doctors advised as little physical activity as possible.

From my few years at St. Patrick's, I was used to seeing people praying. I did not even bat an eye at seeing Bill on his knees. After all, Bill was Catholic. Catholics were always praying.

That picture of Bill Monahan, a tough Irishman, humbly on his knees praying to the God of the universe, was tucked away in the back in my mind. God brought it to the fore on several occasions over the years. As that seed and others grew, the legend tended to shrink.

Another seed
Coach Jason "Red" Greer

My association with Tucson High School Coach Jason "Red" Greer that week at the All-Star Game would also prove to be meaningful to me later on in my life.

Coach Greer was one of the most highly respected high school coaches in the state of Arizona. His Tucson High School football teams were year-in and year-out always one of the top two or three teams in the state.

That past high school season, 1951, was the first time Bisbee High School had beaten Tucson High School in football. In one of the high-lights of my high school career, we beat Tucson High 21-12 on their Tucson home field. The state newspapers called it, *"The upset of the decade."*

When the game was over in the midst of the wild celebration of Bisbee High School players and fans, Coach Greer forced his way through the joyous crowd. He sought me out to shake my hand. He personally congratulated me on a fine game.

A week or so later, I received a nice letter from Coach Greer congratulating me once again. Coach Greer included a picture of me running with the ball during our upset of his team. He even autographed it, "Hadley, a picture of you 'in action' against Tucson High.....from Coach Jason 'Red' Greer". I have that cherished picture in my scrap book to this day.

It wasn't until one summer evening twenty-some years later that the picture and letter from Coach Greer took on a much deeper meaning. I was on my way back to my home in Flagstaff, Arizona after taking my daughter, Susie, and a couple of her friends to a cheer-leading camp in Arizona's White Mountains. As I drove along surfing the radio, I heard a Christian station interviewing a well known Christian personality. Something was said that made me pause and listen. The host of the program had said something like, "So it was your high school coach who was most responsible for you trusting in Christ?" The interviewee said, "Yes. Coach Jason 'Red' Greer had a huge Christian impact on me!"

I was a baby Christian at that time and hearing Coach Greer's name in a Christian context brought tears to my eyes. Through a hand shake, a letter and a picture from a losing coach, I had formed a concept of what a true sportsman was. I was to be reminded of Coach Greer's example many times during my future coaching years.

Coach Greer modeled for me the Christian coach I hoped to be.

CHAPTER TWO

The University of Arizona
1952-1954

The pride of your heart has deceived you.
Obediah 3

SEPTEMBER, 1952

My two years at The University of Arizona were the most miserable of my life. They had a most adverse effect on my search for significance. For many years after, my outlook on life was jaded. I have tried many times over the years to erase the University of Arizona experience from my memory. Much of the two years is shrouded in a mist.

I had such high expectations upon entering The University of Arizona. I was the legend! I was the focal point of so much of the pre-football season University of Arizona publicity. I was completely unprepared for what was about to happen.

UNIVERSITY OF ARIZONA FOOTBALL

Coach Woodson was in his first season at the helm of University of Arizona football. He was a highly successful coach at Harden Simmons University in Texas before accepting the head coaching position at the University of Arizona. While at Harden Simmons University, two of Woodson's running backs had led the nation in rushing: Doc Mobley and Hook Davis were household names during Woodson's tenure at Harden Simmons University.

Coach Woodson had told me on one of his recruiting visits that I was ideally suited for his offense. I had good size at 5'11" and 180 pounds and excellent speed. He assured me that I would see plenty of playing time as a freshman. Playing time, heck! I planned on being a starter!

I had been the subject of numerous newspaper articles prior to my arrival on the University of Arizona campus. A Bisbee High alumnus, and good friend, Lou Pavlovich (B), was the sports reporter for The Arizona Daily Star, one of Tucson's two major publications. The Tucson Daily Citizen was the other major paper. Abe Chanin was their sports editor. I knew Abe well from his coverage of high school sports during my years at Bisbee High. Both these men knew how to spell my name. They gave me plenty of ink!

Coach Woodson sent all freshmen recruits a letter telling us we had to report to campus on Saturday, two days before the start of official practices. The rest of the team was scheduled to report Sunday evening. Coach Woodson wanted us to have those two days to get familiar with our surroundings and each other before the veterans, the returning players came on board. We were required to attend all three meals each day plus several meetings interspersed between the meals.

At the Saturday breakfast we were introduced to the coaches and administrators who were associated with Coach Woodson. Among the assistant coaches that he introduced was a man who made my Bisbee High School blood boil. His name was Frank Sancet.

Mr. Sancet had been a coach at Bisbee's hated rival, Douglas High School for years, before going to the University of Arizona to be head baseball and assistant football coach. During basketball seasons Mr. Sancet officiated a lot of high school games. Though he had been gone from Douglas High School for a number of years, Bisbee fans still saw black and yellow, Douglas' colors, all over the man. His prejudice towards Bisbee High School was quite obvious when he worked BHS games; because of the number of our Bisbee High School basketball games he officiated, I got to know the man well. And, he me!!

One game in particular Mr. Sancet was worse than usual. He was calling many fouls on Bisbee High and me in particular; our fans were quick to let Mr. Sancet know what they thought of him. Some of the loud screams of displeasure were laced with obscenities and references to Mr. Sancet's ancestry. We all knew Mr. Sancet had rabbit ears. He heard all the uncomplementary loud barbs quite clearly. Unfortunately, they only served to solidify Mr. Sancet's already deeply seeded bias toward Bisbee High School.

As an athlete at the University of Arizona, I was destined to have much closer ties to Coach Sancet. Mr. Sancet was to be my University of Arizona baseball coach. He had built a nationally ranked baseball program and was considered by many to be one of the top college baseball coaches in the country. My relationship with him and his attitude toward me did nothing to convince me that Mr. Sancet ever rose above his immature prejudice toward Bisbee High School. Sancet's coaching techniques and his handling of young college athletes made a lasting negative impact on me. I learned from him, yes; but what I learned was how I did not want to handle young kids when I began my much anticipated journey into the teaching-coaching arena.

Other assistant coaches that Coach Woodson introduced to the freshmen that first day were Carl Cooper, Vane Wilson, Hank Stanton and Bob Herwig. These four men were quality coaches, in my opinion.

Coach Carl Cooper was one of the finest gentlemen I was privileged to ever be associated with. He was the University of Arizona's head track coach as well as an assistant football coach. He was friendly, kind and had a knack for encouraging his athletes. I always hoped that some of him rubbed off on me.

During the meeting, Coach Woodson encouraged us to go to church on Sunday, which was the next day. Since he didn't tell us we had to go to church I doubt if any of the freshmen took him too seriously except my Bisbee buddy, Bill Monahan and maybe some other Catholics among the freshmen. Catholics always went to church.

Coach Woodson ended the meeting with a reminder that our freshman only time would end at dinner on Sunday evening. The returning varsity players were going to be on hand to welcome us. We all wondered what that meant. What kind of reception would they give us?!

Since my home town, Bisbee, was only 90 miles from Tucson, I had watched a number of the Varsity play in the past several seasons, and was familiar with them by name. To be in the same room together was something else! It was pretty clear to all of us just who the veterans were. They all came in greeting each other with hugs, insults, punches and in general making it pretty obvious that the freshmen were to be seen and not heard.

My Bisbee High School teammate Bill Monahan and I were seated at the dinner table near one end of the room. Suddenly we both were engulfed by a huge mass of humanity! Two massive arms had gone around both of us and squeezed us together so hard that we banged heads. Of course, we couldn't see who had grabbed us but we found out soon enough.

"These two new *Wildcats* are to be treated with respect!", a loud voice announced, "They both are gentlemen, scholars, and tough football players from my home town of Bisbee, Arizona!" With that proclamation, Bill Deen laughed, roughed us up a bit and then shook our hands and told us he was glad to see us. Bill Deen had been a University of Arizona *Wildcat* for the past three years. He had been an all-state tackle for Bisbee High School our freshman year 1948. Monahan and I knew him well. We had watched him closely for the past three years and had seen him develop into a starter for the *Wildcats*. It was comforting to see a familiar face.

After dinner, for a half hour or so we just milled around, shaking hands and being greeted by the returning players.

To be honest, I had some worries that maybe I wouldn't be well accepted due to the amount of publicity I had received in all the Arizona newspapers. My picture accompanied many of the articles so I was pretty well known by all those in the room. I received nothing but warm, sincere, greetings; they were ok guys.

Some of the veterans made some wise-cracks aimed at me. They were joking and I knew it. I knew better than to return the jokes. I just smiled and pretty much kept my mouth closed. Humility was the order of the day for me. When we had our first workout Monday morning I would have my chance then to show them all what the legend could do!

Coach Woodson told the freshman that he considered us one of his best recruiting classes of his coaching career. He told us that if we all stuck together we would certainly bring national recognition to the University of Arizona by the time we were seniors. He encouraged us to be diligent in the classroom; to be gentlemen on campus and to take our positions as *Wildcat* football players seriously. We were expected to live up to the team rules of conduct Coach Woodson and his coaches outlined for us.

He told us quite candidly that in his past experience as head coach on the college level that there was no doubt some among us would not have what it takes to make it on the college level. He said some would probably flunk out, quit for personal reasons or find out that they just weren't cut out to be college football players. He was certain however, that most of us had what it took. There was no doubt in my mind that I was one of the latter. The legend would continue to be an Arizona household name!

We were rudely awakened bright and early Monday morning by Coach Sancet. I could have guessed. Sancet was loudly blowing his whistle as he walked down the isles of sleeping freshman: "It is 6:00 am. Time to rise and shine. Breakfast in 30 minutes!"

After breakfast, we headed to the practice field which was adjacent to *Wildcat* Field, our game field. We freshmen were the first ones there. We all grouped together waiting for the coaches and veterans to show up. We had been told that practice would start at 8:00am promptly.

At approximately 7:50am some of the veterans strolled on the field, cocky and pretty self assured, I thought. Next came the rest of the veterans, and bringing up the rear were the coaches. The coaches walked right by us and went into the locker room underneath the stadium. The team captains who had been introduced to us the night before were seniors Gil Gonzales, an outstanding veteran running back whom I planned on beating out, quarterback Alan Stanton, and guard Jim Donarski who was receiving pre-season All America publicity. Those three led us into the stadium locker room. We were to be issued lockers and our football gear.

Each locker had a player's name neatly printed on a piece of tape on the screened-door. Inside each locker were two brand new, gray T-shirts with *Wildcat Football* boldly emblazoned across across the front. Two towels hung on hangers underneath a shelf which held a small bottle of shampoo, a bar of soap in a soap dish, and two pairs of sweat socks. On hangers in the locker hung our practice shorts and practice shirt. We were to be issued our pads on the next Monday. The first week of practice, by Border Conference rule were shorts and helmets only.

Coach Woodson told us to find our personal locker, sit on the bench in front of it, and wait for further instructions. Those further instructions would come from Ed Thomas, The *Wildcats'* equipment manager. Coach Woodson then introduced Ed to us. Ed was greeted by raucous cheers, jeers, applause and cat-calls by the veterans. Ed was obviously well liked and respected. His domain was the entire underneath part of the west side of Arizona Stadium.

Ed Thomas was one of those men you just couldn't help but like. He was a friendly black man with a head of snow white hair. His speech to us was short, but to the point. We were told that we would be issued clean practice equipment each Monday, Wednesday, and Friday. We would get a clean towel, two pair of clean socks, and a clean jock daily. Ed assured us that he would take good care of us. The veterans verified that with loud applause and many jocular remarks when Ed finished his talk.

On one of the forms we filled out earlier in the week, we indicated the size of football-shoes and helmet size. The shoes did not present much of a problem. The problem, as we got our equipment from Ed, was the fitting of our helmet. We had all been told horror stories by the veterans about getting used to the helmet.

I soon learned that the horror stories were all true! When Ed fit me for my helmet, he told me that he automatically reduces the indicated size we had written on our equipment form by "a tad." My hat size was 7 1/4. Ed gave me a size 7 helmet. The next thing Ed did was to smear a glob of Vaseline on the head-band which was suspended away from the hard inner core of the plastic helmet by an elaborate system of numerous web straps. Even with that, he still had to twist and force my helmet down on my head. "The tighter the safer" was Ed's theory. Ed told us that the thing we had to do each time we put the helmet on before practice was to smear Vaseline on the suspension web-headband. "It'll cut down on forehead blisters," Ed told us. It didn't. After just two days of wearing that thing, my forehead was rubbed raw. Ed's final touch to insure a snug helmet fit was to whack me over the head with a sawed off piece of a baseball bat. "Now, that is a feeling you have to get used to," Ed warned me.

He said the leather helmet I wore at Bisbee High, while being much more comfortable, would not protect my head from the vicious blows I would encounter playing college football. Leather helmets were a thing of the past. Heavy plastic helmets were in. I hoped Ed was right.

In the meantime, I had to endure the agony of an impossibly tight fitting, excruciatingly painful, ten ton plastic bubble forced down and twisted to conform to the size of my egg-shaped head. In short, the helmet was not at all comfortable. Besides that, I had to live with a splitting headache for hours after I took the thing off at the end of practice.

A New Concept for the Legend
Conditioning

Coach Woodson told us that the first practice each morning would be mainly for conditioning purposes. The afternoon and evening practices would be conditioning combined with learning Woodson's offensive and defensive schemes.

We hit the practice field running. We were never to walk on to the practice field. We were to jog a lap around the field and then "stretch out."

I learned an athletic adage my senior year in high school; it would become gospel for me in my coaching career; namely, "Never stretch a cold muscle." One should always jog a lap to warm up the leg muscles before doing stretching exercises.

I learned the hard way the value of stretching daily. In high school, we would jog a few times back and forth across the field, do a few jumping jacks and were then ready to go full steam without stretching. Not a good idea. I severely pulled my ham-string muscle in a track meet my senior year in high school which prevented me from running in the State Track Meet.

After the team was completely warmed up and stretched out that first practice, we were put into groups by positions to run 50 yard wind sprints. Coach Woodson placed a lot of emphasis on speed; he had a manager record the fastest two or three in each group. I was in the group of backs which included the quarterbacks, fullbacks and halfbacks. There were only three quarterbacks who were being considered Varsity; Alan Stanton; Skip Corley and Bruce McCauley. There were four varsity fullbacks; Kurt Storch, Don "Brother Beas" Beasley, Carl Beard, and fellow freshman Bob Jacobs, my Boys' State buddy (B) from North Phoenix High School. The halfback position was where it got very interesting. There were approximately ten of us and counting the wingbacks ("flankers" in Woodson's Wing-T offense), it was closer to 15.

I made sure I lined up as close to Gil Gonzales as I could. Gil was the returning starter and pre-season All Border Conference selection. We ran five - 50 yard wind sprints that first practice. I came in first all five. I was surprised to find out that Gonzales was either third or fourth in each of the sprints. Two small backs named Kenny Cardella and Bobby Umphress alternated coming in second to me each time followed by wing back Bobby Jackson.

While catching my breath one time between sprints, fullback Brother Beas came up beside me and said, "Comet, (a nickname given me by sports writer, Lou Pavlovich) for a white boy, you can really run." He was smiling as he said it, but he didn't smile when he continued, "....but, it takes more than just picking 'em up and settin' 'em down to be a good college running back. Keep your eyes on Mr. Gilbert Gonzales. He is a good one!" I remembered his words and soon found out that Brother Beas was a pretty astute judge of football talent.

That first week of conditioning flew by. According to Coach Woodson we had pretty much accomplished our goals for that week. Our immediate objective was to get ready for our first scrimmage the following Wednesday. We would don full pads on Monday. It was quite a shock to most of the freshman to go out for practice that Monday morning wearing full pads. We didn't feel quite as fast. Our helmets, though, had begun to form to our heads. The sweat and Vasceline soaked suspension web-head band had adjusted to our head size and caused little discomfort.

"Practice: Full Pads"

That was a message we were to see on our posted practice schedule every practice for the next several weeks: "Practice: Full Pads". The first day in full pads we loosened up and stretched just as we had been doing for the past week. However, the coaches and veterans took on a decidedly much more business-like approach. I was to find out rather quickly that the fun and games of high school football were a thing of the past. From here on it was all business

After our warm-up and stretching period, we immediately went to our usual group drills. My group consisted of the quarterbacks, halfbacks and fullbacks. The halfbacks and fullbacks lined up in three lines behind the three quarterbacks. We worked on the quarterbacks vocal cadence and snap-count and the ball carrier's take-off on the snap count. Quickness was of the utmost essence. Coach Woodson emphasized "quick to the hole" meaning that on the quarterbacks first sound of the designated snap-count the halfback should be one step into full speed toward the line of scrimmage. It was a fairly simple drill in shorts and helmets. We were in full pads and this simple hand-off drill took on a mild form of mayhem. Waiting for us at the hand off point were two defensive players each holding a blocking bag. The ball carriers were expected to blast through the two bag-holders whose job was to pummel the ball carrier, knock him down or make him fumble the ball. I ran this drill often in high school so I jumped to the head of the line to show the others how the legend from Bisbee High School did it. On my first attempt, I was met from my waist up to my head with an unmovable mass of two bodies. They refused to let me go through. Being an All-America high school running back, I deftly stepped to the side and went around them. No sweat! I thought I had weathered that challenge pretty well. Coach Woodson didn't.

"Hadley, that is not the way a *Wildcat* ball carrier will hit a hole. You were running straight up and down. You will get your head torn off if you do that when we scrimmage. When you sense you are going to be hit, you are to lower your shoulder and deliver a blow! Please do not ever again run to a hole and try to run around it. You will be met by a number of unblocked people who will delight in tearing you apart. Now, please stand aside and watch Mr. Gonzalez hit the hole properly."

I learned several lessons. First of all, I vowed to never again volunteer to be first. Let somebody else incur the sarcasm of Coach Woodson. Secondly, I learned how a veteran like Gil Gonzalez did it. He literally hit the hole with so much force that he lifted one of the defensive bag holders off the ground! Well, I was still faster than he was.

The rest of that morning's practice, as well as the second practice at 7:00pm that evening, went pretty much the same. A lot of running plays against defensive players holding dummies. A lot of freshman either gaining confidence or else floundering in the throes of doubt. I was never one who lacked confidence. I could hardly wait until we scrimmaged on Wednesday!

Tuesday's practices were a little more intense. We had some tackling drills where the defensive players delivered some hits on the ball carriers at 3/4 speed; meaning we were hit hard but were not taken to the ground. I thought I did pretty well. And, I think Coach Woodson thought so too. I was alternating with Gil Gonzalez at half back. I understood Coach Woodson's thinking. He could not just designate me as the number one halfback because that would be too humiliating to Gil Gonzalez. After all, he had three good years and was pretty well installed at the *Wildcats'* starting halfback. Probably by the first game in a couple of weeks against Hawaii, I would prove to all concerned that the legend was worthy of being the starting halfback.

I was a little disappointed when Wednesday's practice schedule was posted on the bulletin board outside our locker room. It said we would have a 45 minute "half-line scrimmage". John Lowry, one of our senior linemen, informed me that meant we would scrimmage only one side of the line against one side of the defensive line. In other words we would run plays to one side of the field only. We had not practiced much on a passing attack, so it would be a run only scrimmage.

My already evident ego got a sudden boost when Coach Woodson said I was the starting halfback for the first series of plays. My Boys' State buddy, Bob Jacobs was the fullback who was with me. Our quarterback was senior Alen Stanton. All he would do was hand the ball off to either Bob Jacobs or me.

The first time I carried the ball, I ran through a good sized hole between veterans Bill Deen and Rollie Kuhel; I outran a defensive back to the side line.

Coach Cooper blew his whistle signaling the end of the play. Feeling pretty good about my first carry against live, aiming to injure defensive players, I trotted back to my group of offensive players. No comment from Coach Woodson who was closely observing. I took that as a good sign. I learned in high school to always compliment the linemen when I made a sizeable gain. I did so when I got back to our huddle.

All in all, I felt the scrimmage went well for the offense. I ripped off several good gains as did Bob Jacobs and Mike Kelly. I was rather surprised that not many of the veterans got much action. Gil Gonzalez did not scrimmage at all, nor did fullbacks Kurt Storch or Don Beasley.

Coach Woodson informed us after the 45 minutes were up that by and large, he was pleased with the effort put forth. He said we would do more of the same for the rest of the week and that we would have our first full scale, game-condition scrimmage one week from the coming Saturday two weeks before our home opener against The University of Hawaii *Rainbows*.

Coach Woodson had not spent much practice time on defense. He was an offensive coach. He felt that offense scores the touchdowns and therefore, the offense wins the games. I tended to agree with him. Offense wins games.

That philosophy would plague me my entire football coaching career.

THE SEASON BEGINS

The media build up to the first game of the 1952 University of Arizona football season was pretty much focused on Coach Warren Woodson and the new life he had brought to the football program. His high powered run-oriented offense was getting rave reviews and I seemed to be an integral part of that offense according to my friends in the press, Lou Pavlovich of the Arizona Daily Star and Abe Chanin of the Tucson Citizen.

The Monday prior to our season opener against the University of Hawaii *Rainbows,* the Arizona Daily Star had a three-column picture of "four pre-season standouts": Don Beasley, 190 lb. fullback from Mesa, Arizona, Hadley Hicks, 175 lb. freshman tailback from Bisbee, Arizona, Alan Stanton, 175 lb. quarterback from Clifton, Arizona, and Dave Richards, 185 lb. wingback from West Pittston, Pennsylvania. The caption read "...these four will see much action against the Hawaiians."

I could hardly wait for that first game. I felt very much a part of the team.

The entire team was supportive of me. I got encouragement from the veterans and I felt as though I had earned the respect of my fellow freshman. In every scrimmage I felt as though my performance was every bit as impressive as anyone else's. Coach Woodson, at times, went out of his way to give me encouragement. Gil Gonzalez spoke with me several times about how quickly I was picking up my offensive assignments. It didn't seem to bother him too much that I would probably take his starting position away from him.

Saturday night, September 20, 1952 finally came. Looking back on that evening, it was the beginning of the most dismal time of my athletic career. We beat the undermanned University of Hawaii *Rainbows* 57-7. I carried the ball a grand total of four times. I gained 52 yards total and had a "beautiful" (according to my dad) run of 28 yards called back because of an off sides penalty. I was pretty much relegated to the bench most of the game. Our offense moved the ball up and down the field at will. Gil Gonzalez had over 100 yards rushing, freshman Mike Kelly had 90 yards and Alan Stanton passed for almost 200 yards.

The second game of the season was even more disheartening for me. We ran all over New Mexico A & M 62-12. I carried the ball only two times, one for a 54 yard touchdown in the second quarter. And that was it! Back to the bench for the legend. You talk about being down in the dumps! That was me. My friends and some of my teammates tried to boost my spirits. They said, "Have patience. Your time will come."

What was disturbing to me was that Coach Woodson seemed to be ignoring me in practices. He never did tell me what, if anything, I was doing wrong. My personality was such that I was not aggressive enough to seek Coach Woodson out and ask him why I wasn't getting much playing time. I tried to tell myself that I would see more action the next game.

The next game came and went. I sat the entire game on the bench. We beat the University of Utah 27-0. Gil Gonzalez got slightly injured in the second quarter and freshman Mike Kelly played the rest of the game at tailback. Mike played well but I still felt I had more speed than Mike and could have had more of an impact on the game.

We lost the next game to the University of Colorado 19-34. I carried the ball one time with ten seconds left in the first half and got clobbered for a four yard loss!

The next week we left Tucson to fly to Wisconsin where we played Marquette University. The temperature at the airport when we left Tucson was a balmy 83 degrees. When we arrived in Wisconsin, the temperature was a frigid 46 degrees at 1:00 PM! By game time the temperature had plummeted to 29 degrees. Cold!

By this time Coach Woodson had made me a permanent member of the special teams. Those are the guys who are expected to sacrifice their bodies for the good of the team. I was on the kick off return team. Marquette clobbered us 37-7, which meant they kicked off six times! That meant that I had to throw off the warm side-line jacket and hobble out to our goal line. My legs felt frozen solid. I was praying fervently that they would not kick to ball to me. This was one time the legend did not want anything to do with the football! I got it twice! Both times when I was tackled I felt like every frozen bone in my body was snapped in two. Not much fun!

The remaining five games on our schedule found the legend playing on special teams and wallowing in self-centered depression. We won three of those remaining five games and I saw very little playing time except for special team appearances.

The biggest game on the University of Arizona schedule is always against arch rival Arizona State College (now Arizona State University). Arizona State was loaded that year! And surrounded by controversy.

St. Mary's College, in California, had given up football and some how a number of their more outstanding players found their way to Tempe, Arizona, home of the Arizona State *Sun Devils*.

Rumor had it that Arizona State had some underhanded dealings with the St. Mary's athletes and had convinced them to finish their careers at Arizona State. Rumor also had it that several of those players had used up their eligibility the season before at St. Mary's College. One of those suspected players was their All America running back, John Henry Johnson. John Henry was a 6'2", 230 pound mass of muscle with "tree-stumps" for legs. He was huge, tough, mean and fast! And he saved my life!! The only reason I am here today writing the story is because of John Henry Johnson.

JOHN HENRY JOHNSON SAVED MY LIFE

From the first day of practice back in August of 1952 the entire team was well aware that we would be playing against one of the best running backs in America later that year. John Henry Johnson's reputation of meanness and somewhat unethical playing tactics had been well publicized. John Henry was no shrinking violet. He would just as soon grind his cleats in your face, if you got in his way, as look at you.

For this game I was assigned to the kick-off team. I was the left end. I had one and only one duty on that team: "...do not let anyone get outside you. Hicks, you are to run down the field and ..*do not let anyone get outside you!...*".

Simple enough. Just make sure the ball carrier does not get between me and the sideline. Funnel the ball carrier back into the rest of our players.

When we kicked off to start the game, it was obvious which one was John Henry Johnson. He was number *34*, the massive one standing on the goal line who seemed to just be daring us to kick the ball to him. Foolishly, we did.

John Henry received the ball and started those powerful legs pumping. He was headed straight up the field well away from me. I figured he had been told that the legend was manning the right side and that nobody would ever get around the legend. As John Henry started up the middle, I remember thinking, *"He's probably afraid of me; he knows who I am."*

When John Henry was about, 20 away from me, he suddenly cut sharply to his right and was headed straight towards me! I remember thinking: *"Oh, crap!"*.

It was at that point that John Henry saved my life. He got within five yards of me and cut back into the middle. He was tackled 15 yards on down the field. I did not know who tackled him. I had my eyes closed. Had he kept coming at me he would have simply run over me and killed me. He saved my life by cutting back into the middle, away from the legend.

The rest of the game was nip and tuck. I had a good view from the bench. Arizona State beat us 20-18. John Henry scored all three Arizona State touchdowns and had over 100 yards rushing. We saw more of John Henry than we wanted. We got a preview of a future All-Pro running back, a great football player who today, is enshrined in the National Football League Hall of Fame.

John Henry Johnson played many years for the San Francisco *49'ers,* the Detroit *Lions,* and the Pittsburg *Steelers.*

I have always been thankful to John Henry Johnson; he saved my life.

It Finally Ends

The season ended with a 57-7 win over winless Texas Western (now the University of Texas at El Paso...UTEP) and a 14-19 loss to Texas Tech. I saw very little action in those two games. I felt as though I had let down my family, my friends and to some extent, the people of Arizona. It was very difficult for me to keep my head up. As I walked to my classes in the days preceding the last game, I felt as though everyone I passed was laughing at me. *"Bisbee High School All-American....HA!"* My self-esteem was at rock bottom. Some of my closest friends tried to console me. Two of my teammates said that if I was from Texas I would have been ahead of Mike Kelly. Mike was from Ennis, Texas. Coach Woodson was from Texas.

An overwhelming feeling that I had lost significance dominated my total being. Why hadn't I played more? I was as good as those other guys. No, I was better than those other guys. Why hadn't I played more?

My roommate in Hopi Lodge and long time Bisbee buddy, Charlie Leftault had to endure most of my self-contained pity party. He could only offer one suggestion: "Go talk to Coach Woodson about it."

Coach Woodson had a personal meeting with every player on the team shortly after the season ended. He wanted to evaluate each player's performance during the season and discuss what he expected for next season.

My meeting time with Coach Woodson came several weeks after the season had ended. I went into the meeting with a lousy attitude. I expected a long harangue about how I had let the team down, how I loafed, how I was a big disappointment to him. I had no idea what he would say. I just knew that I did not want to talk to him. I felt I had better things to do than to spend several hours listening to Coach Woodson criticize my performance. The whole state of Arizona was doing that already.

I was trying to work up the nerve to tell him, "Yeah, well, if you had let me play more I would have showed you what I could do." I wish I would have had the nerve to have confronted him with, "If I was from Texas, would I have played more?"

I have to admit that I was surprised when I met with him. The meeting lasted no more than fifteen minutes and all he said was that he had appreciated my attitude during the year. He said he looked forward to having me back for the spring practices. I was one of the more experienced tailbacks returning and I should have an outstanding year next season. When I told him I was planning on going out for baseball, he acted disappointed but was supportive of that. He was no doubt well aware of my baseball potential and aspirations. His last question to me was one that totally took me by surprise. He asked me if I went to church. My reply was, "Sometimes". I had heard rumors during the year that Coach Woodson was very religious. He went to a Baptist Church. He encouraged me to get in the habit of church attendance. Then he excused me. That was the last time I ever spoke with Coach Woodson.

His final comments to me about going to church hung around in the back of my mind for many years. All I could think about at the time, however, was how horrible my life was. I was wallowing in self-pity, depression and loss of self-esteem. It would only get worse.

"The Country Club of the West"

When I chose the University of Arizona over The University of Southern California upon graduating from high school, my uncle who was a huge Southern Cal fan was most disappointed. He said, "Hadley, I never thought you would ever choose 'The Country Club of The West' over the Southern Cal *Trojans!* You know you are going to the biggest party school around, don't you?"

Well, to be honest I was not too concerned about the party aspect of the University of Arizona. But what I was anxious about was the number of cute and rich girls who were purported to abound on campus.

The football team had been practicing for several weeks when the rest of the students started to flood the campus. The favorite gathering place for the football team between practices was the Student Union Building in the middle of campus. That was the best place to evaluate and "eye-ball" the cute girls.

I knew that when I walked in the Union with my studly Freshman football buddies, each of us proudly wearing our gray football T-shirts with WILDCAT FOOTBALL prominently splashed across the front, that the girls would all know who I was.

It didn't take me too many days to realize that most of the girls did not know who I was, nor did they care. I noticed too, that the other macho football players were getting ignored by most of the girls just as I was. Our WILDCAT FOOTBALL chest sign boards seemed to have the opposite effect on the girls. They seemed to be more interested in the "hots", a term some attached to the fraternity men. The hots had the cars and money, and seemingly, the attention of the girls the cute ones, anyway.

That revelation was quite a blow to my ego! I had a hard time believing that the cute girls did not read the sport pages. The legend was in their midst and they were oblivious to the gift that was so readily available. On the advice of my roomie, Charlie Leftault, and Karl Eller, a senior football player, I quit wearing my football T-shirt. I tried to just blend in with the other students. It was painfully obvious that the majority of the girls and the student body in general considered any jock, not just a football player, as nobody special. Freshman jocks especially had to earn the right to be given priority status among the upper-echelon of students. I sensed that right began when one became a hot.

The only ones who seemed to care who I was at the University of Arizona were my Bisbee High buddies Bill Wagner, Hooty Howell and Bill Owen. I ate all my meals with them. I think they were as homesick as I was.

Charlie Leftault was a fraternity man but he wasn't a hot; he was a good guy. Charlie was a Phi Gamma Delta, but he lived in Hopi Lodge with the rest of us "commoners". The hots lived in *The House,* the term by which hots reverently identified their respective fraternity houses. The University's caste system soon became apparent to me. To be someone of importance on campus you had to belong to a fraternity. You had to be a hot.

Why the Big "Rush"?

My Bisbee buddy and roommate, Charlie Leftault, spent the entire first semester of our time together in Hopi Lodge telling me about his fraternity, the Phi Gams or the *Fijis*, as they were commonly referred to.

Charlie was a junior at the University of Arizona and he had been an active in the Fiji house for a year. Charlie was a big man on campus. He was very popular, an excellent student, a varsity basketball player and an all-around good guy. He had me pretty well convinced that I needed to belong to the Fijis.

By the end of that first semester, after an ego deflating football season, I was well aware that to be someone of importance on campus, the fraternity route was the best way for me to go. Wrong! Big mistake!!

"Rush" was the vernacular in fraternity-sorority terms for "kiss-up to those who could enhance the prestige of your house". In short, the actives in a particular fraternity or sorority would fawn over influential potential members. And I ate it up!

Those big shot actives buttered me up and made me feel like I was just what the Fijis needed to make their house the best one on campus. They had me believing that I was the only one they were interested in. Without any doubt that was just what my bruised and battered ego needed.

I was invited to lunch at the Fiji house every Monday. The first lunch I attended was in the middle of the football season and to be among guys who didn't seem to give a rip if I played or not was refreshing. They seemed to accept me as being a huge prize just as I was. The other guys who had been invited to lunch seemed like good guys. They were obviously men of stature, as I knew I was. Possibly they would be invited to become active Fijis along with me.

My first infrequent taste of fraternity life was good. I was made to feel I was something special. Those guys seemed to remember that I was the legend even if football coach Warren Woodson didn't. However, as soon as I pledged to become an active member of The Phi Gams things began to go south fairly rapidly.

When we pledges received our invitations to become proud members of the Fiji pledge class, we were made to feel like very special freshmen. We were on our way to becoming big men on campus. I soon became aware that there was a degree of hypocrisy among some of the active Fijis.

There was an active Fifi in one of my classes. His name was Harry. I had met Harry several times when I visited the house so I felt I knew him. You would never know that Harry realized I even existed when he came into class. Harry usually came in to class after I did; he sat in the same row as I did. In order for Harry to get to his seat, he had to practically climb over me. More often than not, when he shuffled sideways past me to his seat, he would not even acknowledge that I was there. It was rare when he even said hello. Yet, when I went to the special pledge lunches, or any other social functions at the house, Harry greeted me like we were the best of buddies. He gave me hand shakes, pats on the back and great big smiles. I kept thinking, *Phony!*

So You Wanna Be a Legend. So Did I.

I noticed other forms of hypocrisy in the whole Fiji social structure. For instance, a Fiji would get house merit points for dating girls who had stature, both physical and social stature on campus.

It was frowned upon when I dated my Bisbee High School sweetheart, Mary Louise Stensrud. Mary Louise was not in a sorority and transferred from Arizona State College at Tempe that fall. She was not on campus long enough to gain stature. Yet, when I dated Sylvia Sanders, the 1951 Governor of Arizona Girls' State, I got merit points since Sylvia came to campus with "stature".

It was also pretty well known that girls were awarded status if they had a number of squaw dresses. Squaw dresses were very much in on campus and were a sign of wealth. Wealth played a big part on the stature of a girl. A Fiji got more merit points if his date wore squaw dresses. He really got merit points if his date wore an expensive, Navajo Indian squash blossom necklace along with her squaw dress.

THE BLUE ROOM
What a Joke!

Once a week the new pledges were rounded up after the required Monday evening meal and ushered into the dreaded *Blue Room*. The sole purpose of The Blue Room was to break us, to humble us, to show us we were not yet quite human. Only after we became actives would we become worthy of being called "Phi Gam Fijis".

Upon entering The Blue Room, we were told to sit in a circle on the floor. We sat in a darkened room with only a soft blue iridescent glow. Surrounding us, seated comfortably in easy-chairs and couches were a number of the actives. We were required to begin the whole childish experience by introducing ourselves, giving our first, middle and last names. We were told nicknames would not be used when addressing each other.

The actives then went around and introduced themselves by first, middle and last names. We were to memorize everyone's first, middle and last name. We spent a good 45 minutes each session repeating their full names. After the introductions, the actives took turns singling out the pledges individually and telling us what they did not like about us. We were to take these constructive criticisms seriously and work diligently to try to correct the faults we were told about.

One of the actives was a guy I played football against in high school. His name was Curtis Jennings. Curtis and I had had several good natured give and takes about his high school, Safford High, and mine, Bisbee High. We argued the merits of each.

Curtis was a good guy when he wasn't in The Blue Room. In the Blue Room his whole personality was transformed. He became mean and cynical. His first attack on me was, "Hadley Fergus Hicks, you are too 'rah-rah'. You have to grow up. You are no longer in high school. I see you as a child trying to exist in an adult world. Grow up, Hadley Fergus Hicks!" Curtis obviously did not care that I was the legend.

Each Blue Room session lasted approximately 2 hours. Each active got in some good jabs at each pledge in the room. Then, the pledges were required to go around and elaborate on the faults of each other. I am afraid I did not take any of this very seriously. Once when I was supposed to rip into my Bisbee buddy and fellow pledge, Frank "Paco" Day, I got off to a bad start when I called him "Paco". One of the actives immediately called me down for that. He told me Paco was his nickname. I was reminded that I was to respect my fellow Fijis and not call them by their nicknames.

I replied by going into an unsolicited explanation: "Paco was born in Cananea, Sonora, Mexico and his given Mexican name is Paco and his American nickname is Frank. At Bisbee High we always called him Paco. All the teachers called him Paco."

The active wasn't at all impressed with my explanation. He shouted at me, "The trouble with you, Hadley Fergus Hicks, is that you live in the past. You are no longer at Bisbee High School. If you want to be a Fiji, you must remember that! And to become a Fiji, you must abide by the standards established by many fine and revered Fijis before you. So shut up and get serious!"

From that point on my sarcastic reply when I was told to be constructively critical of a fellow pledge was, "Sorry, I don't know any of them well enough yet. But I am sure that as soon as I get to know them I will have many uncomplimentary remarks to make about these, my fellow underlings."

The actives made it pretty plain that my attitude needed adjustment. However, I was not too worried about being "de-pledged". I was too big a catch for the Fijis. I was the legend. They wanted me too badly.

The only thing that would keep me from ever becoming an active and a member in good standing in The House of the Fijis was....

My Academic Standing

I could not believe how lacking in compassion both my high school teachers and my university professors were! I could understand my high school teachers being so unreasonable. After all, they were high school teachers who had lived in my home town of Bisbee, Arizona for many years. They all knew my parents.

The college professors did not know me from Adam. Sure they had heard of "Hadley Hicks, All American". However, in their classes, I was a number. When I was absent from class, the senior assistant for that class merely looked down each row of desks. Upon seeing my empty desk, he would put a check mark in the absent column by desk #32, my assigned desk. So very impersonal!

It took me a month or so to realize I was not doing very well in most of my classes. Football took a lot of time.

Freshman footballer, big John Mellekas took a lot of time too. He often came in my dorm room to insist I go with him to get some pizza, a new craze at The University.

Big John, a freshman tackle from Los Angeles, did not know a lot of people at the U of A. I felt I needed to befriend big John. He could have gotten homesick and left. Had that happened, the U of A would have lost a future All Conference and professional football player. I exhibited compassion for big John, something my college professors knew nothing about. They would not understand me going for pizza with big John so frequently and letting my classroom assignments slide.

Truth be known, the fault that I was doing poorly in my classes was not mine at all. The University of Arizona did not have a very competent advising system in place. I graduated from Bisbee High School fully intending to become a history teacher. To become a history teacher one had to take history classes. I knew that. Yet, the day I was advised, the day I signed up for first semester classes was the day senior football players Kurt Storch and Karl Eller offered to help. They sat down on my cot in East Dorm at Arizona Stadium where we were housed during pre-season practice. I expressed concern about getting the right classes. The ones I could pass.

Kurt and Karl, being seniors and big men on campus, both had some suggestions about cinch freshman classes I should take. The two seniors football players had been around for four years and must know something. I signed up for the classes my personal advisors suggested and was enrolled in The University of Arizona *Business College* my entire first semester! I couldn't learn to be a history teacher in the Business College. So, that is why my grades the first semester were pitiful!

The second semester of my freshman year wasn't much better.

I enrolled in one history class, my desired major. The class was listed in the academic catalog as A Shorter History of England. It was a disaster! An ancient professor "conducted" the class, and I mean *conducted*. He did not teach.

He shuffled into each class period looking like death warmed over. He would place a thick notebook on the podium, open it to the lesson for the day and then began to read and read and read. He read until the bell rang to dismiss us. If I would have to endure more of that to be a history teacher, there was no way I would be a history teacher.

I passed my first semester Freshman English Class with a C-, my highest grade that semester. According to those in the know at The Fiji House, the second semester English was quite a bit more interesting and easier than first semester.

My roomie, Charlie Leftault suggested that I take Speech 101. He said I would get second semester English credit for Speech 101. That Speech class turned out to be a life changing experience for me, though I would not realize it until several years later.

The Fijis were eager to have me become an active. The actives said my first semester low grades would not keep me from becoming an active. I would go through the second semester as a pledge, then I would be voted on the first semester of my sophomore year and become a full fledged Fiji! A big man on campus!

I received a dark blue Letter Sweater with a large red and white "A" for sitting on the bench in football. My first college letter. I was confident I would earn a letter in baseball and possibly one in track my second semester of my freshman year. That would be 3 Varsity letters my first year! Very few college athletes could claim that distinction. The legend would make his presence known at The U of A, yet!

UofA Track Coach
Carl Cooper; a True Class Act!

"Hadley, we'll talk about track when the football season is over. Let's just try to concentrate of beating Arizona State tonight." He probably did not realize it at the time, but Carl Cooper told me what kind of man he was when he spoke these few words to me. The *Wildcat* football team was eating the pre-game meal just before we went to the dressing room under *Arizona Stadium* to get ready for our annual Big Game with Arizona State.

Skip Corley and I seated ourselves near coach Cooper. During the meal I had asked Coach Cooper if he could use another long jumper on the track team. I said I was sure that baseball Coach Sancet would let me practice a few broad jumps after baseball practice at times. After all, I was Arizona state broad jump champion my Junior year of high school with very little practice time. I was just sure Coach Cooper would get all excited about the legend volunteering to lend my talents to the track team. Coach Cooper's surprising reply to my comment startled me.

Coach Cooper exibited a trait that evening that made him a class act and a valuable assistant to football Coach Warren Woodson. Coach Cooper proved his loyalty to his immediate authority, Coach Woodson, and to the University of Arizona football program. Coach Cooper was focused on the task on hand, namely to beat Arizona State. His track program was on hold until the football season was over.

The full impact of that brief conversation with Coach Cooper did not come full circle until years later when I was confronted with the choice of being loyal or not to my authority. A great assistant coach will display loyalty to the head coach and the program. I would learn that truth the hard way.

After the football season, Coach Cooper did encourage me to speak with baseball Coach Sancet and get his permission to do some broad jumping in home meets Coach Sancet said that was fine with him as long as it did not conflict with home baseball games. Since I was relegated primarily to the freshman baseball team it worked out well.

The track team usually held home meets under the lights. I did get some points in the broad jump and Coach Cooper even had me on a few relay teams. I earned a letter in track my freshman year, thanks mainly to Coach Cooper's encouragement.

We had the same arrangement my second year. Though I played more regularly with the *Wildcat* varsity baseball team my sophomore year, I was still able to earn a letter on the *Wildcat* track team. I have always been thankful to Coach Carl Cooper for allowing me to participate in UofA track. His encouragement and kindness meant a lot to the legend who was struggling to find some purpose and meaning to life at the University of Arizona.

UofA Baseball
Frank Sancet Style

I felt pretty certain that when I walked into Coach Sancet's office for my first official visit as a member of the nationally recognized University of Arizona baseball program that all the childish Bisbee High-Douglas High animosity would be forgotten. Coach Sancet would welcome me with open arms. Wrong!

My first taste of University of Arizona baseball went pretty much as the football season went. I played in a few Vasity games, enough to letter. By and large I was relegated to the freshman team. I did not make any of the Varsity "away" games.

I found out very quickly that Coach Sancet pretty much had his Varsity squad set. Freshman practiced separately from the Varsity. We occasionally scrimmaged them. For the most part, Coach Sancet ignored us.

I was to play a bigger part in UofA baseball my sophomore year; however, my dream of being a professional baseball player was slowly being eroded. I had a very difficult time dealing with Coach Sancet and his neglect. All my athletic life I had been chewed out, complimented and encouraged; never neglected; never ignored. I wanted to feel needed. I needed to feel I had significance.

Sophomore Year
1953-1954. Shrouded in a Mist.

Psalm 69:20 says, *"Scorn has broken my heart and has left me helpless. I looked for sympathy, but there was none, for comforters, but I found none."*

That psalm pretty much sums up my struggle to find significance after such a disastrous introduction to the life after Bisbee High School that the legend had been dumped into. As bad as that first year was, my second year would be even more destructive to my huge ego and self-concept.

It was the most miserable year of my life. My high school sweetheart and best friend, Mary Louise, had gotten married. I had always assumed that Mary Louise and I would be married when I graduated and established myself as a professional athlete. Typically, I ignored Mary Louise while I was so self-absorbed in my own efforts to continue to be the legend. Her marriage was the big blow that sent me into the abyss of self-pity. I tried hard to bury my hurt by the only way I knew how. I went overboard in my quest to be a big man on campus.

I was certain that I could still establish my status as the legend on the football team. Certainly Coach Woodson would recognize my capabilities. I was determined to be more aggressive and assertive in practices. I would find a way to get Coach Woodson to realize that my speed and quickness would be very valuable to his high powered offense. That quest was halted before it ever got started. In a physical examination at the end of the 1953 baseball season, the team physician advised me to forego football my sophomore year due to a swollen, sore and weak left knee. The knee had begun to bother me during baseball season. It was an aggravation of an injury caused by a childhood disease which hadn't bothered me for years. The doctor said a lay off from football would get the knee back to normal for the 1954 baseball season.

I do not exaggerate when I say that my sophomore year, 1953-1954, was shrouded in a mist. I could not even remember when it came time to outline this book whether I had even been in school that year. While perusing the University of Arizona's 1954 annual, *The Desert,* I found I was indeed enrolled in school.

What else I found as I went through *The Desert* rekindled memories I had suppressed for years. I had become a hot, a fraternity man! My picture was in *The Desert* for being the anchor on the winning *Fiji* relay team in the annual Fraternity Pajama Relay Race. I am pictured clad in pajamas accepting the winner's trophy. A vivid memory was brought back from the dark recess of my mind. I recall running the anchor lap of that relay race in front of some sorority houses. Girls were in every window yelling and screaming as I dashed to the finish line. Very demeaning! The legend, Hadley Hicks, high school All-American football star winning a fraternity pajama race. How far had I fallen!

Another picture appeared in that same 1954 annual that I did not recall at all. I had evidently won, while again showing my prowess as the all-around hot, the legend of the *Fiji House*. Now get this: I won the annual "Twirp Week" race! I crossed the finish line first without being caught by a bevy of beautiful sorority girls. The picture in *The Desert* is a posed shot of two lovely coeds dragging me by my legs each girl fighting to lay claim to the honor of capturing me. I was wearing the winner's crown of *turnip leaves*. That's right. A crown of turnip leaves. Those turnip leaves did not hurt my head nearly as much as my *Wildcat* football helmet! Oh, I was still the legend alright!

THE BLACK MARBLE

My fraternity experience went downhill from there. The straw that broke my back and soured me forever on fraternities was when I proposed that my good friend, Pete Najera, join the *Fijis*. Pete was an excellent student and very popular on campus. He seemed interested in becoming a member of the *Fijis*. I brought Pete to lunch at the Fiji House numerous times. He was always greeted with respect and made to feel much at home. Before Pete could be accepted to go through "Rush," he had to be voted on by the active members of the Fiji house. The night Pete was voted on has always been vivid in my memory. The bitterness it left in me lasted for years. I was thankful Pete was not present when the vote took place.

I had to officially nominate Pete before the voting process could begin. I nominated Pete and spoke highly of his qualifications. Then some of the actives voiced their opinions of Pete. Pros and cons as to Pete's character had to be thoroughly hashed out before the vote took place. The voting started when "the box" was brought out. The box was full of white marbles and one black marble. The one black marble was separated from the numerous white marbles.

As the box was passed from one active to the other, each would drop a marble in the box. If only one of the actives did not want Pete as a member of the Fijis, that active would drop in the one condemning black marble. The vote had to be unanimous. The box was constructed so that no one else but the holder of the box could see what color of marble he dropped in. As each marble was dropped in the box, it made a loud *clunk*. This verified that each one voted. It was impossible to determine which colored marble the voters had dropped in.

That evening when the box had made it's way around the circle of actives, the black marble was in the bottom of the box among the white marbles. Pete Najera had been black balled! There was only one negative comment made about Pete during the pre-vote discussion time. This concern was expressed by several actives: Pete was not qualified to be a member of the Fiji House because he was Mexican!

I'll never forget how one of the actives voiced it. "Can you imagine what would happen if Pete was accepted as one of us? In several years we would have a few more Mexicans among us. On Mothers' Day we would probably have a couple of Mexican ladies scattered among our mothers. That could be embarrassing for those few Mexican ladies."

I could not believe what I was hearing! I had never before experienced prejudice towards Mexicans. My best friend all though high school, Tony Silva was a Mexican. We lived in Tucson, Arizona, United States of America. We interacted with Mexican people all the time. Yet, because just one black marble showed up in that box, Pete Najera had to be told he was not good enough to be a Fiji.

Pete Najera went on to graduate from The University of Arizona as the outstanding ROTC student on campus. Pete had a distinguished career in The United States Army. He served in Vietnam with distinction. He retired from The United States Army as a major. Yet, Pete was not good enough to be a Fiji!

To the best of my memory, I did not set foot in The Fiji House after that night!

THE COLLEGE WORLD SERIES

OK, where was the legend to go from there? Well, I still had my second season of baseball in front of me. Maybe I could regain some semblance of self-esteem on the UofA baseball diamond. Unfortunately, Coach Sancet was still at the helm.

I made the varsity team and started a number of games when regular outfielder, Gus Stiles, had a class and couldn't be there for the start of the game.

In one game that I remember well, I made a good running catch in deep left-center field for the third out. That catch prevented the opponents from scoring several runs. When I ran into the dug-out, most of the players rushed to congratulate me. Even assistant coach, Kenny Coopwood, congratulated me. All I got from Coach Sancet was the back of his head. Not one word.

I learned much from Coach Sancet that day. I learned how not to encourage a player! I learned how to break a player's heart. And there was more to come. At the end of that season our UofA *Wildcat* baseball team won the Border Conference title and won the district tournament. We qualified for the College World Series in Omaha, Nebraska!

It was and still is the goal of every Division I baseball team and player to go to Omaha for The College World Series. It is a thrill that is never forgotten. In a team meeting shortly after we qualified for The Series, Coach Sancet announced that due to budget restraints two members of the team would have to be left behind. Guess who was one of those players to be left behind? Yep, the legend was left behind. Guess which player left that meeting with tears in his eyes?

The two team captains, Hugh McMullen and Rudy Castro, later went to Coach Sancet to plead my case. Coach Sancet said that besides the budget restraints, he wanted to leave me home so I could attend summer school to bring my grade point average up. I felt that was a pretty flimsy excuse. Summer school did not start for two weeks and the team would be back from The College World Series in time for me to attend. It was many years before I could forgive Coach Sancet. He was never one of my favorite people.

I was not the brightest guy in the world, but I saw the handwriting on the wall. I was not destined to increase my status as the legend at the University of Arizona.

Two weeks after the season ended, I had volunteered for the military draft.

CHAPTER THREE

My Pride Restored at Ft. Ord
1954-1956

*I have seen his ways and will heal him;
I will also lead him, and restore comforts to him.*

Isa. 57:18a

My first experience of army life occurred during the summer of 1950 when seven valiant and patriotic Bisbee High School students joined The U.S. Army's Organized Reserve Corps. When the seven of us signed on the dotted line, communists all over the world shuddered.(B)

The Korean War broke out the Sunday after we arrived at Ft. Ord. We spent eight miserable weeks going through basic training with soldiers who would actually go to Korea. Some of them would never return. Since we were still in high school we were sent home at the end of our basic training.

Captian Turqueza; Leadership

This time when I reported for duty, the Korean War was winding down. The threat of combat duty was not an ever present reality. The legend eagerly looked forward to putting in two years as a U.S Army "Grunt".

Ft. Ord was located on the beautiful Monterey Peninsula near Monterey, California. I had grown to love the Monterey Peninsula during my previous stint in the Organized Reserve Corps in the summer of 1950. Due to the 1950 summer experience I went in with rank. Instead of being just a lowly recruit with no rank, I was automatically assigned the rank of private E-1. I was designated platoon leader and had privileges the ordinary recruits did not have. The recruits had to bed down in a musty barracks with bunks; I shared a room with another E-1. I got to be the first one of my platoon in the chow line. I loved the responsibility of leading my platoon. I took pride in leading and found out I had natural leadership qualities.

Our Company Commander, Captain Turqueza, exemplified leadership. He was only 5'5" inches tall and maybe a robust 130 pounds. But he commanded respect. He spoke with authority. When he spoke, we listened. It could have been the shiny machete he always carried that encouraged us to listen. I will never forget my first introduction to Captain Turqueza. It was 5:30am on our first morning after reporting for duty to Company A of the Sixth Infantry Division. We were all lined up in a military manner for roll call as we were been instructed by our company first sergeant, Sgt. Victor Valesquz. I knew from my previous experience in 1950 that this line up for roll call would be a daily occurence until Basic Training was over.

It was a typical Ft.Ord morning; cool, damp, and foggy. I was not at all looking forward to hearing the dreaded command to *"DROP!"* In 1950, that command meant we dropped to the fog moistened, cigarette butt, phlegm covered cement surface of a company street and immediately gave the required 50 push-ups.(B)

This morning was to be different. Pleasantly different. Instead of "DROP!", we heard Sgt. Valesquez shout, *"ATTEN---HUT!"* We immediately snapped to and stood quietly at attention.

What we witnessed next was, I am sure, firmly embedded in each of our memories. We saw the double doors of Company Headquarters open and the small, wiry Philippino Captain emerge into view.

His first action was to thrust his right arm in the air with his shiny machete gleaming in the morning fog. He shouted, "I have killed many Japanese when fighting for my homeland. I hate war. I hate killing. But, I will kill if I am forced to." At this point, Captain Turqueza slowly lowered his machete.

You could have heard a pin drop. Not a sound. We were all wondering what he meant when he said, "I will kill...if I am forced to." The Captain then broke into a smile and said, "You are lucky. I only use this (indicating his machete) now to dig dandelions out of my wife's garden!" We didn't know if we should laugh or sigh in relief.

We all learned to love and respect Captain Turqueza. He was present at most of our training exercises and often demonstrated his proficiency in hand to hand fighting, use of the bayonet, hand grenade throwing, and forced marching. He was in superb condition for a man who must have been in his fifties. We had no doubts that he had killed many Japanese.

One day Captain Turqueza erased any doubts as to his manliness that some of us may have had. Sunday dinners in Company A were always special occasions. We usually had a fare out of the ordinary; roast beef, fried chicken, baked ham, and sometimes steak! We were always welcomed and encouraged to bring guests, visitors like a mom or dad.

This one Sunday, we heard a loud, *"ATTEN---HUT"*. We immediately jumped to attention. Captain Turqueza walked into the dining room escorting the most beautiful woman most of us had ever seen! Obviously his wife.

Mrs. Turqueza was a good six inches taller than her husband. She had long, slim legs and long black hair. I fell in love with her immediately. But then I remembered the Captain's machete which he had with him incidentally.

Captian Turqueza proudly introduced his wife to us and then pulled out a seat for her. They sat at a table two down from where I was seated. Their coupleness was obvious.

The usually raucous dinner time banter suddenly became subdued and polite. It was obvious to all of us that Mrs. Turqueza was the most important person in the world to the Captain. I noticed that when all the soldiers finished eating and had taken their trays and utensils back to the kitchen area, they politely went to Mrs.

Turqueza to thank her for honoring us with her presence. Something about the Captain's obvious love for her demanded we do that.

Captain Turqueza was an easy man to follow. I learned much from him. Instead of yelling and cursing at us to make us improve, he encouraged.

One time in a grueling one mile obstacle race against several other Company A platoons I led my platoon to first place. As Captain Turqueza presented our platoon the first place ribbon, he looked me square in the eyes and said, "Private Hicks, you are a fine soldier. Fine soldiers lead by example." I was flattered and proud that he complimented me, but also proud that he knew my name.

I did have to go through the dreaded Basic Training again, but I knew what to expect this time. As platoon leader it was my responsibility to insure my platoon did not receive any "gigs", a black mark against us at weekly inspections. As an example, a gig was given if a soldier's bunk was not made properly. The inspecting officer may at any time drop a quarter on any bunk that didn't look like it was made tight enough. If the quarter didn't bounce when it hit the top blanket, the guilty soldier who had made the bunk received a gig. A gig could be given if a soldier's combat boots were not shined so that the inspecting officer could see his reflection in the boot's toe.

My platoon was awarded several "Commander's Citation" ribbons due to outstanding inspections. These long brightly colored ribbons were attached to our Company's identifying flag. This small streamer-like flag attached to a long polished pole is called a *guidon*. Our company's guidon was bright blue with a large gold A. It had quite a few citation ribbons attached. I was privileged to carry our Company guidon at our monthly Sixth Infantry Base Parades. I loved those parades! I could strut with the best of them as we passed in review before the Ft. Ord brass each month. I was a good soldier!

Toward the end of our eight weeks of Basic Training we were all eagerly awaiting our orders for permanent duty assignments. We knew that some of us would go to Korea, some would go to Japan, some would go to Europe and some would be given Stateside assignments. When my orders came I was told to report to Special Services at Ft. Ord. There I got my special orders. I was to report to Coach Bill Abbey, The Ft. Ord *Warrors* football coach when I got back from leave. It seems that a former Arizona State College football player who had played for Ft. Ord the previous two years had recommended me. The player's name was Virgil Savage. I knew his name well. He was a standout for Arizona State and he knew of my high school reputation. Virgil somehow knew that I was at Ft. Ord for Basic Training and recommended me to Coach Abbey. I never got to meet Virgil as he was discharged from the army shortly before I finished Basic Training. I have always wished I could thank him. My quest for significance was to get a big boost from my experience with the Ord *Warriors* football team.

I was a bit uneasy when I first got home on leave. I was afraid to meet old friends for fear they would quiz me about my pitiful experience at The University of Arizona. I was afraid they would ask why I quit. However, for the most part I was still greeted as Bisbee's legend. My time at home with my family, my dad and mom, younger sister and baby brother, granddad and uncles was very special. I always felt loved by my family.

Upon returning to Ft. Ord, I was assigned to the Clerk Typist School. I was told I would work mornings as a typing instructor. I had to laugh at that assignment. I had received a D= (that's a double minus!) in high school typing. Now I was to teach soldiers how to type! I soon found out it was an assignment I could handle.

My teaching was a joke; it involved going into the typing classroom, taking roll, then telling the soldier/students to open their text books to such and such a page. On my signal they were to do the exercises. I then timed them in each exercise. At the end of the allotted time I instructed them to go to the next exercise. Their work was graded at the end of the class time by a grader. It was a piece of cake for me! At noon I went to the chow hall for lunch. After lunch, I had two hours to kill before reporting to The Ft. Ord *Warriors* football stadium. Afternoon practices started at 3:30pm.

THE FT. ORD *WARRIORS*

I heard a lot about The Ft. Ord *Warriors*. Year in and year out the *Warriors* fielded outstanding football teams. The *Warriors* had even played in the Salad Bowl in Phoenix on New Year's several years before. I recall reading about how strong the Ft. Ord team was that year. They featured the great Ollie Matson, former University of San Francisco All American and then current Chicago *Cardinal* All-Pro.

I was not at all prepared for what I found I was going to be a part of. The 1955 Ft. Ord *Warriors* were the finest football players I was ever privileged to join. We had professionals sitting on the bench! At our first meeting I was aghast at who my teammates were. As they were introduced, I found my self wondering just what in the world I was doing there. Sure, I was a legend. More than a few of these guys were Legends**,** with a capitol L**!** Many of them had professional experience. Some of them were former college All-Americans. For the most part, they had all had several years of college experience. *What was I doing there?* I would be cut after the first work out I was sure. However, there were only 39 players in attendance. Coach Abbey announced that he would not cut anybody from the team. I was a *Warrior* through default. I was the least experienced player in the room. All they knew about me was that I was from the University of Arizona. My bench time at the U of A was not mentioned.

How is this for a line up of football talent? Football fans from the 1950's will remember many of these names:

Sam Baker, 6'2", 215 lbs. fullback, Oregon State and Washington *Redskins*

Dewey Brundage, 6'3" 210 lb. end, BYU and Pittsburg *Steelers*

Rudy Bukich, 6'1", 192 lbs. quarterback, USC and L.A. *Rams,* Chicago *Bears*

Paul Cameron, 6'1", 195 lbs. halfback, UCLA and Pittsburg *Steelers*

Charles "Tiny" Grant, 6'5" 265 lbs. center, Utah and Green Bay *Packers*

Jim Dublinski, 6'1" 220 lbs. center, University of Utah and Washington *Redskins*

Ron Miller, 6'4", 210 lbs. end, University of Southen California and L.A. *Rams*

Robert Peviani, 6'1" 215 lbs. tackle, University of Southern California and N.Y. *Giants*

Jimmy Powers, 6", 190 lbs. quarterback/def. back, University of Southern California and S.F. *49ers*

Gerald Perry, 6'4", 235 lbs. tackle, University of California and Detroit *Lions*

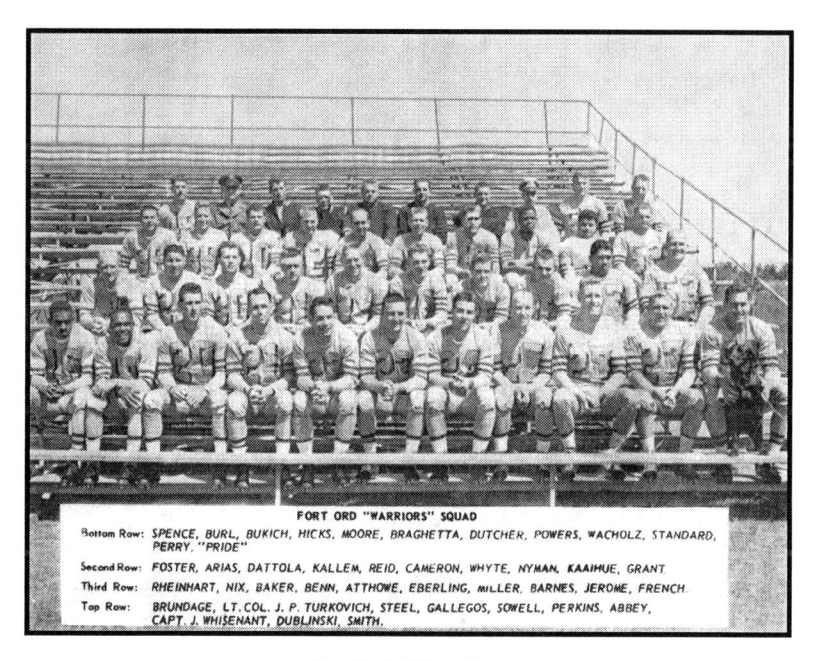

FORT ORD "WARRIORS" SQUAD
Bottom Row: SPENCE, BURL, BUKICH, HICKS, MOORE, BRAGHETTA, DUTCHER, POWERS, WACHOLZ, STANDARD, PERRY, "PRIDE".
Second Row: FOSTER, ARIAS, DATTOLA, KALLEM, REID, CAMERON, WHYTE, NYMAN, KAAIHUE, GRANT
Third Row: RHEINHART, NIX, BAKER, BENN, ATTHOWE, EBERLING, MILLER, BARNES, JEROME, FRENCH.
Top Row: BRUNDAGE, LT. COL. J. P. TURKOVICH, STEEL, GALLEGOS, SOWELL, PERKINS, ABBEY, CAPT. J. WHISENANT, DUBLINSKI, SMITH.

Ft. Ord, *Warriors*
United States Military National Champions

Paul Cameron was the most widely publicized football player in America. He made everybody's All America team while a playing for Coach "Red" Sanders at UCLA. He made the NFL All-Rookie team in 1954 as a defensive back for the Pittsburg *Steelers*.

Sam Baker was known as "Mr. Touchdown" while making All America at Oregon State in 1954. He was one of the all time "characters" in professional football. Sam's trade mark gesture was to throw both arms in the air signifying "touchdown" whenever he entered a room or came into the presence of a group of people. He was not what you would call "shy". Sam was a punter, place kicker and fullback for The Washington *Redskins* for many seasons.

Jimmy Powers was one of the finest team leaders I have ever been associated with. He was our "coach on the field". He and Rudy Bukich shared the quarterback duties. When Powers didn't start at quarterback, he was a starting defensive back, the position he played extensively with the San Francisco *49ers* from 1950-1953.

Rudy Bukich was touted to have the strongest throwing arm of any professional quarterback for several seasons.

Others on the team signed professional contracts after getting out of the Army. These included:

Alex Burl, half back, a world class hurdler at Colorado State, signed and played with the St. Louis *Cardinal* Football Team.

Julian "Sus" Spence, a tough defensive back from San Houston State, signed and played with the St. Louis *Cardinal* Football Team.

Robert Reinhart, quarterback from San Jose State, signed with the Toronto *Argonauts* in The Canadian Football League.

Emery "Big Em" Barnes defensive end from the University of Oregon, signed with the San Francisco *49ers*. "Big Em" was built like a *Greek God*. He was 6'5", 225 lbs. with rippling muscles and not an ounce of fat.

Stanley Wacholz, an end from San Jose State, had a professional try-out.

In addition to these greats, we had a number of outstanding college players who contributed to the near perfect season we had. At the end of our season on December 17, 1955, the Ft Ord *Warriors* were named United States Armed Forces National Football Champions. We beat The Pensacola, Florida Navel Air Station *Goshaws,* in The Poinsettia Bowl in San Diego, California.

I will say this about the legend. I was the second fastest back on the team. I took second place to Alex Burl in all the wind sprints. I got plenty of playing time because the *Warriors* put most of the games away by the second quarter. All of us got into most of the games. We all contributed to the success of the team.

For the first time since graduating from Bisbee High School, I felt I had significance. I was a contributing member of a National Championship team. I was relaxed and did not feel any pressure to be the legend. No one knew me from Adam. I was just "...number 21, Hadley Hicks from the University of Arizona."

The game I remember the most was our preseason battle with the the National Football League Western Conference Champion, Los Angeles *Rams*.

The *Rams'* coach was the legendary Sid Gillman. Gillman took his orders from a guy named Bob Hope, The *Rams'* owner. Their quarterback was Hall of Famer Norm Van Brocklin. Their fullback was All Pro "Deacon" Dan Towler and All Pro "Tank" Younger was one of their halfbacks. The *Rams* had All Pro Tom Fears at one end and All Pro Andy Robustelli at a defensive end position. Needless to say, The *Rams* were tough!

The *Rams* beat us 32-14 in a well played game. I got in for one play. I went in as a defensive back in the fourth quarter. Coach Abbey told me not to let anyone get behind me. We played a zone defense which meant I did not have one particular man to cover. I just had to cover my deep middle zone and not "let anyone get behind me."

When the *Rams* snapped the ball, I read the line blocking and recognized a pass was coming. As I dropped back to my zone and I kept my eyes on quarterback, Norm Van Brocklin. I had an uneasy feeling when I saw that Van Brocklin was looking straight at me. *Oh, oh, why me?*

Then out of the corner of my eye I caught a glimpse of a yellow *Ram* jersey deep in my zone, behind me! Van Brocklin threw a bullet straight over my head. I jumped

So You Wanna Be a Legend. So Did I.

and stretched as high as I could. Doing so I managed to barely deflect the pass. In the process the ball hit the little finger on my right hand and shattered it.

I remember looking down at my finger and thinking, *Hmm...doesn't look right.. looks like a roller-coaster.* The finger was so broken out of shape that it looked like an up and down roller-coaster track. I ran off the field holding my hand and immediately looked for trainer, Sgt. Pat Gallegos. Pat just kind of smiled and said, "It's broken, Hadley". My one play against The *Rams*. Had I been in for a few more plays I probably would have been killed.

A few weeks later we scrimmaged the San Francisco *49er* rookies and beat them soundly, 24-6. I did not play in that scrimmage.

I wish I had a program because I know they had some future big name pros on their team. The one name I remember was Dicky Maegle who was an All American from Rice University. Maegle gained national fame when he was running for a touchdown against The University of Alabama in the Cotton Bowl. When Maegle was in front of the Alabama bench, Tommy Lewis, an Alabama player, jumped off the bench and tackled Maegle. Lewis gained national fame for that illegal tackle and for his comment as to why he did it. To reporters after the game, Lewis said, "I guess I just have too much Alabama in me." Each year during the Cotton Bowl a re-run of that play is shown.

The only regular season game we lost was to the tough Ft. Sill, Oklahoma *Cannoneers*. Their team was comprised of most of the undefeated 1950 University of Oklahoma *Sooner* football team. Household names from that team were: fullback "Buck" McPhail; quarterback Eddie Crowder; halfback Leon Heath; and halfback, Billy Vessels, Oklahoma University's first Heisman Trophy winner.

We played the *Cannoners* the last game of the season, two weeks before we were to play for The National Military Forces Championship. We were outscored by Ft. Sill 35-20 in probably the hardest fought football game I can ever remember being involved in.

Paul Cameron gave a most gutsy performance. Paul's index finger on his right hand had been horribly smashed by a car door several weeks earlier. I will relate that story later on in this chapter. Paul could not use his right hand to its fullest capacity. Cameron was an outstanding passer as well as a runner. Obviously he could not pass.

Paul played tailback on UCLA's single wing offense. Cameron could run or pass equally well. For this Ft. Sill game, Paul was not a passing threat.

The injured and heavily padded and bandaged right index finger prevented Cameron from carrying the ball in his right hand when running to his right. This is a serious handicap for a running back. Running backs are taught to always carry the football in the hand *away* from the defense.

One play in particular stands out in my memory. Cameron had been gaining good yardage against the very rugged *Cannoneer* defense. Time after time, he swept around one end or the other to pick up valuable yardage. The collision between Paul Cameron and the defensive backs could be heard all over the packed to capacity Ft. Sill stadium. Paul lowered his shoulder and met the defender head on. Nothing fancy. Just hard, smash mouth football.

On the one play that stands out in my mind, Paul Cameron was sweeping around left end. The defensive back came up to meet him head on. We all braced for the inevitable collision. Cameron going full speed, lowered his shoulder. The defensive back "broke down" in a tackling position more than willing to once again put a solid hit on Cameron. At the last moment, just as the defensive back was going to deliver his blow, Paul hurdled the defender! He ran 40 more yards for a touchdown without being touched. Great play!

Paul Cameron was the complete package! He was big; the program listed him at 6'1", 205 pounds. I believe he was a good five to ten pounds heavier than that. He was fast. I have seen him run away from some good defensive backs. We could never gage his speed from what he did in practices. Paul Cameron was not a practice player. Many times I heard Coach Abbey threaten: "I'll send your butt to Korea, Cameron, if you don't start hustling!" After each chewing out Cameron would just nonchalantly walk back to his position. Paul knew, we all knew, that Coach Abbey was not about to send the great Paul Cameron to Korea! Coach Abbey should have known not to make a threat he would not back up.

Cameron was awesome to watch when he was running with the ball; he ran with authority. He ran with a distinctive style. In trying to describe what he looked like when he ran, one of Paul's teammates said, "He looks like a young colt stallion; he gallops and glides." That is as good a way to describe Paul's style as any. He *gallops and glides*. He was such an effective runner, a punishing runner, that his other football talents are often overlooked.

Paul Cameron was a proficient passer. Playing for "Red" Sanders' UCLA teams, Paul was a triple-threat back. He could run, pass and kick. Yet, as good as he was on offense, Paul Cameron may have been a better defensive back. He was a starting defensive back for the Pittsburg *Steelers* his rookie year and earned *Steeler* "Rookie of the Year" honors. For the Ft. Ord *Warriors*, Paul Cameron, in just spot appearances as a defensive back, intercepted 11 passes to go along with his 1,450 yards rushing and his 15 touchdowns. Paul Cameron was the real deal!

A good case could be made that the Ft. Ord *Warriors* did not go undefeated because of Walt Disney. I really believe we would have beaten Ft. Sill had Paul Cameron been able to pass. His run or pass threat was almost impossible to defend. Paul had a Disney owned ZORRO, Inc. limousine door slammed on his right index finger; he could not pass in the Ft. Sill game. Here is how all that came to pass, a little pun there:

A Tour of *Disney Land*
Gratis Walt Disney

Our outstanding end from the University of Southern California, Ron Miller was married to Diane Disney, Walt Disney's daughter. A lot of perks came our way because of Ron's relationship with Walt Disney. One perk was a guided tour of Disney Land by the head man himself. In 1955 shortly before Disney Land opened officially, Walt Disney gave a number of us a guided tour. The Ft. Ord *Warriors* were in Los Angeles for a football game with the Marine Recruit Depot.

So You Wanna Be a Legend. So Did I.

When we made these trips we were usually away from Ft. Ord for a week at a time. With time to kill, Ron Miller had arranged for his father-in-law, Walt Disney, to provide a limo to be at Ron's disposal. Ron announced to the team at breakfast one morning that he had arranged for a tour of Disney Land, his father-in-law's new theme park. You have to understand that Disney Land was not a well known entity at that time. Only 10 or 12 of us showed any interest in taking the tour. I was all for it.

Ron had one of the ZORRO, Inc. limos at The Marine Recruit Depot. Henry Braghetta, a fullback on our team from Fresno State was our "Bussey". Henry Braghetta and an army bus were always available to take a load of us anywhere we wanted to go. Most of us who wanted to go to Disney Land piled into the bus. Ron Miller, Paul Cameron, Jimmy Powers and Robert Dutcher, a guard from UCLA and one of Cameron's close buddies, were in the limo.

As Ron Miller drove the limo out of The Marine Recruit Depot parking space by our barracks, I noticed the limo had a large ZORRO, Inc. sign on both doors. Walt Disney owned the rights to the ZORRO trade mark and productions. Those guys had a ZORRO, Inc. limo to drive around in. I was impressed.

Ron Miller told us we would meet at the main entrance to Disney Land at an appointed time. Henry Braghetta drove the bus into the huge Disney Land parking lot in front of the main entrance right on time. Ron Miller and the ZORRO, Inc. limo contingent had not yet arrived.

As we waited, the man himself, Walt Disney, walked up to us and congenially introduced himself. He told us he was pleased to have us as his guests. After we introduced ourselves to Mr. Disney and talked awhile the others in the limo had not yet appeared. We began to get worried about Ron and those in the ZORRO, Inc. limo.

Soon however, Ron Miller came driving up in an empty limo. He was obviously distraught. We could see concern on his face. He explained that they had decided to stop along the way for some snacks. While they were getting out of the limo, Paul Cameron had the car door slammed on his finger. The door had completely closed with Paul's finger still in the door. Ron had to get back in the limo and open the door from the inside. He told us the finger was a bloody mess. They took Paul to the nearest emergency room. Jimmy Powers and Robert Dutcher stayed at the emergency room with Paul. Miller drove back to tell us what happened. There was not much any of us could do. Ron got in the limo and went back to the emergency room. Walt Disney took the rest of us on a personally guided tour as he promised.

We were with Walt Disney for about four hours. He bought us lunch at one of the restaurants on Disney Land's Main Street, USA. He laughed and joked with us and was a most congenial host. One thing I noticed about Walt Disney was how all the vendors and workers at Disney Land called him by his first name. Walt Disney seemed to know all their first names as well. He was an impressive man.

Ron Miller worked for his father-in-law and Disney Productions for many years. Well into the 1980's before the big Disney shake up, the name Ron Miller could often be seen as the producer for many of the Disney films.

It wasn't until much later that night that Ron Miller, Paul Cameron, Jimmy Powers and Robert Dutcher got back to the barracks. Cameron came in with his arm in a sling. We were told the sling was just for comfort. The index finger was heavily bandaged. Paul said he'd be ok. He said he would be able to play in the game that weekend. He did. We routed the Marines and Cameron had his usual one-hundred yard plus game. Paul Cameron was one tough football player.

OFF DUTY HOURS
Exciting!

The Ft. Ord *Warrors* were young men, not young boys. I was the youngest one on the team. I had two years of college. Most of the team had graduated from college. Many of them were married and had families. Because of the physical maturity of the team, Coach Bill Abbey had loose training rules. "Be on time... for whatever" pretty much summed up the extent of Coach Abbey's expectations. I was a part of what amounted to a professional football team. We were definitely a step above most college football teams.

My first real eye opener came at half time of our first game. We were playing at home against the formidable Ft. Carson, Colorado team which featured former Michigan State and Los Angeles *Ram* tackle Bill Quinlan**.**

The *Warriors* were up by 21 points at half time. We had the game under control. I wasn't sure what to expect at half time. Coach Abbey could get fired up and emotional at times. I figured he'd come in with a "..now, don't get complacent" speech. He'd no doubt try to fire us up for a second half which could see possibly the Ft. Carson team mount a comeback.

The first out of the ordinary, confusing thing I noticed was Al Dattola, a halfback from The College of the Pacific going straight to the large refrigerator located in a far corner of the locker room.

"Bring the whole case, Al", yelled John *Whitey Buckeye* Standard**,** a washed-out blond fullback from Ohio State. Al did just that. He brought the whole case of beer and set it on a table in the middle of the room. Being pretty much a straight arrow at that time, I was rather surprised. Sgt. Pat Gallegos, our fine trainer, brought out a tub of iced sodas for those of us who did not yet imbibe in adult beverages. Then to top off our half time, a private from the concession stand brought in a tray loaded with hot dogs, hamburgers, cold cuts, bread and condiments. Coach Abbey and his assistants, Charlie Sewell**,** a former player and coach for the University of Texas *Longhorns,* and Ray Perkins, a former player and coach for the University of Arkansas *Razorbacks,* did not make an appearance until about three minutes before the start of the second half. When someone commented on their absence, trainer Sgt. Pat Gallegos, winked and said they were "...discussing second half strategy.." in the coaches' office. So much for an organized plan of attack for the second half.

Quarterbacks Jimmy Powers and Rudy Bukich did discuss what they thought could still go for the second half. As with most of our games, our talent could fairly well dictate the final result.

So You Wanna Be a Legend. So Did I.

There was one half time about mid-way through our season when Coach Bill Abbey had to make a hurried entrance into the middle of our half time snack period. Coach Abbey was a successful junior college coach in his civilian days before getting drafted. Like all successful college coaches, Coach Abbey had aspirations of moving up the ladder and landing a prestige university coaching job. The success of this great Ft. Ord *Warrior* team, plus the team the year before featuring the great Ollie Mattson generated quite a bit of favorable publicity for Coach Abbey.

Unknown to us, Coach Abbey had applied for the vacant head coaching job at Brigham Young University in Provo, Utah. BYU was a straight laced Mormon university. As fate would have it, a contingent of Brigham Young University officials paid a surprise visit to Ft. Ord this particular weekend.

We had just settled into our customary half time routine. A few of the guys popped a couple of beers. The usual case of beer was on the table in the middle of the room. With the musty stench of a football locker room permeated by the nauseating aroma of beer hanging heavy throughout the locker room, Coach Abbey charged into the room. He was pretty much out of control. He started grabbing beer out of nearby hands; he was trying not to yell, but his voice was well above the whisper he intended. "Get this room cleaned up quick! BYU officials are coming in here! HURRY!!"

Not many of the guys got too excited about the whole situation. No matter how many bottles of beer could have been hidden, the aroma of beer could only have been dissipated by opening all windows and doors and letting the overnight Ft. Ord ocean fog roll through.

In less than a minute after Coach Abbey's panicked tirade, three distinguished gentlemen, all in overcoats and accompanied by Special Services Commander Lt. Col. J.P. Turkovich, entered the room. After a hurried introduction of the BYU officials by Coach Abbey, the group was quickly ushered out of the room. Coach Abbey could be heard to mumble something like," ...let us show you the rest of our football facilities....". I have often wondered how much influence this surprise visit to meet Coach Abbey had on the BYU officials decision to not offer the head coaching position to Bill Abbey.

Whenever the Ft. Ord *Warriors* played an away game, we always left several days ahead of the game. Usually we flew in United States Military Transport aircraft. Since we were staying for most of a week's time at the military base we were playing we needed transportation while we were there. Lt. Col. J.P. Turkovich wired ahead and a bus was available to us at our destination. We traveled first class!

The first airplane flight in a United States Military Air Transport was one I will always remember. Interestingly and surprisingly to me, the United States Military Transport aircraft were always "manned" by at least one, sometimes two, female flight attendants. These young ladies were members of the Women's Army Corps, or WACs, as they were called. They were attractive and personable. They often had civilian experience as flight attendants. Needless to say, they had their work cut out for them trying to avoid the clutches of these *Warriors*. Nothing ever got out of hand. The young ladies laughed and kidded with all of us. After we were in the air for an hour or so on our first flight, one of the flight attendants came in from the pilot's compartment and announced rather matter of factly that we had lost power in one of our four engines.

"Not to worry," she said. "We can safely reach our destination with only three of our four engines."

I was seated next to Emory "Big Em" Barnes, all 6'5", 225 pounds of him. When the young lady announced the good news about three engines being all we needed to reach our destination, Big Em was quiet for a minute. Then without turning his head to the left or the right he said, rather quietly, "If we can make it on three engines, why do it have fo'?" I thought that was a good question.

I have mentioned that Big Em was an impressive physical specimen. His six foot-five inch, lean muscular body was a mass of rippling muscles. Big Em was always the object of turned heads and stares of amazement wherever we went. Understand now, that Big Em was not the biggest of the *Warriors*. Charles "Tiny" Grant was 6'5" and 265 pounds. Gerald Perry was 6'4", 245 pounds.

Even when surrounded by this mass of humanity, Big Em still stood out. Big Em was one of the few smokers we had on the team. One day, when we were eating in the Marine Recruit Dept. chow hall, Big Em startled all the gawking Marine recruits who were eating near us.

Ok, try to picture this: You are one of the young Marine recruits. Maybe just off your farm in Iowa. You are still in awe by what your new Marine life has had in store for you so far. You, along with your fellow Marine recruits, are totally impressed with the group of Army football players who are eating in your chow hall. One in particular stands out. He is a huge ebony skinned, handsome, muscular *Greek god!* He is smoking a cigarette. As you stare at him, he looks right at you; takes the cigarette out of his mouth; still staring at you. Instead of putting the cigarette out in the butt-can provided at all the tables, this Greek god still looking right at you, slowly brings the cigarette up to his eye....and ...still looking at you grinds his cigarette out *in his eye!*

He had very nonchalanty shut his right eye and ground the cigarette out on the closed eyelid. We had of course seen him do that before. We still marveled each time we watched him do that. You can imagine the looks of astonishment on the faces of the recruits who had seen Big Em for the first time at his entertaining best. It was a sight to behold. We *Warriors* all acted rather nonplussed. No big deal; wait until you see him play football!

Obviously, we loved playing away from home. We had time to kill. We would practice for an hour and a half. That left the rest of the day for us to sight-see. The away games we enjoyed the most were with Ft. Bliss, Texas; the Marine Recruit Depot in Los Angeles; San Diego Naval Training Center; and Camp Pendleton near San Diego.

If you are an astute student of geography you can probably figure out why these military bases were so attractive to the Ft. Ord *Warriors*. Ft. Bliss was near El Paso, Texas just across the International Border from Juarez, Mexico. The others, the Marine Recruit Depot, San Diego Naval Training Center, and Camp Pendleton are all in Southern California. They were just a short bus ride with Bussy Braghetta to Tijuana, Mexico.

Across the Line

My experiences across the line into Mexico prior to my adventures with the Ft. Ord *Warriors* had been limited.

I grew up in Bisbee, Arizona, which was only six miles from Naco, Sonora, Mexico. As a youngster, I traveled to Naco with my mother several times on her excursions to purchase cheap liquor(B). Mother, as I have mentioned, was an alcoholic. She found the bulk price for rum, tequila, and *cervesa* (beer) quite a bit cheaper than she could get at Bisbee liquor stores. I enjoyed going with mother as she patironized Rochin's Curio Shop and Bar. Mrs. Rochin was a nice lady. She always gave me some *dulce* (candy) and a toy from the curio shop.

It wasn't until I was in the seventh grade that I heard some of the older and more worldly kids whispering about going to Naco. Evidently there was much more to Naco than Mrs. Rochin's Curio Shop and Bar. I began hearing playground talk about night clubs and *prostitute houses*! As I got older and began to excel in sports, I heard emphatically that head football Coach Waldo Dicus would kick anybody off the football team if they were caught across the line in Naco after dark. I had such a tremendous respect and fear of Coach Dicus that I stayed away from Naco.

When Bussy Braghetta unloaded his bus full of Ft. Ord *Warriors* on the American side of Tijuana, Mexico, for the first time, I had an idea what was in store. Getting across the line was no sweat. We went as a group, all of us in our civies. We told the custom official "Tijuana no mas", meaning of course, that we were not going any deeper into Mexico than the city limits of Tijuana. We were going to have a good time, contribute to the economy of Tijuana and, hopefully not get too rowdy. We heard about the cockroach infested Mexican jails. Stories abounded about the number of American soldiers who got a bit too inebriated or too boisterous and were thrown in jail overnight.

It usually took a good chunk out of the soldiers' wallets to pay the fine to be released the next morning. For safety's sake we hung together in groups of five or so. We had been warned that drunks, both Mexican and American, could be belligerent. Any lone *gringo* was fair game. We were safer in small groups. Plus, Mexican pickpockets were notorious.

Besides the size of Tijuana, two major differences between Naco and Tijuana were immediately obvious. Naco, Mexico, was a small, one dusty Main Street town. Some of the bars were scattered well away from Main Street.

Tijuana, Mexico, was a poorman's Las Vegas, Nevada. It was Las Vegas, Nevada in beggars' attire. It was Las Vegas, Nevada, without garbage pick up. It was filthy, but the bright lights and tackey colored fronts tended to hide the filth.

The streets of Tijuana were lined on both sides with stationary cars. Each car had one or more bored looking Mexicans *hombres* leaning against the hood. Each car had a homemade sign reading *TAXI* either screwed, glued, or painted on it. As we passed each taxi, the driver made a very weak effort to entice us to let him show us the best places for fun.

The second major difference between Naco and Tijuana was the abundance of Mexican street urchins that swarmed around us in Tijuana. These little kids seemed to range from four or five up to mid-teens. They all begged us for candy, money and a promise that for one dollar they would let us meet their sister. To the best of my knowledge none of the Ft. Ord *Warriors* took them up on their offer.

It was on this first trip to Tijuana that I made a close friend who had a positive impact on my life. My teammate Joe Nix, a tough defensive end from The University of Colorado, took me under his wing. Joe was married and had one child. He was religious. He made sure that I did not get led astray as we visited various dens of inequity in Tijuana. I found a kindred spirit in Joe. He did not drink nor was he interested in the girls of the night who swarmed around us in every dive we visited. We were both straight arrows yet we had fun. We drank our Cokes and were as rowdy and having as much fun as those who favored the plentiful adult beverages which were sold at highly inflated prices.

Sometime early that first evening, I took on the role of UCLA All American, Paul Cameron. It seems that some of the Mexican kids found out that we were the Ft. Ord *Warriors* and that All-America Paul Cameron was one of the *Warriors*. It didn't take Paul long to get fed up with all the attention and autograph signing he was doing.

Finally we agreed that I would become *Paul Cameron*. Whenever some of the Mexicans came up to us wanting to know which one was Paul Cameron, they pointed to me. I signed, *atantamonte, Paul Cameron,* which someone told me was Mexican for *sincerely*. I am sure that to this day there are Mexican old men in Tijuana who have my *Paul Cameron* signature framed in their home. I thoroughly enjoyed all the attention I received. It reminded me of my days as the Arizona legend.

I have to admit that the entertainment in each of the dives we visited was interesting to say the least. Each place had its own style of entertainment. There were bands of all kinds; Country Western, Rock and Roll and contemporary Mexican.

Comedians trying to make the big time were featured in some of the places. For the most part, they were horrible. Bob Hope had nothing to fear from what we saw in Tijuana.

Of course, strippers were in abundance. A riot nearly broke out in one of those noisey stripper dives. Jack "Whitey Buckeye" Standard and several of the *Warriors* were seated almost on top of the stage. Joe Nix and I were seated with three others four tables away from Whitey Buckeye's table. The stripper on stage at the moment was in a skimpy outfit comprised of a few large artificial feathers strategically placed over her mostly nude body. As she was doing her thing in time to the music, she slithered up too close to Whitey. The temptation was too much for a semi-inebriated Whitey Buckeye. He took out his cigarette lighter and lit the dancer's nearest feather on fire.

Pandemonium broke out! The dancer screamed; the master of ceremonies ran to her and valiently tried to put the fire out. The ever present Mexican *policia* who were near by ran up just as Whitey Buckeye and his table made a mad dash for the nearest exit. They avoided a night in the Mexican jail by the skin of their teeth. Joe Nix and I and the others at our table sat still trying to be as inconspicious as possible. The master of ceremonies was able to extinguish the fire seemingly without any harm to the dancer. The next act came on and the show continued. Joe and I and our group sat around for a few minutes until things had calmed down. Then we, too, quietly left.

SAM BAKER

Sam Baker had a way about him. He was with one of the groups one minute and the next he disappeared. He got off the bus at Tijuana with the rest of the *Warriors*. He was in a few of the dives with us early in the evening. But all of a sudden we noticed Sam was nowhere to be seen. He just disappeared. When someone asked where he was, those who knew him best just shrugged and said, "That's just Sam."

Sam made national news when he was drafted by the Washington *Redskins* out of Oregon State several years earlier. He showed up for the opening day of training camp with all the other *Redskin's* rookies. The next day he disappeared; he remained absent for the first week.

The police and the *Redskin* coaches seached high and low for Sam. He just disappeared off the face of the earth. The newspapers, TV, and other media carried stories of "suspected foul play in the professional football player's suspicious disappearance." Sam's whereabouts was a mystery.

One day, Sam just reappeared! He went about his job of being one of the *Redskins* outstanding rookies. Where he had been, to the best of my knowledge, was never revealed publicaly. Rumors were rampant. Even those closest to him never knew where he had been. He had just disappeared.

As our evening on the town in Tijuana drew to a close we wandered back to the bus in groups of fours and fives. When roll was taken by Bussy Braghetta the only one missing was Sam Baker. We waited around for an hour or so and then Bussy drove us back to the Marine Recruit Depot barracks. We were all in bed by 2:00 am. All of us but Sam Baker!

Suddenly, about 4:00 am the lights in our barracks were flipped on to a loud shout of, "HAVE NO FEAR! MR. TOUCHDOWN IS HERE!....LET ME TELL YOU WHAT HAPPENED TO OLD SAM!"

For the next hour or so Sam Baker had us all in stitches as he embellished his story in a dramatic fashion. He had gone into one of the dives all by himself and gotten into an argument with some patrons of the place. One thing led to another; Sam had to lay a few of them out before the *policia* took him away in a squad car. While transfeering Sam from the squad car to put him in jail, Sam broke away from his captors. Sam could run. He out ran both police and their bullets. They shot at him, he said. Coming to the barbed wire fence which separated Mexico from the United States, Sam said he literally vaulted over the fence. He had ripped pants to prove it. After several hours, several city bus rides and a taxi, Sam made it back to the Marine Recruit Depot. No worse for the experience. Those who knew Sam best said they had no doubts his story was true.

In the game against The Marine Recruit Depot that weekend, I got an up close and personal glimpse of Sam Baker, football player extraordinary. Sam was a gifted and powerful punter, as well as a fast and punishing runner. As usual, the *Warriors* had a comfortable lead at half time. Sam did not have to punt the entire first half. In the locker room at half time, Coach Bill Abbey told me that I would do the punting the second half. I was a decent punter but not at all in the same league with Sam Baker. Since most of the second stringers were in the game much of the second half, we had to punt on our first possession. It was fourth and about four yards for a first down. As I went back into punt formation, I was thinking, *Only four yards for a first down. Heck, I will fake a punt and run for it. I'll pick up that first down, no sweat.*

Bad thinking. I faked the punt, took off running and was tackled two yards from a first down. Needless to say, Coach Bill Abbey had a few choice words for me! The least of which was, "Hicks, that was pitiful! Don't ever do that again. Baker, you punt."

It was well into the fourth quarter when we had to punt again. 4th and 8. As Sam ran on to the field to punt, he ran by me and said quietly, "Hadley, watch how old Sam does it." Sam faked a punt and ran 50 yards for a touchdown. On his way back to the bench, Sam walked by me and winked. Sam Baker was a great football player.

The Warriors Take in a Bull Fight

Most of us had never been to a bull fight. We got our chance to see one when we played Ft. Bliss, Texas, later in the season. Ft. Bliss is near El Paso, Texas. Just across the Mexican line from El Paso is Juarez, Mexico. Juarez is a Tijuana clone; lots of bright lights, lots of waiting taxis, questionable sanatary practices and many young urchins. The night we visited Juarez, we saw signs advertising a special bull fight featuring the world famous Mexican comedian, Continflas. That was a must see for the *Warriors!*

The entire team showed up at the Juarez Bull Ring on the appointed day. It was a hot day. Most of us had our shirts off; many carried jugs of wine. We got tickets for the shady side of the ring. These were more expensive than tickets for the sunny side. We wanted to go first class.

However, by the time we were in the ring for an hour or so, the sun was now bathing the shady side in sweltering heat. So much for going first class. The heat seemed to cause a rapid increase in the effects of the wine on the *Warriors* who were guzzling the stuff. They got vocal. We were all rooting for the bulls. Whenever a bull seemed to get the best of the matador, we all yelled for the bull. We booed loudly at the matador when he stuck a *banderilla*, a sharp knife in the end of a foot long spear, in the poor bull. We obviously favored the underdog bull!

When the first matador was introduced to the crowd we witnessed the grand spectacle of his entrance. He arrogantly strutted to the center of the ring amidst several loud trumpet blasts. The brave matador was accompanied by several mounted, garishly dressed *novilleros* or novices. Wanna' be matadors. Loud applause and whistles from the crowd seemed to give the matador an exalted opinion of himself. What a cockey guy! The *Warriors* booed him vociferously.

We were delighted when on the first pass of the bull the matador was too close to the bull's massive head. The matador was thrown head over rear-end and landed unceremoniously in a heap. Our *Warrior* cheering section went crazy. This brought disgusted looks from the numerous Mexican *aficionados* seated around us. To the credit of the matador, he got up, dusted himself off and finished off the bull rather easily, much to our disgust. Horses came on the scene and dragged the dead bull off.

Several of the *Warriors* paid their respects to the dead bull by standing with their hats held respectfully over their hearts.

The highlight of the day was when Continflas was introduced. He was a favorite of the Mexian people. He was Mexico's Charlie Chaplin. Continflas was a riot. From the moment he was introduced, he brought the house down with laughter. He was dressed in baggy overalls. He had a floppy felt hat pulled down over his ears and a 'Clark Gable' style mustache. To watch him shuffle to the middle of the ring was comical. We noticed that he did not seem to have the matador's necessary weapons to properly defend himself from the angry bull. When the trumpet sounded and the bull made his appearance, Continflas merely turned his back to the bull. Suddenly tuning around, Contefelous walked towards the bull seemingly daring the bull to charge him. It got deathly quiet. The bull stood snorting and pawing the ground. Continflas turned away again and began walking away from the bull. As he walked away, he turned and whistled at the bull. He waved his hat. This seemed to inflame the bull to action. The bull charged.

By this time, Continflas had reached one side of the ring and was standing in front of one of the protective wooden barriers, a *la barrrela protectora*. We all just assumed that when the bull got within a few feet of him that Continflas would merely step behind the protective wooden barrier. As the bull got within twenty feet or so of Continflas, the brave "matador" simple reached inside his baggy pants and pulled out a .45 pistol. Taking careful aim, Continflas pulled the trigger; a loud *"BANG"* was followed by a red-flag which unfurled out of the muzzle. Continflas then deftly danced behind the protective barrier. The bull applied breaks and sped away looking for someone else to do battle with. The crowd roared their approval. The *Warriors* did not at all approve of Continflous' method of bull fighting. We thought he was a coward. Continflous walked off to a loud chorus of boos from the *Warriors*. We gave Continflas a standing, united show of contempt as he took his bows. Several of the *Warriors* even displayed the universal sign of disapproval.

There were a few minor leaguers to follow Continflas, but the *Warriors* did not get to see any of them. A dozen or so of Juarez's finest *policia* did not approve of our loud and sometimes obscene cat-calls. They rounded us up without much ceremony and ushered us out. They threatened to jail the bunch of us. When they saw the size and number of us though, they just told us to leave and not come back. Seeing that each of the *policia* carried guns we did not offer any resistance. All in all, the *Warriors*, thoroughly enJoyed our first and for most of us, our last bull fight.

THE NATIONAL ARMED FORCES CHAMPIONSHIP

On our third trip to San Diego we did not have the free time we had when we played the Naval Training Center or Camp Pendleton. The *Warriors* were selected to represent the West in the fourth annual Poinsettia Bowl. Our opponent representing the East was the Naval Air Station *Goshaws* from Pensacola, Florida. The winner would lay claim to the title of The National Armed Forces Champion.

The *Warriors* and the *Goshaws* had each lost only one game (our loss to the LA *Rams* did not count). All the other military teams lost at least two games. Both teams were treated royally by the San Diego Chamber of Commerce Poinsettia Bowl Committee. We were guests of the committee at numerous banquets, luncheons, and even one evening at the theatre. We got a little culture. It wasn't a movie theatre but rather it was a live theatrical production of the musical *OKLAHOMA* which we all enjoyed.

My most memorable experience of the whole Poinsettia Bowl weekend occurred the day after we had seen *OKLAHOMA*.

The *Warriors* had held a brief 10:00 am practice. After lunch we had the rest of the day to sight see around the beautiful city of San Diego. One of the perks offered us were free tickets for a boat cruise of San Diego Bay.

I had taken this cruise several years earlier shortly after I graduated from Bisbee High School. A pretty girl from Flagstaff, Arizona, Pauline Roland, and I dated a few times and we become good friends. Pauline's mom and dad invited me to spend a weekend with them in San Diego. I remembered that experience in San Diego fondly.

It was on that weekend trip when I took the cruise with Pauline and her mom and dad. I enjoyed the cruise so much with Pauline that I talked Joe Nix into going on it with me this time. Joe and I both thought the cruise would be a welcome change from all the hussle and bussel of the running around we were doing.

It was relaxing. Joe and I found a semisecluded spot along the cruise ship's deck railing. We leaned against the railing and enjoyed the beautiful San Diego Bay and shoreline. We saw many naval ship yards, the battle ships, destroyers and other naval vessels which we found intriguing.

What I enjoyed the most was just talking to Joe. What a great guy. His outlook on life captivated me. Joe was a devoted husband and he spoke so lovingly of his wife, Laura and his young son, Joey. Joe shared his heart with me. His goal in life was to provide, in his terms, "a godly environment" in which to raise his family. I had never heard anyone speak in this manner. Joe wanted to find a coaching position in a wholesome area, preferably in Colorado or Arizona. Joe's desire was to coach wrestling. Besides being a stand out football player at The University of Colorado, Joe was a great college wrestler. He loved working with kids and felt he had a lot to offer working with young people. I soon realized that Joe's philosophy of life differed greatly from mine.

I wanted to go back to Arizona and make a name for myself. I wanted to be a great, well known college football coach. I wanted to show people that my reputation as a legend in Arizona was still in tact.

When I shared this with Joe, he did not laugh or belittle my goal. He encouraged me to "go for it". His advice was, "Hadley, what ever you do, do it with all your heart. Be the best football coach you can be. Be a coach that people will look up to. Remember, you will be working with young people. Young people will have parents who love them. Always put the young people ahead of your win-loss record. If you do that the parents and the young people will respect you. Respect is much more important than your win-loss record."

Joe's advice went a long way towards giving me a different outlook on my future as a coach. It took awhile, but over the years his words of wisdom took root.

So You Wanna Be a Legend. So Did I.

Though Joe and I crossed paths several times in the ensuing years, I never did thank him for helping to mold my coaching philosophy.

With our 35-13 rout of the Pensacola Naval Air Station and our undisputed National Championship, my experince as a Ft. Ord *Warrior* was now in the books. It was been a great ride, one I would never forget.

To be associated with such an array of football talent was the thrill of my life. I have written about the great professionals on that team. There were also guys on the bench who were starters for some good college football teams. All of us felt we had contributed in many ways to the success of The *Warriors*.

It was heart warming for me to be accepted for who I was. Never once did I ever feel I was just one of the insignificant guys on the bench. Paul Cameron, Sam Baker, Gerald Perry, all the big names let me know that I was part of the team, a valuable part. My self-esteem got a huge boost while playing on a National Championship football team!

A Life Changing Moment

Shortly after I started practicing football with the *Warriors* my duty assignment was changed from the Clerk Typest School to the mail room for Company B of the 6th Infantry Division.

The mail room! What a great job that was. I was working with Private Glenn Sterley. Glenn was from New York and was as gung-ho Army as I was. We took our job as mailmen seriously. I reported for mailroom duty immediately after breakfast each day. Glenn and I sorted all the out-going mail into large canvas bags. I then loaded the canvas bags into a jeep and drove to the Post Mail Room. I picked up the several bags of mail for Company B and drove back to the Company Mail Room. Glenn and I then spent several hours sorting the incoming mail and then distributed it into the designated mail boxes.

On one of my morning trips to pick up the mail I stopped at a near by PX (Post Exchange. The soldier's version of Wal Mart) to get a donut and a cup of coffee as I often did. As I walked in I noticed a civilian servicing the juke box. I thought he looked familiar. The more I watched him, the more I was sure I had seen him before. Being the gregarious guy I am, I went up to him and asked if we had met before. He got a most astonished look on his face. He looked at my name stenciled on my jacket. He said, "Hadley Hicks! The Bisbee Comet! I am Dan Yurkovich from Ajo, Arizona."

Immediately I knew who he was. Dan Yurkovich had been a successful basketball coach at Ajo High School in Arizona. He coached the Arizona Class A All Star Basketball Team in Flagstaff, Arizona the summer I played in the Arizona All Star Football Game. The game I dazzled the fans with my 35 yards rushing.

Dan and I sat down and had a cup of coffee while he told me what he was doing in Northern California. Dan suffered a heart attack in 1953 and had to retire from coaching. His father-in-law ran a vending machine business in Monterey, California. and Dan had been working for him for the past several years. Dan invited me to dinner at his house for the following weekend.

One thing led to another and Dan Yurkovich, his family and I became close. I often spent the weekend with them. I kept my civilian clothes at their house. I baby sat their two kids and became a part of their family. Dan Yurkovich was going to be instrumental in my future teaching-coaching career. All due to a chance meeting at a PX at Ft. Ord, California! Talk about coincidences!

FT. ORD *WARRIOR* BASEBALL

A month after the football season I got orders to report to Special Services for assignment to the baseball team. Needless to say, I was excited about the prospect of playing baseball again. After all, I still had professional aspirations. If the *Warrior* baseball team was as loaded with professionals as the football team was, I was in for a great experience.

I found out quickly that the baseball team was not the same caliber as the *Warrior* football team. After my once in a life time experience as a member of a National Championship Team, *Warrior* baseball was pretty much anti-climactic. We had only one player with any professional experience. Bill Giddings had had some professional experience in the Cleveland *Indians* minor league system as a good middle infielder. Bill Giddings was to be our coach. Giddings was a good leader. He was enthusiastic and loved baseball with a passion. We did have a number of players with college experience. The *Warriors* were a good team; we won most of our games.

We had a great schedule, over 40 games against some of the best teams at the college level in California including a series of games against Stanford, the University of California, UCLA and the Univesity of Southern California. We split with Stanford, winning one and losing one. The University of California fell to us twice though the newspaper account of the games indicated most of the Cal. team was comprised of freshmen. The *Warriors* lost two to the *Trojans* of Southern California. UCLA also clobbered us in two games.

Every military base, no matter how large or how small, fielded a baseball team. We played most of the military teams in California; Casssel Air Force Base, Hamilton Air Force Base, 52nd Artillery from Cassel Air Force Base, the Presidio of San Francisco, the Army Language School just down the road in Monterey. You name them, we played them. And we beat most of them. Our won-loss was something like 30 wins-10 losses. Records were not a high priority for the *Warrior* baseball team.

Baseball was low key at Ft. Ord. We did not get over-flow crowds like we drew for football. Yet, we played hard, were excited to play, and took pride in our achievements. Most importantly we had fun! Billy Giddings told us something I tried to remember when I had the chance to coach baseball, "Baseball is meant to be fun. If you do not enjoy playing then don't play. Always play hard. Always wear your uniform proudly. No shirt tails hanging out. No hats on backwards. Baseball has a long and proud history. Do not disgrace the game by giving it less than your best!"

So You Wanna Be a Legend. So Did I.

Mamma's Chicken Wings

As much fun as I had playing baseball for the Ft.Ord *Warriors*, I had even more fun playing for the Salinas' *Mamma's Chicken Wings*.

One day after a brief practice on a rare day off, Bill Giddings approached John Hauch our left fielder, Harry Micheels our number one pitcher, and me, our center fielder. Giddings was hush-hush as he cornered the three of us. He explained that there was a Negro owned bar-b-que restaurant in Salinas, just 20 miles away. The restaurant was organizing a baseball team to play in a semi-pro league in the Salinas area. Bill explained that he ate in the restaurant on numerous occasions and was friends with the owner.

When the owner found out Bill Giddings had played a little pro ball and was the coach for the Ft. Ord team, the owner presented a proposition to Bill. The owner told Bill that if he could get three or four Ft. Ord players to play on the restaurant's team, the restaurant would pay gas-mileage plus give each player a free bar-b-que meal after the game. Bill was told that it had to all be on the "qt". It could not be known that we played on the Ft. Ord team. That would be against the Salinas' league rules. Bill had been told the league was rather loosey-goosey about that rule. It sounded like fun to us so we all said we would do it.

Several evenings later that week, John Hauch, Harry Micheels and I loaded into Bill Giddings' car for a trip to Salinas and *Momma's Chicken Wing Bar-b-Que Restaurant*. A special dinner had been arranged so we could meet the owner and the other players. We anticipated that we would probably be the only white guys on the team. We were right.

When we walked into *Mamma's Chicken Wing* the first thing I noticed was the noise! Then I saw the crowd. It was wall to wall people. Some were dancing, some were playing pool, some were sitting at a bar drinking beer, some were feeding nickles into a juke box which was cranked up full decibel. They were all black.

When we four whities walked through the swinging doors, every head in the place turned to look at us. It was no big deal to them. They resumed making noise immediately. We had been inside barely ten seconds when a heavy, full bosomed black lady waddled through the crowd and embraced Bill Giddings. "Mr. Billy, I am so glad you were able to get away! And these handsome young'ens must be your friends."

With that she proceeded to give each of us the same smothering, motherly hug she gave Bill. We felt at home immediately.

"Come on back to the eatery. We can't do any talking or eating with all this commotion."

With that pronouncement we followed her through the crowd; through a door into a large dining room. There were several black guys already there. When we walked in, they got up and came over to introduce themselves. They seemed like good guys, very friendly and accepting of us. We found out that the lady who had greeted us was "Mamma"*.* She was the owner.

After a very tasty all we could eat bar-b-que chicken meal, Momma wanted to know the life histories of her new additions to *The Chicken Wings*. When I told them I was born and raised in Bisbee, Arizona, Momma let our a loud shriek and yelled: **"Honey don't you be joshing me!! Why child, I fed fried chicken to every**

nigger at Ft. Huachuca for pretty near three years back in the 40's; land sakes, you from Bisbee, Arizona!"

Momma explained she had been owner-cook for a fried chicken restaurant in Fry, Arizona just outside the main gate of Ft. Huachuca. Ft. Huachuca is just 45 miles from Bisbee. That solidified my standing with Momma. I was one of her boys from that day on.

We played our games for *The Chicken Wings* every Sunday afternoon. Our team mates were great guys. None of them had ever played what could be called organized ball before. They were strictly sand-lot ball players. Several of them were fine athletes and all of them were coachable; eager to learn. Under Bill Giddings leadership, we conducted a couple of informal baseball clinics for the team. It was surprising to me to see how quickly the guys caught on to the basic rudiments of the game.

Bill's biggest problem with them was to get them to quit hot-dogging it. They loved to show-boat; do the unpredictable and often the stupidist things. Some would try to steal third base with two outs. They would swing at a ball over their heads with a count of three balls and no strikes.

Once with two outs and a runner on third, an easy two-hop grounder was hit to our third baseman; he threw to the catcher to get the runner going home. He got him ok, but not without a collision between the runner and our catcher. A simple, easy throw to first would have gotten the batter for the third out

But they learned. By the end of the season in early August of 1956 we had a pretty good baseball team. It was gratifying to see how these kids became proud of playing smart baseball. They quit hot-dogging it for the most part. They hustled and played with passion as Bill instructed them. I had noticed too, how they copied much of what Bill, John, Harry and I did. We were the veterans and they looked up to us. We had significance.

The games were fun but the after game meal was the highlight of the day! Win or lose, Momma fed us like kings. We were required to give animated reviews of the games while we ate. This always was accompanied by much laughter. If one of us got a key hit or a home run, he was made to get in front of the room and pantomime the event. If one of us made an error or a bone-head play, one of the other guys would act it out accompanied by much hooting and hollering. It was great fun. Baseball *The Chicken Wings'* way.

Often over the years as I thought back to that summer, I got a lump in my throat remembering Momma and her *Chicken Wings*. I never remembered the names of any of the players as we only saw them on Sunday afternoons. The couple of clinics we held were such loosey-goosey affairs, that names were not important.

The games were intense; we played hard for nine innings and then went to *The Chicken Wing Restaurant* for a few hours of great bar-b-que chicken, laughter, and fun. Sadly, I did not have a camera; video was still a thing of the future. What I wouldn't give for a few pictures of Momma and her *Chicken Wings*!

Our won-loss record? We won some and lost some. We had fun. We played hard. That's all that we cared about.

MY FUTURE AS A MORMON?
Almost.

It was always tucked away in the back of my mind. That nagging thought; what would I do when I got out of the Army in August? I got depressed just thinking about it. I knew for sure I did not want to go back to the University of Arizona. My two years there had been miserable.

My time playing football and baseball at Ft. Ord helped restore some of my self-esteem. I no longer wallowed in self-pity. Instead I dwelled on my prospects for finding some college where I could excel and once again feel I had significance. I wanted to feel needed and loved.

One day in early spring of 1956, I had a letter from Coach Max Spilsbury (B) telling me he was one of the finalists for the head coaching job at Brigham Young University. The same job Ft. Ord *Warrior* Coach Bill Abbey had applied for.

Max Spilsbury was one of the finest coaches in Arizona. He had had two consecutive undefeated seasons at Bisbee High School in 1954 and 1955. Besides being an outstanding coach, Coach Spilsbury was a Mormon. Rest assured his teams did not guzzle beer at half time, nor even drink Coke.

Coach Spilsbury told me that if he got the job at BYU that he wanted me to go with him. He guaranteed me a full ride scholarship.

Coach Spilsbury told me I could play football as well as baseball at BYU. Their baseball program was well established and highly respected. That sounded good to me!

I always held Mormons in high regard. I admired the way they emphasized family values. I liked the Mormon girls I knew at Bisbee High School. I had even dated one Mormon girl from Flagstaff, Arizona after I graduated from Bisbee High. The thought of marrying a Mormon girl and settling down to a career as a high school or college coach sounded appealing.

I did not know anything about the Mormon religion, or any religion for that matter. I was longing for significance. I wanted a family. I was twenty-two years old. BYU sounded like the ticket for me!

However, that bubble was popped shortly after I got the letter from Coach Spilsbury. I read in the San Francisco newspaper one day that BYU hired a new football coach; it wasn't Max Spilsbury. I was very disappointed

Back to the drawing board. What was I going to do? My Ft. Ord baseball coach, Bill Giddings once told me I had professional baseball potential. He said he could get me a try out with a professional team and he felt assured I could land a pro job somewhere. I was not getting any younger and if I wanted to play professional ball, I had best do it soon. Thankfully, I was smart enough to realize that I had to get a college education before anything else. That was my number one priority right now.

Shortly after Coach Spilsbury was turned down for the BYU position, he landed the Arizona State College at Flagstaff head football coaching position. He called me at Ft. Ord and said I had a scholarship there if I wanted it. The only draw back to that offer was that Arizona State College at Flagstaff did not have a baseball program at that time. I loved baseball and wanted to go somewhere where I could play both football and baseball. It was about that time that I got a call from a man named Frank Kush.

FRANK KUSH.

I had just walked into the The Company B Mail Room with the morning's mail. Glenn Sterley handed me the phone, indicating with a shrug of his shoulder that he did not know who was on the line. "This is Private E-2 Hicks, Sir!" We were taught to always answer a phone call formally punctuated with a clipped and emphatic *Sir!* It just might be an officer.

In this case a very forceful and friendly voice said, "Is this Hadley Hicks, the Bisbee Comet?" I was taken back for a moment. I did not recognize the voice. I assumed it was one of my Arizona buddies recently arrived for basic training at Ft. Ord.

So, I responded accordingly with a rather crude, and what I thought was a clever impromptu retort. The friendly voice became not so friendly, "Watch your language, Private Hicks! My name is Lieutenant Frank Kush."

Oh, oh! An officer! I had blown it! But, before I could stutter a feeble reply, Lieutenant Kush laughted loudly and again, in a friendly voice said, "Relax, 'Bisbee'. My name is Frank Kush, and I am a lieutenant, but this is not a military phone call. I am assistant football coach at Arizona State College in Tempe. Our Head Coach, Dan Devine asked me to contact you. Are you free for a cup of coffee at the PX?"

Even before laying eyes on the man, I liked Frank Kush. His sense of humor, and his authoritative voice exuded sincerity. I liked being called "Bisbee". I was eager to visit with him. We agreed on a time to meet at the PX just across the street from Company B. When I arrived, Frank Kush was there waiting for me. Fifteen minutes after sitting down with Coach Frank Kush over coffee and donuts, I was sold on becoming an Arizona State *Sun Devil*!

I strongly considered transferring to Arizona State even before visiting with Coach Kush. I hesitated due to the fact that the Arizona State baseball program had been dropped in 1953. Coach Kush assured me that the new athletic director at Arizona State, Clyde Smith , was going to resurrect the program. Mr. Smith had in fact already found a coach, a gentleman by the name of Mel Erickson, a physical education instructor at Arizona State agreed to step in temporarily as baseball coach until a full time coach would be hired, probably in two or three years.

Coach Kush said he was certain that I could get "some scholarship money" for baseball as well as for football. The National Collegiate Association of Athletics (NCAA) rules stipulated that an athlete who was on the government's GI Bill receiving money to attend school was restricted on the amount of scholarship money a college could provide. Since I would be getting GI Bill money for my military service, only so much money could be given for participating in football and baseball. Coach Kush told me that Arizona State's football coach, Dan Devine, had said that if I agreed to transfeer to Arizona State, I would receive the NCAA's allowable amount for football as well as baseball. Coach Devine had no problems with me playing baseball. He was certain, Kush said, that new baseball coach Mel Erickson would be more than glad to give me some baseball money as well.

So You Wanna Be a Legend. So Did I.

The forthrightness and sincerity of Coach Kush was all I needed. My Army discharge date was late August. I verbally agreed that I would report for Arizona State football practice in September. We visited for well over an hour. Kush was at Ft. Ord with his Army Reserve Unit for two weeks of summer training. He had received his commission as a First Lieutenant when he graduated from Michigan State University in Lansing, Michigan. He then spent four years in the university's Reserve Officers' Corps (ROTC).

The coach had done his homework. He knew about my Bisbee High School career and my reputation as a legend in Arizona. He also knew about my dissatisfaction with my two years at the University of Arizona

Coach Kush was very upfront with me. He told me that Coach Devine had recruited some very good running backs his first year at the helm of Arizona State in 1955. Coach Devine had compiled an enviable record of 8-2-1 that first year.

I would have my work cut out for me. I was not promised a lot of playing time as Coach Warren Woodson did at the University of Arizona. Coach Kush just said an opportunity was there for me to be highly successful. He was convinced that Coach Devine was going to build a nationally recognized football program. They wanted me to be a part of that. And, so did I.

With a week to go before my military discharge, I was ordered to report to the Ft. Ord Holding Depot. If you are ever on an Army base chances are you will see soldiers dressed in work fatigues all over the base. They will be washing windows, mowing lawns, mopping floors, sweeping rooms, policing areas for cigarette butts, and doing other sundary seemingly trival jobs. One thing that will be common with all these soldiers. They will all have smiles on their faces. They are in The Holding Depot waiting to be discharged. They are going home to civilian life!

These "short-timers" are fair game to be ordered around by any soldier with authority and rank to undertake even the most measly jobs. One of the first soldiers I ran into upon reporting to The Mustering Out Depot was an Arizona acquaintance, Bill Johnston. Bill and I had gone through Basic Training together. He was deployed to Europe upon graduating from Basic Training. We were both glad to see a familiar face!

At dinner that night, Bill and I devised a plan that got us through the next several days without breaking a sweat. When we woke up the next morning, Bill and I went to the supply room and checked out some working tools. Bill got two mops and I checked out a broom and a rake.

The first thing we did then was to walk down to the main PX with our working tools over our shoulders. Anybody seeing us would deduce that we were either going to a job or returning from a job. Wrong on both counts. We were going to the PX to have a good hearty breakfast. We went inside, stacked our tools in a corner near our table and made outselves comfortable. We bought a copy of the San Francisco *Chronicle* and spent several hours reading what was happening on the outside.

When we got bored eating and reading, we picked up our tools and walked around the base for an hour or so. We saw quite a few fellow short timers busy working. We just walked by like soldiers on a mission. We always ended up at a PX for a snack or maybe something heavier. Nobody ever bothered to ask us where we were headed. We looked bent on a mission with our working tools over our shoulders. Neither of us felt at all guilty about shirking our duty.

Several months before my August of 1956 Army discharge date, I called my dad in Bisbee and asked him to be on the look out for a decent second hand car. I needed a car at college I reasoned.

Dad called me just a few days before I reported to The Holding Depot; he bought a 1952 Cheverolet that he felt was in excellent shape. I had sent him money I saved out of my Army pay check. Dad had made up the rest. My mother was going to drive the car up and we would drive back to Arizona together. Mother arrived the day before I was officially discharged. I had reserved a room for her in one of the numerous guest houses on base.

After Bill Johnston and I signed all the required documents swearing we had not stolen any government property, that we had had all the necessary shots to protect us from the germ infested civilian life we were entering, we shook hands and went our separate ways. We agreed we would get together in Phoenix someday. We never did.

Since I had several weeks before I was to report to Arizona State football camp, Mom and I were in no hurry to get back to Arizona. We toured the beautiful Monterey Peninsula, had a hurried lunch with my Arizona friend, Dan Yurkovich and then we headed up for two memorable days in San Francisco. That time with my mother was very special to me. Mother, though being an alcoholic, had been on her best behavior while driving the car all the way from Bisbee, Arizona. I was very worried about that. While we were in San Francisco, we went to a number of night clubs which advertised good entertainment. Mother would have one or two beers while thoroughly enjoying the floor shows. I was proud of her. She did not get drunk, or "tight" as dad called it. We had a wonderful time driving down The Pacific Coast Highway #1.

We stopped often to walk quiet, secluded beaches. Mother always wanted to live near the ocean. She hated Bisbee, Arizona. She had been born and raised there and often said, "....and I will die there!" She did.

I truely believe our trip together from Ft. Ord to San Francisco, down Highway #1, to Arizona was a highlight of her life.

I was so glad I was able to share that with her. It was a wonderful way to finish my 21 months in The United States Army.

CHAPTER FOUR

Arizona State *Sun Devils*
1956-1958

Not that I have already attained or am already perfected; but I press on that I may lay hold of that for which Christ Jesus has also laid hold of me.

Phil. 3:12

    The La Mesita Motel is located half way between Tempe, Arizona and Mesa, Arizona. *The La Mesita* was owned by the uncle of a good friend of mine from Douglas, Arizona, Dan Pollak. When Dan read in the Arizona *Republic* newspaper that "Hadley Hicks, 1951 All America football player from Bisbee High School had commited to Arizona State University,--" he had contacted my dad in Bisbee

    Dan told dad to tell me he was saving me a room at *The La Mesita* for the several weeks until football camp started. That sounded like a much better arrangement than staying in a dorm on the campus of Arizona State. Besides Dan Pollak, my best high school buddy from Bisbee, Tony Silva, was staying at *The La Mesita*. The three of us roomed together. We had a blast! None of us drank but we ate a lot of Mexican food. We consumed Cokes and Pepsi's. We went to movies. But mostly, we lounged around *The La Mesita* swimming pool ogling the girls who came and went at the motel.

    One afternoon we were soaking up the sun when we noticed a car from Canada drive up to the office of the motel. Three cute Canadian girls got out and went in the office to register. The three of us looked at each other and were thinking the same thing. *I hope there is a room available for them.* There was.

    The girls drove their car around to the room they had been assigned. Not wanting to appear forward, neither Dan, Tony or I offered to help them with their luggage. But, the three of us held a hasty conference and decided we'd offer to take them dancing after they had eaten dinner. We did not have enough funds to take them to both dinner and dancing.

    We didn't have to work too hard at making the date. The driver of the car, Mary, came up to us and asked us if there was a good restaurant near by. We told Mary that the best restaurant in the area was a popular Western style restaurant which had a large cage in front with a live puma or mountain lion in it. They couldn't miss it we said.

By this time, the other two girls came out of their room. We politely asked them if they would like to go dancing with us after they ate. They agreed. My life has not been the same from that day to the present!

When the three Canadian girls drove off, Dan, Tony and I hustled into our room, took hurried showers, shaved, put on our best smelling foo-foo juice and dressed in our cleanest Levis and shirts. We drove Dan's uncle's Chrysler to the Western restaurant. We made sure we saw the Canadian license plate before we parked by the caged puma and waited for the girls to finish dinner. We saw them coming out of the restaurant. Before they could get to their car, we drove up, politely introduced ourselves which we had not done properly at the motel. We told them there was a nice dance parlor on down toward Tempe near the Arizona State Campus.

The six of us squeezed into Dan's uncle's Chrysler and we went dancing.

We all got along great. We talked and laughed a lot. None of the three girls drank alcohol so we had that in common. They were rather surprised as they thought all "cowboys" from Arizona were beer drinkers. They were genuinely surprised that none of us were cowboys. We grew up in houses, not ranches like they believed. They were surprised that they hadn't seen any wild Indians yet. For the most of the evening, we just sat around the table and enjoyed talking with each other.

We found that the other two were named Betty and Joan. I was seated between Joan and my buddy, Tony. In one moment of time as I turned to say something to Joan she turned and looked in my eyes. The light reflected off of the most beautiful pair of blue eyes I had ever seen. I was in love! After an hour or so, we drove back to the motel and all six of us went swimming. I could not take my eyes off Joan. I pretty much kept my cool and did not make a fool out of myself. We swam and talked until after midnight when Dan's uncle insisted all swimming cease for the night.

The girls were leaving early in the morning headed for Carmel, California to study some of Frank Lloyd Wright's architecture. Betty was planning on going to architectural school. We said polite good bys, thanks for a fun evening, and went to our rooms. I couldn't just let my feelings for Joan go like that. I wrote her a note and told her I would love to hear from her again. I gave her my mailing address at Arizona State. I stuck the note under the windshield wiper of Mary's car. I went back to bed and wondered if I would ever hear from Joan again. Little did I know!

Sun Devil Football
The Legend; Older and Wiser

When I reported to The University of Arizona football camp right out of Bisbee High School, I went in with a horribaly inflated ego. I was the greatest football player in the state of Arizona. The newspapers told me that. I was going to come right into Coach Woodson's program and make an immediate positive impact.

When I reported for my first meeting with Arizona State's Coach Dan Devine, I entertained no such self consuming thoughts. My valuable time spent with the Ft. Ord *Warriors* made it pretty clear to me that I was not a great football player. I was on that Ft. Ord team with a number of authenticly *great* football players. I knew I was an above average football player but there were a lot more out there who were

So You Wanna Be a Legend. So Did I.

better. I walked into Coach Devine's office thankful for a chance to be a part of his program. I wanted to contribute any way I could. As I shook hands with Coach Devine, my first thought was, *This man is smooth!* I felt as though I was shaking hands with a successful banker

Coach Devine was sitting behind his desk in a short sleeved shirt, wearing a tie under a blue vest. His blue coat was drapped over the back of his swivel chair. Coach Devine was polite, business like, not overly friendly and he got right down to the basics. He told me he was glad to have me be part of his program. He explained right up front that the only financial aid the football program could give me was a percentage of the cost of books. The GI Bill was going to pay for most of my schooling and National Collegiate Athletic Association (NCAA) rules prohibited the football program from giving an Army veteran on the GI Bill over a certain amount. With the GI Bill, along with what little football and baseball could offer, I was pushed to the limit financially. I had no problem with that. I told Coach Devine that I would be fine financially. All I wanted was a chance to play some more football and baseball. I was thankful for anything Coach Devine could give me out of his football scholarship budget. After we talked for maybe 15 minutes, Coach Devine politely brought the meeting to a close. He told me when the first team meeting was to be held, we shook hands and I left.

It was pretty obvious to me that I was not going to be fawned over. Hadley Hicks, legend, was no big deal to Coach Dan Devine. I was just one of the new guys. And that was fine with me. I was hoping my introduction to Arizona State *Sun Devil* football would be like it was at Ft. Ord. I wanted to be just plain old "Hadley Hicks, number.... whatever." But, unfortunately, that was not to be!

Shortly after the *Sun Devils* commenced practices, my name began to appear in the Arizona *Republic* and the Phoenix *Gazette,* the two Phoenix newspapers. I have to admit that I did have a much better baptism of fire to *Sun Devil* football than I did to University of Arizona football.

Gene Mitcham, a fine football player from North High School in Phoenix had been a starter for Coach Devine in 1955. Mitcham was being touted as a pre-season All America pick.

I was listed on the depth chart as number two at wing back behind Mitcham. However, Mitcham had a pretty severe groin strain and did not participate in full scale scrimmages. I started at wing back in most of the scrimmages. I was seeing much more action in practices than I ever did at The University of Arizona, and my performance was quite a bit more impressive. Headlines in the sport pages began to feature "Bisbee's Hadley Hicks". One of them even refered to me as "Bisbee's Legendary Hicks....". Another called me a "Whiz".

In the *Sun Devils* first full game-conditioning scrimmage, I had touchdown runs of 94, 61, and 51 yards. One write up of that scrimmage the next day said, ..."*THE QUIET GUY STEALS THE SHOW.* Taking advantage of his now considerable football experience, he (Hicks) made professional use of his eyes and blockers, as well as his legs, in one of the best individual shows ever associated with this pre-season dress rehearsal."

All in all, I was feeling rather pleased with my return to college football. I was more mature and football wise due to the invaluable time spent rubbing shoulders with such an extraordinary group of football talent that I was blessed to be a part of at Ft. Ord.

I harbored no expectations that I was a "shoe-in" for a starting position in the Arizona State *Sun Devil* lineup. I did feel certain that I would see considerable playing time. I realized right off the bat that I would not play in front of Bobby Mulgado or Leon Burton at left half back. These two would go on to enjoy *Sun Devil* careers seldom matched. I did envision myself getting in quality playing time at wingback and possibly on the kick-off return and punt return teams.

1955 *Sun Devil* starter Gene Mitcham's slow to heal groin injury was preventing him from getting in as many repetitions in practices as a starter should get. I got the lion's share of reps at Mitcham's spot during practices and scrimmages. Even if Gene Mitcham's injury was sufficiently healed by the first game for him to start, I felt certain that I would still get in substantial playing time.

The football team was housed in Hayden Hall during the pre-season practice time. Hayden Hall was the men's dorm to which I was assigned for the year. I was able to move in the first day of practice with a sense of permanence knowing I would not have to move again once pre-season practices were over.

The first person I met when I checked to Hayden Hall was Mrs. Wilson, Hayden Hall's Dorm Mother. That was certainly a new concept for me. I could not imagine a woman riding herd on a bunch of rowdy men. Mrs. Wilson was such a sweet, gentle lady, soft spoken and easy going. Yet she made it very plain that she was a no nonsense lady. Mrs. Wilson commanded respect without demanding it. Her motherly demeanor endeared her to all of "her boys".

When I introduced myself to Mrs. Wilson upon signing in, she said, "Oh, Hadley Hicks! Your roommate, Ed Hickcox, has told me so much about you. It is so good to have you with us!" And with that she gave me a welcoming hug. Mrs. Wilson went on to explain that my roommate, Ed Hickcox, was a senior at Arizona State and was Mrs. Wilson's third floor Assistant Student Resident Director. Ed, whom I had never met, was a native of Douglas, Arizona. Bisbee and Douglas are only 30 miles apart in Southern Arizona and are intense, bitter rivals in athletics. Ed told Mrs. Wilson about my legendary reputation. Ed was still on summer vacation and would not be back for a number of days. I was going to have room #310 all to myself for awhile and I welcomed that. I had spent several weeks rooming with Dan Pollak and Tony Silva at the *La Mesita Motel* and as much fun as the three of us had, I was still looking forward to some quiet thinking time. I had much to think about.

Sun Devil football consumed all my time daily from 7:00 am until late evenings. Sometimes I did not get back to my dorm room until close to midnight. We had meetings, practice, meals, more meetings, and more practice every day. Coach Dan Devine was a task master much like Coach Warren Woodson had been at The University of Arizona. Coach Devine was very strict. There was to be no drinking of alcoholic beverages, no smoking, and a curfew was imposed and rigidly adhered to. Coach Devine's assistant coaches lived in Hayden Hall with us during pre-season practice. They had room heck every night at a designated hour. All players had better be accounted for.

The back field coach was Tom Fletcher. He was to be my position coach. I spent several late evenings after practices when I couldn't sleep talking football with Coach Fletcher. He was friendly and easy to talk to. I felt he and I would get along pretty well. And we did during pre-season practices.

When I would finally hit the sack late in the evenings too exausted to sleep, I had lots of time to think. I often found myself thinking about Ft. Ord *Warrior* buddy Joe Nix and his wise and mature advice. I resigned myself to the fact that the legend was not going to be a professional football player. The time I spent with Bill Giddings and the Ft. Ord *Warrior* baseball team also convinced me that at age 23, time was running out on me if I was considering professional baseball. Joe Nix told me on several occasions that whatever I decided to do with my life, I had best find something I would enjoy doing. I knew I would enjoy teaching and coaching.

I entered The University of Arizona with the desire to teach history as Jack "The Rock" Miller had done at Bisbee High School. My one history class at The University of Arizona titled *A Shorter History of England* and conducted by a boring relic who read to the class for 45 minutes dissuaded me from majoring in History.

Coach Devine told the team that we would be registering for classes in a day or so. I knew that I had to declare a major at that time. I knew that most of my life would be spent in class rooms teaching high school youngsters. Joe Nix had said, "Find something you would enjoy doing." What would I enjoy doing? The answer came to me completely out of the blue one evening as I lay in bed after a hard practice.

What one class did I enjoy at The University of Arizona? One class and one class only! The Speech 101 class taught by Dr. Sparks! It was almost four years since I had taken that class or even thought of Dr. Sparks. As I lay in bed that evening, Dr. Sparks' name and face flashed across my mind like a movie credit. How I enjoyed that class! The most pronounced memory I had of that speech class was my UofA football teammate Don "Brother Beas" Beasley giving a *speech to inform* on the "Techniques of Playing Catcher". Don Beasley had the class rolling in the aisles with his unintentionally humorous depiction of a baseball catcher. Now that is the kind of class I could really enjoy teaching. That brief one hour's meditation alone in my Hayden Hall dorm room put into motion the course I followed for the next twenty-plus years. I enjoyed every minute of it thanks to the sage advice of Ft. Ord buddy, Joe Nix. And thanks to Brother Beas and Dr. Sparks, my Bisbee buddy and University of Arizona room-mate, Charlie Leftault was the one who suggested that I take Dr. Sparks' speech class. Those four would never know how much they unwittingly influenced the legend.

One afternoon after lunch my roommate, Ed Hickcox, and I were on our way back to our room when Ed noticed that there was a letter in our mail box. Taking the letter out, Ed handed it over to me. "For you, Hadley," he said. It was the first letter I had received. I never even got letters from home as I called home probably two or three times per week. Who could be sending me a letter? I looked at the return address and read, "Joan Fallis, Melrose Avenue, Toronto, Ontario, Canada". Who in the world? Then it hit me! *Joan!....blue eyes....the Canadian girl.*

That one letter from Joan Fallis began what quickly developed into a long distance romance. It was a daily occurance; get a letter from Joan, answer that letter the same day, get another letter from Joan the next day, answer that letter the same day, etc, etc, etc.

Before I could verbalize "I am in love", I had Joan a room near campus in *The Teepee Motel* for two days in December. Joan was flying to Tempe, Arizona to spend Christmas vacation with me and my family in Bisbee. The legend still worked fast! Needless to say, I was pumped! But, Joan's visit was still months away. A lot would transpire before then.

FOOTBALL SEASON OF 1956
More of the Same

The first *Sun Devil* football game for the 1956 season was less than a week away. So far, my chances of seeing action looked good. Starter and All America candidate, Gene Mitcham was still hobbled with a groin injury. He and I got most of the reps at wingback-right halfback in practice. There were three other right halfbacks and they each got a few reps during the week. None of the other three were very big or very fast. It looked like Mitcham and I would see most of the action against Wichita State from Wichita, Kansas, our first opponent.

The morning of our first game finally arrived on Saturday, September 22, 1956. I was excited. Wichita State was favored in some quarters as the *Sun Devils* had struggled to a 20-20 tie in Wichita the year before. The Wichita State *Wheat Shockers* were reported to be a bigger and stronger team than the 1955 edition. Ed, my roommate, aroused me out of a fitful sleep by announcing, "Hey roomie, you are famous. I didn't know I was rooming with a legend!" Spread out on the desk before me was the morning editon of The Arizona *Republic*, Phoenix's morning newspaper. There on the sports page beside a long article discussing the *Sun Devils'* first game, was a large three column picture and article about me! The headline under my picture read: "Bisbee's Legendary Hicks to See Plenty of Action in Demon, Wichita Grid Tilt." Under that headline was a lengthy, very complimentary, well written article extolling "Bisbee's famed Hadley Hicks". The author got carried away and compared me to Red Grange and Jim Thorpe. He wrote, "What Red Grange was to Illinois and what Jim Thorpe was to little Carlisle, Hicks was to Bisbee..." I was flying high! At the *Sun Devils'* team breakfast, some of the guys razzed me about the article. Most were gracious and merely said, "Nice article, Hadley."

Coach Devine had announced the starting line up at our last practice. Gene Mitcham was to start at right halfback. I was expecting that. Mitcham was the returning starter. He was being plugged for pre-season All America honors. But, he was still severely hampered by his groin injury. I had never seen him run at full speed. He was an enigma to me. He was friendly enough, but never went out of his way to encourage me or give me pointers. He knew he was the stater. He felt confident that I was not going to take his position away. He was right.

We beat Wichita State 37-9. I got in for a few plays. I did not carry the ball one time. Coach Devine was not pleased with our efforts, especially my effort on one play.

On that play, I was in on defense. We were playing a zone defense and we had a substantial lead. Wichita State threw a long pass. I had been taught at Ft. Ord that when the pass is in the air the ball belongs to anyone who can catch it. As soon as the pass by the Wichita State quarterback was thrown, I left my zone and went for the ball which was thrown in a teammate's zone. When I jumped for the ball, I did not catch the ball, but tipped it to the Wichita State player who was behind both my teammate and me. The Wichita State player scored on that play.

In the postgame analysis of the game, Coach Devine reamed me out pretty well. He made it clear that first: I should have stayed in my zone. Second: I should have caught the ball. Coach Devine was upset that Wichita State had scored. That was pretty much the story of the rest of the season for me. Gene Mitcham started and played most of every game at right halfback. He never did regain full speed. He had an average season.

In spite of all the pre-season publicity, I played sparingly. I did return a punt for a 50 yard touchdown against San Diego State. It was called back because of a clip on the play. We were ahead 54-0 at the time.

The game that was the biggest disappointment to me was the *Sun Devils'* annual grudge match against in-state rival University of Arizona *Wildcats* in Tucson.

During the week prior to that game a couple of articles appeared bringing up the fact that I had played for the U of A my freshman year before I went into the army. It was to be a big game for me. The *Sun Devils* went down to Tucson and won 20-0. I did not play.

The Arizona State *Sun Devils* finished the 1956 season with an excellent record of 9-1. Our only loss was a humiliating 0-28 defeat at the hands of a weak University of Texas at El Paso (U.T.E.P.) team in front of our home town fans. Some speculated that Coach Devine had allowed the team to overlook U.T.E.P. because we were playing "THE BIG GAME" against the U of A the following week. I had never seen Coach Devine so livid as he was in the locker room after that crushing defeat at the hands of U.T.E.P. He was near tears as he raved on and on about how U.T.E.P. "did not belong on the same field with us and how an undefeated season was no longer possible." He told us how crucial it was for the prestige of the *Sun Devil* football program that we win our last two games. We must beat the University of Arizona the next week and the University of Pacific the last game of the season. We had to finish better than the *Sun Devils* did the year before. In 1955, Coach Devine's first year at the helm of Arizona State, the *Devils* went 8-2-1. Coach Devine got his wish. The 1956 *Sun Devils* finished 9-1. The next year, 1957, would even be better. Coach Devine would get his first undefeated season. 10-0.

DAPPER DAN DEVINE

There was just something about Coach Dan Devine that did not ring true. From the first moment I shook hands with him in his office in late August, 1956, I did not feel comfortable. There was something about his eyes. They just kind of bored into you.

His mouth was set in a permanent combination of a smirk and a half smile. I got the feeling Coach Devine regarded me as just another body to be utilized in whichever way would best benefit *his* Arizona State College football program. I did not sense even the slightest degree of sensitivity.

Don't misunderstand me. Coach Dan Devine was an outstanding football coach. I learned about coaching football from him. He was a master game strategist.

He was highly organized. The third and fourth games of the season proved to a future wanna-be coach like me that I could learn from Coach Dan Devine.

Our third game was against a fairly weak New Mexico State team. We won 28-7 with a lackadaisical offensive effort. We did not look like a well polished football team. We ran primarily wide sweeps to both sides; very few passes. In the locker room after the game Coach Devine revealed his strategy to us. The game the following week against The University of Idaho in Moscow, Idaho was being billed as real barn-burner.

Both teams were quick. Idaho had the size, however. Their team was led by a future Green Bay *Packer* All Professional, offensive and defensive lineman, Jerry Kramer. Few teams could run inside effectively against Idaho. The Idaho coaches who watched movies of the *Sun Devils* running wide against New Mexico State figured, logically, that Idaho could expect the same. Lots of wide plays and maybe just a few long bombs from quarterback, Dave Graybill. The *Sun Devils* wanted to run away from their great defense led by Jerry Kramer. Coach Devine had other plans.

The *Sun Devil's* 41-0 romp of the Idaho *Vandals* was a textbook football clinic, masterfully orchestrated from start to finish. The *Devils* took the opening kickoff and methodically ground out 87 yards for a quick touchdown. Bobby Mulgado and Leon Burton picked up huge chunks of yardage by running quick hitting plays right up the middle of the vaunted Idaho defense. Quarterback Dave Graybill mixed in a few short, quick passes just to keep the defense honest. As the game progressed Idaho realized they had to bunch their defense in the middle to slow down our quick hitting plays. When they did that, quarterback Graybill ran either Bobby Mulgado or Leon Burton on a wide sweep. However Idaho tried to defense us was of no avail. The *Sun Devil* game plan covered anything Idaho came up with. Coach Dan Devine clearly showed his coaching genius in preparing our Arizona State *Sun Devils* for this key game. I was an admiring student as I sat on the bench and watched the strategy unfold.

One early season newspaper article quoted me as saying, "This is the best coaching staff I have ever been associated with." I was, of course, referring to Coach Devine and his coaching assistants. And, I was getting in a dig at Coach Warren Woodson and his assistants at the University of Arizona. And, I was, of course, displaying my sour grapes. At the time I said that I was riding high in the midst of my stellar early season practice performances. I felt that what I said carried some clout.

I felt pretty certain at that time Coach Woodson and the entire student body at the University of Arizona would be in mourning over the loss of the Bisbee legend. They just didn't appreciate me when they had me. I was way off base to say what I said. Both the UofA and A.S.C. had excellent coaching staffs. My sour grapes were merely starting to ferment.

Coach Dan Devine was not a hands-on coach. He spent a large portion of practice time 50 feet above the rest of us. His moveable tower was situated in the center of the practice field. He could view all that was going on from that location. It seemed to me that Coach Devine's assistant coaches did most of the on the field coaching.

Coach Devine had some good assistant coaches: Al Onofrio was the ends' coach, Tom Fletcher coached the backs, Frank Kush was line coach, and Cecil Coleman coached the freshman team and assisted Coach Devine with the Varsity quarterbacks.

Both Coleman and Onofrio were outstanding football players for Arizona State College in their undergraduate years.

Coach Dan Devine highly organized the practices starting with a 30 minute warm up and stretch period, through the 15 minute group time, the 30 to 45 minute team time, a 30 minute specialty team time and finishing with 15 minutes of conditioning time. Everything was by the clock

One of the team managers posted the practice schedule in our locker room before practice every day. We knew that practice started on time and ended on time.

This was a trait of Coach Dan Devine's that I tried to emulate my entire coaching career. I attempted to be highly organized. I tried to conduct all practices "by the clock".

Once the practice started, Coach Devine usually climbed up to his 50 foot tower. He had a whistle and a stopwatch around his neck. He didn't have a bullhorn with him as some head coaches are pictured to have. Coach Dan Devine communicated with his assistants with his whistle and his soft, low key voice.

When Coach Devine was down on the field, his time was spent usually with the backs and quarterbacks, though he would often go from group to group and comment on this or that. Devine never said a lot, most of his comments were directed to Coach Coleman. Coleman then carried out Coach Devine's instructions. In my view, Coach Dan Devine was not a players' coach. He was very impersonal in his interactions with his players.

He did have a few favorites. Just a few. These seemed to be a couple of the second and third stringers. Every now and then he would crack some jokes directed at these certain few. I noticed, too, that his "favorites" would get brief playing time in most of the games. Just a play here and there. Not a lot of playing time, but more than I was getting! In fairness to Coach Dan Devine, the players who were his starters were obviously the best at those positions. To this day, however, I cannot figure out why Coach Devine started and played injured senior Gene Mitcham as much as he did.

Mitcham had had a great career at A.S.C. He was touted for pre-season All America honors. Gene Mitcham was obviously hampered by his groin injury. I don't think he ever was 100% all season.

Mitcham played most of every game. Whenever he was given a breather for a few plays, he was not spelled by me. Yet, all pre-season I was the one getting most of the action at Mitcham's righthalf back position. And, according to many newspaper reports, I was one of the most outstanding players going into our first game with Wichita State. And, yet I saw very little action. I could not figure it out

Against Wichita State I was in for just a couple of plays. I did not carry the ball once. I did play a few defensive downs. I did tip a pass to one of the Wichita State players that led to a touchdown for them. We won handily; 37-9. Why wasn't I playing more? Was it because I was not very tough on defense? Was it because I was not assertive enough? Maybe I was too much of a quiet guy. I couldn't figure it out.

The entire season was like that first game. In ten games, I don't remember ever once carrying the ball from scrimmage. I was in on a few kick-off return teams. In the San Diego State game I returned a punt 50 yards for a touchdown which was called back because of a clip. That was the only punt I caught all season. The next to last game of the season was one I had looked forward to well before the season started. We were playing our down-state rival, my former team, the University of Arizona *Wildcats*. The entire State of Arizona gets excited about this game each year. It was The Big Game.

I admit I was selfish. I wanted to play in the game to get revenge. I wanted to play and do well just to show Coach Woodson and the *Wildcat* fans that I was better than they thought. However, by game time my chances of playing did not look good. We had our first loss of the season the week before when a so-so Texas El Paso College upset the *Sun Devils* 0-28! Our undefeated season was out the window. Coach Devine had emphasized "undefeated season" all year. He was in shock.

The week of practice for the UofA game was intense to say the least! By game time the entire team was sky high. I felt great. My legs felt fresh and strong. If I could only get in for a few plays. Maybe get an opportunity to return a kick-off or a punt. The game was played in Tucson. A lot of my Bisbee friends were there. I knew that they would be rooting for The UofA to win. I knew too, they were hoping to see me play. But, I didn't. Not one play. I was very, very disappointed. The Arizona State College *Sun Devils* won 20-0.

My most humiliating moment as an athlete came the following Monday at practice. My teammates knew how badly I wanted to play against my former team, the U of A *Wildcats*. None of them quite knew what to say to me. Most of them said nothing which I appreciated. Monday practices were usually pretty laid back after a game on Saturday. That Monday, after we warmed up and stretched, we got together to run some team-offense.

As the first team huddled to call the first play, Coach Dan Devine said, "Wait a minute. Hicks get in here." I was not expecting that. I put my helmet on and got in the huddle.

Coach Dan Devine then said something which bothered me for years: "Hadley, I really wanted to get you in against the *Wildcats* but I just forgot about you." I was shocked! I didn't know how I should react. All I could do was mumble something like, "That's o.k. We won." Coach Devine then turned to quarterback Dave Graybill and said, "Run Hadley on a few sweeps." As the team huddled and quarterback Graybill was calling the play, end Clancy Osborne whom I was huddled next to, reached behind me and patted me on the back, Clancy's way of saying he understood how I felt. I appreciated Clancy's gesture. I ran two plays and then Gene Mitcham came in and I was back to the sidelines. I thought that said a lot about Coach Dan Devine. His sensitivity to the feelings of a player left much to be desired. I tried to remember that as I worked with young athletes in my coaching career.

We won our last game of the year against the University of Pacific 19-6. We ended the year with nine wins against one loss. That was the best record an Arizona State *Sun Devil* team had in many years.

Coach Dan Devine was the Border Conference Coach of the Year. Coach Devine was the "Toast of Arizona". He was much in demand for speaking engagements throughout the Southwest. It was during this time he picked up the monicker *Dapper* Dan Devine. He was never seen in public without being decked out in a dark blue three piece suit. His hair was always neatly combed. Coach Devine was always poised and articulate when speaking to an audience. He was smooth.

So You Wanna Be a Legend. So Did I.

My end-of-the-year meeting with Coach Devine spoke volumes to me about *Dapper Dan*. My opinion of Coach Devine was verified. He was out to feather his career. His players were just so many rungs in the ladder Coach Devine was climbing on his way up to coaching greatness.

When I knocked and walked into his office at the appointed time, Coach Devine got up from his seat behind his desk and shook my hand. That took me totally by surprise! He was more friendly to me than than at any other time during the season. He got right to the point. He began speaking about "next year". Not one word about the past season. Not one word of encouragement or exortation about my contribution to the successful season

He told me how much he was looking forward to having me contesting for a starting spot next season. He told me he wanted me to report for spring practice in excellent shape. *Spring practice?* I told Coach Dan Devine that I was going to play baseball in the spring. I was getting a partial baseball scholarship and felt obligated to the baseball program.

I loved baseball and was looking forward to being a part of the *Sun Devil* baseball team. Coach Devine countered by saying that my only chance to be a contributing member of the *Sun Devil* football squad next season would be to come out for spring practice. I repeated my felt obligation to the baseball program and the scholarship money I was receiving from baseball coach Mel Erickson.

Coach Devine's cool, poised demener seemed to take a turn toward impatience and anger with me. He said, "Hadley, if money is the problem, I can make up what you get from baseball. I will increase your football scholarship money. You will be right where you are now."

I replied, "But Coach Devine, you told me last fall that according to NCAA rules, football could only give an Army veteran on the GI Bill a maximum amount. You said the amount I was getting was the maximum. Anything over that would be in violation of NCAA rules."

Coach Devine then said something that really bothered me. He said, "Don't worry about that. We have ways we can get around the rules."

I assured Coach Dan Devine that I was going to play baseball in the spring. I would not be participating in spring football practice. Coach Devine dismissed me without a hand shake and without getting up from his desk. That was my last official face to face meeting with Coach Dan Devine. I did run into him one other time several years later.

Coach Devine left Arizona State University in 1958, the year the State of Arizona Legislature granted Arizona State College at Tempe "University" status.

Coach Devine went to the University of Missouri at Columbia, Missouri where he immediately put the Missouri *Tigers* on the football map. Coach Devine's 1966 Missouri *Tigers* were undefeated. They beat Florida in the Sugar Bowl on New Year's Day 20-18 to claim the National College Football Championship.

At the National Football Coaches' *Coach of the Year Clinic* at Anaheim, California in January of 1967 I ran into Coach Dan Devine once again. I was coaching at Prescott High School in Prescott, Arizona at that time. I had not seen Coach Devine for eight or nine years. Dan Devine had become a big name in the coaching ranks. He was one of the most successful coaches in the country. Coach Devine was a keynote speaker at the *Coach of the Year Clinic* in Anaheim, California.

I had been bragging to my Prescott High coaching cohorts about playing for Dan Devine at Arizona State. They never asked how much I got to play and I never told them. I was anxious to see him again and hear him speak. I held his coaching skills in high regard and told my coaching buddies as much. I knew I would pick up some good coaching tidbits from his talk.

My coaching buddy Wayne Howell and I went into the Anaheim Auditorium as soon as we got there so we could save seats up close to the stage. As we walked into the auditorium I immediately spotted *Dapper* Dan Devine seated in an isle seat. Alone. I said to Wayne, "Hey, there's Dan Devine."

Coach Devine was dressed in his customery blue three piece suit looking as dapper as ever. As I walked up to him I held out my hand and said, "Coach Devine, it is good to see you again!".

Barely turning his head, he just looked at me for a second or so without saying a word. Thinking he may not have recognized me, I said, "Hadley Hicks. Arizona State."

Coach Devine gave me a "dead fish" hand shake and said, "Yes, hello Hadley." Period! Not "How are you?", "How is your family?" "Where are you now?" Nothing! That was it.

I said in parting, "Congratulations on a great season." He did say, "Thank you." As we walked away, Wayne Howell said to me, "He is not very friendly is he?"

No, he wasn't. Coach Dan Devine was a great football coach. But, he wasn't personable. I often wondered if he ever got close to any of his players. Did he have any intimate friends? He always seemed like a loner. I always found him aloof and impersonal. I will say this for him. He knew what he wanted and he went after it. He obviously wanted to be a great football coach. He was that. He was highly successful at the University of Missouri going 93 wins-37 losses-7 ties in 13 years.

He then had a short three year stint with the NFL Green Bay *Packers*. Dan Devine finished his coaching career at the University of Notre Dame where he won another National Championship in 1977. Coach Dan Devine was indeed a successful football coach. I probably learned more coaching techniques from Coach Dan Devine than from any other coach I played for. He also made me realize what my good Army friend, Joe Nix, meant when he said I would be working with young people who had parents who loved them. I wanted to be a coach who was respected by my players and their parents. I wanted to be a coach who could treat his players as human beings and not objects for self-advancement. I wanted to be able to look a kid and his parents in the eyes and let them know I truly cared.

Coach Dan Devin did not model that kind of a coach.

So You Wanna Be a Legend. So Did I.

"Dapper" Dan Devine
"Here's your spot on the bench, Hicks. Now, stay there!"

FRANK KUSH.
"The Meanest Coach in America"   •

    I liked Frank Kush from the minute I first talked to him on the phone and first saw him in the Post Exchange at Ft. Ord, California.
    I received a phone call from Frank Kush earlier that morning. He said the Arizona State College *Sun Devil* coach Dan Devine asked him to contact me about a possible transfer to Arizona State College at Tempe when I was dischaged from the Army. I walked into the Post Exchange not knowing what to expect. Nor, did I know what Frank Kush looked like.
    He introduced himself over the phone as a Lieutenant. So I went in looking for an officer. As always the Post Exchange was crowded with soldiers drinking mid-afternoon coffee or eating a late lunch. I took maybe two or three steps inside and as I was looking around I heard a pleasant voice calling, "Hey, Bisbee....over here!"

Frank Kush was seated at a table in a far corner of the Post Exchange. He was dressed in a brightly colored, open necked, sport shirt.

When he stood up to shake my hand I saw he was wearing khaki civilian pants. He was also wearing a broad grin that immediately exuded warmth and openness.

I like this guy! was the first thought that went through my mind. Coach Kush said he recognized me as I walked through the door because I looked just like a "Bisbee hard-rock miner." He laughed when he said it. Coach Kush and I sat and talked for over an hour. He told me about himself, that he had played football for Michigan State University. I found out much later that Frank Kush had made All America his last year at Michigan State. He came with Coach Dan Devine to Arizona State College the previous year, 1955, as the *Sun Devil* line coach.

Coach Kush told me he had grown up in a hard working Pennsylvania Polish mining family. He was one of 15 kids. Coach Kush obviously knew the rigors of hard work. Coach Kush knew the value of a college education. He also knew that football was one way a youngster could get that education. Football kept Frank Kush out of the mines. He was interested in Bisbee, Arizona because he, too grew up in a small mining town, Windbar, Pennsylvania, about the same size as Bisbee. He said, "Don't ever go back to the mines!"

I was impressed with Coach Kush. He did not have a pat recruiting talk. He told me about Coach Devine and the program they were going to build at Arizona State. Coach Kush promised only one thing. He promised that if I wanted it bad enough that I would get a quality education at Arizona State. After an hour or so and a couple of cups of coffee, Coach Kush and I shook hands and parted. His last words to me were, "I hope you will join us at Arizona State, 'Bisbee'. We small town boys need to stick together! Even after I was a part of the *Sun Devil* football team, Coach Kush still called me "Bisbee". I kind of liked that.

When Coach Dan Devine left Arizona State University in 1958 to take over the University of Missouri program, the administration of ASU made a very wise decision. They appointed 29 year old Frank Kush as head football coach. And, as the saying goes, "The rest is history!" Frank Kush became one of the greatest college football coaches of all time. His 22 year won-loss record at ASU was phenomenal 176-54-1! He took the ASU *Sun Devils* to six major bowl games. ASU won five. In 1975 the *'Devils* went 12-0 and won the Fiesta Bowl by beating Coach Tom Osborn and his Nebraska *Corn Huskers*. That year, ASU was consensus number two in the nation. The National *Coach of the Year* for 1975 was Arizona State's Frank Kush.

During his 22 year span as head coach at Arizona State, Coach Kush sent an unbelievable 129 players to the National Football League. A number of them became household names: Dnny White, Curley Culp, Art and Bennie Malone, Charlie Taylor, Bob Bruenig, Woody Green and John Jefferson ("JJ"), just to name a few. The success Frank Kush achieved at Arizona State and the number of players who went to the professional ranks obviously made the *Sun Devils* a high profile program.

Soon the public was wanting to know how a small town Polish miner's son could achieve such success. The media investigated and Frank Kush was soon tabbed "The Meanest Coach in America". CBS even did a special on Coach Kush before one of ASU's bowl games. The special was titled, *The Meanest Coach in America.*

So You Wanna Be a Legend. So Did I.

Frank Kush's personal work ethic was instilled in his teams. It was said that the Arizona State *Sun Devils* were worked harder than any other college team in America.

A small mountain in north-eastern Arizona was named "Mount Kush". This mountain was adjacent to the *Sun Devil* pre-season training camp in Payson, Arizona.

Horror stories abound about the number of players who were required to run up and down this steep mountain. The slightest little mistake, a missed assignment, a dropped pass or a slow first step, was a mandatory trip up Mount Kush for the guilty player. Being late for a meeting was several trips up Mount Kush after the team had made a few conditioning runs already. The players hated a Frank Kush practice session. One player was quoted as saying, "At least Coach Kush treats us all the same....like dogs!"

I had a personal experience with Coach Frank Kush in October 1962 which sets him head and shoulders above many head college football coaches in my estimation.

I was coaching and teaching at Carmel High School in Carmel, California. One of my teaching and coaching compadres was a San Jose State College graduate named Jim Agan. San Jose State was just down the road from Carmel about 60 miles.

Early that summer I read that Arizona State University was going to play San Jose State at San Jose the coming football season. Needless to say, the "needle" went to work. I gave it to Jim Agan whenever the opportunity arose. I reminded him that I had graduated from Arizona State and had even been on the football team. I went so far as to boast that Coach Frank Kush was a personal friend of mine. "Ok, big shot," Agan replied, "if you and Kush are so tight see if he can get us two tickets to the game."

Not one to ignore a challange, I got on the phone to Coach Frank Kush's office at ASU. When his secretary answered the phone I identified myself and asked to speak with Coach Kush. No sooner had his secretary said, "Just a moment, please" than I heard his familiar voice saying, "Bisbee! Are you in town? Where are you...?".

I had been away from ASU for four years and he still called me "Bisbee"!

After we shot the bull for a few minutes, I told Coach Kush what I was calling about. He explained to me that it was too early to be able to tell if he could get tickets for away games. Coach Kush told me to call two weeks prior to the game and he would have two tickets if at all possible.

Two weeks before the game I called Coach Kush's office again. I again identified myself to the secretary only this time she told me Coach was out of his office. But he had left a message should I call and he wasn't in!! The message from Coach Kush told me that if I would call the hotel the team was staying in on the morning of the game that he would have tickets for me. He gave the name and phone number of the hotel. Jim Agan was impressed with my relationship with Coach Frank Kush!

Jim and I got to San Jose early the morning of the game. We went to the hotel rather than calling. It was close to 9:00a.m. when I called Coach Kush's room from the registration desk. When he answered the phone he genuinely seemed glad to talk to me again. He said for Jim and I to wait in the lobby and he would be right down with the tickets. When he came off the elevator he greeted me with his usual "Hey, Bisbee....good to see you!" He shook Jim Agan's hand and asked him a few questions before asking us if we'd had breakfast. We said we had. He then said he had breakfast with the team at 7:30, but that he could use a cup of coffee; he'd buy if we wanted to join him. We did and enjoyed an hour or so gabbing about things in general as well as his outlook for the game. He ribbed Jim Agan about having to sit with the Arizona State fans at the game.

As we were getting ready to leave, I asked Coach Kush about Art Dickenson the popular ASU trainer. Art Dickenson and I had become good friends through my association with him when I was a member of the ASU football and baseball teams.

Coach Kush said Art was along on the trip. When I asked Coach Kush to give Art Dickenson my regards, both Jim Agan and I were floored by Coach Kush's response.

Coach Kush said, "Hey...I'll tell you what. You two show up about three hours before game time; come to our locker room and you can come in for our pre-game taping. You know how much Art likes to gab when he is taping. He would enjoy seeing you."

Then to top it off, Coach Kush gave me his field pass. "Take this just in case they won't let you in the gate so early. And, Bisbee, don't you dare lose it....they may not let me on the field."

Jim and I got to the gate and got in without any trouble. We found where the ASU locker room was. Coach Kush greeted us; introduced us to a few of the players who were standing near by and then took us to the Visitor's Training Room. When Art Dickenson saw me he gave me a big hug like we were old buddies. We had a good visit with Art while he taped the players.

We were in the locker room when Coach Kush sent his specialty players (punters, kickers, receivers, quarterbacks) out on the field for warm up.

He then talked to the rest of the team and we were in the background for that. There was nothing emotional or firey about his talk. Just a matter of fact meeting about the business at hand for that evening's game.

The rest of the team went out on the field about 45 minutes before game time. Jim Agan and I said a quick good bye to Coach Kush, thanked him for the tickets and we left to go to our seats.

What a guy!! He wasn't even my position coach while I was on the ASU *Sun Devils* team. He seemed to take a personal interest in me since he had recruited me while I was at Ft. Ord. He made it a point several times during the season to encourage me even though I was just another not so important member of the 1956 *Sun Devil* football team. Yet, four years later he still called me *Bisbee*. He treated me like a person of some significance. I had no problem adopting Coach Frank Kush as a coaching role model!

After 22 years at Arizona State University, Frank Kush quit due to a controversary that I don't know enough about to get into.

He coached several more years in the professional ranks before retiring to Tempe, Arizona where he worked for a number of years as Executive Administrator of Arizona Boys' Ranch, a residentual facility for delinquent boys. He served in several capacities on Arizona State University Alumni Board.

Frank Kush was named to the College Football Coaches' Hall of Fame in 1995.

As far as I am concerned Frank Kush was inducted into my Hall of Fame that October day at San Jose State College in 1962.

So You Wanna Be a Legend. So Did I.

Frank Kush

Campus Life
"Arizona State Cowboy College"

One of my first thoughts as I stood in a long line the first day of class registration was, *Where are all the squaw dresses?* Lots and lots of pretty and cute girls. But no squaw dresses. I did not see one squaw dress the whole time I was registering.

At the University of Arizona a squaw dress was a status symbol. A girl wearing a squaw dress at the UofA was letting observers know she was stylish. She had class. She may even be wealthy. She was definitely worth getting to know.

I would soon found out why some at The University of Arizona in Tucson refered to Arizona State College at Tempe as *Arizona State Cowboy College*. Arizona State College was not "The Country Club of the West" and I looked on that as a good thing!

Sitting at lunch in the college cafeteria that afternoon was an eye opener. I was seated at a long table with a few of my new friends from the football team.

What I noticed right away was that the football players, the jocks if you will, were not shunned by the girls. At the UofA, the jocks for the most part, took second place to the hots, the frat boys. The table where I was seated was a mixture of football players and several girls. Charlie Mackey *Sun Devil* team captain and tackle John

Hickman were at my table. I was introduced by Charlie to two of the closest girls. They were friendly and did not seem at all to mind sharing a table with football players.

As I looked around the cafeteria I could not pick out the hots from the ordinary run of the mill student. At the UofA I got pretty good at picking out the hots. Most of them had an exalted sense of superiority. Most of the hots dressed stylishly at the UofA. At ASC, the majority of the men wore Levis and T-shirts. I assumed that was why ASC was called a cowboy college by the UofA. The thought ran through my mind that maybe ASC did not have fraternities and sororities. It took me several days to realize that ASC did indeed have fraternities and sororities. And, as far as I could tell, there were just as many of them at ASC as at the UofA.

In fact, "rush" at ASC was a big deal. Rush is when all the fraternities and sororities compete to get new students to pledge to join their particular fratenity or sorority. However, rush at ASC was not nearly as competative or as cut throat as it was at The UofA. The pressure to join was low key. At Arizona State College one did not have to belong to a fraternity or a sorority to be a somebody. Girls were not awarded status due to wardrobe. Few girls wore squaw dresses to class. Those who had squaw dresses wore them on special occasions. They weren't worn around campus to impress others. The girls I met at Arizona State were for the most part just plain Janes. And, I might add, the men were for the most part were just good ol' boys. The plain Janes and the good ol' boys were what set ASC apart from the U of A; what set the cowboy college apart from the country club of the West. I was much more comfortable around the cowboys.

One area where I did notice a certain amount of pressure at Arizona State compared to The U of A was in the area of religious organizations. One of Arizona State's fine football players, John Allen had just returned to Arizona State from the two year mission that Mormon men are required to take. After practice one day, John and I were talking together as we were showering and dressing. I asked John about his mission trip and told him I was disappointed that Coach Max Spilsbury from Bisbee did not get the head football job at Brigham Young University, the well known Mormon university. I told John how much I respected the Mormon religion. Soon we were in a serious discussion about the merits of Mormonism compared to other religions. John did most of the talking.

I knew a little about Catholicism from my days at St. Patricks Grade School (B) but zip about any other religion, much less Mormonism. He told me he would get me a <u>Book of Mormon</u> so I could read up on the religion. John even offered to take me to church with him if I'd like. John was nice; not at all pushy. He did not push the "going to church" thing which I was grateful for. John did give me a <u>Book of Mormon</u> one day after practice. I made an attempt to read it but just couldn't get into it. It seemed to be a sort of history book about a bunch of Indian tribes I had never heard of. I didn't get very far into it and, John never did ask me if I read it. John was a nice guy. All the Mormons I knew were nice people.

One day walking back to Hayden Hall after class with my roommate, Ed Hickcox, a man named Elmer Lappin stopped us and asked Ed and me if he could visit with us for a minute. He was a very pleasant man, older than most students and had a physical deformity. He walked with a noticeable limp. Ed and I were in no hurry and Elmer had such a pleasant personality that we agreed to visit with him for a few minutes. The three of us sat on a nearby bench and Elmer explained that he was Campus Director for Campus Crusade for Christ. Elmer explained that Campus Crusade for Christ was a Christian outreach to college students. I wasn't real sure what he was talking about.

The ASC Chapter of Campus Crusade was just getting underway for the fall semester and Elmer invited Ed and me to lunch at his home the next day to hear more about the organizaton. Ed declined the invitation explaining to Elmer that he was a Catholic and belonged to The Newman Club, a Catholic organization. I didn't know why that made any difference but I didn't say anything to Ed. I agreed to go. Elmer said he would meet me the next day, same time, same place.

Elmer and I met again the next day as Ed and I were on the way back to the dorm. I walked with Elmer to his home just a few blocks from campus and found several other ASC students were already there. We were served a nice lunch by Elmer's very lovely wife. As we ate, Elmer asked each of us about our backgrounds, specifically our religious backgrounds. I explained to Elmer that I went to a Catholic grade school for a number of years and knew a little about the Catholic religion although I didn't consider myself a Catholic. I explained that being a football player I just did not have time to go to church. I was pretty tired on Sundays after the football games. Yeah, right, tired from sitting on the bench. After we had eaten our dessert and were preparing to leave Elmer asked each of us to consider if we were indeed Christian. I did not feel uncomfortable at all when Elmer asked if he could pray for us before we left. I don't remember what he prayed about, but I do remember thinking about the question he had asked us, the question about if we were sure we were Christians. As I thought about it, I was pretty sure I could call myself a Christian. I believed in God. St. Patrick's Church in Bisbee saw to that. I was born in America which as we all knew was a Christian nation. I was as good a Christian as the next guy.

I met Elmer Lappin only one more time after that. On my way back to the dorm one day I saw Elmer sitting on the same bench where I first met him. We talked awhile. Elmer said something that kind of bothered me. He invited me to Campus Crusade's next meeting. He said there would probably be a few students I knew. Then he mentioned one of my football teammates whom Elmer said was a Christian. He would probably be at the meeting. I knew this teammate fairly well. We had our lockers close to each other in the football locker room. This particular football player was a pretty good cusser. He talked about women in a crude way and he liked to go to parties on the weekends. He did not at all act like my Army buddy, Joe Nix, who I knew was a Christian.

I felt I could qualify. I was not much of a cusser. I did not like to party. And, I had a lot of respect for women. Elmer Lappin was a nice man

But, I was not too excited about joining his Campus Crusade for Christ. It was probably a lot like some of the fraternities. I had made up my mind from my UofA *Fiji* fraternity experience that I was not cut out to be a "hot"; nor a Campus Crusade for Christ guy.

Registration went fairly smoothly. Lots of long lines. But, at least I got help planning my class schedule. I actually had one of the professors help me.

At the University of Arizona, two of my football teammates got me signed up for business classes the first semester. I knew at the time that I wanted to be a teacher and a coach. The Business Department just didn't cut it.

At Arizona State College when I said I wanted to major in Speech I was sent to a professor named Dr. White. I would get to know Dr. White well over the next two years. Dr. White got me enrolled in the Education Department with a declared major in Speech and Drama. I questioned Dr. White about the drama part. Dr. White explained that drama was a natural spin off from Speech.

The first semester, I was signed up to take a class in *Interpretative Reading*. I had no clue what that was. Dr. White said I would enjoy it.

The class in *Interpretative Reading*, Dr. White explained, was one of those spin off classes. My professor was Dr. Mary Lavin. She and I got to know each other well. Her class was a blast!

"Interp." as *Intrepetative Reading* was called was much like drama/acting. We picked a story and read part of it to the class. As we read it, we had to read with feeling. I was not much of a reader at that point in my life so I did not have much of a backlog of books at my disposal. I had seen a great movie that had been taken from a book. It was <u>No Time for Sargeants</u> starring Andy Griffith. Andy Griffith played a hillbilly who was drafted into the Army. I saw the movie while I was in the Army at Ft. Ord. It was a riot! I checked out the book from the library and began to prepare for my first live stage performance.

I picked out a scene from the movie that just cracked me up. The hillbilly soldier tried to describe via a hand written letter to his family back home in the hills about going to his first football game. He didn't understand it at all. He told his family that "what it was called was football". He couldn't understand why the"big cow pasture the game was played in had lines painted all over it." He couldn't understand why "the one who had the funny shaped pumpkin kept running away from the other players who wanted to take it away from him; he didn't think the ones playing the game were very nice to each other." He couldn't understand why the "men in the striped shirts kept taking the pumpkin away from the one who had it and putting it back on the ground." One thing the hillbilly really liked about his experience was "the big 'arnge' drink he bought."

Of course the story was written in hillbilly language and I had to immitate that as I read and acted it out. I found out that I was a bona fide ham.

The class laughed at my presentation and that really pumped me up! I got a B+ on the reading which was better than any grade I ever got on anything at The UofA. Come to think of it, it was a better grade than anything I ever got at Bisbee High School.

Dr. Lavin said she really enjoyed my reading. She did tell the class that we had to diversify. We couldn't pick the same *genre* for all our readings. I had to ask the guy sitting next to me what "genre" meant. He said the thought it meant we had to read different types of books. So I did.

So You Wanna Be a Legend. So Did I.

The next one I did was a scene from "Cyrano de Bergerac", the sword fighter with the big nose; it was a good movie. For my final reading I did the entire poem, "Casey at the Bat". That was the hardest reading I had to do all semester! For each character in the poem I had a different colored baseball cap. Each character had a different voice.

I had to time the putting on and taking off of the hats with the dialogue. It had to "flow" as Dr. Lavin said. My reading did flow. I got an A on my final. All in all, *Intrepretative Reading* was an enjoyable class. I got an A in it. The legend was on a roll, academically anyway.

The most difficult class for me was *Methods of Acting*. Dr. White had the class spend a lot of time studing the various playwrites; the guys who wrote the plays we were going to read. The only one I had ever heard of was William Shakespeare. I soon became familiar with a lot more of those guys; at least by name; Tennessee Williams, Moliere, Thornton Wilder, and others. I felt pretty intellectual rattling off some of those guys' names to my roommate, Ed Hitchcock. Ed was impressed. I could tell.

The hardest part of acting for me was memorizing the lines. Most of my on stage presentations involved a lot of making up as I went along or "ad libbing" as Dr. White called it. I never did get very good at memorizing my lines. Memorizing was always difficult for me.

I did do a decent job on my final acting performance that sememster, however. One of my class mates, a little guy named Albie, and I were paired up for the final.

We were assigned to do a scene from Shakespeare's *Julius Caesar*. The scene we did was the famous "et tu, Brute" scene where Brutus stabs and kills Julius Caesar. Albie was Brutus and I was Julius Caesar.

I really got into that scene! When Albie pulled the rubber dagger out of his cloak and stabbed me you should have seen me die. I grabbed his shoulder and as I slowly slid to the floor I uttered, "et tu, Brute?"

I let it be known to the audience that I was incredulous that my dear friend, Brutus was in on the conspiracy to kill me. I'll bet it took me a good minute to die! I thought I did a great job.

Dr. White said I over did it. The perfomance was not believable he said. Albie and I got an over-all grade of B for the scene. I got an individual grade of *B-*. I was satisfied. My disappointment at not seeing much playing time for the Arizona State *Sun Devil* football team was somewhat eased by the success and enjoyment I realized as a student. I knew I had made the right career choice by selecting Speech as my academic major.

Because of my intense desire to become a well known football coach, I chose Physical Education as my academic minor. The only Physical Education class I took that first semester was *Methods of Physical Education*. It was in this class where I first met Dr. Rudy Lavik. Dr. Lavik was the instructor that semester for *Methods of Physical Education* and as I would find out, was one of the most highly respected professors at Arizona State College. Dr. Lavik had been around A.S.C. for a long time. He started his tenure at A.S.C. in 1933 when he was appointed football coach. He became a legend at Arizona State. Dr. Lavik was an intelligent man. His classes were demanding. He would not allow a student to slide by. Students had to "bow the neck" as he said. We had to always do our best. Dr. Lavik was well read. He was familiar with many of the playwrites I was studying in my Drama Class. He loved to talk about World War I and World War II.

Most of all, Dr. Lavik loved to talk sports. He was a walking encyclopedia of sports. He could quote statistics back to the days of Bronco Nagerski, Red Grange, Knute Rockne, Wee Willie Keeler, Babe Ruth, Kenshaw "Mountain" Landis, and many others I had never heard of. In addition, Dr. Lavik was a physical fitness nut. He religiously followed a daily regime of running, push-ups, sit-ups and pull-ups. He even pitched batting practice to the *Sun Devil* baseball team as I was to find out.

Dr. Lavik's class on *Methods of Physical Education*, more than any other Physical Education class I would take, cemented my desire to be a coach. He emphasized to his students the importance of fair play, abiding by the rules of the game, sportsmanship, team work, physical fitness and making the game fun for the participants. Dr. Lavik said, "Anybody could be a coach. But, only a person with those attributes could be *worthy* coach, one who was respected and admired."

Dr. Lavik's philosophy was much like my Army buddy, Joe Nix's philosophy. I subconsciously vowed that I too, would become a *worthy* coach. I would "bow my neck" to do so.

1957 was a milestone year for the legend**.** I was able to intelligently handle my lack of football success. I found out I could diligently study and make good grades.

I was part of an Arizona State *Sun Devil* baseball team that was the beginning of instilling respectability and a winning attitude in the baseball program at ASC.

I got the first part-time job of my life and I was able to save some money via a "delayed gratification" concept I stumbled upon. You see, I realized I must save some money for my *HONEYMOON!!!* Yep, the legend would be getting married in 1957!

Joan Pauline Fallis, the beautiful, blue-eyed Canadian girl with whom I had carried on an intense letter writing romance flew down from Toronto, Ontario, Canada to spend a few days with the legend. I reserved a room for her at *The Tee-Pee* motel just off campus. Joan was impressed with the motel. Her room was situated at the very top of the huge Indian teepee shaped structure. There were three of these structures on the motel grounds. It looked just like a picture book Indian encampment, complete with a bar-b-que grill in the center of the teepees. Pretty impressive for a Canadian girl who was enthralled with The West and legends, cowboys and Indians, and me.

I found it pretty amazing just how well Joan and I hit it off after such a brief one evening encounter the previous summer. That summer evening was followed by what soon became a passionate, intimate, transparent sharing of our lives via mail. When Joan got off the airplane at Phoenix's Sky Harbor Airport our embrace felt as natural as if we'd known each other for years. We spent several wonderful days together visiting beautiful Oak Creek Canyon and Sedona before driving to Bisbee and a weekend with my parents, sister and brother. They of course, were very loving toward Joan and made her feel right at home. My mother was on her best behavior and did not embarass me by getting drunk. I warned Joan beforehand that Mother was an alcoholic and I had no clue how she would behave. Joan was a bit nervous but seemed at ease with all of us.

After a tour of historic Bisbee on Saturday, Joan and I set out for Agua Prieta "warm water" Mexico just across the Border from Douglas, Arizona. Agua Prieta was a miniature Tijuana, Mexico of my Fort Ord *Warrior* days. We thoroughly enjoyed the evening dancing to the music of Mexican *mariachis* and eating Mexican food which was a real novelty to this Canadian beauty. Joan especially liked the tacos and did not shy away from them even when I told her the rumor about "no dogs seen on the streets in Agua Prieta".

When Joan and I got back to my home about 1:30 a.m.. I parked my car in the back alley near our garbage cans where I often parked when I got home late. I was thankful that our garbage can lids were all in place. A pretty pungent odor was noticable if the cans were uncovered. It was a perfect cool winter night. Cold enough that Joan had to snuggle close for warmth. A bright moon was bathing the alley in a bright yellow glow, and the garbage cans did not smell! A perfect setting for a PROPOSAL!

The legend moved fast. Before either of us knew it, we were engaged! We set the wedding for the following summer in Toronto, Canada. No sense wasting time.

The first thing I did the next morning was to go into the bedroom Joan was in. I woke her up with a kiss and asked her if she had changed her mind. She hadn't. I kissed her again. I left when my mother yelled and told me to get out of Joan's bedroom and let her get dressed for breakfast.

Joan and I drove back to Tempe on Sunday afternoon. We had just enough time on Monday to buy an engagement ring before her flight left Sky Harbor Airport Monday evening. My head was in the clouds for several days after Joan left. I knew I had the perfect girl for a wife. I found significance at last. She loved me as I was. She was not at all impressed with my reputation as a legend. I would have plenty of time to tell her all that after we got married.

Shortly after the 1957 ASC football season ended, a *Sun Devil* team mate, Tom Delaney, and I were driving back to campus from Phoenix. We noticed a large sign near a construction site. The sign read:

<u>**TO OPEN SOON**</u>

BILL JOHNSON'S
BIG APPLE RESTAURANT
"We don't fool you, we feed you!"

HELP NEEDED!

Tom and I didn't discuss it long. We both were looking for part time work. We turned around and drove up to a mobile home situated on the construction site. We saw a sign on the front door of the mobile home which read, *"APPLY INSIDE."* I knocked on the door. A pleasant female voice told us to, "Come in, please." We did and it was at that moment when we first met *Rabbit*.

And that was how she introduced herself. "Rabbit". No last name. Just "Rabbit". Rabbit was an attractive lady. Tiny with a slim, petite figure, Rabbit was dressed in cowgirl garb; western female jeans, chaps, cowgirl boots, and a western hat hanging down behind her neck. A bandanna was tied neatly around the collar of her colorful western shirt.

Rabbit was all business. Her interview was brief and to the point. She was the on-site manager of *The Big Apple*. Bill Johnson was the owner. The opening date for *The Big Apple* was scheduled for late November. Rabbit told us that Bill Johnson's *Big Apple* was going to be the largest Western Style Bar-B-Q restaurant in the entire Valley of the Sun, the whole Phoenix area.

We were impressed with her sales talk. We were soon signed up as Bill Johnson's *Big Apple's* first employees. We were hired as bus boys! The first bus boys in the history of what was to become a long standing Phoenix landmark, "Bill Johnson's *Big Apple!*"

And, what a fun job that was! Tom and I worked the same shifts. We usually were working the 6:00p.m. untill closing shift. The doors closed at 12:00 midnight. By the time we swept the place down and cleaned up the area, we were off by 1:00a.m. or so. The floors were easy to clean as the entire surface of the floor was covered with saw dust, easy to sweep up the old and sprinkle on the new.

Tom and I worked closely with the waitresses. Most of them were nice ladies, fun, but zealous of their working areas. They were very vigilant when the bus boys cleaned off their tables. The tips belonged to the waitresses! One bus boy was fired on the spot by Rabbit when he was seen pocketing some change left for the waitress.

We could eat one meal per shift free; anything on the menu except steak and ribs.

My favorite menu item was their famous deep dish apple pie ala mode! The Big Apple motto, "We don't fool you.We feed you!" was faithfully adhered to. Shortly after opening officially in January of 1957, Bill Johnson's *Big Apple* became the place to eat in the Phoenix area. Tom and I began to work when the doors were first opened for business in early December of 1956. The Grand Opening was huge "bash" on January 1, 1957; New Year's Day! Tom and I were rather disappointed that we would be working on New Year's Day as that was "football day". We would miss *The Sun Bowl, The Rose Bowl, The Sugar Bowl, and The Orange Bowl!* But; not to worry! Bill Johnson had set up several television sets around the huge dining room. He was a shrewd business man.

The place was packed. The customers enjoyed delicious food while watching the games. The "carry out business" was very brisk as well.

Tom and I missed little of the games. We were able to "bus" tables, load our carts with dirty dishes, wipe off the tables, talk with customers, all while keeping track of the games via the various TV sets. The only employees who did not get to watch the games were the kitchen help, the cooks and the dishwashers. Bill Johnson did not want the cooks distracted. *"We don't fool you. We feed you"* was a motto Bill Johnson took seriously; all of his employees were trained with that motto in mind.

SUN DEVIL BASEBALL
The Foundation

I noticed the sign as I was going into the cafeteria for breakfast one day in early February. It was a hand written sign on note bookpaper. It read:

So You Wanna Be a Legend. So Did I.

BASEBALL PLAYERS
PRACTICE WILL BEGIN MONDAY.
REPORT TO THE BASEBALL FIELD AT 3:30 P.M. SHARP.
Coach Mel Erickson

That was my first indication that Arizona State Baseball under the direction of Mel Erickson was going to be on a much lower profile than what I experienced at the U. of A. under Coach Frank Sancet.

After breakfast, I picked up Tom Delaney and we headed in to Bill Johnson's *Big Apple*. This was to be my last weekend shift as I had already given my notice to Rabbit earlier that week. I knew that baseball would be starting soon.

I was telling Tom about the sign when it hit me! "Where is the baseball field?" I had never given that a thought. I could not recall seeing any lights, a fence, anything that resembled a baseball field since I came on campus over six months ago. Tom wasn't sure either. All we could figure out was that the baseball team must practice and play at one of the local high school diamonds.

WRONG! Arizona State baseball was not so fortunate as to play on a bonafide baseball field with grass infield and a fence. For years the baseball team, practiced and played on what was commonly known as "the ROTC Drill Field". And the Physical Education Classes used the area for their P.E. activities. I would run into a similar situation years later.

A well hit ball to left field would bounce off of the Arizona State Gymnasium wall. A well hit ball to center field could conceivably hit a student walking to or from the parking lot. A well hit ball to right field could be expected to be picked up by a kid playing in his front yard in the residental area just off campus. If the catcher turned quickly to go after a passed ball, he might run face first into the wire backstop only a few feet behind home plate. The back stop was hastily constructed for the P.E. classes' softball games

Baseball at Arizona State resembled a "club activity"; it was not at all emphasized like a Varsity sport. That fact was made more obvious as the season progressed. I was surprised at the turnout at 3:30 that Monday afternoon. There were over 100 in attendance. The few who got there first were seated in the bleachers just behind the team benches. The rest of us were standing around on both sides of the bleachers. At 3:30 sharp, the door to the P.E. Locker room just behind the bleachers opened and I got a glimpse of a man who would have a positive influence on my life in the next two years.

Coach Mel Erickson walked slowly up to where all of us were standing. He got right to the point. He gave a brief introduction and then we assemble to groups according to our positions. Catchers over here, pitchers over there, and first basemen over there,

Then came the first "Mel-ism", and it wasn't the last I witnessed in the next two years. Coach Erickson told us to take a lap around the field. The field encompassed several acres The leaders of the pack determined what "around the field" meant. What none of us could figure out was why Coach Erickson grouped us according to position. The position groups get blended together in the lap around the field. When we got back from our lap, Coach then went into his first-meeting lecture.

We stood around for an hour as he went over the college eligibility requirements, the care and respect for the equipment we would be issued, and our tough schedule which would start in just two weeks' time. Coach Erickson then got personal. He told us how much he loves baseball, and how he had agreed to coach the team in 1955 after Baseball Hall of Fame inductee Jimmy Foxx turned down the job.

Coach told us he was a doctoral student who had some minor league playing experience. He jumped at the chance to get back into baseball as a coach. Plus, as I learned later, he came cheap. Rumor had it that Coach Erickson was not getting a salary.

His love for the game became very obvious as the season progressed. It was also obvious to us that he loved his players as well. The last item in his first lecture was to introduce Dave Graybill, the team captain. I knew and respected Dave Graybill. He was The Arizona State starting quarterback last fall and one of Arizona State's greatest all around athletes. I was looking forward to playing on the same baseball team with Dave Graybill. However, I did not recall seeing Dave in all the mass of the 100+ players. Again, a Mel-ism. He hollered, "Dave Graybill, wherever you are?" Coach was obviously expecting Graybill to raise his hand. No hand. No reply. Graybill was not in attendance. Coach Erickson then said something like, "Well, Graybill will be here shortly. He is our team captain for this season."

We proceeded to practice. All 100+ of us, with little semblance of organization. We played catch. We played "pepper". We ran bases. Then we took batting practice. We numbered off by fours and batted in numerical order. Those not batting scattered all around the field to retrieve hit balls. Coach Erickson was our batting practice pitcher. He threw each pitch right over the plate. It didn't take too long to have each player swing at five pitches and bunt two before we went through the entire bunch.

At the end of practice team meeting, still no Dave Graybill. Before Coach Erickson sent us in, one of the players asked a good question, "Coach, when are you going to cut?" Coach's response was another Mel-ism, "Oh, you'll take care of that." I had no clue what he was talking about. The next day at 3:30 there were only 30 or so players. Dave Graybill was one of them.

Somehow the team had been whittled down to a managable number.

My guess is that those who did not come back were mostly new to Arizona State. Probably they were disenchanted with Coach Mel Erickson's "organizational skills".

Dave Graybill later told me he had been to two of Coach Erickson's first day practices. He waited until the second day to show up this year. He said it always takes the new guys awhile to get used to "Mel-babe" as Coach Erickson was dubbed by Graybill and the veterans who had played for him in the past. I soon found out that even though the Arizona State baseball program was considered by the college administration to be a "club activity" along with ladies soccer and intramural football, the players who came back the second day took baseball very seriously. After the first few days of practice, I could see we had the potential to be a good team. We were not as polished as Coach Sancet's U. of A. *Wildcat* teams but we were head and shoulders above the good Ft. Ord *Warrior* team I was on last spring. And definitely better than *Mama's Chicken Wings*, the semi-pro team I played on in Salinas, California.

It was obvious that Dave Graybill was our coach-on-the-field. Coach Erickson had the practice sequences sketched out on paper and we followed them until we came to a glitch in the agenda. At that point Graybill cornered Coach Erickson and suggest we take another route. Graybill often suggested we devote more time to an area we hadn't worked on as much as we should have.

The first glitch I remember Graybill mentioning to Coach Erickson was one day at practice when we were just about finished taking infield practice. Graybill mentioned to Coach Erickson that we hadn't worked on double-plays as much as we needed to, so Coach Erickson gave the infielders another 10 minutes of double-play work. I was impressed with Coach Erickson's willingness to take advice from one of the players.

Dave Graybill brought his football toughness to the baseball field. His nickname was *Grubby*. I found out why the day we had our first intersquad game with live pitching.

Jim Sims, a fine, experienced, left-handed pitcher with excellent control, pitched for one team and Graybill pitched for the other.

What a contrast in styles! Sims was poised, methodical, and unemotional. Graybill, on the other hand, was herky-jerky in his motions, he talked to himself and the batters. He just reared back and threw as hard as he could. Seemingly, he had no idea where the ball was going. It could just as well be headed for the batter's head as across the plate. The batters did not dare dig in at the plate when Graybill was pitching. They had to hang pretty loose

After just one inning of pitching Dave Graybill was a filthy mess. I never did figure out how he got so dirty so fast. He was just such an intense competitor and did everything full blast and to the best of his ability. When Dave had to slide into a base, not only did he raise a cloud of dust, he dug a trench several feet in length. His uniform was often in shreds after a game or an intense practice. *Grubby* fit Dave Graybill to a "T".

By the Saturday morning practice at the end of our first week, a starting line-up began to emerge. As I mentally compared the teams I was part of at The University of Arizona, I could see we were not in same class as *The Wildcats,* skill and experience wise. But I could see, too, that we had something *The Wildcats* lacked.

My new Arizona State College teammates exhibited more hustle and a desire to improve than any team I had been a part of. I learned a valuable lesson for my future coaching career that year: in some cases *attitude* is of more value to a team than *skill*.

Our first Saturday morning full scale scrimmage encouraging to me. I felt that for me to get a good shot at professional baseball, I had to be on a good team. I had to be a leader and one of the best players on the team.

Bill Giddings, the player-manager of The Fort Ord *Warrior* baseball team told me that he felt I was the player on that *Warrior* team with the most potential to be a professional. Giddings tried to convince me to go to a major league tryout camp as soon as I got out of the Army. He said that at my age the baseball clock was running down.

I felt good about my chances on this Arizona State team. I was the fastest one on the team and pretty well had the center field position nailed down. Though I was not a power hitter, I felt I could hold my own with the bat. I was a decent hitter the two seasons I played at the University of Arizona and I believed I had improved while at Fort Ord. I was a pretty good bunter and with my speed had drag bunted for a number of hits while at Fort Ord. All in all, I felt good about my immediate future with the Arizona State *Sun Devil* baseball team.

Our season started with a bang. We won nine out of our first ten games. We swept Grand Canyon College, San Diego Navy, Colorado State, and the University of Utah, before losing one of three against a good University of Wyoming team.

"A Gamer"
Royce Youree

I would be remiss if I did not credit Royce Youree for much of the solid foundation this *Sun Devil* team laid for the future.

When one speaks of "hustle" and "athletic desire", Royce Youree automatically comes to my mind. If I had one player upon which to build a winning baseball program, I would choose Royce Youree.

I first became aware of Royce during the 1957 ASC basketball season. Royce was a mainstay on the *Sun Devil* basketball teams for several years. What impressed me the most about him was the trememdous hustle and all out effort he put into every minute he was on the floor. His enthusiasm and desire to compete was highly contagious.

Royce played baseball with that same intensity. Above all else, Royce was a fighter. I can't count the times Royce came to the defense of our little, cocky second baseman, Don Baniewicz. Don was made out of some of the same stuff Royce was. He was a hustler. He played a spirited second base. He enjoyed coming down on top of a sliding opponent and applying a glove in the face tag. Most of the opponents did not appreciate Don's over aggressive style of play. Often they would come up swinging. Don had sense enough to cower and wait for Royce to come to his rescue. Royce, a third baseman, was close enough to Don that he would plow into the opponent before Don came to any harm. Youree would sometimes inflict bloody wounds. Umpires and teammates usually broke up the fights before too much damage was done.

The fight that Royce Youree will be most remembered for occured in 1958. The *Sun Devils* were in San Diego playing The Naval Training Center. Three or four Marines were in the stands verbally abusing Royce for his aggressive style of play. The verbal abuse continued for nine innings. Youree took it. When the game finally ended with the *Sun Devils* winning, Royce wasted little time sprinting into the stands where he took on the surprised Marines. Those nearest the battle say that Royce was the winner hands down. Military Police and most of the *Sun Devil* team broke up the fight.

So You Wanna Be a Legend. So Did I.

Berry Sollenberger, long time Arizona sports historian called it "the most famous ruckus in Sun Devil baseball annals." When Royce was asked if he was hurt, he replied, "Naw, there were only three or four of them."

Royce Youree was a truly a solidifying agent on our baseball team. Royce's eagerness to coming to the rescue of Don Baniewicz many times during the season told us he would do the same for any of us. We became a united team under Royce's leadership. That unity carried the 1958 *The Sun Devils* to a school record 19 wins.

The 1957 season saw the *Sun Devils* defeat arch rival University of Arizona *Wildcats* for the first time in modern history. Royce was the catalyst for that win as well. He led the way with his hustle and never-say-die attitude. Royce's stellar defensive play at third base kept the *Wildcats* from scoring in two consecutive innings to preserve our 4-3 win. With runners on second and third, two outs in the ninth inning the *Cats* threatened to tie or win the game. Royce ended the game with a hustling, diving catch of a pop fly into short left field. Royce Youree was a "gamer".

The 1957 *Sun Devil* baseball season was much more rewarding and enjoyable than was my *Sun Devil* football experience.

Though we started off by winning nine of our first ten games we slowed down as we got into the heart of of our schedule. Our overall record was an modest 15 wins-16 losses-1 tie; not great but for a team not officially recognized by the administration we did well. Our 4-3 win over our bitter rival, University of Arizona *Wildcats* opened some eyes. 1958 would be even better.

I was happy. I had a good season. My 36 total hits led the team. I tied with four of my teammates for most hits in a game with four. I tied with right fielder, Bill Mead for grand slam home runs with one; I led the team with 110 total at bats; I tied first baseman John Jacobs, and Dave Graybill with 22 runs batted in; I led the team with runs scored with 29; and I tied short stop John Regoli with 12 stolen bases. Dave Graybill had the team's highest batting average of .400. My batting average was average. I hit a decent .341. That put me in the middle of the pack somewhere.

The handwriting on the wall told me I would have to greatly improve in 1958, improve in all categories if I wanted to have a professional career in baseball.

The hand writing on the wall in this case was my god-father, Roy "Hard Rock" Johnson (B). Roy was a close family friend. He had coached for the Chicago *Cubs* major league baseball club for many years and was now the *Cubs* West Coast Scout. His territory included Arizona. Roy covered several *Sun Devil* games and he always made it a point to seek me out and visit. Roy made it pretty clear that my statistics would have to improve for him to offer me a professional contract. He said "next season" would tell the story.

Roy and his lovely wife Fanetta lived many off-seasons in my home town Bisbee. Some of those off seasons Roy worked in the Bisbee copper mines. He got his nickname "*Hard Rock*" from that experience. Miners who worked with a sledge hammer and a chisel were known as "hard rock miners". They drilled holes in *hard rock* to place dynamite sticks in place for blasting.

Roy and Fanetta loved Mexican food, especially my mother's Mexican food. Mother was a great cook. Her tacos were the talk of the town. Roy often brought members of the Chicago *Cubs* to our Bisbee house for a taco dinner.

My love for baseball was nurtured by rubbing shoulders with well-known professional baseball players. Dizzy Dean, Gabby Hartnet, and rookie Ernie Banks were just a few of the pros. who graced our living room enjoying tacos as well as passing on baseball stories and fundamentals of the game. (B)

MY WIFE JOAN

In all honesty my mind was not always focused just on *Sun Devil* baseball in 1957. I had an upcoming wedding. I knew 1958 would be a better season for me. I would be a married man, settled down, much more mature and focused. As usual the legend moved pretty fast.

Our torrid letter writing romance was in full throttle. We set a date for the wedding. Joan's dad had a summer job waiting for me in one of Toronto's largest lumber yards. Joan found several dresses she wanted me to check out. I told her to pick out the one she liked best; she would be beautiful in any of them.

My dad and mom drove up from Bisbee to see our last 1957 *Sun Devil* game. When they saw Roy Johnson they had a boisterous reunion. When Roy was excited he was loud. He hadn't seen dad and mom in several years. The handshakes, hugs and back slaps were heard all over the stands. Roy was one of our family.

I told dad and mom about Bill Johnson's *Big Apple* and their great bar-b-que ribs. Dad suggested we go there for dinner. Roy thought that was a good idea. He suggested, "We'll let Mr. Wrigley pick up the tab." Mr. Wrigley of "Wrigley chewing gum" fame owned the Chicago *Cubs*. Mr. Wrigley paid Roy's salary.

After we ate and were waiting for dessert, dad sprang a huge surprise on me! He handed me an envelope with a nice *Sun Devil* key ring inside. I looked puzzled. "What is the key ring for?"

Dad's reply floored me: "You will need keys for your wedding present. Mom and I are buying you and Joan a hot off the assembley line 1957 Chevrolet!"

Dad was not the emotional type. He was pretty cool about it. Mom cried when she saw my stunned reaction. I couldn't believe it; a new Chevy! How lucky could a guy get? I was marrying a beautiful girl. We were getting a brand new car. I just knew that even though I wasn't going to be a pro football player, maybe not even a pro. baseball player that my search for significance was on the right track. I would have a perfectly satisfying marriage and my coaching skills would land me a prestigeous coaching position at Arizona State.

Dad had arranged for Joan and me to pick up the new Chevrolet at the Chevrolet factory in Flint, Michigan. I had no clue where Flint, Michigan was. Dad knew it was fairly close to Joan's home, Toronto, Canada. Dad thought it would be special for us to pick up the Chevrolet right off the assembly line. He was right. It was very special.

Joan and I tried to coordinate our plane flights to arrive in Flint as near as possible to the same time. We did pretty well. Joan only had to wait for me for an hour or so. We took a taxi to a motel and we got separate rooms. I was still a "straight arrow". We would be married August 16. We could wait.

We got to the Chevrolet factory shortly before the whistle blew to indicate the day's work was to begin. We checked in at the head office. The nice lady looked at all the papers dad had given me. She indicated all was in order. We went to the waiting area the lady had indicated. We were the only ones there. Joan and I just looked at each other, held hands, and kissed a few times.

I tried to look as cool and unemotional as possible. I was so cool that when our names were called I let Joan get to the window first. We were going to watch a beautiful, black Chevrolet roll off the assembly line. It did; it was beautiful!

The man handed me the keys, said "Congratulations" and walked off. Still as cool as possible and being the gentleman I was, I gave Joan the keys and said she could have the honor of driving it off the line. She was nervous and didn't bang into anything. She made me drive it to the motel. She said she didn't like to drive in city traffic.

I was a bit hesitant myself. I figured though that driving a beautiful, shiny black Chevrolet in city traffic would be a "cake walk" compared to looking football great John Henry Johnson's pumping tree-stump legs head on.

Joan and I alternated driving our wedding present for the rest of the way to Toronto, Canada. What a joy to drive.

What a joy to know my future was to be carefree. I had a loving wife-to-be. I had the whole world at my beckon call. The legend was finding significance.

Canadians are a bit different.

Joan's dad and mom were very nice people. Ethel Fallis, Joan's mother, met us on the front porch as we drove into the driveway. I liked her instantly. She greeted me with a hug and a warm welcome. She ushered us into the house and immediately went to the basement door to tell Joan's dad that we had arrived. He came up slowly and greeted me in a rather casual, but friendly manner.

Her dad, Clair Fallis, was a retired elementary school principal. I got the feeling he somewhat disapproved of me when I told him I was going to be a high school teacher-coach. "One can make much more money on the university level", he replied. "You won't make much money instructing physical education activities in American high schools. You will need to begin working on an advanced degree. Once you get your doctorate degree you will provide nicely for Joan and your children."

That exchange was destined to be repeated numerous times. Mr. Fallis just could not understand American infatuation with competative athletics.

What really got Mr. Fallis' attention was our new 1957 black Chevrolet. He was a car nut. I have never known anyone as obsessed with automobiles.

Mr. Fallis had a note book with a detailed log on all the cars he ever owned, the amount he paid for them, the dates he purchased them, and the dates they were maintainced, the mileage when new tires were needed. You name it, he had it recorded.

Mr. Fallis' first piece of advice regarding our new '57 Chevy was to always have several dust rags in the trunk of the car. Each morning before getting in the car I should wipe all the dust off the outside body.

His vocabulary took some getting used to. He cautioned me to be sure to check "the rad most frequently". "The heat in Arizona," he said, "would cause the rad to seethe well above the recommended celsius level." It took me awhile to catch on. When I did, Mr. Fallis' advice made a lot of sense. Check the water level in the radiator often. It got hot in Arizona.

As a teacher and later an elementary principal, Mr. Fallis was a hard nosed disciplinarian. His encouragement to be a stickler for discipline played an important part of my classroom management in later years. He advised me to insist that the students were to stand up whenever an adult came into the classroom. He felt the students should stand at their desks at the beginning of each class period. They were to remain standing until the teacher told them to sit down. For some reason I just could not see me insisting on students standing like that in an Arizona classroom.

I didn't dare knock the Canadian educational system. Joan was a product of that system. She graduated from high school with outstanding academic standing. She attended the University of Toronto for her "fifth year". She earned a degree in Medical Technology. Joan explained to me that the fifth year was an intensive year of advanced study in her selected area. She chose medical technlgy as she loved chemestry and laboratory work. She was confident that she could get a job as a lab technician somewhere in the Phoenix, Arizona area. I had one more year before I received my B.A. degree in Education. Her income would allow us to enjoy life as newlyweds. My Military G.I.Bill money would not hurt either.

Joan and I had a week of leisure before my job in the lumberyard started. We made the most of it. We traveled to Stratford, Ontario and took in an evening of their famous "Summer Shakespearean Festival". I impressed Joan with my familiarity with the renowned English playwright and poet.

We enjoyed a few evenings with some of Joan's friends. She wanted to show off her American catch. I was an immediate hit when Joan told them I was from Arizona. They all asked about my ranch, did I ride horses, were the Indians still a problem? They were a bit disappointed to find out all those Western movies they loved were exaggerated and outdated. They were especially disappointed that I grew up in a house and not a ranch.

The highlight of that first week was the Fallis Family Reunion. The event was held at the Fallis' country cabin some 40 miles outside Toronto. There were over 100 in attendance. I was the center of attraction.

Mr. Fallis told most of the family that I was going to be a teacher. That seemed to make me o.k. None of them asked me about my athletic endeavors which disappointed me. I wanted them to know where my real talents and aspirations lay.

My introduction to Joan's family was a real joy. They were good people, the salt of the earth, one might say. I was proud to be included in the family.

Welch's Lumberyard was one of the largest in all of Eastern Canada. Mr. Fallis and Mr. Welch had been long time friends. I had no trouble gaining summer employment. I didn't even have to go through the interview process. I walked into Mr. Welsh's office Monday morning and was welcomed by a cordial elderly gentleman. I found out immediately that Mr. Welch was all business.

Our initial meeting was brief. Mr. Welch gave me a tour of the area of the lumberyard where I was to spend the next two months, the railroad unloading dock.

My job was to assist unloading lumber from railroad boxcars. It was to be the most physically challanging job I would ever have. It also proved to be one of the most enjoyable and interesting jobs I would ever have. My work companions would make the job one I would never forget.

I worked each day with three men whom I would grow to love and admire. Two were Dutchmen straight from Holland and the other was German, a former member of the Hitler Youth Corps.

The Dutchmen were Jon Van Gent and Cor Kammerman. Jon was an elderly man, of slight of build and outgoing. He had a great sense of humor. Cor was much younger than Jon, probably my age. He had recently been married. Cor, too, was friendly and outgoing. He was tall, handsome and blond.

William was the German. I never did learn his last name. William was aloof. He did not speak unless spoken to and he kept to himself most of the time. When I spoke to him he always had a friendly response. His English was passable. William willingly shared with me some of his experiences in war time Germany under Hitler's rule. William was a young boy of ten or twelve when his family coerced him into joining The Hitler Youth Corps. His family felt they would be safer if one of them was part of the Nazi regime.

William told me he could not believe how Germans believed all the lies Hitler told them. William was so much under Hitler's spell that he would listen to his parents' conversations hoping to hear some mention of anti-Nazi opinion. He would have been rewarded handsomely had he been able to turn his parents over to the Nazi authorities. To speak negatively about any of Hitler's administration was considered treason punishable by death.

Almost thirty years later William still carried German prejudice towards their World War II enemies. He did not care at all to converse or socialize with Dutchmen, thus his aloofness towards Cor and Jon. This aloofness carried over into our work, yet, we were a very hard working and competent group.

Our job was to unload newly arrived train box car loads of lumber. The lumber was all cut to one length and packed tightly into the box car. Our job was to unload it for cutting into prescribed lengths. That was the hard part, unloading it.

One of us, usually Cor or I would have to climb to the very top inside the boxcar, lying flat on our stomachs on top of all that lumber we would have to work the pieces free to slide them down to our co workers waiting on the dock below.

It took about an hour before we had unloaded enough lumber that the one lying on top could get on his knees, a few more hours before he could stand up without bumping his head on the boxcar's roof. The unloading was easier after that.

We usually unloaded one and one and a half box cars before lunch. The summer heat and humidity in Eastern Canada was worse than even my beloved Arizona. It became horrific inside a lumber loaded boxcar. Lunch was a most welcome break.

The four of us usually ate lunch in the shade of an empty boxcar. Jon, Cor, and myself in one corner; William in another corner. It was at these lunch down times that I was able to dig into personal histories of my three new friends. I was the only one who would seek information from William. I was the only one William would respond to.

Jon and Cor both related snippets of their war time experiences under Germany's domination. During these emotional and personal times William would usually leave the boxcar. Jon and Cor then spoke very freely. Their families suffered horribly. Jon's mother and father both died during the early stages of World War II. I never learned how. Cor's family all survived and came to Canada at the end of The War. They met Jon shortly after coming to Canada and became close friends. Cor's family was the only family Jon had. Cor and I became good friends. Joan and I were invited to his home for dinner once. It was then that we met Cor's sweet and gracious wife, Agnes.

I have often thought of my summer job and my three Canadian friends. Cor and I vowed to stay in touch after Joan and I left Toronto. We exchanged a few letters over the years. Sadly we lost touch with each other after I began teaching.

August 16, 1957. Our Wedding Day

The ceremony was held in a church within a few blocks of Joan's home. The church was Joan's family's church. She grew up in that church. I don't remember much about the ceremony but have fond memories of the reception held in Joan's home after the wedding. My dad and mom were there as was my little sister, Cathy.

My Scotish granddad, Big Bobby was there. Big Bobby was my mother's father.

He was a Fergus; Robert Fergus. Big Bobby was cocky, humorous and a show off. He was the life of the reception. Joan's family was all crowded into the Fallis' home.

Big Bobby had a chair in the center of all the activity. He was usually surrounded by a bevy of Joan's elderly aunts. He let it be known pretty quickly that he settled in Nova Scotia, Canada for a few years after coming over from Scotland

He then moved to Bisbee, Arizona to work in the copper mines. His greatly exaggerated stories of the hard times in Arizona captivated the ladies. Luckily Joan's parents did not serve alcoholic beverages at the reception or Big Bobby's stories would have become possibly a bit risque. Big Bobby was a hard drinking copper miner; an alcoholic, as was my mother.

I made a hit with Joan's family during the reception when I had to give a brief speech. During the speech I got a little emotional. I told everyone how proud I was to have Joan as my wife. I thanked Joan's dad and mom for raising such a beautiful daughter and for instilling in Joan the attributes I was searching for in a wife. I left out the part about how I knew Joan would support my quest to become a teacher-coach of significance. I got a lot of "oh's" and "ah's" from Joan's relatives when I closed the speech with a brief prayer to "the man upstairs". They knew I was a religious man and would take good care of Joan.

I had one disappointment on my wedding day. I had invited my three lumber yard buddies, Jon, Cor, and William to come to the wedding and the reception. Jon and William did not attend. I was pleased yet saddened to see Cor and Agnes among the long line of relatives and friends as Joan and I left the reception. They had not come in the house. Joan and I were so busy ducking rice that I did not stop to give my good friend Cor and his wife Agnes a good-by hug. Though we did write each other a few times, I never saw Cor again, nor Jon, nor William.

Our honeymoon started in Cape Cod, Massachusetts. Joan and I spent several days enjoying the beach, the great eating places and the tourist attractions.

Since we were in Massachusetts I wanted so much to at least drive by Fenway Park, home of the Boston *Red Sox*. I told Joan that possibly I would someday play there. We had to hurry back to Arizona as *Sun Devil* football practice was starting soon. I knew head coach "Dapper Dan" Devine would not wait for me to show up.

The summer of 1957 was one I would remember all of my life. I gained a beautiful, devoted wife. I had a brief but meaningful friendship with three men at Welch's Lumber Yard.

A New Perspective

The 1957-58 school year would prove to be a year of finally getting my act together, a year of realizing that significance was found in who I was. I was Joan's husband. Being a legend was not as important to me now.

My search for significance as a "great college football player" was laid to rest after just one week. It was pretty obvious that Head Coach Dan Devine had no plans for me. At the first team meeting when Assistant Coach Tom Fletcher took roll my name was not called. When Coach Fletcher finished calling roll, he asked: "Anybody I did not call?" I sheepishly raised my hand along with a few others. Coach Fletcher murmured under his breath, "Oh yeah. Hicks". He then added my name to the list, reluctantly so it seemed to me.

We practiced in shorts and helmets that first week. I was still one of the fastest on the team. I finished second to Leon Burton in most of the conditioning sprints. When we did our team drills I did not get into any of the drills. I mainly stood around in the background and watched. Some of my friends from the previous year offered encouragement and pats on the rear. They were concerned about their own place on the team however, to pay too much attention to me.

I found it interesting that my attitude had undertaken a major change from the previous season. I was not at all upset that I was being ignored at practices. *Hadley Hicks legend* was replaced by *Hadley Hicks husband*. I eagerly looked forward to the end of practices so I could go home to my wife.

Joan always greeted me with a warm hug and a kiss. Sometime during the dinner she had prepared she would ask how the practice went. I told her that I was disappointed that I was not getting any practice time. Somehow though that was no big deal either to Joan or to me. Our new life as Hadley and Joan Hicks took precedence over everything.

Joan loved her job as a laboratory technician at the Mesa Community Hospital. Mesa, Arizona was just a few minutes down the road from our one bedroom home in Tempe, Arizona.

I found a new lease on my academic life. My speech/debate classes occupied most of my daytime hours. Football practices after a few days were put on the back burner. I was eager to get as much knowledge as I could to prepare myself for teaching.

Joan was a big help. My toughest class was *kinesiology*, the study of the body's muscle functions. Much memorization of muscle *origin* and *insertion*, where the muscles were attached to which bones and what their effects were on bone functions. Joan grilled me by the hour. Memorization never did come easy for me. It was especially tough when I was distracted by the beautiful one grilling me.

A phone call one evening from my Ft. Ord *Warrior* teammate, Jack "*Whitey Buckeye*" Standard encouraged me to put the brakes on any thoughts of football significance that may have been lingering in the back of my mind. Jack was calling from the Tempe Greyhound Bus Station and was looking for a place to sleep for the night. He wanted to know if it was too late to "walk on" at Arizona State since he was looking for a place to play football.

Joan and I got in our 1957 Chevy and drove to downtown Tempe and picked up Whitey Buckey. I was glad to see Jack and proud to introduce him to my new wife. Joan was curious as to where he got that nickname. Jack explained his Ft. Ord teammates were responsible. He played one season on the Ohio State University *Buckeye* football team. Jack's white complexion along with his striking blond hair did the rest. Thus: "*Whitey Buckeye*".

Jack was always a free spirit. He told Joan and me that he was traveling around trying to find a school in which to enroll and "play some football". The more we talked the more I saw Jack as a good prospect for my friend Max Spilsbury at Arizona State College in Flagstaff. I told Jack about Max, a United States Marine during World War II. (B) He was highly decorated and like all Marines, Max was tough. He coached tough and expected his players to play tough. The more I talked the more Jack liked what he heard. I told him Joan and I would drive him to Flagstaff the next day. We needed to get away for a weekend. It would do us good.

I decided then and there my football playing days were over. I doubted that the *Sun Devils* would miss me at the Saturday morning practice. I did not need the Arizona State *Sun Devils* to provide me with significance. The *Sun Devils* certainly did not need me.

We drove to Flagstaff the next morning and arrived as the Arizona State College *Lumberjacks* were finishing their morning practice. Seeing Coach Max Spilsbury and some of the *Lumberjacks* was almost like going home to Bisbee. I knew many of them and they knew me. I was still a hero to them.

Max attended high school in Bisbee before his Marine tour of duty. Many of Max's *Lumberjacks* were tough football players from Bisbee. They had played for Max at Bisbee High School and knew what to expect. Max knew what to expect from them as well. Max prided himself in recruiting tough football players and Bisbee football players were tough.

Max seemed genuinely glad to see me. He was impressed with Joan. He told me she was too good for me. With that he grabbed me around the neck and roughed me up a little. Then turning to Jack he said, "And who is this tough looking hombre?" I told Max that his name was Jack "Whitey Buckeye" Standard. Max liked that. He said, "Anyone with a name like that has to be tough."

Over lunch in the Arizona State College cafeteria I explained to Max that Jack would like an opportunity to try out for the *Lumberjack* football team. I told Max about Jack and I playing together on the Fort Ord *Warrior* National Championship team. I spoke highly of Jack's toughness as a fullback.

Max and his *Lumberjacks* were leaving the next morning for a week long trip to Mexico. The *Lumberjacks* would put on several football clinics for interested Mexican coaches. At the end of the week the *Lumberjacks* would play the University of Mexico team in a regulation football game using American rules.

Max explained that Jack could not go along due to legality reasons. Jack hadn't registered in school, he didn't have a physical exam and wasn't an official member of the Arizona State College football squad. Jack was to register for classes and get all the paper work done by the time Max and the team returned from Mexico.

Before Joan and I got in the car for our return trip to Tempe, Max took us to the dorm where Jack would be housed for the time being. Max set Jack up with a temporary cafeteria ticket. I could tell Max was excited at the possibility of having a tough former Ohio State *Buckeye* playing for him. He told Jack they would get together as soon as the team returned from Mexico, and gave Jack $100 of his own money to tide him over for the week.

With that Joan and I said good by to my Fort Ord *Warrior* teammate. We both got crunching hugs from Max. As we got into our car, Max thanked me for bringing Jack to Flagstaff.

Max and his *Lumberjacks* left for Mexico early the next morning. Max never saw Whitey Buckeye again, nor did he ever see his $100 again, nor did I ever see my Fort Ord *Warrior* teammate again.

1958
No more *"Mel-isms"*?

We heard the rumor during basketball season, "Baseball coach Mel Erickson was being fired. The 1958 season will be his last."

The rumor appeared to be pretty valid. Jim Sims, our number one pitcher going into the season told me about it first. Jim's father was Head of Arizona State's Maintenance Department. He was pretty much in the know about goings-on in the higher levels of the administrative network. Jim said his father told him that it was not a secret. Coach Erickson was to be replaced by someone with more baseball experience.

The Arizona State Athletic Director was Clyde "Character Builder" Smith. Mr Smith had never been popular with the *Sun Devil* baseball team. We did not think Mr. Smith did enough to aid our baseball program.

It was obvious to many of Arizona State's athletes that Mr. Smith favored football. One sports reporter for a local newspaper had this to say about the administrations's interest, support and financial backing for baseball: "On a scale of 1-to-10... it would be -10."

Clyde Smith came to Arizona State College in 1952 as head football coach. His record was a so-so 15-13-1.

Upon being appointed Athletic Director in 1955 Smith immediately began to improve the football program. Smith's first positive move was to step down as head football coach. He then replaced himself with Dan Devine, a brilliant move.

It appeared Smith's next move was to get rid of baseball Coach Mel Erickson. With the 1958 season in front of us with a "lame-duck" coach the entire team was incensed.

We knew that Coach Erickson volunteered to coach the *Sun Devils*. His compensation, if any, was minimal. We knew too that Mrs. Erickson was in poor health. We could only speculate on the stress Coach was going through. He was a private person. He never complained to us about the dirty deal he was getting. The team to a man vowed to give Coach Erickson the best possible going away present we could, a winning season.

At the first practice session a record number of prospects reported; 149. The majority were "walk-ons" who had not been recruited. The veterans were amazed at this turnout. We thought that with the rumor of Coach Mel Erickson's dismissal most would not be too eager to play under those circumstances. Most new comers, however, said that with the Arizona Board of Regents officially granting Arizona State College *University* status, more emphasis would be placed on baseball. All of us were proud to be on the first Arizona State University baseball team.

University status was an incentive to us. For way too long Arizona State was considered just a step above a junior college. *Sun Devil* baseballers had a once in a life time opportunity. We could begin taking steps to put our baseball program on a level with the University of Arizona *Wildcats*.

We began to make heads turn in 1957 when the *SunDevils* beat the U.of A. 4-3 behind Dave Graybill's superb 4-hit pitching performance. We followed that up with another win in 1958. We could sense the tide turning. We were on our way. The attitude on the team was one of determination. We were determined that win or lose we would make Arizona State University *Sun Devils* a team to be reckoned with.

That first practice session was memorable in that our first "Mel-ism" of the season got us off to a good start. It occured during outfield practice. Coach Erickson was hitting fly balls to the outfielders. He was standing in foul territory near first base. Our first baseman, John Jacobs was shagging the balls for Coach as the outfielders threw them back. It was always fun to watch Coach Erickson hit fly balls. He was not blessed with the skill needed to hit fly balls consistantly. Often he would swing and miss, Sometimes he would hit a high fly ball behind him. John Jacobs the first baseman would catch that one.

When he did hit a fly ball in the direction of the outfielders grouped in right field it was anyone's guess who should catch it. Coach Erickson would usually yell an outfielder's name. That outfielder was expected to catch the ball wherever Coach hit it. Coach yelled, as an example, "Hadley Hicks wherever you are." I then had to take off after the ball. Sometimes it was right at me. Other times I had to run halfway across the field to get to it.

So You Wanna Be a Legend. So Did I.

The season's first, but by no means last "Mel-ism", was initiated by first baseman John Jacobs. As John gave Coach Mel a ball to hit to the outfield, John said, "Coach, hit one to Kim Frasier."

As Coach tossed the ball in the air to hit, he yelled out, "Kim Frasier, wherever you are." He hit a long fly ball towards the grouped outfielders who were all dying laughing. Kim Frasier graduated the year before.

Coach Erickson's last season as head baseball coach was memorable for us in a number of ways. Besides another big win over a superior University of Arizona team we were able to give Coach Erickson a winning season. Our 19 wins were an all-time record for the *Sun Devils,* we won ASU's first ever no-hit game 15-0 pitched by 4 pitchers and outfielder Bill Mead hit a monstrous 450 foot home run off of the men's physical education building in deep left field. Royce Youree took on The Marine Corps and won after *The Sun Devils* had beaten the Naval Training Center team in San Diego and shortstop Benny Ruiz set a *Sun Devil* record for hitting safely in 22 straight games.

These were just a few of the memorable moments we left Coach Erickson with. We had one more memorable moment to give.

HONORING COACH MEL IN TUCSON

Even though it had not been announced officially by the ASU administration it was common knowledge that Coach Mel Erickson was being relieved of his coaching duties after the season. Outfielder Ken Toney and I were team co-captains. We decided that we should do something for Coach that he would remember for a lifetime.

After conferring with the rest of the team we decided we'd do something a bit different, a bit out of the ordinary. We took up a collection among the team and bought Coach a beautiful plaque with all our names engraved on it. The plaque expressed our thanks for Coach Erickson's devotion and personal sacrifices to Arizona State over the past few years. We decided the best time to present the plaque to Coach would be at home plate before one of the last games of the season.

Now here is the kicker. One of Coach Erickson's last games as *Sun Devil* coach was to be at the University of Arizona's *Hi Corbett Field* in Tucson. We thought this would be the most appropriate time to honor Coach Erickson.

I called UofA coach Frank Sancet and made arrangements for a microphone to be available at home plate before the game. Coach Sancet agreed to set that up.

Just before the game was to start our entire team gathered in a semi-circle around home plate. Coach Erickson was dumb-founded. When we called him to come forward he did so reluctantly.

I explained to the large crowd that the *Sun Devils* wanted to show our appreciation to Coach Erickson. We wanted to do it in Tucson since our administration at ASU was unappreciative of Coach.

The Tucson fans were great. They gave Coach a standing ovation. The U.of A. team gathered outside their dugout and applauded as the presentation was made.

Coach Erickson was crying unashamedly, the first time any of us had seen him show emotion.

I wish I could say we won the game. We didn't. The *Wildcats* beat us 2-1. That game was memorable to me in that I was the recipient of the last ever "Mel-ism." With the score 1-2 *Wildcats* I was lead-off batter in the top of the ninth inning. U.of A. pitcher Dave Baldwin was still throwing 90 m.p.h. fast balls. I had to get on base to get something started. I got on base alright.

One of Baldwin's fast balls clobbered me in my left thigh knocking my legs out from under me. I got up quickly and instinctively hobbled to first base. While standing on first rubbing my thobbing thigh I looked at Coach Mel who was coaching at third base. I couldn't believe it! Coach Erickson was giving me the *steal* sign! I could barely walk and he was giving me the *steal* sign.

I called "time-out", turned to our dugout and yelled for a pinch runner. Ev Cope, speedy reserver outfielder, came in to run for me. As I gimped to our dugout several teammates came out to help me get back to the dugout. It wasn't until after the game that many of my teammates found out that Coach Mel had given me the steal sign. We all had a good chuckle over that; after the game.

"Mel-Babe"

I personally had a decent year, nothing great. My statistics were not as good as in 1957. I felt I contributed to the success of the team. I felt good about my leadership. Ken Toney and I were able to keep the attitude of the team at a positive level.

We competed hard in every game. Our opponents respected us. We exhibited good sportsmanship and we played with pride. We established a reputation for all-out competative intensity. That attitude would be passed on to future *Sun Devil* teams. We left them with something to build on.

My "Cup of Coffee"
Professional Baseball
Summer 1958

My godfather Roy Johnson, scout for the Chicago *Cubs,* was on hand for one of my last college baseball games. After the game he presented me with an envelope with Chicago *Cubs* letterhead. Opening it I found an official Chicago *Cub* contract to one of their minor league affiliates. I was stunned! I had given up on ever playing professional baseball. My 1958 season statistics were lower than my 1957 season, and my '57 season was nothing to brag about.

Roy explained that he took it on himself to draw up the contract knowing that I wanted to be a baseball coach someday. He said, "Hadley, a summer in a professional minor league would be great experience for you. Since you want to coach your learning opportunities would be boundless." How right he was!

Joan and I learned that we were to be parents early in the 1958 season. We were overjoyed! The baby was due sometime in the summer, sometime during my professional baseball season.

As Joan and I discussed the professional opportunity for us we both agreed the contract came at a good time. I would not have to worry about a summer job. Joan would be able to take the summer off from Mesa Community Hospital. We hadn't even considered how much money the professional contract was offering me, but we knew that professional baseball players made good money.

As I scrutinized the fine print in the contract I saw: "Sect. 2. For the service aforesaid subsequent to the training season the Club will pay the Player at the rate of $350 per month...".

WOW! We knew that we could live pretty well on that. Joan would not have her Mesa Community Hospital salary coming in, but we reasoned that many of my meals would be paid for by the *Cubs*. We would make it. Plus, the *Cubs* would pay mileage to wherever they assigned me.

The contract required me to report to the Carlsbad, New Mexico *Potasher* club. Carlsbad, New Mexico was a short one day drive from Bisbee, Arizona.

Joan and I would spend a few days at my home before reporting to the *Potasher* club. My dad and mom were excited for us. I was to be a professional baseball player, not exactly at the major league level but a professional player none the less.

Joan and I along with our dog *Snoopy* enjoyed the trip to Carlsbad, New Mexico. We even took the time to visit Carlsbad Caverns, one of America's leading tourist attractions. At one point during the tour of the Caverns they turned the lights out. The darkness was enveloping! We could *feel* the darkness. We had never experienced anything like that! After four or five minutes the lights came back on. Joan was startled to find that her tie-on maternity dress had come untied; it had fallen down to her ankles.

Joan was approximately eight months pregnant and her pregancy was pretty obvious.

Joan was mortified. Pulling up her dress and surrounded by a number of fellow tourists. Her bulging belly was partially covered by her very thin slip. How embarassing.

A ONE NIGHT STAND.
Carlsbad, New Mexico.

After finding a motel room and getting Joan settled down, I reported to the *Potasher* club house. I was pleased to see a familiar face. University of Arizona outfielder Dick Griesser was my lockermate.

I knew Dick since he was a freshman when I played my last season for the *Wildcats* in 1954. I competed against him for the past two years and he and I always hit it off well. As we dressed for the pre-game workout we had a good talk. I was glad that he was to be a teammate since I wanted to pick his brain. His experience for four years on a nationally ranked University of Arizona team would be an asset to me since I was determined to get as much baseball knowledge as possible. Dick gave me one important tip as we took outfield practice before the night's game.

During outfield practice a coach would hit ground balls to the outfielders in their respective playing positions. Dick and I were in centerfield. As I got my first ground ball I decided to show off my throwing ability and I threw it on a straight line to the third baseman. *"Great throw,"* I thought. Dick informed me that outfielders should always throw *through* a designated infielder. Never throw over an infielder to the designated base as I had done. Outfielders should throw the ball to an infielder head high on the infielder's throwing arm side.

The infielder would line up with the designated base the ball was to be thrown. If the infielder is told to "cut" by the catcher, he will cut off the ball and throw it to a base to keep a runner from advancing. If the ball is thrown over the infielder's head by the outfielder, as I did, the infielder has no chance to cut the ball off. Lesson well learned. Thanks Dick.

After our pre-game infield/outfield practice we went back to our locker room while the other team took infield/outfield. I noticed Dick was a bit disgruntled. He wispered to me, *"Pancho (*nickname for U of A coach Sancet*) always made us watch the other team's infield/outfield pre-game. We watched for arm strength, which ones we might take an extra base on."* Dick felt the *Potasher* manager was not in the same league as Sancet. Probably not, Sancet was one of the best.

I knew I would learn a lot of baseball hanging around Dick Griesser and the *Potasher* club. It was not to be.

As I was getting ready to join the team in our dugout for the beginning of the game, one of the Carlsbad *Potasher* front-office personnel handed me an envelope. I was to report in two days to Pulaski, Virginia. I was being transferred. I was to be a Pulaski *Cub*. I said a hasty "good by" and "good luck" to Dick Griesser, packed my belongings and went back to the motel to tell Joan we were going south. We loaded up that evening, made sure *Snoopy* was comfortable on top of our belongings in the back seat and we headed for Pulaski, Virginia. It was to be a summer neither of us would ever forget.

My significance was to be greatly enhanced; not by my baseball prowess, however.

Pulaski *Cubs*

My instructions were to report to *The Pulaski Hotel* before noon. We had no trouble finding the hotel. It was located in the center of town and was the city's most impressive and famous building. The hotel dated back to pre-Civil War days. It had a rich heritage the locals were proud of.

When I told the lady at the front desk my name she said I needed to contact Hershel Martin, the manager of the club. The lady gave me the number of Mr. Martin's room. My knock on the door was answered by a pleasingly plump and friendly lady. I introduced Joan and myself to her. She smiled, hugged us and said, "We have been expecting you both. Welcome.", then yelled, "Hersh we have company!"

Mrs. Martin told us her name was *Ad* and that is what we were to call her, Ad.

She told us we were to call Mr. Martin anything but *Mr. Martin*. He hated that name. About that time Hershel Martin walked into the room. I liked him immediately.

He said, "Hickey, I am so glad to meet you. 'Hard Rock' (my god-father) told me a lot about you. And Joan, the pleasure is all mine."

Several things were pretty obvious right from the start. Ad was going to "mother" Joan through her pregnancy. She seated Joan in an oversized easy chair and put her cardigan sweater over Joan's legs. Ad explained that she kept the window air-cooler turned up full blast all summer. She said that Pulaski's heat and humidity was intense. "A lady in your condition has to be careful not to get chilled. I cool off the room as much as we can stand."

It was obvious, too, that Hershel would call me "Hickey". I got the idea he liked "Hickey" better than "Hadley". I found out during the course of the season that Hershel Martin's nickname was *Red*. I never found out why he was called Red. His hair was not red.

Hershel played with the New York *Yankees* during the World War II years. Rumor was that Hershel substituted for Joe DiMaggio while the great *Yankee* Hall of Famer was away in the U.S. Military. Hershel was still a fine baseball player. He could cover a lot of ground in the outfield. He scrimmaged with us several times. We were especially impressed with his hitting ability.

Hershel loved to hit. Every batting practice Hershel got in his share of the cuts. He did not hit with a regular bat, he used his own personal bat. Hershel's personal bat looked like a regular game bat, but he drilled out the core of the bat and filled it with lead. It was heavy! Several of us picked it up when Hershel wasn't looking and we tried to swing it. It was impossible to swing it with any authority.

Instead of using a common fungo bat to hit his infield and outfield drills Hershel used his leaded bat. We saw him hit balls off the outfield fences during batting practice using his lead weighted bat. He didn't swing it hard, he swung it quickly. His swing was a thing of beauty. It was effortless, it was smooth and his head was steady, looking at the ball. His arms were fully extended and his weight was over his back leg. It was his *Yankee* swing. He told us that all he knew about baseball was learned while with the *Yankees*.

Joan and I stayed in a comfortable room in the hotel for a few days. Ad picked out a nice place she wanted us to look at. It would be available in a day or two.

While I went to the Pulaski Baseball Field for my first work out with the team, Ad and Joan looked at the place. Joan liked it.

The locker rooms for the home team *Cubs* and the visiting teams were in a long wooden barracks-like structure. One large shower-room separated the home team locker room from the visitors' locker room, both teams used this shower. The *Cubs* were in the Appalachian Rookie League which consisted of the Bluefield *Orioles*, the Salem *Pirates*, the Wytheville *Cardinals*, the Johnson City *Phillies*, the Roanoke *Reds*, and the Pulaski *Cubs*.

Hershel Martin was a great guy to play for. He was laid back and never yelled or screamed to make a point. But, his word was law. What he said went.

Once on a long trip back from an away game Wayne McGee a left-handed pitcher, committed a Hershel Martin no-no. He expelled flatulence which woke up most of the sleeping players. Hershel was driving the bus and he immediately stopped. We were on a lonely winding mountain road somewhere in the middle of the Appalachian Mountains. McGee was ordered to get off the bus immediately. He did so.

Hershell drove us the rest of the way back to Pulaski. McGee was left to get home as best he could. And he did. He hitchedhiked home and was there to greet the bus when Hershel pulled into the hotel's parking lot. He beat the bus back. Hershel laughed and congratulated McGee but assured him that if it ever happened again Wayne McGee might never get home.

I expected since Hershel Martin played major league baseball that his signals would be rather complicated. They weren't. Hershel never coached at third base as most managers do. He gave all his signals from the dugout.

His signal for steal was merely a whistle to get the baserunner's attention. When their eyes met Hershel gave a slight waving motion towards second base, his index finger pointing to second. The baserunner had no doubts as to the manager's intention for him, head for the next base on the next pitch. The opposing manager had no doubts either. His signal for bunt was to hold both arms in front of his chest and give a slight pushing motion with both arms, like when one bunts. Hit and Run was a steal sign to the runner on first and a verbal, "Hit behind him" to the batter. We didn't need team meetings to learn the signals.

The *Cubs* as an organization emphasized bunting throughout their farm team system. The *Cubs'* traveling bunting instructor was a guy named Rogers Hornsby. Hornsby, as any baseball fan will know is a member of Baseball's Hall of Fame. Rogers Hornsby was inducted into Baseball's Hall of Fame in 1942. He was one of baseball's all time greats. Hornsby was with us for a couple of days. Besides his emphasis on how to correctly bunt he worked a lot with us on hitting. I wish I took notes when he lectured us. I tried to file much of it away in the back of my mind.

Most of his teaching was via demonstration. He had a pitcher pitch to him and he demonstrated the point he was trying to make. He gave us way too much information for us to maintain or utilize all of it.

Hershel Martin told us to just key-in on a few of his points and work on those few. I did that. I knew when I swung at a ball and missed that my weight always ended up on my front foot. Hornsby emphasized keeping your weight back. I never heard that before. When swinging at a ball the batter's weight should stay on his back leg. I worked on that but it took me quite a while to get the concept.

Once I got the concept of keeping my weight distributed over my back foot my swing generated more quickness. By keeping the weight off my front foot my balance was steadier. When I swung with my weight over my front foot I often ended up off balance. I was much slower getting out of the batters' box which made me a step slower getting to first. With my weight back when I hit a ball, not only was I well balanced but my back foot gave me a good push towards first. It all made sense to me.

I know most of my teammates also got some good pointers from Rogers Hornsby. If he hadn't spent that time with us, we probably would have been much worse than we were.

We were not a very good baseball team. For most of the season we were at the bottom of the league in hitting. Our team average was a pitiful .228. Our shortstop Gary Johnson, was our best hitter. He was around the .330 mark. He was flirting with first place in the league in hitting most of the season. He ended up in third place.

We were a good team defensively. Our fielding average was .992 which put us in third place at the end of the season.

As pitiful as we were we were not the worst team in the Appalachian League. The Bluefield *Orioles* held that distinction. They finished fifth, dead last. We finished two games ahead of the *Orioles* in fourth place. The Johnson City *Phillies* ran away from the other four teams, finishing first by a comfortable margin. Their leading player was shortstop Danny Cater. Cater went on to a fine Major League career, twelve years with seven different teams.

My first real taste of racial prejudice occured while playing professional baseball with the Pulaski, Virginia *Cubs*. Ernie King, a Black kid from California, was our regular leftfielder. I have much admiration for Ernie. He had to endure racial taunts all season long, mostly from a few of our own fans. One elderly man was especially vocal. He came to every game with his dog on a leash. He and his dog sat behind our dugout along the third base line. He took delght in harassing Ernie. With Ernie's each at-bat the man yelled various racial insults, his favorite being "Throw the nigger a water melon!" There were times when Ernie would get close enough to his "uncle", as the team referred to him, that the man would get his dog to growl at Ernie. Even though the man was in the stands behind the screen, he was still disconcerting to all of us, especially Ernie.

When we saw this guy and his dog coming in from the front gate, we'd tell Ernie, "Hey Ernie here comes your uncle and his brother." Ernie would just smile.

Playing in other cities was especially hard on Ernie. When we ate either our pre-game meal or our post-game meal we took Ernie to the Greyhound bus station. Ernie went inside and ate by himself, the rest of the team would go to a nice restaurant. None of us thought much of it. That was just the way it was. Not until years later did I get convicted. I should have gotten off the bus and eaten with Ernie.

The episode I recall the most vividly was during one game in Bluefield, Virginia against the *Orioles*. I was in centerfield and Ernie was in left. Suddenly, "ping", dust kicked up between us. I looked at Ernie. Ernie looked at me. Again, "ping", more dust kicked up. This time Ernie and I realized some nut was in the forest behind us shooting a rifle. Though the shots kicked up dust well between the two of us, it was not very comfortable. Especially for Ernie. His eyes were as wide as saucers. When the inning was over Ernie and I set a record for sprinting to our dugout. Ernie beat me by a wide margin. When that half inning was over Ernie refused to go back out to leftfield. I was hesitant but I did. No more shots. We heard later that the police ran the shooter or shooters off.

Susan Marie Hicks
August 23, 1958

Joan was eight-plus months pregnant when we arrived in Pulaski. Joan and I were rather a novelty in Pulaski. I was the only married ball player. Joan was the only pregnant young lady who came to all our games. Joan was our best fan. Win or lose she was yelling for all of us. She knew all the players by first names. We had most of them over for dinner. The players all loved Joan who added much significance to my status on the team.

The management of the ball park also knew Joan. She was given the royal treatment when she came to the ball park. Joan's seat was three rows up behind home plate, directly in line with my centerfield position.

According to the doctor's calculations our baby was due in August. One home game early in August I experienced a false alarm that was as real as any mother's.

Joan usually needed to go to the bathroom during the seventh inning. She was like clock work. I noticed her getting up from her seat behind home plate and begin the long walk through the stands out to the ladies' bathroom near the main entrance to the park. It was never more than five or ten minutes when I'd see Joan walking back to her seat.

In this one particular game I had just taken my position in center field in the third inning. Before the first pitch was made Joan got out of her seat and began to walk to the bathroom rather hurriedly I thought. And only the third inning! I panicked! I almost shouted, *"Time out! I am about to become a father!"* I kept my cool however and my eyes glued on the ladies' bathroom door. *"What is going on in there? Is she alright? Is the baby coming? Isn't anyone going in there to help her?"*

It seemed like an eternity until Joan came walking out the door and headed back to her seat. It hadn't been an eternity. It had been merely one-half of the third inning. My first conscious moment was when leftfielder Ernie King said, "Come on Hicks. That's three outs." The *Cubs* had made three outs and I was not aware of any of them. The opponents could have hit a ball right at me and I would have been oblivious to it.

I must have still had a blank look on my face when I got to the dugout. Manager Hershel Martin looked at me and asked if I was ok. When I explained to him what happened he told me to take the rest of the game off. I did gladly. I had the chance to ask Joan if she was ok. She said she was. She pointed to her empty juice bottle she always had at the games. That explained her hurried trip to the ladies' bathroom.

A game or two later the *Cubs* began an extended road trip. We were going to play a three game series with the Salem *Pirates,* three games with the Wythville *Cardinals,* and the league leading Johnson City *Phillies* before heading home. I was a nervous wreck knowing our baby was due at any moment. Manager Martin realized this and benched me for most of those games. He told me he knew how I felt. He had experienced much the same thing with the birth of his two children Johnny and Betty. The only difference, Hershel Martin was playing in the Major Leagues when his kids were born.

During the games I was on the bench I sat as close to Manager Martin as possible. It was during these times that I learned a lot of baseball. I would pick his brain about every conceivable baseball fundamental I could think of.

Hershel Martin gave me one piece of advice that was to stay with me all my coaching career. One time when we was discussing the art of hitting he told me this: "Hickey, hitting a baseball consistantly is the most difficult thing to do in sports. My advice to you is to watch the good hitters. Watch what they all do the same that you do not do. If their stance is different than yours copy theirs for awhile. If it helps you, keep it. If their swing is different from yours copy it for awhile. If it helps you, keep it. But watch and learn. Experiment. Sooner or later you will stumble on something that will improve your hitting."

So I did, I sat and observed. It proved beneficial. It made me into a pretty good hitter. My last several weeks of the season was a turning point for me. If I had learned how to hit earlier in the season no telling what kind of season I would have had.

We no sooner got to Johnson City for our three game series than Hershel Martin got a phone call. Mrs. Martin took Joan to the hospital. Our baby was due at any moment. Manager Martin got me in the team bus and drove me to the nearest bus station. He took $10.00 out of his pocket and said for me to get the first bus going to Pulaski.

That bus ride was the longest bus ride I ever took. It seemed like an all day trip, it was probably about four hours.

I got to the Pulaski Hospital in time to welcome my beautiful baby daughter Susan Marie Hicks into the world. I had tears in my eyes as I looked at Susie wrapped securely in a blanket, cradled in Joan's arms. That precious little baby would change our lives forever. Little did we realize what joy Susan Marie Hicks would bring us.

August 24th, 1958 was a very special day for the Hadley Hicks Family.

Shortly thereafter an article appeared in the Southwest Times, Pulaski's daily newspaper, written by Sports Editor, George Akers. The article summed up much of what my one season in professional baseball did for my search for significance. Here are a few quotes from that article:

"Since the arrival of seven pound and one-half ounce Susan Marie at the Hicks' home, Pulaski Cubs center fielder Hadley Hicks has hit the ball more consistently and harder than any other time in the season. Whether 'Poppa' Hicks had the jitters previously or whether he rose from his slump one will not know. But one thing is for certain, he has been hitting the ball better. The 23 year old father from Bisbee, Arizona has hit safely nine times in eight games.

"In the ball game following the arrival of his daughter, Hicks collected a pair of singles in three times to the plate in the Cubs' win over the Bluefield Orioles last Sunday. He had one of Pulaski's four hits in the locals' loss to Salem in the second game. Hadley added a single in Pulaski's win over Wytheville Tuesday Night. He also collected one of the Cubs' five hits in their loss to the league leading Johnson City Phillies in the night cap of the same game.

'Poppa' started the extra base knocks Thursday night when he blasted a round tripper to aid in Pulaski's 7-6 win over the host Bluefield Orioles.

Friday night the right hander led the game off with a single and smacked a home run in the big fourth inning outburst that enabled to Cubs to knock off the second place Wytheville Cardinals 9-5."

Mr Akers' article was a bit misleading. Yes, I was much more relaxed after Susie was born. However, the real reson I hit the ball better was not because I was relaxed. I hit better because Manager Hershel Martin had benched me for several games. His advice to *"Watch the good hitters....watch what they do that you don't do...."* was the best single piece of hitting advice I got.

What I learned by watching the good hitters while I sat the bench was to assist me in my later years of coaching baseball. It was to make me a pretty good hitting instructor. And, it allowed me to be a much better hitter as the 1958 Appalachian League drew to a close.

Every coach I had in baseball preached that the hitter should not hitch. To hitch meant to drop your hands and the bat below where the bat was originally positioned as the hitter got ready to swing at the pitch. A hitch was an up and down movement with the hands. A cardinal sin in hitting was to hitch.

I learned from some of the very good hitters in the Appalachian League that all of them hitched**.** Only they all hitched in a backward and forward movement, not in an up and down movement. Their arms and bat were moving in sync with the pitcher's wind-up. "Time the pitcher" is an addage one often hears from good batting instructors. As the pitcher begins his movement to deliver the ball the hitter should be slowly moving his arms and hands back in sync with the pitcher. Some of the great hitters can wait until almost the last second before the ball gets to them that their hands and arms begin to "cock", that is to prepare for the swing. All of them have a degree of backward and forward movement in their arms and hands before they swing.

Hershel Martin was a wise man. I wish I had taken written notes on his teachings. His knowledge would have filled volumes. Hershel was also a very loving and gentle man. Hershel and his wife Ad were very kind to Joan and me.

Mr. Akers had this to say about Hershal Martin and the *Cubs* as he finished the article I quoted above:

"I would like to take this opportunity to say 'thanks' for having the privilege of working with the 1958 Cubs. I have especially enjoyed meeting and working with the Hershel Martin family. "I feel this year's Cubs are one of the finest groups of lads to come to Pulaski to work in the Appalachian League."

I guess to be honest I need quote what else Mr. Akers said about me as he finished his section on "Poppa" Hicks:

"Hicks has fattened his batting average over the last couple of weeks. He is now batting **.226.** Nice going Hadley!"

That was pitiful. A .226 batting average; not exactly the stuff to enhance my reputation as an Arizona legend, nor is it worthy of a professional baseball contract.

I am glad I don't know what I was batting before Susie was born. Obviously I was not destined for significance as a major league baseball player. My brief cup of coffee in professional baseball player was finished.

Pulaski, VA. *Cubs*

Susie made it a significant summer, one Joan and I would never forget.

Joan and Susie flew to visit Joan's parents in Toronto, Canada after the season was over. Our dog *Snoopy* and I piled in our 1957 Chevy and headed back to Arizona. I had one more semester at Arizona State University to finish my BA Degree. I was to complete my Student Teaching requirement, then my dreams of becoming an outstanding teacher and coach would begin to be realized.

When I arrived back in Arizona my first task was to drive to Bisbee to visit my parents for a day or so. Sadly I had to leave *Snoopy* with them as dogs were not allowed on campus at Arizona State. *Snoopy* was a great companion for us. He was Susie's watchdog. *Snoopy's* ears perked up when Susie made baby noises. I shed a few tears as I drove away without *Snoopy*. My trip back to campus would be lonely. I was anxious to get back. I would prove to the people of Arizona that the legend was still alive and kicking. Just wait until I put all my knowledge, maturity and know-how to good use. I was now an "old man" athletically speaking. My dream of becoming a great professional athlete had been realistically put aside. There was no age limit however, on great coaches. The legend still had goals to pursue.

BACK ON CAMPUS

Before Joan and I left Tempe for the summer, we applied for an apartment at Arizona State University's *Victory Village.* Victory Village was ASU's married military veteran student housing complex. Victory Village consisted of three rows of military constructed buildings, each section was converted into two, three or four, one bedroom apartments. The apartments were comfortable and convenient for a couple with a child or two, if one overlooked the cockroach population and the thin walls between apartments My first task after getting the key to our apartment was to get what little furniture we owned out of storage. Ed Hickcox, my Hayden Hall roommate, helped me move the furniture into the apartment. Joan and I owned two comfortable easy chairs, a couch, a kitchen table with four chairs and a bedroom chest of drawers. A decent double bed came with the apartment. Side tables were orange crates from the local Safeway After dusting and mopping the wooden floors, washing the two large windows in the living room and the one small window in the bedroom, the apartment looked "homey". I wanted the apartment to look nice for Joan and Susie when they got back from Toronto. I decided to get a few flowers for the kitchen table.

Our apartment was on one corner of a four apartment complex. Thus we only had to be concerned about the thin walls on one side.

Jack and Ann McCusker and their month old baby boy Robbie were our neighbors. They were great neighbors and we became close friends. Robbie's crib was up against the wall next to our bed. It only took me two nights to move our bed to the other side of the room. I figured Susie's crib could be head to head with Robbie's crib. They could cry each other to sleep.

Jack and Ann lived in Victory Village for a year. They knew the ropes. One thing Jack told me was that the only cockroach preventative was to step on one when you saw it. That was the only thing that would prevent that particular roach from coming back. Jack said the cockroach poison sold in the stores seemed to serve as a population stimulant. There was no way to get rid of them. Cockroachs were a permanent fixture with the apartment.

Jack warned me about the huge swamp cooler in our living room window.

He told me when it was turned on after being off for weeks or months as our's had been, I could expect a massive swarm of mosquitos to be blown throughout our apartment. Mosquito spray and a fly-swatter were a must. Jack was right. I battled the critters all day and night for weeks after Joan and Susie came home. We tried to put a net of sorts over Susie's bed each time we put her down.

Joan and Ann McCusker became very close friends. They walked the babies in their strollers around the complex. On nice days which were common place in Tempe, Arizona, Joan and Ann spread blankets on a large physical education field near our apartment. In the midafternoons the PE archery classes were gone and the grassed area was perfect for mothers and children to gather.

Early morning on weekends I got my golf clubs and went to the physical education field. It was a perfect place to drive golf balls. I took up golf when I was in the Army at Fort Ord and learned to love it.

Sometimes when Joan needed a break I would take Susie in her stroller to the field. Her stroller had a basket on the back that held about 50 golf balls. I'd hit them all, then push Susie in the stroller to shag the balls. Susie loved it.

Victory Village. What a great place for young married college students! All of us were in the same financial boat. We lived on our G.I. Bill income. The couples with a second income were the "high rollers".

There wasn't much partying on the weekends. Those with a TV invited neighbors over to watch "Lucy", "Sgt. Bilko" or possibly a movie, on Sunday evenings it was "The Ed Sullivan" show.

Hamburgers and hot dogs were grilled on the several charcoal grills scattered around the neighborhood. It was "bring your own meat." If the host was a high roller, a bottle of beer was sometimes offered. If not Coke or Pepsi was the usual liquid refreshment.

After the kids were put to bed the adults sat around and talked. The men shared "war stories" and the women talked about what women talk about. Sometimes a game of Monopoly or Scrabble was played if the talk got stale. The evenings usually broke up before midnight. We were all in our mid-twenties and getting older. We needed our sleep.

I loved a good practical joke; even when it was played on me. I played one on our neighbors, Jack, Ann and Robbie McCusker that back-fired on me. I picked up one of those "tail-pipe torpedoes" you could get at gag shops. Put one of them in a car's tail pipe and when the car started up the loudest most obnoxious whistle was emitted. The only way to get rid of it was to either speed up and try to blow it out or stop and dig it out with a screwdriver.

Late one Saturday night when it was dark and nobody could see me, I put one in the McCusker's tail-pipe. I went to bed anxious to watch the fun when they started up their car to go to church the next morning. The fun started earlier than I anticipated. Somewhere around 6:00 a.m. Joan and I were awakened by a loud scream from Ann next door. Ann was yelling, "Hurry Jack! We have to get to the hospital!"

By the time I got my pants on and went to the front door, Jack, Ann and Robbie were getting in their car. I yelled to see if I could do anything. Ann yelled back that

Robbie was having a convulsion, they were on their way to the hospital emergency room. I wasn't about to take the time to warn them about the "tail-pipe torpedo". They found out soon enough. The noise as Jack sped out of the Victory Village parking lot reverberated all over the ASU campus. I heared the loud whistle for blocks as Jack got closer to the hospital. I felt like a jerk.

Joan and I were on pins and needles waiting for the McCuskers to get back. We were concerned for little Robbie. I saw them drive up to their parking place.

They drove up quietly. Somehow Jack got the torpedo out. They walked up with semi-smiles on their faces. We knew Robbie was o.k. Joan made me confess that I was the guy who put the torpedo in the tail-pipe. Ann was a little miffed, but she was happy that it turned out well. Robbie would be o.k. All Jack said was, "Where did you buy that thing?" I still think it was a good joke. It was just that the timing was poor.

Victory Village and the large field were located where Grady Gammage Auditorium, Arizona State University's well known civic center now stands. The Grady Gammage Auditorium was one of internationally known architect Frank Lloyd Wright's last masterpieces. The auditorium was constructed in 1964. I am certain that there are thousands of former Arizona State College students who drive by Grady Gammage Auditorium and get a lump in their throats. I know I do. Victory Village.Many fond memories were born on that special piece of real estate.

STUDENT TEACHING
"Uncle Fred Flits By"

I heard horror stories about student teaching experiences by prospective teachers, stories about being turned loose the first day in a classroom of unruly junior high kids, of having a supervising teacher who sat in the back of the classroom reading a newspaper while the student teacher floundered with a lesson. They were stories which made me wonder if I really wanted to student teach. My student teaching experience was great. It wasn't what I expected, but it was great. I was assigned to teach Speech at Phoenix Union High School in downtown Phoenix. Phoenix Union was the largest high school in Arizona, three or four thousand students, ninth through twelfth grades.

My instructions from the Arizona State University Education Department said to report to Mr. Richard L. Olsen. Mr. Olsen was the Department Head of the Phoenix Union High School Speech, English and Drama Department. He was my Supervising Teacher. He would decide if I was qualified to become a public school teacher and he tested my debating skills immediately. "Very pleased to meet you, Mr. Hicks. Please sit down." Before I could reply the next words out of his mouth floored me! "You are going to direct the Junior class play next November. It is a comedy by Christopher Sergel, *Uncle Fred Flits By*."

After a moment of stunned disbelief I stuttered some weak retorts. "Mr. Olsen, I am not qualified. My major is Speech. Mr. Olsen, I have never been in a play in my life, Mr. Olsen, please don't make me direct a play."

I honestly don't remember what I said to Mr. Olsen. Whatever it was took Mr. Olsen completely by surprise. He couldn't believe that someone who was majoring in Speech and Drama at Arizona State University would turn down an opportunity to direct a high school play.

After a half-hour of discussing the issue, Mr. Olsen gave in. Actually he was pretty nice about it. He could have been much more insistant. He was the supervisor, I was the student teacher. I was at his mercy. He probably realized that his department's reputation was at stake. He also realized that with me as director he would have to take over the reins after the first few rehearsals anyway. I became the Junior Class Play's Assistant Director, that I felt I could handle.

My duties were simple. I listened to the students say their lines and at times I played one part and read the lines.

I worked closely with Nina Johnson, student director. Nina was a senior. She had experience in school drama productions. I never admitted this to anyone but Nina would have done a much better job directing the play than I would have. Nina, in my opinion, was even more effective than Mr. Olsen. The cast of actors were Nina's peers. Perhaps this is why the cast responded to Nina so readily.

November 6, 1958 finally arrived. *Opening night.* The Phoenix Union Auditorium was crowded with relatives and friends of the cast. Quite a few Phoenix Union High School faculty attended as well. I was surprised that so many faculty members supported Mr. Olsen's Drama Department. I would be pleased if the schools I teach in will be as supportive of each other's endeavors. I was beginning to realize that teamwork and loyalty will breed success, even in the thespian arena.

I did enjoy my work with Mr. Olsen. He was good at delegating authority. Mr. Olsen made it clear that he was "where the buck stopped" to quote President Harry Truman. Student director Nina Johnson and I each had a role to fill. Mr. Olsen told the cast members that when Nina or I issued an order they were to "hop to". I felt that I was an integral factor in the success of the play. I am sure that Nina Johnson felt the same way.

One negative about my time spent with *Uncle Fred Flits By* was that I did not get to spend much time with the other two members of the Speech, English and Drama Department, Mrs. Dorothy Gillespie and Mr. Lyle Loosle.

In Mrs. Gillespie's speech class I sat in the back of her room and observed. A few times Mrs. Gillespie asked for my imput on one of the speeches. Once or twice she allowed me to evaluate a speech. I critiqued the student without imput from Mrs. Gillespie. That was good experience for me. Mrs. Gillespie's constructive comments to me were appreciated.

Mr. Lyle Loosle taught English Literature Classes. One day at lunch Mr. Loosle told me he was just beginning a unit on A.B. Guthrie, Jr.'s *The Big Sky* novels.

I had to admit to Mr.Loosle that I had never heard of either the author, A.B. Guthrie, Jr. or his *Big Sky* novels. Mr. Loosle jumped at the chance to briefly educate me on some of the most unforgettable stories of the Western frontier. He invited me to sit in on his afternoon literature class any chance I got. After attending just one of Mr. Loosle's classes I was hooked on Western Literature. A.B.Guthrie, Jr. became one of my favorite authors in later years.

I got to know Mr. Loosle pretty well. We ate together many lunch periods. Mr. Olsen and Mrs. Gillespie ate lunch in their respective classrooms. They liked a degree of privacy. Mr. Loosle and I enjoyed our time together. Besides his enthusiasm for literature, Mr. Loosle loved his students. He had a heart for the kids, especially the ones from disfunctional homes. Often Mr. Loosle would point out a kid at lunch and he would be near tears as he told me about that kid's home life. I wish I could have spent more time with Mr. Loosle. I feel I could have learned more about teaching from him. As Mr. Loosle and I parted the last lunch we were together, I stuck out my hand to shake his. I was going to tell him how much I enjoyed knowing him. I wanted to thank him for his input into my student teaching experience. Instead of grasping my outstretched hand he hugged me. He said something so softly I didn't hear it all. It sounded like *God bless you, Hadley*. That was special to me.

I felt a twinge of nostalgia as I said good-by to Mr. Olsen. I had enjoyed my student teaching experience. I did not have as much "hands-on" experience in the class room as I would have liked though I did observe and take mental notes. I felt I could handle most classrooms. All I received to show for my efforts was a certificate signed by Mr. Olsen indicating that I had completed the required number of student teaching hours, nothing else. No evaluation, just the certificate.

BOBBY WINKLES.
Building on The Foundation

Little did I know as I walked into the office of the new Arizona State University *Sun Devil* baseball coach that I was walking into the presence of coaching greatness. The new coach's name was Bobby Winkles**.** I never heard of him.

Our former coach, Mel Erickson, whom we all dearly loved was a "no namer" as well.

I do admit that when I read Bobby Winkles' resume' in the *Arizona Republic* I was impressed. The man at least played some baseball. Coach Erickson's baseball experience was somewhat limited. Winkles' baseball history included four years collegiate experience at Illinois Wesleyan University where he earned a bachelor of philosophy degree. Upon graduation, the Chicago *White Sox* signed Winkles to a minor league contract. He played shortstop in *the Sox's* system with Memphis, Charleston, Colorado Springs, Indianapolis, Tulsa and Winkles spent one winter in Venezuela where he was a teammate of baseball great, Luis Aparacio**.**

While playing in the Texas League with Tulsa, Bobby Winkles was the leagues' All-Star selection at shortstop. In one season he handled over 800 chances in the infield. He was known for his quickness and flawless fielding ability.

Some Winkles' followers will argue that had he not signed as Arizona State University head baseball coach in 1959 he would have been called up to the Chicago *White Sox* Major League club. Many of ASU's future opponents wished that he had gone into the Major Leagues. Winkles built a baseball dynasty upon the solid foundation *The Sun Devils* of 1957 had built.

When I walked into Bobby Winkles' office, before I could introduce myself, Winkles said, "You look familiar. Wait a minute." He got up from his desk and went

So You Wanna Be a Legend. So Did I.

to a team picture of the 1958 *Sun Devils*. After looking it over for a minute he turned to me, stuck out his hand and said, "Hadley Hicks. Very glad to meet you. You look just like your picture. Have a seat."

The next hour went by quickly. Bobby Winkles seemed to know about me. He complimented me on my career as an Arizona State *Sun Devil*. He told me he liked what he heard about my leadership; he liked that I was a hustler. The first time he asked me a question and I answered by saying. "Yes, Sir**",** Bobby WInkles broke into a huge smile. "Hadley I wish we had you coming back. You are the type of player I could use to continue the *Sun Devil* tradition of 'gentlemen on and off the field.' All my players will answer questions with a 'yes sir' or a 'no sir'. None of this 'yeah' stuff. All my players will address me as Coach Winkles."

As I visited with Bobby Winkles there were no doubts in my mind that Coach Winkles meant what he said. His very presence, his confident voice exuded respect. He did not come across as arrogant or over-bearing. He was matter of fact. It was either his way or the highway.

When Coach Winkles found out that I finished my student teaching requirement in the fall he asked me a silly question, "Hadley would you be willing to participate in some of our practices this spring? We could use you in scrimmages and drill sessions."

I answered with a quick and positive, "Yes sir!" The dozen or so of Coach Bobby Winkles' practices that I attended proved to be as beneficial to me as they were to the *Sun Devil* team. What a learning experience!

Much of what I took away from Coach Winkles' handling of practice sessions would prove to be invaluable to me. My future football and baseball coaching philosophy along with my future classroom management philosophy were each woven together. They were shaped by what I learned from Bobby Winkles.

What I learned was not just gleaned from those few practice sessions. I attended several coaching clinics over the years where Coach Winkles was a featured speaker. As his success with the Arizona State University *Sun Devils* became more and more widely publicized Winkles was more in demand as a speaker. While on a speaker's platform Bobby Winkles emphasized his team disciplinary code more than he did his teaching of baseball fundamentals. To him team discipline was more important to team success.

Examples: hustle every minute on the field, never argue with an umpire over a close call, never throw a bat or a helmet in disgust, no *Sun Devil* wears long hair or sideburns, players run to and from their positions every inning, a *Sun Devil* who has struck out will trot back to his dugout with his head held high, a *Sun Devil* who has been issued a "'walk" by the opposing pitcher will sprint to first base, he will not walk.

Coach Winkles' reasoning for all this imposed discipline was simple. Obedience to imposed discipline would lead to self-discipline. Discipline makes the difference between a good player and a great player, discipline holds a team together when its down and can bring it back to victory. Self-discipline leads to a winner in life.

Coach Winkles said, "Each player is offered the choice of playing by my rules or not playing at ASU." Winkles reasoned that obtaining an education should be forefront in a player's mind. Some players came to ASU believing they would spend the rest of their lives on a baseball diamond. Winkles did all he could to dispel that kind of thinking. He was known to leave a player behind on a road-trip if the young man was sluffing off in one of his classes.

Winkles believed that every kid on his team should be treated as an individual, no two of them are the same. "Some kids need a kick in the can once in awhile; others need a pat on the head," was an axiom Winkles adhered to.

I heard Coach Winkles speak at Little League functions around the state of Arizona. One of those occasions was in "Little League happy" Prescott, Arizona. Prescott had an outstanding Little League program. Hundreds of kids and parents were involved. Prescott took it's Little Leagues very seriously.

I heard Bobby Winkles speak at one of their banquets. He laid it on the line to the parents. He told them Little League baseball should be for the kids, not for the egos of the parents. If he was in charge of a Little League program, he stated, there were several rules he would insist on. Number one: all bleachers and stands for the spectators would be built 50 yards away from the playing field. Number two: all the games would be played at 3:00 p.m. Wednesday afternoons so many of the fathers could not attend.

Bobby Winkles had an outstanding 11 year tenure at ASU. His *Sun Devil* teams' rang up an enviable win-loss record of 524 wins, 173 loses. The *Sun Devils* won the National Collegiate Athletic Association (NCAA) Baseball championship titles three times, 1965, 1967, and 1969.

A number of his players went on to stellar careers in Major League Baseball. Of the most notable were: Reggie Jackson, "Mr. October" of New York *Yankee* fame; Rick Monday, while playing for the Chicago *Cubs* in Dodger Stadium in 1976 gained world wide fame by preventing a protester from burning the American Flag; Sal Bando, after a Major League career which he earned four time selection as an American League All-Star, and a three time World Series Champion, became General Manager of The Milwaukee *Brewers*.

After a successful career at Arizona State, Bobby Winkles spent several years as a manager in professional baseball. Winkles was the manager of the California *Angels* in 1973 and 1974 and the Oakland *Athletics* in 1977 and 1978.

My guess as to why Bobby Winkles did not stay in the major leagues longer is that major league players are spoiled. They make so much money that they would not respond to Winkles' style baseball. Bobby Winkles would not tolerate a player of his hot-dogging it to first base after hitting a home run.

I had the pleasure of attending Bobby Winkles' induction into The American Baseball Coaches Association Hall of Fame. The Induction Dinner was held in conjunction with The American Baseball Coaches Association's annual baseball clinic. It was held in Dallas, Texas in 1997. Just as I was entering the dinner hall I ran into Bobby Winkles. He seemed genuinely pleased to see me. Bobby was with his lovely wife, Ellie. He introduced me to Ellie as "Hadley Hicks one of the *Sun Devils* who way back in 1958 paved the way for me at ASU". I was so proud that he even remembered my name. It had been years since I had last seen Bobby Winkles. Bobby invited me to sit at the table adjacent to his.

As I was getting seated Bobby Winkles got a huge grin on his face. The distinguished gentleman walking up to greet Bobby Winkles had an equally huge grin on his face. Bobby said, "Sal, it is good to see you. Thanks for coming." It was then that Winkles turned to me and said, "Hadley, this guy is not some wealthy Wall Street financier. This is Sal Bando who got to play for ASU before he made it big in the pros."

Bobby then introduced me to Sal Bando. "Sal this is Hadley Hicks one of ASU's finest outfielders. He was right up there with Reggie Jackson and Rick Monday. And only two of those guys could catch a fly-ball," an obvious dig at Reggie Jackson's well known defensive deficiencies.

MEMORABLE PHONE CALL
From Bobby Winkles

On April 27, 2007 I received a phone call I will not forget. When I answered I heard a familiar Arkansas drawl, "Hadley. This is Bobby Winkles." I have to admit I got choked up when he told me why he was calling. He wanted to thank me for being a part of his success at ASU. Bobby said that my leadership and attitude was a "foundation for success". He was appreciative of everything that my teammates and I did to get the ASU baseball program to the point where it was when he took over in 1959. His job was made easier, he said.

I know that Bobby Winkles made a number of such phone calls. Many of my teammates received a call, John Jacobs, Benny Ruiz, Roger Kudron, Bill Mead, John Rigoli, Jim Sims, and Royce Youree. Others I am sure were honored to get a call of "thanks" from Bobby Winkles. Bobby Winkles did indeed build a baseball dynasty upon the foundation laid by the *Sun Devils* of 1958.

CHAPTER FIVE

Carmel High School
Carmel, California

Declaring the end from the beginning...
Saying "My counsel shall stand,
And I will do all My pleasure."
Isaiah 46:10

Lone Cypress
Picture credit: Doug Lumsden

*I'd like to state before I die
That teaching's been a total high.
For I have felt, like those who paint,
That inner glow that warms a saint.
To most, I fear, this glow's denied,
For it is not composed of pride
Nor does it deal in recompense
In what is an accepted sense.
It isn't something one can earn,
By merely watching students learn
And sharing as their eyes reveal
The utter wonder that they feel."
Buzz Rainer
Carmel High School*

My First Steps Towards
Coaching Significance

What a fantastic place to begin a teaching-coaching career! The job just popped up out of the blue. I came back to our apartment in Victory Village on the ASU campus fresh from a promising interview. The city of Scottsdale, Arizona was opening two new high schools. I interviewed for a teaching-coaching position in one of the schools. The administrator I interviewed with seemed positive. They needed teachers and coaches.

My wife Joan met me at the door. She was excited. She handed me a slip of paper with a note: "Call Dan Yurkovich in Carmel". Joan had his phone number written at the bottom of the note. I was to call Dan's work phone sometime during the day.

Dan Yurkovich was the guy from Ajo, Arizona whom I ran into in a Post Exchange at Fort Ord, California. Dan and his family took me in while I finished out my Army hitch.

I wasted very little time returning Dan's call. A familiar voice answered the phone; "Carmel High School. This is Dan Yurkovich".

'Yurkovich! What in the world are you doing at Carmel High School? You were changing records in juke-boxes the last time I saw you!"

Dan chuckled at my surprise. He explained that he became friends with the principal of Carmel High School. When a job opened that Dan qualified for, he applied and got the job. "Hicks, I am the varsity basketball coach and Senior class counselor. I have pull so treat me with respect!" Dan went on to explain that a coaching position was open at North High School in Salinas, California. Salinas is located 30 miles south of Carmel. I had fond memories of Salinas, California. It was in Salinas where Momma's Chicken Wing bar-b-que resturant was located. Great memories!

Dan said that if I could get a flight to Monterey, California in the next few days he would call the North High School athletic director, Don Norgard and set up an interview.

Monterey, California was the hub of the Monterey Peninsula. Carmel was just over the hill from Monterey about five miles. Salinas was about 25 miles south.

Joan mentally checked our budget and concluded that if the plane ticket was not expensive I could do it. I called the airlines and the ticket was priced within our budget. I reserved one for the next morning. I called Dan immediately and gave him my arrival time. He took care of the rest, "Including", as he said, "a suite at The Yurkovich Hotel."

I was excited to get back to one of my favorite places in the world, The Monterey Peninsula. I had many good times there during my two Army stints at Fort Ord.

I spent a sleepless night and mentally formulated my interview with Don Norgard. I would humbly tell him of all my achievements in Arizona. I would let him know that I was the only Arizona athlete to letter in football and baseball at both the University of Arizona and Arizona State University. I wouldn't bother to mention my bench time at both places. I would mention my co-captaincy of the ASU baseball team and my summer of pro-baseball. I would let him know that I was a potential outstanding coach. I would no doubt be looking into a major college coaching position within the next five to ten years. He could have me for at least that long.

Two days later I was in Salinas, California and memories of Momma and her Chicken Wings flooded my mind. If I got a job in the Salinas school system I vowed to take Joan and Susie to have some of her bar-b-que chichen. Momma would would be excited to meet them. First I had an important interview to take care of.

The interview went well. Mr. Norgard was a nice man. He would be easy to work with. He told me he would submit my name to the school board which makes all the hiring decisions and would give the board a favorable report. Mr. Norgard said that he would get back with me within the next few weeks. After giving him my resume' along with several letters of recommendation, I shook his hand, thanked him for his time and drove back to Carmel in Dan's car which he had loaned me. Dan had told me to drop by Carmel High School on my way back. Since the interview with Mr. Norgard was mid-morning I got to Carmel before Dan left for the day. Though I had never visited Carmel High School I had driven by it many times. As one leaves Monterey driving up the hill on Highway #1 one can't miss the entrance to Carmel High School. There is a stop light where Ocean Avenue and Highway #1 intersect. Most travelers either go on down Highway #1 to Big Sur or they turn right on Ocean Avenue down a long hill to the quaint village of Carmel. At the bottom of the hill through downtown Carmel is beautiful Carmel Beach. The white sand on the beach is both unique and breath taking.

Turning left at the stop-light leads into the campus of Carmel High School. The sign identifying Carmel High School is a large round section of what must have been a huge tree. Boldly painted in the middle of the round section of tree was:

So You Wanna Be a Legend. So Did I.

Tour bus drivers taking a load of tourists down scenic Highway #1 are known to say as they drive by Carmel High, "And on your left is Carmel High School where they serve martinis at lunch."

Of course that wasn't true. I am sure though that some of the tourists believed it was true as the grounds of Carmel High School looked like a plush country club with beautifully groomed green lawns bordered by stately Monterey Pines, Spanish adobe buildings with ivy covered walls and walk-ways. It is a beautiful school.

School was out for the summer and no students were around. Dan Yurkovich and another man were outside seated on a cement, ivy covered wall when I drove up. Dan waved me to a parking space near where he and the other guy were talking. Both Dan and his friend were engaged in a relaxed conversation. Both were seated on a knee-high wall that seemed to go around the outside of the school. They were leaning against ivy covered pillers, feet up on the wall facing each other.

When I walked to where they were seated neither one got up to greet me. Both were too relaxed. Dan introduced me to a man whom I would get to know well, Warren Edwards, the principal of Carmel High School.

Warren Edwards didn't beat around the bush. He said, "Good to meet you Hadley. Dan has told me a lot about you. Come in to my office and let's talk. We may have a better proposition for you than North Salinas High School." With a quizzical shrug of my shoulders to Dan I followed Mr. Edwards inside to his office.

After approximately one hour I had verbally agreed to be a teacher and a coach for Carmel High School. Mr. Edwards said he had a Speech class opening and possibly two non-college prep English openings. The administration of Carmel High School wanted to start a lightweight football program. They already had a lightweight basketball program. Mr. Edwards said that possibly I could coach the lightweight basketball team as well.

I had no clue what Mr. Edwards meant by "lightweight". To my knowledge no such designation was applied to Arizona high school teams. Edwards explained to me what determined if a player was a lightweight. It was based on an exponent system the kid's date of birth, grade in school and his height and weight. Conceivably a senior in high school could be on the same team as a freshman.

It sounded interesting but I wanted to coach varsity teams. I asked what my chances were of coaching on the varsity football team or the varsity baseball team. Mr. Edwards told me about the Carmel High School football program. Coach George Mosolf was the head coach and also the "Dean" of Northern California football coaches. His Carmel High football team ended the past season undefeated. They were undefeated in the last 23 straight games. Pretty impressive. His coaching staff had been together for years. A newcomer like me would have to earn his way to the varsity. Edwards said that was not likely to happen any time soon. Coach Mosolf would not give up his head baseball coaching position either.

"What about the JV team? Could I maybe coach them?" Mr. Edwards then told me about Buzz Rainer. Rainer had been JV coach for a number of years. His JV record was almost as good as Mosolf's varsity record. Rainer would die before giving up JV football. Buzz also coached track but it was out of necessity. Nobody else would take the job. He liked track o.k. but he loved golf. He was an avid golfer as I found out.

I left Mr. Edward's office in a semi-dazed condition. I had driven into Carmel High School's parking lot excited about a possible varsity football coaching position at North Salinas High School. I left wondering just what I had verbally agreed to at Carmel High. Lightweight football coach? How in the world does one coach a pigmy team? How would I ever climb the ladder to a college coaching position? But I had to admit, it would be exciting to coach for a few years at Carmel High School, Carmel-by-the-Sea.

I got to know Yurkovich's wife and children when I was in the Army at Fort Ord. It was good to see them again. Patty Yurkovich, Dan's wife, said she first saw me years ago when I was playing in the Arizona All-Star football game in Flagstaff. Dan was coaching the Arizona Class A basketball all-stars that same year.

We hadn't met at that time but Patty knew who I was. Their two children, Donna and Danny grew quite a bit since I saw them three years earlier when I was at Fort Ord. I even babysat them a time or two and they both remembered me. They even asked me to read them a bedtime story that evening.

So You Wanna Be a Legend. So Did I.

After dinner I quizzed Dan and Patty about living in Carmel, the people, Carmel High and it's students. Dan and Patty said that many of the kids came from upper-class wealthy families. For the most part they were bright, hard working kids. They were motivated to do well as their fathers before them had done. He said they were easy to coach. Dan had coached basketball the last season and had a winning record.

Dan told me that Fort Ord and the Army Language School in nearby Monterey had military families living in Carmel; many had high school age children. I would find that I would reap the benefits of those military family offspring many times over the next few years.

When my flight home arrived at Sky Harbor Airport in Phoenix, Joan and Susie were there to greet me. Joan was excited about my new job. Even though I had not signed a contract, Mr. Edwards assured me my job was in the bag. We could pack up our belongings and get on the road he had said. We did. Joan and I spent the next few days packing and tying up loose ends at Victory Village.

We headed out for Carmel, California early one morning. We got as far as Yuma, Arizona before Joan got tired. She was several months pregnant with our second baby. Being pregnant did not prevent Joan from swimming in the pool at the motel in Yuma. Susie got her first taste of swimming that evening. She loved it. Susie let me hold her on my lap to come down the waterslide. She squealed with delight and didn't mind getting her face wet.

What a lucky guy I was. A beautiful wife, a beautiful little girl, one unknown on the way and a teaching-coaching position in one of the most desirable locals in America, Carmel-by-the-Sea on the beautiful Monterey Peninsula. Could it get any better than that? The head football job at Arizona State University would have to wait.

Joan, Susie and I stayed with the Yurkovich's our first week in Carmel. Dan had lined up a couple of small houses for us to look at. Buying a house was out of the question. Carmel was an expensive village to live in. We saw a house to rent that we thought would fit the bill. It was a small one bedroom house just half a block from downtown Carmel.

We were within walking distance of anywhere in town except for Carmel High School which was a mile up Ocean Avenue. We were only two blocks from Ocean Avenue, the main drag through Carmel. All the shops and restaurants were either on Ocean Avenue or one of the side streets. We felt we found the perfect place.

Dan Yurkovich was good friends with Mr. Bill Wakefield the Athletic Director of the Carmel Unified School District. Mr. Wakefield got me a job directing summer activities at the Carmel High School gymnasium.

The Carmel School District had a full slate of summer activities from grade school kids' basketball leagues in the mornings, to high school basketball leagues in the afternoons, summer swimming lessons in the mornings and afternoons and adult volley ball leagues in the evenings. I didn't work the evenings as my days were full.

Halfway through the summer I was startled one afternoon to see Mr. Wakefield come in the gym with a man I recognized immediately, Bing Crosby!

Mr. Wakefield loved playing the big shot. He and Bing Crosby walked close enough to my table for Bing Crosby and I to exchange smiles. No introductions.

Wakefield was all business. He showed Bing Crosby the activities taking place in the gym, then took him outside and watched the swimming activities.

After about an hour, Mr. Wakefield came back in the gym alone. He walked up to where I was operating the timeclock for a game in progress. He stood near my table for a minute before he said, "Did you recognize that man I was just with?"

I can play games too. I said, "Nope. Didn't pay any attention. Who was he?"

Wakefield couldn't belive I hadn't recognizied one of the most famous people in America. "That was Bing Crosby. He lives on The Seventeen Mile Drive and is a big contributer to our Recreation Department. In fact our main Recreation Building in Carmel is 'The Bing Crosby Recreation Center'. You'll be glad to know he is a big fan of CHS."

"No kidding. Pretty lucky to have a guy like that involved with our community. He's a singer isn't he?" I am sure that when Mr.Wakefield walked away he was thinking, *"He didn't even know who Bing Crosby is. Hicks is a real hick from Arizona."*

I met two other Carmel High School faculty members that summer who would play important roles in my life over the years. The first one was Dick Lawitzke Dan Yurkovich came by the gym one day and said for me to come outside with him. He wanted me to meet someone. We went out to the swimming pool; Dan pointed out a large man smoking a pipe and painting a corner on the deck of the swimming pool. Lawitzke looked like a football coach. He was 6'2" tall and weighed around 240 pounds.

What a friendly guy! I liked him immediately. Dick said he had been looking for a chance to meet me. Before I went back in the gym I found out that Dick Lawitzke was JV football line coach and JV basketball coach under Dan Yurkovich. He taught Driver Education. He was working on his PhD in Driver Education.

A few days later I met Buzz Rainer the head JV football coach and track coach, another friendly guy. Buzz walked into the gym looking for me. He too seemed eager to meet me. Buzz was easy to talk to, and interesting as well. Buzz was what I called an intellectual, a serious student of the classics and a published poet. Later that summer Buzz got me to read the first full length novel I ever read cover to cover, <u>The Mysterious Island</u> by Jules Verne. I thoroughly enjoyed it and was hooked on reading from that time on.

The summer went by quickly. Joan and I spent many hours pushing Susie in her stroller up and down Carmel's beautiful business district. Dan Yurkovich worked for the Carmel Police Department in the summers. Joan, Susie and I walked to the Police Station almost every evening just to visit with Dan. On these evening walks we met many people whom we would grow to love over the years.

I met many of the students I would shortly be coaching. They were all nice, polite kids, so much so that I began to wonder how Carmel High School won so many games. I always heard that "nice" kids won't win for you. Boy was that wrong!

It was a Carmel High football tradition for the football coaches to meet for dinner at Coach George Mosolf's house a few weeks before the season got under way. Buzz Rainer and Dick Lawitzke picked me up. I had never met "Coach Mo" as he was fondly called but I liked him immediately. He was an older man probably in his mid 50's. and

So You Wanna Be a Legend. So Did I.

one of the most successful football coaches in Northern California. I heard that he turned down a few college jobs in his day. I knew I could learn a lot from him.

During the evening after dinner and over a glass of wine Coach Mo told each of us what he expected. He mentioned that Coach Don Craig would not be at the meeting due a prior engagement to attend a concert in Monterey. Coach Craig worked with Coach Mo for so many years that he didn't need to be reminded of his duties.

Coach Craig proved to be one of the classiest gentlemen I met. He was an excellent Spanish teacher. Some called him the most genuine, sincere, and intelligent member of our Carmel High faculty.

Don Craig's trade-mark dress was a black top coat worn over a two-piece suit. He wore a dress hat to finish off his defining stylish attire. He didn't dress up to impress anyone. That was just Don Craig. He dressed like that for school most every day, including his sideline duties at Carmel High football games. Don Craig had class.

Coach Mosolf was heard to say that Don Craig was responsible for Carmel High's football success over the years. Coach Mo called him a football genius. Some of Don Craig's contemporaries call him a "genius" period.

Coach Mosolf's main agenda for the evening was to go over name by name the kids expected to turn out for football that year. One of the main reasons for the year- after-year success of Carmel High football was how well the personnel were identified.

As an example: Danny Holman a skinny kid who would be a freshman in the fall. Coach Mosolf said Holman was the varsity quarterback of the future. Coach Buzz Rainer was excited about having Holman on his JV team.

Coach Mosolf said, "No". His feeling was that Danny Holman was still too immature to step into the intense rigors of JV football. He said he thought it best that Holman get his feet wet with my lightweights. Danny's father, a well known Carmel music instructor died earlier that summer. Coach Mosolf did not want too much pressure on Danny too soon.

This discussion was an eye-opener for me. I soon learned the reason the CHS JV team was so strong year in and year out. Coach Mosolf let Coach Rainer keep a number of juniors, kids who were good football players but who would probably be backups on the varsity. Carmel High always had a number of one-year varsity letter winners, kids who had played varsity football only their Senior year. They played two or three years on the JV team. A lot of the sophomore and junior kids could be varsity players on our opponents' teams. At CHS only the best athletes in school played on the Carmel Varsity. It was tradition. To be a CHS varsity player was to be among the best. All the kids took great pride in being a CHS football player, regardless of the level, lightweights, JV, or varsity. That pride was instilled in the football program years before by Coach Mosolf and Coach Don Craig.

During the discussion time I asked Coach Mosolf if he wanted the lightweights running the varsity's offensive plays. Coach Mo told me to run whatever offense and defense I wanted. "Just make sure they line up in a straight line," he said with a chuckle Then he said something that made a lot of sense to me. He said, "Hadley, just make sure the kids have fun. Never take a win or a loss too seriously. That is why I want Danny Holman on lightweights. I want him to have fun." I was to find out soon that Danny

Holman not only had fun but he made it fun for all of us. On the way home Buzz told me Coach Mo lets him pretty much have free rein with the JV offense and defense. Coach Mo wanted the JV's to have the same method of numbering and calling plays. Otherwise Coach Rainer was on his own, as I would be.

The Carmel area was first settled in the 1700's by Father Junipero Serra, a Catholic Jesuit priest. He founded Mission San Carlos Borromeo. The original Mission is still a tourist attraction in Carmel. Legend has it that Father Serra still holds mass there every midnight. That's questionable.

Much of the tradition and legend of Father Serra is found throughout the Carmel and Monterey Peninsula boundries, and many Jesuit Spanish names are still in use.

I wasn't fond of one of the Jesuit Spanish names Carmel High School inherited. Our teams' mascot was a wimpy looking *Padre* with a sweet grin on his face. "The Carmel High School *Padres*". How quaint. Our *Padre* mascot didn't look at all like an athlete much less a *tough* athlete. He is pudgy, obviously very much out of shape. How in the world could I as a coach inspire my team with, "All right team. Go out there and fight like *Padres!*"

Oh, well. I got used to it.

The Carmel High School *Padre*

First Day of School
Let 'em Know Who's Boss

I didn't go as far as my wife's father suggested I go. Mr. Claire Fallis, a strict Canadian public school administrator, told me I should insist my students stand when I walked into class. They should remain standing until I told them to sit. They must be taught respect for authority.

I didn't quite go that far.

Principal Warren Edwards told all teachers he wanted us to stand at the door to greet all students as they entered the class room. The classsrooms opened to an outside hallway, the ivy covered ceilings were supported by ivy covered pillars. It was always cool and refreshing standing outside my classroom. I loved it.

First Period warning bell rang at 8:00 a.m. That first day of school I was standing in the hallway next to my open door. As each student entered my room I greeted them with a smile and a "Good morning." I wasn't too surprised when most of them answered with a pleasant, "Good morning, Mr. Hicks." I got to know some of them during my summer hours working for the Recreation Department.

I was still the new kid on the block. I had to establish my ground rules. I came on pretty firmly. I told them that when the tardy bell rang they were to be in their seats and not talking. I would take roll by reading their names until I knew them all by sight.

They were to answer with a firm "Here, sir". They were to address me as "Mr. Hicks" or "Coach Hicks". They were never to reply to a question with "Yeah" or "Nope"; always "no, sir" or "Yes, sir". If they had a question or a pertinent comment they were to raise their hand. I would call on them when it was appropriate.

That seemed to work pretty well. None of them rolled their eyes or snickered. I spent the rest of the period discussing my expectations for the Speech class. I did all the talking. I told them they would have plenty of time to do their own talking as we started their speech assignments.

The rest of the time was spent seating the students by alphabetical order. They were to sit in their assigned seats until I determined a change should be made. For the most part the students were pretty quiet as they changed seats.

With about 15 minutes of class time left I asked if they had any questions or comments. Most of the questions were about the kinds of speeches they would be giving. I anticipated this. I explained each category of speech in such a way that the speeches sounded interesting to them. There would be some humorous speeches, some serious speeches and speeches which required lots of research. For most of the speeches the students would be able to use outlined notes. A few would have to be memorized. On some they would be given the topic with just a minute to prepare. I guaranteed that the class would be fun and interesting if they put effort into preparation.

Most of the students seemed to be excited about the class. Others would probably drop the class.

My other two Speech Classes went pretty much the way the First Period Class went. They seemed like great kids; eager to participate and polite. I knew I would enjoy my Speech Classes. I felt certain that I had chosen the best, most enjoyable subject to teach. I said a silent thanks to University of Arizona Professor Dr. Sparks, my roomie Charlie Leftault and football teammate Don Beasley. All three planted the thought in my mind.

My two non-college Prep. English Classses might be something else. The students seemed to be not quite as energetic, or engaged. They were polite enough just not enthused about school. I got the feeling they were there because thay had to be.

When I went over my class expectations a few of the boys slouched down in their seats and seemed to be thinking *"Yeah, I've heard this before."* When I told them they were to be in their seats and quiet when the tardy bell rang, I seemed to sense a *"Ha!*

That'll be the day." attitude from the same boys. I knew they would test me. A few of the boys were football players and they seemed to be more with it, more attentative. They knew I was a coach and I felt that made a difference.

I was warned by Dan Yurkovich that I would have to crack down on the non-college kids right off the bat. Let them know "how the cow ate the cabbage" day one and don't let up. That was going to be hard for me to do. Some of them seemed like great kids; some obviously from non-functional homes. They would be a challange.

I knew my reputation was at stake. If these kids got the best of me I would have trouble all year long. Once respect was lost it was tough to get it back Yurkovich had told me.

CHS *Padre* Football
A Proud Tradition

I knew I was walking into something special. All summer long the chatter among the kids at the gymnasium was centered around football. Freshman to-be were talking about going out for football or they were being asked, "Are you going out for football?"

When the kids found out that I was going to be one of the football coaches I took on a new significance. I was peppered with questions about my background. Where was I from? Did I play football? What position? I had ample opportunity to humbly let them know that I was pretty well known in Arizona.

Most of the grade school kids eyed me from a distance. They didn't want to get too close at first. The older kids, the high school kids, wanted to be buddy-buddy with me. I had to subtly squelch that. Dan Yurkovich advised me to not let any get too personal. He said some would try to dominate my attention and I shouldn't have any favorites.

The Mission Trails Athletic League (MTAL) of which CHS was a member allowed a week prior to start of school for "shorts and helmets only" workouts. The workouts were specifically geared towards conditioning. Coach Mosolf conducted our workouts with all kids together, varsity down through lightweights. The workouts allowed the coaches to evaluate the new talent and to judge the physical condition of the returners. It was also a chance for me to judge the coaching techniques of my fellow coaches. I was especially eager to watch Coaches Mosolf and Craig in action. Once school started and the season got underway I would be on my own. I kept my mouth shut and observed. I did only what I was asked to do.

In the Coaches' locker room after the workouts I got my chance to pick the coaches' brains. I asked a lot of questions. Sometimes we stayed for two hours or so discussing various coaching techniques.

The coaches were not too big on exact fundamentals. As long as a kid could get his job done. He was not coached on doing it exactly "this way". The coaches did not over-coach. Coach Mo told me that over-coaching was a habit many new coaches brought with them. "Keep it simple" was the best way to go. I found that to be true over the years.

So You Wanna Be a Legend. So Did I.

These after workout discussion sessions were especially valuable to me when personnel were discussed. The strengths and weaknesses of each kid were gone over in detail. I was pleasently surprised at just how much detail the coaches went into discussing the pros and cons of the various kids. I again witnessed Coach Mosolf carefully evaluating where best to place certain kids; Varsity, JV or Lightweight?

Coach Mo was always thinking about "next year". Would another year on the JV's make a certain junior a better player next year? Or would he be more valuable to the Varsity this year? I noticed Coach Rainer pushed pretty hard for as many juniors as possible to be placed on his JV squad. Rainer and I would have a heated discussion about a certain Danny Holman in just 2 years hence. I would be glad I took note of Coach Mosolf's philosophy.

THE FIRST DAY
Full Pads

Coach Mosolf was organized. He got each kid's helmet well fitted during the pre-season conditioning workouts. On the first day of full pads Coach Mo had a locker for each varsity and junior varsity player with his helmet, pads, practice pants and shirt neatly hung up. Each kid furnished his own football cleats.

The varsity and JV players were grouped together on three sides of the locker room. My Lightweights had to take what was left. For some that meant they had to pile their equipment on top of a JV locker. That was inconvenient and made for some overcrowded areas. It was just a fact of life that they lived with without too much complaining. There were always several younger kids who quit after the first day or so; that lessened the crowding.

The first day in pads was quite an experience for me. After I dressed in my coaching clothes I was just killing time gabbing with the other coaches when Coach Mo came in with a grin on his face. "Coach Hicks, you'd best go out there and help your young charges get dressed. They need you!"

It was a funny sight. These were freshman. None of them ever played organized football before. They had no clue how to put on the pads. For the most part they had very little problems with the shoulder pads. They were astute enough to realize that the unlaced side of the shoulder pad was the side that went in front. What proved to be a major problem for most of the kids was putting the thigh pads in. The thigh pads are to be placed in right and left pockets inside the legs of the football pants; the right thigh pad fits in the right leg pocket; the left thigh pad fits in the left leg pocket. Sounds easy enough.

What complicated it for the kids was that each thigh pad had an elongated portion on one side of the pad. The elongated portion was to go on the outside of each thigh, away from the groin area. The opposite portion of the pad allowed for an unobstructed fit against the groin area. If the pads were put in the wrong leg pocket the groin area had the elongated part of the pad jabbing into the groin. Very uncomfortable. Very dangerous.

Then there were the few boys who had never worn a jockstrap. Believe it or not they tried to put the jock on backwards! Again, very uncomfortable. Very dangerous.

As each one of our players got dressed correctly he went outside the front door of the gymnasium and waited. When they had were all dressed correctly and were outside I conducted a final inspection.

We were finally ready for our first ever organized football practice. The players were nervous as was to be expected. They had never experienced real football practice. I was also nervous. I had never experienced real football practice as the coach.

My lightweight team had it made! We were told we would not practice with the varsity and the JVs. They were both on Bardarson Field, Carmel High's beautiful homefield. Neither varsity or JV team had lost a game on that field in quite a few years.

I was happy to have our own practice field. We practiced on the Girls' Physical Education field outside the main entrance of the gymnasium. This was the field the tour bus drivers looked on as plush country club landscaping. It was in the shape of a bowl. It made a perfect practice field.

We always had an audience for our practices. When school was out for the day, the school buses were parked just above our practice field. Students often waited for the buses or their ride home by sitting on the side of the bowl, a perfect place to watch us practice. Parents of the players would sometimes sit on the soft grass and watch their boys practice. Many would bring a blanket to sit on while they watched us.

After explaining our stretching exercises and going through them a few times I got down to serious business. I grouped the players by positions they indicated they wanted to play. I then ran them through some agilty exercises to test foot speed and agility. I used a note-pad and a pencil to take notes. Each player had a piece of athletic tape across the front of each helmet. His last name was written on the tape in Magic Marker. This helped me greatly in identifying the kids as they went through their agility exercises. Though I knew a lot of them they were hard to recognize wearing helmets.

Before ending practice I went through some pass-receiving drills. Even those who wanted to be linemen had to go through these drills. I came away from those passing drills with a couple positive conclusions: Danny Holman could throw a football! There was no doubt who my quarterback would be!

I was able to identify three fairly decent receivers Holman could throw to. Pat Olmstead who was to catch our first touchdown of the season was a good looking receiver. Lynden Mahrt had good speed. Al Tegtmeier was a tall gangly kid who could catch. The CHS lightweights would present a passing threat, I was sure of that.

To end practice we ran 25 yard sprints to give me a gage on the individual speed of the players. A few of them could run well. In my opinion Terry Bishop had running back potential. He was big for a freshman, maybe 155-160 pounds on a sturdy frame.

I was pleased when practice was over. I felt we had the possibility of having a decent football team. I saw that there was what I would call good over-all speed. I was concerned in only one area after the first day. Our offensive line candidates were not impressive. But it was only the first day.

I sent them in on a positive note. We got together in a large huddle, hands either together or on a shoulder. We counted to three and on the "three" we all yelled together *"Padrecitos"*. I had to explain to some of them before we yelled what *Padrecitos* meant. "Little Padres". They liked that. They all went inside happy. They had survived their first official Carmel High football practice.

As I walked off the field I noticed that one of the young men who had been watching practice was waiting for me by the gym door. He introduced himself as Bill Dickens. Bill's younger brother was one of our lightweights, Kenny Dickens. Bill told me he had played some high school football in another state. He noticed I was the only coach on the field. He asked if I needed help.

After speaking with Bill for a few minutes I asked him to come inside. Before I told him I would greatly appreciate his help I wanted to find out the legality of an outsider helping me coach.

We went inside as the Varsity was just coming in. I introduced Bill to Coach Mosolf. After explaining what Bill had asked to do, Coach Mo said it was perfectly legal but before any decision was made Bill and I should get together and visit. If, after visiting, I felt Bill would be a good fit for my needs than Coach Mo would be all for it.

Bill and I had a good visit. We sat on the bleachers inside the gymnasium and basically talked coaching philosophy. I made it clear that I had to be the head coach. I would consult with Bill but I had to make the final decision on matters we discussed. Bill would be the line coach. He felt he knew enough about line-play to be a help. He said he would probably drive me nuts with questions. I liked that. That showed me Bill had enthusiasm and was eager.

After an hour or so we shook hands. Bill would be at our next day's practice. I told him I would introduce him as the *Padrecitos* line coach and to be there at least half an hour before practice was to begin. We needed to be on the same page with our practice schedule. I would write out a tentative schedule and we would discuss it when he came in. I was excited. Bill was a nice young man. He seemed honest and sincere. My first impression of Bill was a positive one. I liked him. I had my first coaching "staff"!

The first two weeks of practices went well. Bill and I were slowly but surely beginning to feel comfortable with each other. We put in our offensive system first.

I told Bill that what we were going to use initially was the basic Arizona State *Sun Devil* offense, line up in the T formation; shift sometimes to a wing-T one side or the other; shift sometimes to the single wing formation, the same single wing formation that I hated so much when I had to use it in the Arizona All-Star Game. At Arizona State it was a thing of beauty. I hoped it would be the same for the *Padrecitos*. It was.

The first test for our lightweights was on Wednesday of week three. We had a full scrimmage against our CHS JVs. Our little lightweights were scared to death. Coach Bill and I were nervous as well. We knew we could hold our own against another lightweight team. But against our JVs?? We would find out.

The scrimmage was held on our practice field, the "upper-field" as it was refered to by the varsity and JV coaches. It was agreed that the lightweights would run the first series of plays. We would run as many plays as we could until we either made a 1st and 10 or lost the ball on downs. It didn't take us long to make a first down. In fact we scored a touchdown on the first play of the scrimmage! We completely took the JVs off guard. We lined up in the T formation. When Danny Holman signaled for the backfield to shift to the single wing the JVs jumped off sides. On our "do-over" we again shifted. This time the JVs did not jump off sides.

When we shifted from the T formation to the single wing, quarterback Holman who had lined up with his hands under the center to get the ball, merely took 2 quick steps to his right; he was now directly behind our right guard. The right half back shifted to a foot behind and two feet outside our end on the right side. Our left halfback shifted to directly behind the center about five yards deep. Our fullback shifted a foot or so to his right; he was four feet back of the line of scrimmage, behind our right tackle and parallel to our left halfback. When we had finished with the shift, our backs were in the shape of a "box".

On quarterback Holman's signal the ball was centered to left halfback Terry Bishop. Bishop got the ball, ducked his head running hard toward our right guard, making it look like he was going to run up the middle. On the snap of the ball qurarterback Holman had turned his back to the defense and faced halfback Bishop.

Bishop running directly toward Holman handed the ball to him. This hand off was very difficult for the defensive secondary to see, bodies going all directions.

The movement of halfback Bishop towards the line of scrimmage fooled the defensive backs into thinking the play was a run up the middle. The defensive backs came flying up to make the tackle. Holman got the ball and ran in a crouched position until he was about eight yards deep. He turned around and hit wide open end Pat Olmsted for an easy first-play touchdown. Lightweights 6- JVs 0.

The JVs were stunned!

I should have called the scrimmage off at that point, should have made up some excuse. Our kids had to get home for dinner or something. But I didn't.

I wish I could say the Lightweights went on and scored more than the JVs. Official scoring was not kept; we scored three times all on Holman passes. The JVs scored four or five times. Their bigger, stronger line and backs dominated our little kids. It was obvious which was the better team, and the more experienced.

I made one big mistake in this, my first under-fire test. In the coaches' locker room after the scrimmage JV Coaches Rainer and Lawitzke had some good things to say about the Lightweights. Coach Dickens and I were feeling pretty good. Then Coach Mosolf asked this question, "Did all your kids get to play?" Long pause. "No sir, I don't think so."

"Remember what I told you, Hadley. Make sure the kids have fun. That means all the kids. Get them all in one way or another, even if for only one or two plays."

I felt pretty sheepish. Coach Mo brought me down to earth pretty quickly. That was a mistake I tried hard not to replicate over the years.

The season went by quickly. We won one game, lost two and tied one.

The one game we tied was a "moral victory". We played the Live Oak *Acorns'* Junior Varsity team. The were one of the biggest JV teams in the league.

Coaches Mosolf and Craig had seen them play when they went on a scouting trip. They gave Bill and me a good scouting report. The one weak spot Mosolf and Craig felt we might capitalize on was Live Oak's lack of "fire". They gave up pretty easily and did not play with intensity. We felt if we could get in the first couple of hits we might take some fire out of them.

So here is what we did to insure we got in the first good hits. We told our tough little nose guard Jack Hinchcliff to line up directly in front of the Live Oak center, nose to nose. On the first syllable, the first sound the quarterback uttered, Hinchcliff was to fire out as quick and as tough as he could and drive the center back into the quarterback. Hinchcliff did it beautifully. The center and quarterback did not know what hit them. We gladly took the five yard penalty. But, Hinchcliff was not finished. He was to do exactly the same thing the next time the quarterback uttered a sound. Hinchcliff clobbered them again, another five yard penalty. This time I yelled at Jack Hinchclff to "Be alert. Wait until the ball moves!" I put on a good show of being angry with Hinchcliff.

On the third attempt by Live Oak to run a play, Hinchcliff had been instructed to fake a quick movement at the center. Hinchcliff did; the center flinched and jumped off sides. The five yard penalty was called on Hinchcliff for drawing the center off sides as was correct. I immediately sent in a substitute for Hinchcliff and when he came to the sidelines Coach Dickens and I both got in his face pretending to chew him out. The charade was a success except as we were "chewing him out" Hinchcliff was smiling. He was proud of his perfomance. We sent Jack Hinchcliff back in after a few plays. From that point on the Live Oak center and quarterback were a little antsy. We made them somewhat fearful of our quick hitting nose guard. Offensively they were pretty inept. Defensively they were tough.

We did not generate any kind of offensive threat. Their big defensive line kept our offense well in check. Quarterback Holman was sacked almost every time he went back to pass. He did get off one long pass to speedy end Lynden Mahrt for the only score of the first half. We led 6 - 0 going in at half time. The second half was more of the same. With a couple of minutes left to play it looked like we might pull an upset. Our 6 - 0 lead looked fairly secure. We had the ball in our own territory. If we could pick up a first down or two the clock would wind down. It was not in the cards. One of our backs fumbled. Live Oak recovered. They scored the tying touchdown with less than a minute left. Their extra-point attempt failed. Final score 6-6. We played well for the most part. We could have won it. Live Oak played poorly. They should have won it.

I learned a lesson I was well aware of. I had just never seen it so well exibited as it was in that game. *Attitude!* The difference was like night and day: Live Oak was listless. They walked to and from the huddle, no hustle. Our kids were hustling, clapping hands, yelling, encouraging each other right up to the end. When our kid fumbled we did not get down. We played all the harder with our backs to the wall. Coach Dickens and I were proud of them. We told them so.

Though we did not play many games the number of scrimmages we had with the JVs gave our youngsters good experience. The JV Coaches Rainer and Lawitzke felt good about scrimmaging us. They said we gave their starters more competition than their reserves did, more even than a few of their scheduled opponents. The JVs were undefeated in league play. We were proud to have contributed to their success.

The CHS Varsity was undefeated again. 8-0. Coach Mosolf, Coach Craig and the *Padres* won 31 straight games. Quite a record. How far would the win streak go? It was anybody's guess.

Though my Lightweight team did not have a winning season I still felt that I earned my stripes as a Carmel High School coach. All of our opponents were JV teams. We were the first MTAL school to field a Lightweight team. We held our own with the other teams. We lost two close games, won one, tied another one. I looked forward to bigger and better things. I was not to be disappointed.

"Coach" Hicks.

It was sometime around the fourth or fifth week of school that I suddenly realized that most of the students were calling me "Coach" Hicks. It was no longer "Mr." Hicks as it was for the first few weeks. It was now *Coach Hicks*. Each time I was referred to as "Coach" I stood a little taller. I felt respected. I felt like I was accepted as one of them. I felt- I don't know- I felt significant.

Even my two classes of non-college English kids called me "Coach Hicks". I discovered that my disciplinary measures in those classes occured less frequently. They accepted "Coach Hicks" as the classroom authoriy much more readily than they did common, ordinary "Mr. Hicks."

MICHAEL HADLEY HICKS
November 19, 1959

Our second child, Michael (Mike) H. Hicks, came into the world with much less fanfare than did his big sister. Susie was born during the height of my professional baseball career, my two and a half month "cup of coffee" in the Chicago *Cub* farm system. Susie got lots of attention and adoration from the baseball fans in Pulaski, Virginia. Mike got some hugs and kisses on the cheek from our CHS faculty friends.

For Mike's first year when Joan took Susie and Mike to our CHS activities, Susie was in her stroller. Mike was in a car seat on the back of Susie's stroller. Some of the Carmel High girls "ooh'ed" and "ah'ed" over Mike; Susie got the cutesy talk and tickles. She responded with smiles and cute baby talk. She even sat on the cheer leaders' laps during quiet times at the basketball games. Mike just drank from his bottle, sucked on his pacifier, and slept.

Mike came into his own his second year. By this time Susie thought she owned the Carmel High football stadium and the gymnasium; her baby brother infringed on her territory. Mike liked to tag along with Susie at first. Susie tolerated him.

When Mike discovered that the male athletes were somewhat special with me, he coveted some of the attention I gave them. Soon Mike was a regular at practices and games. Susie could care less about practices- no fans, no cheerleaders or pom-pom girls. Mike spent much of his practice time playing catch or kicking the football with any unoccupied player or manager. He loved it. What joy Mike was to give us for the next forty six years.

HADLEY HICKS
Head Carmel High School Football Coach

Several weeks after my second lightweight season finished I was hit square between the eyes with a life altering change of status. It happened so very, very suddenly. One minute I was sitting in the CHS Faculty Room minding my own business. The next minute I was in Principal Warren Edward's office. My head was swimming with a multitude of thoughts about my future

So You Wanna Be a Legend. So Did I.

Principal Edwards called JV Head Coach Buzz Rainer and me into his office. When Buzz and I were seated, Edwards closed the door to his offfice. He got right to the point. Head Football Coach George Mosolf had been relieved of his duties. He was being assigned to the Carmel Middle School as Physical Education Teacher.

Edwards then unloaded this bomb shell on Buzz and me. "Men. One of you will be the next Carmel High football coach. Which one of you wants it?" Buzz surprised me. He quickly answered, "Not me!" I looked around the room. There was no one else in there but Buzz and me. Buzz turned the job down. I soon found out why.

Afer discussing particulars for awhile Buzz and Mr. Edwards shook hands with the new CHS football coach. They both wished me luck and said they would help me any way they could.

I was stunned. I must have sat there a good hour digesting all that this assignment entailed. One of the first main items to chew on was the fact that Coach Mosolf had won 31 straight games. There would be tremendous pressure on the new coach to continue the tradition. I was sure that when the rest of the MTAL football coaches heard that Mosolf was no longer at the helm of CHS football there would be a huge sigh of relief from all of them.

During our discussion I asked Buzz if he would be my assistant coach. Buzz said, "No," and he explained why he did not want to be elevated to the varsity. Buzz and Coach Mosolf had been friends for years. Buzz felt a certain loyalty to Coach Mo. He did not want to replace him in any way.

I found out later from the District "grapevine" that Coach Mosolf was relieved from his duties as Varsity Head Football Coach for some issues which were controversial. I never did find out what I could call the "truth" of the issues so I didn't try to explain the situation. All I knew or cared to know was that I had a huge job ahead of me.

My first job was to put together a coaching staff. I asked Coach Don Craig long time assistant to Coach Mosolf if he would consider staying on as my assistant Coach Craig being the class act he was graciously declined. He said sincerely that he would be glad to offer advice should I ask it of him, but it was time for "new blood" to take over. I had much admiration for Don Craig for his dedicated loyalty to Coach Mosolf. As it turned out I ended up with the best choice for an assistant coach. I talked Dick Lawitzke, CHS JV assistant to Buzz Rainer into coming up to Varsity. I told him I needed his experience. And boy did I ever!

Coach Lawitzke knew offensive and defensive line play as well as most high school coaches in the area. He was a tough task master. He blended in well with my easy-going mannerisms.

Listen to how Bill Stowers, one of Carmel High's best ever football players, described the first time he ever saw Coach Lawitzke:

"I reported to two-a-day practices at Carmel High in the summer of 1962. One of the first things I remember seeing was a Carmel High coach walking down the stadium steps to the field snapping a bull whip and yelling at everyone in sight. That guy with the bull whip was to be my line coach for the next two years, Coach Dick Lawitzke"

Coach Lawitzke wielded that bull whip for the entire first practice session each year. It left no doubts as to who was the linemens boss. He definitely got his point across.

Coach Dick Lawitzke
"Making his point."

When Dick Lawitzke agreed to move up to the Varsity with me that left a huge void on Buzz Rainer's JV team. I had several calls from potential candidates around the area for the position. The only name I seriously considered was Jason Harbert Jason was an assistant at Monterey High School; he had grown up in Carmel and was a CHS graduate. Jason was laying the ground work for a CHS position for several years. He applied unsuccessfully for various teaching and coaching openings. This opening fit the bill! Jason Harbert was to be a bulwark for Carmel High School for many years, both athletically and academically.

FOOTBALL 1961.
"The Streak" Finally Broken.

I learned quickly what the adage "Albatros around your neck" meant. From the first day it was announced that I was to replace Coach Mosolf as Varsity Football coach I got the question:, "CHS has a 31 game winning streak. Think you can extend it?"

That was the topic of conversation with everyone who frequented Jim Kelsey's "*Rinky Dink*" coffee shop. The *Rinky Dink* was the Carmel place-to-go for a cup of coffee and expert analysis on all subjects dealing with CHS athletics.

A sports reporter from the San Jose, California *Mercury* newspaper phoned me with this dumb question: "Coach Mosolf is the dean of Northern California football coaches. Do you think you are qualified to replace him?" That was one of those "dammed if you do and dammed if you don't "questions. Answer, "Yes, I am qualified," and I am arrogant. "No, I am not qualified," and I have no confidence.

Thankfully my good Arizona friend Dan Yurkovich, CHS basketball coach had been around the block a few times. He gave me good advice on how to handle the pressure I experienced. It was was simple. He told me to answer those questions with a great degree of humility. He said regarding the win streak to say something like, "That is an unbelievable streak accomplished by an outstanding coach. I will try the best I can. "Period! End of discussion. Dan said to answer any question about being qualified to replace Mosolf with, "I personally don't believe anybody can replace Coach Mosolf. He is a legend." Period! Dan gave good advice regarding handling my first post-Mosolf CHS football team. He told me to not try to change too much too soon.

I incorporated some of the Arizona State *Sun Devil* offense into my lightweight team's offense. Dan did not think that would be a good idea for my first CHS team. I needed to prove myself before making any drastic changes away from the success of Mosolf's scheme of things. Mosolf used a basic T formation with an occasional wing or flanker one side or the other. His style was straight smash-mouth power football, not a lot of passing.

Dan Yurkovich told me somethng else I became a firm believer in: "adapt your offense and defense to the personnel you have on hand." On paper I did not have the personnel for a power-type offense. From what I could see my kids were not big. A few I knew were quick. I'd have to work with what I had.

Graduating from Coach Mosolf's last team were a quality bunch of large, powerful linemen. Chief among them were the outstanding Wilkin twins, John and Chris. Their father was "Wee Willie" Wilkin who made a name for himself with the Washington *Red Skins* professional team. Wilber "Wee Willie" Wilkin was considered to be one of professional football's outstanding linemen during the early NFL days. To quote one newspaper source: "'Wee Willie' was 6'1, 265 pounds and ran the 100 yards in 10.5 seconds. He was the most dominate tackle in the NFL from 1938 to 1945."

"Wee Willie's" two sons were made from the same mold. Both were well over 6' tall and both over 220 pounds. John and Chris were heavily recruited by California universities. John Wilkin went to Stanford where he played for several years. Chris was tragically killed in an auto accident soon after graduating from Carmel High School.

Just before he graduated Chris came up to me one day and sincerely wished me good luck with the *Padres* the next year. He said he doubted that I would be able to "replace me and John." Chris did not say this arrogantly. He was not an arrogant kid. He said it matter of factly. They would be difficult but not impossible to replace.

Not only did I have to replace the Wilkin twins I had to replace a Northern California icon, long time Carmel High School Coach George Mosolf. I had much to live up to. Not only did Mosolf's teams win but they did it with class and polish. They always looked good. They were *poised,* an attribute I had always admired in Dan Devine's Arizona State *Sun Devil* teams. I was determined the Hicks coached CHS *Padres* would exhibit that same poise.

"Replacing me and John" was the first order of business for the new Carmel High football coaching staff. Coaches Lawitzke, Rainer, Harbert and I met sometimes three or four times per week all summer. We spent time discussing and sometimes arguing philosophy.

I had a hard time disagreeing with Coach Mo's winning philosophy. I was determined though that I would disagree in one area. Mosolf often kept a good junior player down on the JV team. That strengthened Coach Rainer's JV team and got the junior player well seasoned for the following year's varsity competition. Fine and good; but if that junior was the best player, the best athlete in school, he was going to be on the varsity.

Danny Holman was the best player in school for the past two seasons; he had an outstanding freshman season on my lightweight team. He was even better the next season with Coach Rainer's JV team. He **was** going to be the CHS Varsity quarterback.

Rainer fought me tooth and toe-nail over this.

Buzz insisted that Danny was not ready for the Varsity; he was too skinny, he was not athletically mature. Buzz even went so far as to insist that Danny's grades would suffer from all the stress of keeping the streak alive. And on and on and on.

What finally put the issue to rest was the evening Joan and I were invited to Rainer's house for dinner. When Buzz had come to our house to invite us he brought an expensive bottle of wine "just as a gift". After he extended his invitation to dinner and went home, I said to Joan, "Baloney! This bottle of wine and the dinner invitation is to give Buzz another chance to sway me about Holman. He feels that if I am in his territory for a nice meal, conversation and wine that I will relent when he brings the Holman arguement up again."

Let Buzz tell the story in his own words. This version is from an article which appeared in the January 1, 2000 Monterey *Herald* newspaper. It is part of a full front page article on the untimely death of Danny Holman.

Here is Buzz's version of how Danny got on the CHS Varsity in 1961:

"He was so skinny we had to tape thigh pads to both sides of his legs," said Buzz Rainer, Holman's junior varsity coach at Carmel. "I convinced varsity head coach Hadley Hicks that Danny was too small to play with those huge linemen. But then I went home and told my wife that with Danny, we could beat anyone on the Peninsula, including our Varsity.

"So we had Hadley and his wife over for dinner right before the season. My wife says to him, 'Hadley, Buzz says that with Danny on his team he could beat you any day of the week.' I said, 'Honey, you just put Danny on the Varsity.' "

The pre-season Mission Trail Athletic League (MTAL) football coaches' "Liars Banquet" as I called it met in Salinas, California a week before the football season began.

So You Wanna Be a Legend. So Did I.

Coaches from several other conferences besides the MTAL were in attendance. Coaches in attendance included head coaches, some assistant coaches and even some JV coaches. They came from the Monterey Peninsula high schools, several Salinas high schools and schools from a Catholic league totaling 15 or so high schools total.

In addition to all the coaches many Peninsula newspapers had representatives there. Some even came from the San Jose, California area 80 miles away. The coaches' banquet was a big deal and always held in one of Salinas' larger hotels' banquet hall.

The purpose of the meeting was to hear the head coaches detail the prospects for their teams' chances for the upcoming season. Each head coach was asked to speak about his team. He was expected to go over the personnel they had returning and what newcomers looked promising.

All the head coaches and the sportswriters would vote on how they felt the teams would finish at season's end. There were two polls; coaches poll and sportswriters poll. To be voted first in either poll was a "kiss of death." Thus, the lies. The coaches who were loaded downplayed the fact. Nobody wanted to be voted first.

When it was my turn to review our prospects I was fairly honest. I bemoaned the loss of All Northern California tackles John and Chris Wilkin, all-league running backs Mike Draper and Frank Mayo, quarterback Russell Wise. I said we would have a fair running game. Halfbacks Terry Bishop, transfer student Dennis Hermanson, J.T. Thomas. These three would give us fair speed.

My only lie: I said that Senior Bob Larson looked like our quarterback. He had done a good job for our lightweight team my second year. I knew that Bob could be a starter for some of our MTAL opponents. He would be reliable backup for Danny. I didn't say that though. I hoped to not have to talk about Danny Holman. I didn't want any adverse pre-season publicity on him. I almost made it. As I was about to sit down a coach asked about the "skinny kid that was quarterback for the JV's." I said, "That is Danny Holman. He will be in the mix somewhere." Yes, he would. That was not a lie.

Our season opened at home against perennial door mat Gonzales High School. We were unimpressive in a 12-0 easy win. Coach Lawitzke was responsible for our preparation for that game. I hate to under estimate a team but Lawitzke talked me into toning down our offense. "Just keep it simple," was his advice.

Since our home games were played Saturday afternoons due to the fact that Bardarson Field does not have lights, we have the advantage of scouting opponents on Friday nights. Our entire coaching staff scouted Gonzales' inter-squad scrimmage the Friday night a week before our scheduled league game with them. Scouting scrimmages was legal under MTAL rules. All of us to a man concluded that Gonzales would not be much of a test for us. Still I hated to be too confident.

Our offense ran a scaled down attack. Holman threw only a few passes. All of them were complete for short gains. Our defense was able to shut down Gonzales effectively. It was obvious to the experienced eye that we were holding back and not showing all we had.

There was one pleasant surprise which seemingly came out of nowhere. In order to hold down our offensive production I put in 130 pound running back Steve Fairfield. Fairfield was a senior; the fastest player on the team. He had never played football before. I put him in toward the end of the first quarter. On his first carry he sped 38 yards for our second touchdown. He was untouched. The next time we had the ball, Fairfield had two long beautiful runs but did not score. Had I kept him in he would certainly have scored one or two more touchdowns. I took him out before half time. Lawitzke and I both agreed that Steve Fairfield would be a welcome addition to our future offensive plans

We were happy with the win, my first as the new CHS head coach. When Lawitzke and I went for coffee at the *Rinky-Dink* the next Monday some of our Monday quarterbacks told us we would have to play much better the next Friday night.

Our next opponent was the Hollister *Haybalers* at their place. They were the pre-season picks to win the MTAL. They were an experienced team, big and slow. The "slow" part was what Lawitzke and I keyed on. Their stands were packed. Hollister had not beaten Carmel in years. This was to be their year. We could sense the excitement in the air. It was electric. The Hollister crowd completely drowned out our 100 or so faithful who made the trip to root us on.

When the *Haybalers* rumbled on to the field for their pre-game warm ups, Lawitzke and I looked at each other. *"Big"* was our unspoken thought. Our kids were too busy getting ready to play an important game to notice the huge *Haybalers* at the other end of the field. Dick and I both sensed our kids were pumped.

Last week's game was merely a warm up for tonight. Our week's practices had gone smoothly. We established our game plans firmly in their minds. Our running game was to be quick hitting dive plays with fullback Rick Baldwin, halfbacks Terry Bishop; Steve Fairfield, J.T. Thomas and Dennis Hermanson hopefully picking up chunks of Hollister real estate. When the slower Hollister defense bunched up to stop the quick dives we would run wide with our speed. We felt we could counter any defense Hollister threw at us.

Fairfield was a surprise starter. Steve looked great in the week's practices. He seemed to have picked up our offense quickly. Coach Lawitzke and I were still concerned about his size and durability. Could he hold up against the pounding? We were soon to find out.

We received the kick-off and for all practical purposes the game was over. Our offenses' first drive was a thing of beauty. We marched down the field five or six yards at a time.

As we neared the Hollister goal line their defense bunched up to stop our next quick dive play. I had been calling most of the plays; on this one I let Danny Holman call it. He faked a quick dive to Baldwin. The defense swarmed in to stop it. Holman straightened up and hit wide open end Al Tegtmeier for an easy ten yard touchdown. That was Holman's first pass of the entire eighty yard drive, his first pass as a CHS Varsity quarterback. The Hollister crowd was noticeably quiet.

We were off to the races!

The Hollister defense was in a quandry. Steve Fairfield and Dennis Hermanson ran wide sweeps to both sides, picking up good yardage.

When the *Haybaler* defense spread out to stop our sweeps we ran quick hitting dive plays or Holman hit them with quick passes over the middle. Our offense was unstoppable. The half-time score was 14-0.

Coach Dick Lawitzke proved to any doubters what an excellent defensive coach he was. His defensive game plan was executed to perfection. Lawitzke realized that the size and strength of the Hollister offensive line would be too much for our smaller kids to handle for a full game.

Dick worked all week during our defensive practice segment with our defensive linemen playing just a step deeper than usual. Instead of our defensive linemen lining up nose-to-nose or head-to-shoulder on the Hollister offensive line Dick had them line up just a bit deeper than normal. This little adjustment made it easier for our smaller, quicker kids to get a head-start. The strength of the Hollister line was nullified. By the time the Hollister behemoths took one step our kids had taken several and were in the Hollister backfield causing havoc. The Hollister quarterback was sacked repeatedly; their running game was mass confusion. When the final gun sounded we had won going away, 28-0. Our reserves played much of the final minutes. The Hollister crowd had thinned out considerably.

"The Streak" was intact; CHS was unbeaten in 33 straight games.

The following Monday Dick and I were anxious to hear what the experts had to say down at Jim Kelsey's *Rinky-Dink*. Kelsey was chomping at the bit to tell us what he heard about our win while he was shopping in Monterey Saturday morning.

Jim ran into Nick Albert one of the popular sports figures in Monterey. Nick was the brother of Danny Albert head varsity football coach at Monterey High School.

Nick did a lot of officiating at high school games. He was the Head Linesman at our Hollister game the night before. Nick told Jim Kelsey that in his opinion Carmel High School executed as well as any CHS team he had seen. He was very impressed.

Lawitzke told me that if the talk at the *Rinky-Dink* was so flattering the parents and the rest of the town were saying the same ego inflating things. We needed to be cautious of our kids getting the bighead.

Our entire student body was still flying high Monday. The topic of conversation in all the classes was the big win over Hollister; "the Streak", and the upcoming game Friday night vs King City.

King City! Picked second to Holllister to win the league championship. They were always tough, especially tough on their own turf.

Coach Lawitzke and I knew we could not rest on our laurels. We had to get our kids back down to earth quickly. We had a lot to do to prepare for King City. They were an unorthodox offensive team. They ran the single wing offense exclusively and they ran it well. When the single wing is run well it is difficult to defend.

As it turned out our battle with King City was going to be for the MTAL Championship. Both teams were going into the game with identical 2-0 records. King City was favored by 12 points, primarily because they had a powerful running attack featuring 220 pound fullback Jim Mankins. The sports writers figured this game would be high scoring. One predicted a seesaw 39-32 King City win. He was wrong. It was a 14-13 King City win.

"The Streak" was over after 33 straight wins. King City would be MTAL Champ. By one point!

Our kids were devastated. We played hard against a physically superior team. We had a few chances to win but just couldn't get it done. To be honest King City had several chances to score a time or two more. Our kids denied them the opportunity with some hard nosed, aggressive defense. We had played even with them most of the evening. Despite such a low scoring game the fans were kept on the edge of their seats the whole evening. Vicious tackling by both teams stopped key attempts at picking up first downs. Both teams punted five times each. There were few first downs by either team.

King City scored its first touchdown on their only sustained drive of the first half. Mankins scored from three yards out late in the first quarter. The extra point kick was right down the middle.

CHS scored early in the second quarter. Holman picked the King City defense apart with several short passes. We got down to the King City 15 yard line. Running back Rick Baldwin pushed it across. Baldwin's extra point attempt was good. Going in at half time the score was tied 7- 7.

Mankins and King City pretty much controlled the ball in the third quarter. The rugged King City fullback carried over from the CHS 5 yard line with seconds left in the quarter; kick good. King City led 14-7 as the 3rd quarter ended.

The *Padres* got the ensuing kick off and generated a drive which took four minutes. Facing a third down and eight, Holman hit end Pat Olmstead over the middle for a touchdown. Rick Baldwin's extra point attempt was partially blocked. 13-14 King City.

With just minutes left King City and Mankins ran the clock out. King City won by one point!

Jim Mankins, King City tailback was a man among boys. What a physical specimen! He later played with the Green Bay *Packers*. He was a good one.

THE SPIRIT WHICH IS EXCLUSIVELY OURS

Our principal Warren Edwards felt the need to call an assembly the next Monday morning. Mr. Edwards told me before first period on Monday that he sensed a negative attitude among the students. He asked if I thought it would be good for both of us to talk to the student body and try to lift their spirits. I agreed.

The assembly was just before lunch. The students were quieter than usual as they came into the gym. Mr. Edwards spoke first. He did a great job putting the one point loss into the proper perspective. He complemented the students for their outstanding sportsmanship. It was a disappointing loss yet the students conducted themselves in a manner which brought pride to Carmel High School. There were no crass, crude remarks directed toward the King City students or fans. They were a good team and won the game fairly against a most worthy opponent. He said he had already written a letter of congratulations to the principal of King City High School.

Football is just a game. We lost; time to get back to the business at hand, namely getting a quality education which will reap dividends on down the road. He encouraged the students to hold their heads high. They still were members of the greatest high school in the State of California.

So You Wanna Be a Legend. So Did I.

Mr. Edwards ended his speech with this comment: "And by the way. I added a post-script to the letter I wrote to the King City Principal. I wrote, 'P.S. Wait until next year!' "

That last comment did it. The students were on their feet yelling their heads off. "Wait 'til next year!!"; "Wait 'til next year", over and over.

It was my turn to speak. It seemed like five minutes before the students quieted down. When I was finally able to make myself heard, I started with this comment:

"Thank you, Mr. Edwards. Students, what a great guy Mr. Edwards is. I don't know if you noticed Mr. Edwards immediately after the game last Friday. I did. I happened to look in the stands where he was seated. Guess what he was doing? He was throwing handfulls of confetti into the air! I thought to myself, what a guy. Throwing confetti. Here we just lost the most important game in years and Mr. Edwards is showing that he can still celebrate that he is a Carmel High *Padre*. What a great show of support by our principal!"

Continuing I said, "Mr. Edwards was waiting for me by the locker-room door as we went in. I went up to him and said, 'Mr. Edwards I appreciated you showing your good sportsmanship and support for the team by throwing that confetti in the air after we lost.'

"Mr. Edwards' reply?

Hicks, that was not confetti. That was your contract!"

Mr. Edwards' enthusiastic speech and my light humored opening comment seemed to settle the students down. They were eager to hear what I would say about the loss and the end of "the streak".

I spoke briefly, maybe ten minutes. I spoke positively about our team. We never quit. Never for a moment did we think we were going to lose the game. Even when the final gun went off we knew that we did not lose, the clock just ran out on us.

I told our students how proud of them I was. I told them that they were the best student body in the State of California. We had more games to play. I knew they would be fully behind us, supporting the *Padres* as they had done all year. It was then that I ended with a statement which would become a motto for CHS *Padres* for quite a few years. I had not planned this statement. It just came out.

I said, "Students, never forget that you represent Carmel High School. What you, we, represent is 'A Spirit which is exclusively ours'. "

For some reason that just caught on. I know that for a number of years CHS students and faculty alike often referred to that *Spirit* in their writings and discussions.

Coach Buzz Ralner the resident poet put the quote to verse for publication in the school newspaper. Tom Poulos a very tough guard for the *Padres* refered to the motto in an email I got from him in 2006. He rememberd using the motto in a pep rally when he as CHS Student Body Vice-President introduced some guests from bitter-rival Pacific Grove High School. To quote Tom, "To keep a lid on things I distinctly remember saying to our students as I was about to introduce the PG people, 'I want you to show our guests from Pacific Grove the respect and spirit which is exclusively ours.' The CHS crowd went nuts although things did stay relatively under control."

When the assembly ended I walked out of the gym with Mr. Edwards. He took my arm and directed me toward his car.

"Hadley I want to take you to lunch. We have more to talk about."

"Oh, oh." I thought. *"Maybe he really did shred my contract."*

Mr. Edwards drove to *The Hearthstone* a nice upper-scale restaurant. My wife and I had walked by it several times and wished we could afford to eat there just once. Mr. Edwards made a comment that this discussion was one he didn't want the experts in the "Rinky-Dink" over hearing. Needless to say, I was more than curious.

After we had ordered, Mr. Edwards startled me with, "Hadley, if you ever tell anyone what I am going to say, I will call you a liar! The one point loss, the end of 'the streak', were the best things that have ever happened to Carmel High School in a long, long time! The football program had created a monster. Some of the glow has been taken off the other sports.

'My biggest concern was that academics have taken a back-seat to football.

Do you know how many football players over the past several years have talked teachers into elevating their grade just so they can be eligible for next weeks game? Quite a few. Even some teachers got caught up in the 'keep the streak alive' mentality. I have attended administrative meetings around Northern California where principals from other high schools have queried me about 'the streak'. Has it affected our student body attitude toward academic excellence? Hadley, it has. It is a very subtle thing. It was getting more and more noticable after each win. The loss to King City was just what we needed. You played them tough right up to the end. You could have won the game several times. It was just not in the cards. All streaks have to come to an end. You could have lost by a large margin. That would have left a bad taste in all our mouths. To lose such a close game was not a disgrace. You, Lawitzke, and the team can be proud of your performance.

Hadley, I like your philosophy. Some of the teachers and some of our students have told me how you emphasize academics to the kids. You seem to exude a sense of 'do your very best' not just on the football field but in the classroom as well. You have your priorities in order. Keep it up."

I was flattered. I told Mr. Edwards I appreciated his comments and that it wasn't really my contract he shredded after the one-point loss.

We had a great practice that afternoon. Coach Lawitzke and I discussed the practice schedule during our prep period just before practice. We knew that many coaches after a big loss like we had would work their teams to near-exhaustion, punish them for losing. We didn't.

We conducted a typical Monday practice. We sent the kids out in shorts, tee-shirts and helmets. We briefly went through our offensive and defensive schemes for San Lorenzo Valley our next opponent.

We ended the practice with a number of fun games the kids loved. It was always linemen v.s. backs and ends. The favorite which got the most laughs was the relay race we all ran in grade school. The two groups had to race to a stand-up dummy (we used a baseball bat in grade school) and put their heads face down on the dummy and run in a circle around the dummy ten times. Then after they got dizzy they had to sprint back to their group and the next in line would sprint to the dummy. Actually there was no winner or loser; they just had fun.

The King City loss was a thing of the past. I know that in the back of their minds was Mr. Edwards challenge to the King City principal, "Wait 'till next year."

The King City game the next year, 1962, was played on our field. It was a game which went down in the annals of Carmel High football as perhaps the greatest game ever played by a Padre football team.

STEVEN PHILLIP HICKS
April 14, 1961

One year and five months after Joan and I were blessed with our son Mike, Steve unobtrusively joined our family. I had just been appointed CHS Head Varsity Football Coach; then all of a sudden Steve came into the picture. One day he was just there.

Steve was a true wake-up call for me, a most welcome addition to the family as he kept my mind somewhat off of the pressure of "the streak". Steve caused me to seriously consider my responsibility as a father. My three children were much more important than the pressure I inherited from Coach Mosolf.

Steve was great. Susie had a real live doll to play with. Mike was kind of bent out of shape at first. This new kid couldn't even play catch with him. That would come much later.

THE FORT ORD *WARRIORS*
A Big Assist to The *Padres*

One of the first things I did when our season was over was to get in my car and drive the ten miles to Fort Ord.

Art the Gardner made it clear to me one day that the CHS Football Team was in dire need of a qualified trainer. Art was the Carmel High School's grounds keeper; "Art the Gardner" for short. Art liked to hang around the football practices and give the coaches advice when he deemed it necessary.

One day shortly before the crucial last game of the season against rival Pacific Grove High School Coach Lawitzke and I were finishing our practice plan for the day. One of our players came hurrying into our locker room. "Better come quick. Markowitz twisted his knee coming down the steps. Art the Gardner is gonna ruin him!!"

Lawitzke and I both got to the field as quickly as we could. What we saw as we got closer to the field was Jim Markowitz flat on his back. Art the Gardner had Markowitz's leg stretched out straight and was twisting it round-and-round in a circle.

Dick Lawitzke yelled at Art the Gardner, "Stop twisting his leg, you idiot!" Art was not dumb enough to ignore Lawitzke's booming voice. "I'm just trying to help. I used to be a trainer," was all Art the Gardner said as he sheepishly walked away.

Besides having to worry about Art the Gardner wanting to help, we coaches spent too much time taping ankles. All of our running backs and ends had their ankles wrapped if not taped every practice and game. The others who had weak ankles or sprained ankles had their ankles taped every practice as well. We owed it to our players to have someone who was qualified to attend to the injuries which are a part of football.

I knew just where to go. Sgt. Pat Gallegos who was our trainer when I was with The National Military Champion Fort Ord *Warriors* could hopefully help. I knew where to find Sgt. Gallegos without a lot of military red tape. I headed directly to the Fort Ord Physical Fitness and Recretional Complex, the Gymnasium for short.

Sgt. Gallegos was a professional boxing trainer. He worked with a number of well known professional boxers in his "other life" as he said, his civilian life. Sgt. Gallegos was in touch with all the military personnel at Fort Ord who had any prior athletic training experience.

While I was with the Fort Ord *Warrior* football team, Sgt. Gallegos had several experienced trainers working with him. One of them, Private Bobby Brown, was the head trainer for the Houston *Oilers* professional football team for many years after his discharge from the Army. I wasn't expecting Sgt. Gallegos to get me another Bobby Brown. That would be too much to expect. What I got was much better. I got Sgt. Gallegos himself!

Sgt. Gallegos was at every practice the CHS *Padre* football team had for the next three years. He was on the sidelines for every home game. He loved working with our kids. He once told me he enjoyed working at Carmel High more than any other training job he ever had. The CHS kids were special to him. He called them "his" kids.

Sgt. Gallegos' presence was a huge confidence boost for all of us. I had several parents tell me how much they appreciated "Pat" as he was soon called. They knew their sons were in good hands if an injury occured; plus, Pat prevented injuries.

At one of Sgt. Gallegos' first practices I gave him the shock of his life. Pat Olmstead our starting end had been born with a severely malformed clavical (collarbone). It protruded out of his upper chest some two to three inches. It was an ugly looking deformity which did not hamper Olmstead's football participation at all. It did not hurt him nor bother him in the least. The coaches and players were used to seeing it when Pat would shower and dress. Sgt. Gallegos had never seen it.

This particular day when Olmstead came in from practice I had him take his practice jersey and shoulder pads off. I rushed into our training room dragging Olmstead with me. "Sgt. Gallegos! Look at this! Olmstead took a blow to his chest. Do you think we should get him to a doctor?"

I thought Sgt. Gallegos would faint on the spot. His jaw dropped. He let out an expletiv and grabbed Olmstead to put him on the training table for a closer look. Before it went much farther Sgt. Gallegos heard the laughter from the players who had gathered around to watch the fun. Sgt. Gallegos was a good sport. He liked a practical joke as much as I did. As he inspected Pat Olmstead's clavical he was heard to mutter that he had never seen anything like that in all his life.

Carmel High School football was lucky to have Fort Ord close by. Several soldiers who were coaches or college players in civilian life were recruited to assist our program. We had the benefit of additional coaches off and on until they were transferred elsewhere. We usually had them for only a few months at a time. They aided us however in numerous ways.

One of them was a young man by the name of Leon Criner. Leon played college football somewhere in the South. He was a lineman and was a big help to Coach Lawitzke. Leon was with us for a full season. He was an outstanding coach. I would have hired him in a second had that been possible.

Fort Ord was indeed good to us as was The Army Language School which was also situated on the Monterey Peninsula. During my six years at CHS we got welcome assistance from Sgt Pat Gallegos, Leon Criner and several other adult coaches. In addition we were most fortunate to have a number of very fine student-athletes come to CHS via military families located in beautiful Carmel.

By hasty mental calculation I come up with 19 military "brats" who were starters for the *Padres* during my six year tenure at Carmel High. One of them, Bill Stowers whom I have already mentioned was a starting end for the University of California his senior year; Bill had tryouts with the Denver *Broncos* and the Green Bay *Packers*.

Mrs. Romayne Hill
"The Mother Hen"

Had I been consulted as to the qualities needed for high school cheerleaders and songleaders I probably would have described the Arizona State University groups. At least I would have described the ASU cheerleaders. What a bevy of eye-catching lovelies! They made the "Shimmy" the most anticipated sideline routine at the football games. Those girls each put on quite a show.

As the ASU Pep Band loudly began to play "The Shimmy" each girl began to do her thing. It seemed that each young ASU coed in the line probably 10 or so tried to out-do the other. The football crowd on the ASU side loved it! The clapping and shouts of approval rivaled the most steamed up crowd at any Pentecostal revival gathering one could imagine. At Arizona State University all eyes were focused on individual young ladies. Not so at Carmel High School! To be sure the CHS girls were every bit as lovely as the ASU girls, but all eyes in the CHS gym were focused on the group not the individual. I found my self in awe as I witnessed my first CHS Pep Rally. The noise was thunderous even before the rally started. As the students and faculty filed into the gymnasium the four cheerleaders were enthusiasticlly clapping and walking back and forth each one in front of a section of bleachers. Their clapping in time with Mr. John Farr's pep band was eagerly joined by the students as they took their places. The clapping and chants of "CHS", "CHS", "CHS" continued until the Student Body Vice President took the microphone and asked for quiet.

Immediately after the Vice President led in the pledge of allegiance to the flag of the United States of America the pep band struck up.

Right on cue the four CHS songleaders ran into the center of the gym, one from each corner. They met in the middle and began a well orchestrated dance routine accompanied by the crowd's clapping.

From that point on the 45 minute pep rally just flowed. It was sheer clock work from a time of brief pertinent announcements by an administrator, to several lively dance numbers by both the cheerleaders and songleaders to an inspirational message from *Padre* football co-captain Doyle Clayton, followed by more music and cheering and brought to a climax by a talk from Head Coach George Mosolf. There was more cheering and clapping before the Student Body Vice President dismissed the students.

One of the CHS songleaders, Renee Tomasini was in my fourth period Speech Class. I complimented her on the pep rally, how well organized it was. Renee gave all the credit to Mrs. Romayne Hill. Mrs. Hill was the faculty sponsor of the cheerleaders and songleaders. Renee told me how much time and effort Mrs. Hill put into each Pep Rally.

The agenda for a pep rally began with Mrs. Hill consulting with Head Football Coach George Mosolf. How much time did he need for his talk? Did he want one of his players or Assistant Coach Craig to talk? Mrs. Hill next talked to either Principal Warren Edwards or Vice Principal Dorothy Wright. How much time did they want, if any?

She then scripted each band number and dance routine for the cheerleaders and songleaders. Then she consulted with Mr. Farr CHS Band Director. After school practices insured they were ready to go.

Talking with Renee further about Mrs. Hill solidified my respect for the leadership Mrs. Hill provided. Renee affectionately called her their "mother hen". Mrs. Hill insisted that "her" girls always conducted themselves as young ladies should; modest in dress, polite in speech, respect for their elders, and commitment to their roles as student leaders.

Renee said the girls had individual conferences with Mrs. Hill once a month all school year. These conferences served as one-on-one time for Mrs. Hill to further bond with her girls. The girls' Grade Point Averages (GPA) were checked to make sure their grades were not suffering. Mrs. Hill was known to suspend a girl for a period of time if her grades had slipped.

The eight girls who made up the cheerleader and songleader squads were chosen by a student body vote. To be in the running for one of the eight positions all girls trying out had to meet Mrs. Hill's criteria, the top two criteria being a faculty evaluation and a 3.0 or better GPA.

The cheerleaders and songleaders deemed it an honor and a privilege to be chosen. They were held in high esteem by both students and faculty, as was Mrs. Hill. She ran a tight ship. The girls loved her.

At the first Faculty Meeting just before school began Mrs. Hill sought me out and introduced herself. It seemed that my addition to the faculty somewhat eased her teaching load. I was to take several of the non-college Prep. English classes which Mrs. Hill previously taught. She was given three classes in her real love, English Literature. She still had a full load with her cheerleader-songleader sponsorship.

As we talked Mrs. Hill explained that my taking several non-college prep English classes off her plate allowed her spend more time with English Lit. She did keep one non-college Prep. English class as per her request. She dearly loved those kids who often needed special attention and love.

I was encouraged when Mrs. Hill told me she would be available for any help I may need. This was my initial voyage in the area of working with special needs kids. I expressed some reluctance to her about not being officially certified to work with them. I wasn't sure I was qualified. Mrs. Hill responded with a question: "Hadley, do you love kids?"

I believe that was perhaps the first time I was ever confronted with that teaching necessity. I paused, stumbled around a bit before answering in the affirmative.

"Hadley if you love kids you will be great with these special kids." Mrs. Hill was a great encourager.

When I found that my classroom would be just a room away from Mrs. Hill's and that she was available to assist me as needed, I was greatly relieved. There were several times over the next few years when I sought her advice.

At times Mrs. Hill gave me advice without me seeking it.

A month or so after school started Mrs. Hill came into my room and bluntly told me my classroom was too *sterile,* too *blah.* Students learn better in classrooms with color, with *pizzazz.*

Mrs Hill began a two week project to get me to spice up my room a bit. The first thing I did, and this was my own idea, was rearrange my seating arrangement. I moved my desk to the back of the room rather than in front like traditional classrooms. It was much easier for me to watch each student's reactions to speeches from the rear. Students were more cautious of misconduct not knowing if I was watching them or not.

At the end of two weeks even students were commenting on the changes. They did not like me seated behind them and that was good.

They did like some of the pictures I hung up. I found some old pictures of Carmel High School athletes that Coach Mosolf had stored away in the dark recesses of the gymnasium. I even found some pictures of my family that Joan said I could take to my room. I got some "Oh...how cute," comments from a few girls. My kids were cute. Romayne Hill was certainly a mother-hen to me.

Teaching Speech Classes
How Could it Get Any Better?

I knew going in that teaching Speech would be an enjoyable experience. Just how enjoyable I had no idea.

I found out at our first Faculty Meeting that teachers were not required to turn in lesson plans. I heard nothing good about making lesson plans in my Education Classes at Arizona State University. I had a pronounced fear of lesson plans when I reported for my Student Teaching assignment at Phoenix Union High School. Mr. Olsen my Student Teacher supervisor at Phoenix Union, informed me the first day that I would not have to turn in lesson plans. He said he didn't have time to read them. That was fine with me.

In my mind "no lesson plans" left me with room for using my imagination, my ingenuity and my spontaneity.

My discussion with Renee Tomasini early in my first semester at CHS was a case in point. As Renee and I discussed the value of a teacher like Mrs. Hill being involved in students' lives other students joined in. After raising their hands, of course. We had soon discussed several other CHS Faculty who fit the criteria of caring teachers. Mrs. Marquita Bray, Senior English Literature teacher was high on the list as was Mr. Ray Gere, Senior English instructor.

Soon the class was over. I had gone the entire time discussing basically "what makes a great teacher." In retrospect I did not feel that class time was wasted. We had good give-and-take. Some students who were a bit reluctant to speak in class offered their opinions. I had not allowed negative comments about teachers who were not in the good graces of some students. The entire time was definitely up-beat for the class as well as for me.

I had not deliberately planned for the entire class time to be used. It was spontaneous. From that time on after taking roll I often opened all my classes with, "Anybody have anything you want to talk about?"

Sometimes every hand went up, sometimes only one or two, sometimes none. Whatever, some spontaneous warm-up time was always available. I was smart enough to realize that sometimes I was tested. How far could they take me before I realized we were just wasting time? There were times when I flunked the test; I let it go on way too long.

Usually though, I felt the time was well spent. If nothing else I was able to better understand what was going on in some of the students' heads. They spoke from their hearts on many subjects of interest to students of the 1960's, abortion, what about psychedelic drugs?, what about that nut up in Berkley at the University of California, the one using crude and vulgar speech in his protests over the worsening situation in Vietnam. How far should we take the First Amendment regarding free speech?

The students' concerns were unending.

My Speech classes were just that: *speech* classes. The students were encouraged to speak. Most had no trouble doing so. Some had to be encouraged. I think I am safe in saying they all found they enjoyed the classes.

A Shy Student

Sandy Aldinger was one of my shy students. She had to be encouraged in unique ways to fulfill her speech assignments. At times Sandy would get up to speak and before uttering a word she would break out in uncontrolled giggles, and I had to make her sit down to get control of herself. Sandy has fond memories of those times. She recently wrote, "I could never be serious. I remember once you made me give my speech with my back to the class because I couldn't keep from laughing due to the boys in the back of the class. If my memory serves me correctly you once made the class turn around while I gave a two minute impromptu. One September morning you even had a birthday cake waiting for me." Sandy ended her brief note with: "Little did I know how this class would play such an important role in my life as I now speak to groups all the time."

THE DOUGH BOY

Then there was the CHS Dough Boy as in Pillsbury Dough Boy. I forget the kid's name. I will never forget his speech on *"Making Pizza"*. He was a short chubby little freshman. His speech effort earned him the nick name The Dough Boy, at least in that Speech Class. As per my instructions on requirements for *Speeches to Inform* he came prepared. He had a round pizza baking pan, all the pizza ingredients in four bowls; the pre-mixed pizza dough in one, the sauce in another, the toppings in the third, and the condiments in the fourth.

Then came the *coup de grace!* His chef's white apron and tall white chef's hat.

The moment he put on the apron and hat we all mentally *saw* The Pillsbury Dough Boy. The entire class chuckled. He was an exact replica.

The Dough Boy knew he had us in the palm of his hand. He was poised. He began his speech telling us how pizza became so popular in America. He named a few of the popular franchises which have gained nation wide popularity.

He explained that he would make a pizza for us. He demonstrated the important steps to get the pizza just right. When he had the pizza prepared for the oven he would take it to the Home Economic Room where he had a preheated oven ready to go. We would all share in his delicious pizza.

Thinking what came next almost brings me to tears as I recall the events. The Dough Boy oiled the pizza pan. He was so poised. He next sprinkled flour on the table explaining that the flour would keep the dough from sticking to the table. He dumped the pre-mixed pizza dough onto the floured table. Exactly and with poise he explained how the pizza dough was made. The ingredients had to be measured very carefully to get the right texture of dough. He explained that this step was perhaps the key step in baking the *perfect* pizza.

He then made a show of rolling his sleeves up a notch or two. With the utmost of care he placed the large ball of dough in the exact center of the well oiled pizza pan.

He explained that he would next precisely spread the dough to the correct thickness over the entire pizza pan. He did this with ease. The dough spread very nicely and evenly. Until. Until he took his hands off of it! The moment he removed his hands...."*pffthpftht!*".... the entire batch of dough slithered back to its original ball in he center of the pan. The Dough Boy kept his poise. He again spread the ball of dough over the pan. Again...,"*pffthpfth!*" ...back to the center of the pan to it's original ball form

His poise was beginning to waiver. He went through the routine a few more times. The rest of the class including the teacher were getting a bit uneasy. We were feeling empathy for The Dough Boy. On the last *"pffthpftht"* the poor kid completely lost it. He broke down in uncontrollable sobs of frustration. He just sobbed and sobbed. I had one of the girls lead him to the nurse. I was told that the nurse had to have his mother come get him.

We never did get to eat pizza that day.

An Accidental Shooting

The Student Body President Tom Hudson was in my Speech Class one semester. The ingenuity Tom displayed in one speech in particular has left those of us who witnessed the "accidental shooting" smiling and shaking our heads in awe as we recall it. It was an event in class we would never forget.

Tom come to me asking if he could give a *Speech to Inform* on "gun safety". I had to check with Mr. Edwards our principal to see if a student could legally bring a gun to school for a Speech Class assignment. Mr. Edwards saw no reason why he couldn't, especially when I told him the student was Tom Hudson one of our more gifted students.

Tom came to class that day carrying a long leather gun case. When it was Tom's turn to give his *Speech to Inform* he came to the front of the class. He explained he did not need the speakers rostrum as the gun he was going to tell us about was too big; we could not see what he was going to show us from behind the rostrum.

I was rather surprised when Tom pulled out a rifle. I had expected a hand gun not a rifle. But Tom had gotten the principal's ok so I didn't worry about it. Tom stood back from the students in the front desks and went into the speech. He explained he was going to discuss gun safety with us. So far so good. What I did not know and Tom hadn't told me was that he had asked his classmate Jeff Wright to assist him; another surprise. Jeff was seated in the front desk directly in front of Tom.

Jeff was wearing a white polo shirt. Underneath his white shirt Jeff had pinned a baggy containing a mixture of coffee grounds and ketchup.

When Tom got to the part about being careful because some guns have hair triggers', he pulled the trigger. A loud *"bang"* rang out from the blank Tom had loaded in the rifle. Jeff immediately slapped his chest which splattered the coffee-ketchup concoction up his neck and all over his face. His acting was most professional, most realistic.

The reaction of the audience was interesting as the seriously wounded Jeff Wright crumpled to the floor. Two girls seated on either side of Jeff screemed and put their heads down on their desks, semi-conscious. Ray Rhodes seated in the back of the room made a mad dash for the front door. He was on his way to the office to call for an ambulance. George Pollock rushed to the side of the victim and intended to try to stop the blood.

The rest of the class sat in their seats stunned. Some were to say later that they knew all along that the shooting was a fake.

My first reaction which was unplanned was to tell the class to quietly exit the room. I followed Ray Rhodes out the door. I yelled to him as he was running down the walk way, "Ray, it was a joke. Come back." Ray stopped when he heard me. He had taken a step or two to return when he saw the expressions on the faces of his classmates as they came out of class. They didn't think it was a joke. Ray Rhodes immediately turned around and continued his run to the office to call for an ambulance.

Somehow I regained order in my class. The ambulance was never called. The fake was realized when George Pollock got to the victim and smelled coffee and ketchup. The students who had gotten outside silently returned still a bit stunned.

So You Wanna Be a Legend. So Did I.

I explained that it had all been Tom Hudson's way to emphasize gun safety. The class found that the discussion we had over the accidental shooting was practical and educational. They all agreed that it was a worthwhile learning experience. How would they react in an emergency? We had good discussion off and on for several days.

The mother of one of the girls who had nearly fainted did not at all think the lesson was worthwhile. She called Mr. Edwards to complain about the teacher who would allow students to be as traumatized as her daughter had been.

Mr. Edwards consoled her by saying that it would never happen again. Mr. Edwards told me privately that he thought the lesson was great. He wished he could have been in the room to see it. He said to let him know the next time something like that was going to occur in my Speech Class. I promised I would.

Murder in the Classroom

We never had anything like the accidental shooting in my class again. There was however a *"murder in Hicks' classroom"* which is interesting and fun to recall, not at all controversal like the shooting.

We had a few students give brief speeches on "Legalese," the specialized speech of the Law Profession. This prompted numerous discussions which whet appetites for more information on criminal law. This got the students all worked up to try conducting a criminal trial in class.

Here is what we did:

(1) I secretly got Steve Shore to agree to be the murderer. Steve was an outgoing kid. He was a ham. He had lost an eye as a child and wore a black eye-patch.

(2) I explained to the class that in two weeks time there would be a crime committed in the classroom. During the two weeks time the class would give daily *Extemporaneous* speeches during which various students would drop subtle clues as to what the crime was to be, who the victim was to be, and who the guilty one would be.

(3) I chose four students to be my "plants", the ones who would drop the clues. Again I did this secretly. They did not know who the other plants were. Nor did the rest of the class know that there were plants among them.

(4) One of the plants was Mike Escandon**.** Mike agreed to be a plant and also to be the victim. His *Extemporaneous* speeches were faked in that I let him know well ahead of time what the title of his speech was to be. He could then quickly plan how to get clues inserted which would point to a dislike for *"Patch"*. The astute students would pick Steve Shore out as Mike's reference to *"Patch"*.

(5) The victim Steve Shore was one of the plants as well. He was given time to develop his *Extemporaneous* speech. A few comments about Mexican bullies were dropped. Mike Escandon was Mexican and proud of it. He freely talked about his Mexican heritage.

(6) On the day the crime was to be discovered Mike came to class early. I helped Mike get a butcher knife lodged under his right arm pit. It stuck out in back as though Mike had been stabbed. We poured ketchup around the knife and down the back of an old shirt he had worn. Mike then got inside the full-length coat closet in the back

of the room. After Mike was standing inside I closed the door and poured a glob of ketchup on the floor underneath the closet door.

The students came into class as usual and I took roll as usual. Mike Escandon was absent. One of the students said they had seen him earlier in the day but that he looked in a hurry. About that time one of the students noticed the glob of blood beneath the closet door. Upon opening the door Mike the murder victim fell on the classroom floor, stabbed to death. The students immediately knew the crime had been committed.

The first thing I did after getting Mike cleaned up was to appoint various necessary rolls for the trial to be held the following week. I appointed two students as detectives, one student to be the defense lawyer, one to be the prosecuting lawyer, one to be the Judge, and the rest of the class was to be the jury. They would determine the guilt or innocence of whomever the detectives arrested for the crime.

Each student had to present his or her designated roll in the form of a *Speech to Convince*. They had a few days plus the weekend to prepare.

The detectives immediately arrested Steve Shore as the murderer.

I had been talking about the preparations for this speech assignment for several weeks in the Faculty Lounge. A few of the teachers were interested in the outcome.

When the Trial Date finally arrived three faculty members were on hand as the courtroom crowd; Romayne Hill, Buzz Rainer and Peter Lyon were given seats in the back of the courtroom. I had given the three crowd members prior permission to disrupt the proceedings at any time.

The detectives were the first to testify as to why Shore was their suspect. At the end of their convincing testimony Romayne Hill in the crowd started to get emotional. "Steve is such a sweet boy. He couldn't do a thing like that." The Judge had to rap for order. Order was restored.

The trial was over in two class periods. Evidence both for and against acquittal was presented. The jury took two minutes to come up with their verdict. Steve Shore was found guilty. The detectives had to drag Steve Shore, the convicted murderer, out of the courtroom kicking and screaming. Shore was heard up and down the halls of CHS yelling, *"I am innocent. I was framed!"*

The Judge in his mercy put Steve Shore on probation for the rest of the semester.

THE CHS FACULTY
Unique.

To say our faculty was unique is to put it mildly. I cannot find an adjective that adequately describes the faculty of CHS during the early 1960's. Each was a quality educator in his-her own right. Each expressed a genuine love for the kids who walked the halls of CHS. Each made a newcomer like me feel welcome and at home. The sincerity of the Carmel High Faculty was hard to match. Most of us genuinely looked forward to the times during the day when we could go into The Faculty Room. I know I did.

Principal Warren Edwards was an outstanding administrator. He made the difficult decisions quickly after looking at all the factors involved. Sometimes his decisions were not popular. Other times they were just what the faculty ordered. He

So You Wanna Be a Legend. So Did I.

did not always go with the flow; sometimes he went up-stream. It could never be said that Warren Edwards was wishy-washy as some administrators are.

Warren Edwards was also just one of the boys. Warren and his wife Pat were famous for their frequent faculty get togethers. Good food, wine and great fun were the order of the evening. Though wine was served in abundance none of the faculty ever got snockered. The get togethers were always lots of fun, loud laughter and bantering back and forth. Nothing ever got out of hand except for the times we played *"Mr. Hinkle Funnyduster."* Things got somewhat out of hand then.

Mr. Hinkle Funnyduster was a fun and rowdy card game. I have tried for years to get Warren Edwards to send me the rules for the game without any luck.

As best as I can remember each card suit had a name. The "Funnyduster" family I believe were the spades. "Mr. Hinkle Funnyduster" was the ace of spades. My mind goes blank after that. I do remember that when one got a complete hand of one family he was to subtly lay his hand down without anyone noticing. When someone noticed the hand either being laid down or already down, the observant person yelled, threw his cards in the air and dove for the hand being laid down. The object was to get as many loose cards as possible.

If the person who yelled was quick, he-she would find themselves on the bottom of the pile, others trying to grab as many loose cards as possible were not too particular whom they plowed into. It was indeed a rough and tumble game. Rules and common sense forbid pregnant women to play.

Warren Edwards loved a good practical joke. He was in on many that occured at the expense of a fellow CHS faculty member. Here's an example: Chuck Moody was a terrific U.S.History teacher. He was also the lousiest, sloppiest housekeeper on the faculty! His room was always in shambles. His desk was a permanent mess. A report card for one of his students was once not delivered to the student until the student's tenth class reunion. Moody admitted that he found the report card under some papers on his desk while looking for something else.

Buzz Rainer and I also loved a good practical joke. Buzz somehow got hold of a four-hen portable chicken coop. Buzz and I were talking after football practice one day about Moody's messy desk. Suddenly Buzz's eyes lit up! He had a brilliant idea. "Let's get the chicken coop and put it in the middle of Moody's desk. That will send a message." Moody would be fit to be tied when he came into his class the next morning. Great idea, but how do we get into Moody's room at night? Edwards! Warren had master keys to all the rooms. We drove to Warren's house and presented our plan. Warren Edwards loved a good practical joke. He not only had a master key, he went with us.

Students who came into Moody's room first period the next morning swear that Chuck Moody never noticed the chicken coop until one of the hens cackled. Moody had a short fuse. He exploded when he saw the chicken coop and chicken manure spread around his messy desk. His explosion was short lived. By mid-morning break Chuck Moody was in the Faculty Lounge laughing and threatening revenge on any and all who were involved. Chuck Moody was a good sport.

Ray Stumbo another fine History Teacher was not a good sport. Stumbo was called "Mr. Machine" by his students because of the number of history movies he showed to his classes. Stumbo was known to give the students the assignment for a particular movie and then leave the room. He would come back about the time the film was to be over. It just so happened that one time some of Ray's students who loved a good practical joke got to him. The students got hold of a movie due to be shown in Stumbo's class. They expertly spliced a *Looney-Tunes* cartoon in the middle of the history movie.

Ray Stumbo started the movie, then left for coffee in the Faculty Lounge. Upon returning Ray heard laughter coming from his room. He expected to see the students playing hanky-panky and running around his room. To his surprise Ray Stumbo found all the class seated at their desks having good laughs at the cartoon. Stumbo threatened to flunk the whole class unless they told him who the guilty party was.

Ray Stumbo was a good easy going guy. He just could not take a joke. The one thing that really got his goat was to belittle his beloved University of Oregon *Ducks*. Ray was an alumnus of the University of Oregon. He had no sense of humor when it came to his *Ducks*. As fate would have it the Arizona State University *Sun Devils*, my alma mater had a game with the University of Oregon in Eugene, Oregon a few weeks into the football season.

Ray and I had some serious give and take before the game. As game day drew closer and closer Ray Stumbo got quieter and quieter. No joking around, no give and take. Of course, the quieter Ray got the more I needled him. A few days before the game Ray Stumbo would not go near the Faculty Lounge for fear he would run into me. I tried to talk him into a friendly bet; a Pepsi or something small. He would have nothing to do with a bet even though the *Ducks* were playing at home and favored by a touchdown. I got to watch the game on TV and loved every minute of it. I knew Ray Stumbo was watching. He did not enjoy the game; *The Sun Devils* won in an exciting and well played game.

The phone rang almost immediately after the game ended. It was Buzz Rainer. He had another good idea. We'd get a master key from principal Warren Edwards. We'd get into Stumbo's room late Sunday night and get his room ready for some serious rubbing it in first thing in the morning. My daughter Susie had a ragged, frazzled old chicken doll which she seldom played with. I borrowed it Sunday night. Buzz, Warren, and I went into Stumbo's room. We had some maroon and gold crepe paper which was Arizona State's colors. We also had some University of Oregon green and gold.

We hung the chicken from the ceiling against the chalkboard in the front of the room. The chicken was a mess to begin with but when we plucked it a bit more in Stumbo's room it was *really* a mess! We hung some pieces of green and gold crepe paper around the chicken's neck. There was no question that the bird hanging with green and gold colors was a chicken and not a duck.

On the chalkboard below the hanging chicken we wrote in large print the score of the game: *SUN DEVILS 21-OREGON DUCKS 13*

The message came through loud and clear: "the ducks were chickens."

We had also written under the green and gold crepe paper: "Oregon colors: green and **yellow**."

We strung the *Sun Devil* maroon and gold colors around Ray's desk.

Ray Stumbo did not at all think the joke was funny. He stormed into the Faculty Room shortly after he got to school Monday morning. He was fuming. I don't know why but he stood at the door of the lounge and looked right at me!

"Damn you, Hicks! If I knew for sure it was you who called The Oregon *Ducks* yellow chickens I'd get you outside and pound you to pieces."

Of course, I put on my best *"who, me?"* face. I acted the innocent party. I insisted that I was not guilty. Stumbo said, "If you didn't do it who did? I'll go outside with whoever did it!"

It was then that Buzz Rainer brought the house down. He said in all seriousnes, "Ray I think it was Marquita." The Faculty who were in the Lounge cracked up laughing. Marquita Bray was the last person one would ever expect to pull such a childish trick as what Stumbo just experienced. Marquita was gentile and refined. Marquita was sophisticated and nobel, a true lady. She would never belittle a fellow faculty member.

At that point Ray Stumbo turned around and stormed out just as he had stormed in. I was half way afraid that Ray Stumbo would be back with more threats. I hoped he would get over it quickly. He evidentally did. Nothing more was ever said about what came to be known among the few insiders as the "saga of the yellow chicken."

John Rylander was one of those teachers students remember. Rylander seemed to be the perfect teacher for those students who were just experiencing the beginning of the radical 1960's. One of his former students commented that Rylander encouraged independent thinking and interpretation.

Former student Tom Poulos wrote about the mini-political movements which were a part of the growing political awareness of the baby boomers. Poulos made this statement about John Rylander, "Many of our teachers, Rylander leading the way, were proud of us and while not openly encouraging such radical activity, we still knew most were supportive. Rylander was perfect for the times."

Lloyd Miller was CHS Business teacher for years. Lloyd was a member of the Camel High Faculty since it's inception in 1941. Lloyd was appointed Athletic Director shortly after I was hired in 1959. Lloyd told me that he was made Athletic Director to try to keep my lavish spending habits under control.

I learned quickly that if I thought our football program needed four dozen new footballs for the upcoming year I orded eight dozen. Lloyd always cut our athletic orders in half. He was a notorious tightwad.

As much as we coaches griped about not getting what we thought we needed to run a first class program we always had first class equipment. We always had as much as needed, not always as much as we wanted. Lloyd kept the books balanced.

The one place Lloyd was not a tightwad was when he went on football scouting trips with us. He made sure he took us to good restaurants.

We would give him a job to take care of while we were scouting. For most games Lloyd tabulated the substitution tendencies of the team we were scouting. For example, on long yardage situations did the team put in a certain kid and try to throw long to him?

Lloyd did a great job at that. There were times during a game when I could hear Lloyd yelling from the stands, "Watch out!! They just put in number 81. They are going long!" Most of the time he was right.

I considered Lloyd a good friend as well as my boss. He gave me a piece of advice one day that stayed with me my entire teaching career. I was walking to class with a senior girl whom I knew pretty well. She was upset this particular day and was telling me all about it as we walked along side by side. As we neared the classroom she was going to I put my arm around her and gave her a side-by-side hug of encouragement. Lloyd was walking some distance behind and saw my hug.

Later that same day Lloyd came to me and gave me some common sense advice. He said that male teachers should always be careful about outward signs of affection with female students. Lloyd cautioned me that someone seeing my hug could misconstrue my intentions. The female student involved could also misconstrue my intentions. Lloyd told me too that some people not just females find touching to be distasteful. They are averse to touch in many cases. Good advice from a good friend.

I Left My Toothbrush in *Paladin's* Bathroom

Coach Buzz Rainer is Richard Boone's cousin. I had the honor of meeting the great actor who played the part of *Paladin* in the popular TV series *Have Gun Will Travel*. Buzz and I were in Los Angeles for a football clinic. Buzz had told me that he would ask his cousin if we could spend a night with him and his wife. The arrangements were made. Buzz and I got to the Boone's beautiful Beverly Hills home at dinner time just as Boone was getting home from being on location for an episode of *Paladin's* adventures. What a class act Richard Boone and his wife were!

Buzz and I were treated to a simple roast beef dinner in the Boone's kitchen, cooked and served by Mrs. Boone. The four of us sat at a fairly small kitchen table, nothing at all extravagant. The conversation was easy flowing. Boone did not even take the time to get undressed from his day before the cameras. He still had on his dusty jeans, dusty black Western shirt and a dirty, well used bandana around his neck. His pock marked face was all smiles as he related some stories about his life as a well known Hollywood celebrity.

He entertained us with a story about his cameo appearance in John Wayne's movie production of *The Alamo*. You may remember that Richard Boone appeared on camera for maybe one minute. He portrayed the famous Texas military commander *Sam Houston*. Boone said one or two sentences. Then he rode off never to appear in the film again. As Richard Boone told the story he was laughing the whole time. What happened, he said, was that John Wayne called him and asked Boone if he would do him a favor. Boone, of course, said he would. He and John Wayne were close friends. Wayne said, "Richard, my movie budget won't allow me to pay you your asking movie rate; if you appear in a very brief cameo, I will make it worth your while."

So the deal was made and Richard Boone did his friend a favor. Richard Boone then said to Buzz and I, "Let me show you the 'small gift' John gave me."

Richard Boone led us to his garage. He turned on the light and before us was a beautiful, shiny new Mercedes Benz. I had never seen such a beautiful vehicle before. The entire back seat including the floor was lined with lamb's wool. Boone laughed when he showed us the next feature John Wayne had added.

"See these wires?" He pointed to wires running across the length of the back window. "These are defrosters! Defrosters for Los Angeles, California!" Boone seemed incredulous.

My only thought which I did not ask, *If this is a small gift and if John Wayne could not afford Richard Boone's movie rate, just what is his movie rate?*

The four of us went into the Boone's large and comfortable library. A bar running the length of one side of the library was made from an imported hull of some ancient Viking sailing vessel complete with a bearded Viking warrior's wooden head at the fore of the structure. Very impressive.

As Mrs. Boone served us coffee Richard Boone talked about many things. He was not trying to impress us as he talked about his acting roles. The one he said he enjoyed the most was when he played *Abraham Lincoln* on TV's *Playhouse 90*.

Boone pointed to the top shelf of his library which ran completely around the good sized room. He said, "See all those books lining the top shelf? Every one of those books is about Abe Lincoln. I read each one before going on camera."

Richard Boone told us one humorous story before we went to bed. A year or so before, Boone was traveling in Northern California. When he went through Carmel he stopped to gas up. The high school student who waited on the famous Richard Boone looked at him aghast! The kid said, "I know who you are! You're Coach Rainer's cousin!" Boone got a huge kick out of that. He said it was humbling.

Buzz and I left for the football clinic after a breakfast with Mrs. Boone. Richard left for location much earlier. We thanked Mrs. Boone for their hospitality. Buzz gave Mrs. Boone a hug. I remembered Lloyd Miller's advice and merely shook her hand.

That night after the Football Clinic session as Buzz and I were going to bed in the motel we had for the night, I discovered my tooth brush missing. I knew right where it was. And for all I know it is still there.

Three Football Clinics
Food For Thought

I have never been to a bad football clinic. There is always much to be learned. Some of the greatest football coaches in America are often on hand to share their wisdom; never their secrets but their wisdom.

There were three *Coach of The Year Clinics* I attended with my fellow CHS coaches which impacted my coaching philosophy greatly. Two of the COY Clinics were held in San Francisco at The Marriott Hotel. The first one I attended was held at the end of the 1959 season. "*Cactus*" Jack Curtis then coach at Stanford University at Palo Alto, California was one of the speakers.

Coach Curtis took over a lackluster Stanford *Indian* football program. He had much success at the University of Texas at El Paso (UTEP) before coming to Stanford. Curtis came to Stanford with great expectations. His first year was seemingly a turn-around year for Stanford. Coach Curtis with his wide open passing offense surprised many by going 3 - 7; certainly not a great year but much better than expected.

CHS Coach Buzz Rainer and I were eating lunch in The Marriott Hotel's crowded restaurant. Coach Curtis had been the last speaker before lunch. The coaches gave him a standing ovation for an excellent speech; he was extremely motivational. Coach Curtis spoke positively about the future of Stanford University football. We had no doubts that with *Cactus* Jack at the helm, the Stanford *Indians* would once again be a force to be reckoned with in the tough Pac-6 West Coast Conference.

As we ate there was suddenly a hush over the noisy crowd. Coach Curtis had just walked into the restaurant. He was alone and looking for a table. I thought it was humorous as all those at the table nearest to Coach Curtis did everyting but turn the table over trying to make room for him. One of the coaches ran to a nearby waitress asking her to get a chair and menu for the late arriving Coach.

Coach Rainer and I were only a few tables away. When I saw all the adulation heaped on Coach Curtis I remember thinking, "Here is a coach who has it made. He has significance. Someday maybe I will."

Fast forward one year to 1961. Same Coach of the Year Football Clinic. Same hotel and restaurant. It was an almost identical scenario. The same Coach Curtis walked in to the crowded restaurant. This time he walked in as a 0 - 10 losing coach. Few even acknowledged his presence. Poor guy. I felt so sorry for him. How fickle people can be.

It got me to thinking, "If significance cannot be found in people and one's reputation, where can it be found?"

I ran that question through my mind for many years. I felt certain that as a good coach I would find significance. I would not lose it as Coach Curtis seemingly did. I would not make the same mistakes he did. Even with a few losses every now and then I still had my family to support me. I knew I was a good coach. My confidence in myself would see me through any tough times I may have.

Several years later I attended another Coach of the Year Football Clinic. This time the clinic was held at Saint Mary's College in Moraga, California. One of the key speakers was a former All America football player from the University of California. Don Moomaw was a big name in California and especially Northern California. He had a brief stint in Canadian Professional Football. He was a much sought after motivational speaker. What he had to say that day certainly motivated me.

What, if anything Moomaw said about coaching football I do not remember. What I do remember is that he mentioned a newly formed organization which some years later would play a major role in my search for significance. Moomaw was one of the original founders of *The Fellowship of Christian Athletes* (FCA). He said that FCA was beginning to take root in many high schools in the San Francisco Bay area.

I picked up some brochures Moomaw was handing out; I made a mental note to check FCA and the feasibility of starting a CHS *Huddle* group as they were called.

Moomaw spent most of his time discussing the values of coaches having a *relationship* with God. Moomaw said something about Jesus Christ being important in that relationship. I admit I did not understand all Moomaw said but he was the first speaker at an athletic function to mention God that I could remember. God seemed to be important to Don Moomaw. I felt God had always been important to me as well. My early involvement with Catholics in my grade school years (B) emphasized God. I knew just enough about God to understand that He was Someone to fear. From what the nuns and priests told us I knew that God could *zap* me any moment.

Don Moomaw went on to be the Senior Pastor at Bel Aire Presbyterian Church in Los Angeles, President Ronald Reagan's church for many years.

That particular Coach of The Year Football Clinic did not just impact me in the religious realm. An assistant coach from the University of Southern California *Trojans* shared a thought with us which I would have cause to remember many times in my coaching career. He told us to always be aware of the fact that, "After a big loss it was always the kids, the players, who rebounded faster than did the coaching staff."

How well I remember that after CHS's one point loss to King City it took our coaches, me included, most of the week to come back, to be able to generate enthusiasm at practices. The players were ready to move on when Monday's practice rolled around, especially after principal Warren Edwards' fine pep-talk earlier in the day. Edwards' letter of congratulations to the King City principal with his "wait 'til next year" challange was mentally filed away. The players' attitude seemed to be, "Next year will come soon enough. In the meantime we have some games to play. Let's get with it."

"Next Year" is Here.

The 1962 season would prove to be a banner year for the *Padres* in several respects. Senior quarterback Danny Holman elevated himself head and shoulders above any other quarterback in Northern California, in my mind at least. College coaches who scouted Danny his senior year had only one knock against him. He was too skinny. He had to put on much more weight to play big-time college football. They all agreed that he had a Division I arm; his arm right then was as strong as many major college passers.

As a CHS senior Danny was 6' even and weighed anywhere between 150 pounds to 160 pounds. His frame had lots of room for more meat which would come with a strict weight program. We did not have weight facilities at CHS. We did have extra thigh pads. We taped an extra thigh pad on Danny's hamstring area. His legs didn't look so skinny with two thigh pads on each leg.

There was no doubt in my mind that when Danny graduated from CHS that he could go to any of the California Division I universities and play for them. He would be a starter for most of them by his sophomore year. I felt he was that good. I knew that in a good college program Danny would overcome his one major handicap; his high school coach- me.

Unbeknown to Danny or anyone else at the time Danny's skills made me do some serious soul searching. I was a run oriented coach. I copied everything that the great Vince Lombardi and his Green Bay *Packers* football team did. I felt that our *Padre* offense could run the Green Bay *sweep* with the best of them. Most teams we played could not stop it consistantly even when they knew it was coming.

My knowledge of the passing game was limited. I just did not understand the philosophy of the complicated 2, 3, or 4 receiver routes that good football teams employed. The CHS passing game consisted of a couple quick slants over the middle and maybe four or five routes by the two ends and a back. I should have read up on the passing game; I should have talked to good college passing coaches like maybe *Cactus* Jack Curtis at Stanford. But I didn't. I was contented to be only as good as we were. We could win with a few Holman passes and a potent ground-eating running game. I could only coach what I knew.

With a great passing quarterback like Danny Holman we got away with the minimum passing game. Our running game opened up certain passing routes; Danny would take advantage of that.

Danny's passing statistics were not all that impressive because we did not pass as much as we could have had I known how. Danny did not throw a whole bunch of passes. When he did pass I do not remember ever having one intercepted! I feel very sure that had I known how best to utilize the great skills that Danny possessed we would have beaten King City; the missed extra point would not have mattered. "The streak" could have lasted at least until Danny graduated if only I had not been such a one-dimensional coach!

Danny Holman

THE HISTORIC GAME THAT DEFINED DANNY HOLMAN
The Spirit Which Is Exclusively Ours
CHS-19 King City-13
1962

"The Big Game" was finally here. The whole community was buzzing and had been for weeks. The talk in Jim Kelsey's *Rinky-Dink* was more and more animated as the days went by. Rumors were running rampant: I watched practice yesterday; Holman did not look sharp; I heard he has a sore arm; I heard Hicks is going to run Holman on some 'keepers', Kelsey guaranteed a CHS win; Coffee on the house all next week.

The King City *Mustangs* came to Carmel's Bardarson Field riding high. They were again undefeated. Their great Jim Mankins had gone on to bigger and better things at the University of Oklahoma. Mankins had been ably replaced by speedy sophomore tailback Jovious Macklin. Their vaunted single-wing offense was again very potent. They didn't seem to have skipped a beat with the loss of Mankins.

Coach Buzz Rainer's JV Team beat the KC JV's earlier that morning by 14 points. Junior quarterback Al Nishimura led the way with two touchdown passes to Rich De Lorenzo. The tradition at CHS was that if the JV's won their morning game the Varsity would win their game that afternoon. We hoped the tradition would continue.

The stands were pretty well filled by the time the JV game got underway at 10:00 a.m. At 1:00 p.m. kick-off time for the main event both the CHS stands and the KC stands were full. Both roped-off endzones and sideline areas were swarming with anxious fans of both teams.

I was nervous. Coach Lawitzke was nervous. I knew King City Coach Ernie Piper was nervous. Both teams were nervous. My guess however that the most nervous guy in the whole place was principal Warren Edwards. He's the one who popped off about "Wait 'til next year." His comment had been well publicized.

Finally.Kickoff! The football game that went down in CHS History was underway.

The *Mustangs* scored first mid-way through the 1st quarter. The extra point was good. King City 7-CHS 0.

CHS came right back on the running of Dennis Hermanson and the Holman to Tegtmeier passing combo. Hermanson got the *Padres* on the board with a five yard blast up the middle. The extra point attempt failed. King City 7-CHS 6

With a minute to go in the first half King City scored again. Their extra point was no good. The half time score: King City 13-CHS 6.

Our locker room was calm. Sgt. Gallegos, our trainer, quietly went around and checked for injuries. Coach Lawitzke talked one on one with a few of his defensive people. I got Danny Holman with the backs and ends and we briefly discussed what would and wouldn't go offensively the second half.

Now the next part of our half-time preparation I cannot adequately explain. It was just pure chance the way it all came together. Coach Lawitzke made some major changes in his defensive scheme mainly involving defensive personnel John Whittaker, Jim Kelley and David Harris.

Coach Lawitzke felt certain these changes would throw the King City run offense off-stride; they would more likely attempt to pass more. Lawitzke cautioned our tough defensive backs and linebackers to be more aware of the pass in the second half.

Coach Lawitzke's changes did the trick. King City did not score again.

I made only one slight change in our offensive scheme. We had been working on a new pass pattern; "roll right or left, halfback deep." This pass pattern was designed to take advantage of a defense which played a "two deep" defense. Their defensive backs were aligned so that their two deep backs were lined up on the offense's two ends. They did not utilize a safety in the deep middle of the field. All the King City pass defenders played "man for man"; they covered whomever their assigned offensive player was wherever he would go.

What happened next has been bandied around for years. It has been greatly exaggerated, enlarged way out of proportion. Some said the reason we won was because Holman gave a five minute pep talk at half time. Danny did not give a five minute pep talk. Holman was not the "rah-rah" type.

What he said was pure *Danny Holman*. His exact words as he walked by me, "We'll get 'em, Coach." No arrogance, not at all cocky, just plain confidence. Just four words spoken softly to me; "We'll get 'em Coach."

Get them we did, in what some called the greatest half of football ever played by a *Padre* team.

King City came out for the second half fired-up as we knew they would be. Their offense was completely shut down by Coach Lawitzke's defense. Time after time Kelley, Harris and Whittaker led a defensive surge the King City single wing offense could not contain. King City had numerous third down efforts stuffed. Their offense could not solve Lawitzke's chess moves with the CHS defense.

Danny Holman meanwhile was standing with his arms folded quietly waiting for the offense's turn. He knew what had to be done. The offense was a thing of beauty to watch that second half. Hermanson, JT Thomas, Gary Mumford and Terry Bishop each picked up valuable yards rushing against the strong King City defense. Danny Holman stymied the *Mustang* secondary with his pinpoint passing.

On the last play of the third quarter Al Tegtmeier made what I considered the greatest catch I've ever seen by a high school receiver. We were on the KC 30 yard line. Third down and short yardage to go for a first down. King City was expecting another run as we had run it down their throats up to that point. Conventional wisdom said we should run it. Get the first down and drive it on in for a score. However Danny Holman was not conventional. As I was about to send in a running play, Danny was waving me off. I knew better than to argue with Danny Holman. Danny faked a run and sent Al Tegtmeier straight down and deep across the middle of the field.

The KC defense hesitated for a moment as Hermanson was hitting up the middle of the defense on his fake. Danny carried out his fake, dropped back behind good protection from his offensive line and threw a bullet to Tegtmeier cutting deep behind the KC defensive secondary. The pass was higher than usual as some KC

So You Wanna Be a Legend. So Did I.

defenders drifted back after going for the fake. Danny had to throw it high to clear the confused KC defenders. While in full stride Al Tegtmeier leaped for the ball. Holman had thrown a bullet; he had to to get it to Tegtmeier before the KC defense could react. Just as Al left the ground one of the KC defenders recovered enough to get a shoulder into Tegtmeier's stretched out legs. Al Tegtmeier was high in the air when his legs were knocked out from under him. Al caught the ball in both hands just as the ball hit him in the face mask. Al was parallel to the ground as he fell still gripping the ball in his face mask. The impact of Al hitting the ground should have knocked the ball out of his hands. It didn't because the ball was stuck in Al's face mask.

Al later told us he kept his hands on the ball to make sure that if it should be jarred loose from the face mask he would still be holding it. Holman had thrown the ball with such velocity and accuracy that it hit Al's face mask between the plastic protective bar and the rim of the helmet. The ball was wedged in firmly.

Al lay stretched out on the ground holding the ball in his face mask until the referee signaled "Touchdown!". Then comically Al struggled to get the ball loose from his face mask to give it to the referee.

We again missed the extra point attempt. As we lined up for the kick-off the score board seemed to be yelling at us: **King City: 13-CHS: 12.** We had one full quarter to erase the one point deficit. Would this be *de-ja vu* all over again?

Coach Lawitzke and I knew that the game rested in the hands of the defense. If King City could be kept out of our end-zone there was no way they could keep Danny Holman and the offense from scoring, no way except keep the ball away from Danny.

King City's strategy was just that, play "ball-control". They felt that if they could keep the ball for most of the fourth quarter and not give Holman many chances the clock would run out on us. Their single-wing offense was perfect for that strategy; slow developing power football, four to five yards a crack.

It almost worked. King City had the ball much of the fourth quarter. They gave up the ball for the last time with 1:30 left to play.

The King City punter pinned the *Padres* deep in our territory. We had first down and ten to go; we were on our own ten yard line.

Lawitzke and I knew, the whole team knew, the King City team knew, all the fans knew. Danny Holman was going to pass. Danny Holman had to pass. Before going back on the field after KC punted, Danny and I discussed strategy. We had not called "roll right or left halfback deep" the entire game. Now was the time. King City used the same 2-deep defense all game. We had not thrown a pass to one of our backs all game so that would be a suprise to the defense, we hoped.

Danny got the team in the huddle. His poise and calm manner rubbed off on his teammates. Somehow they knew that they could do it. JT Thomas was at right halfback and JT was the best receiver of our running backs. Danny called: "Roll right; halfback deep, JT up the middle for a long one."

When the ball was snapped it seemed to me like both teams reacted in slow-motion. I could see the play develop just as though I was drawing it on the chalk board. Our two ends ran straight down the field for ten yards then broke quickly to the sidelines. The two King City defenders assigned to cover our two ends followed them as we wanted them to. The King City right defensive corner-back was assigned to cover our wing-back, Dennis Hermanson. He did as he was supposed to. Hermanson took him to the sidelines.

The two King City deep defensive half-backs were taken away from the middle of the field by our two streaking ends; the defensive right corner-back covering Hermanson to the sidelines left the middle of the field wide open.

As JT sped out of the backfield and turned upfield he saw nothing but open turf. Holman's pass hit him in full stride. Wide open! JT took three or four steps with the ball when he discovered that the Head Linesman had blown his whistle.

We were off sides! The play was called back. The penalty moved us back to our five yard line. No place for mistakes now. Forty seconds left in the game.

CHS had two time-outs left. I called one at that time. Danny and I discussed our options: we could run "roll right half back deep" immediately; or as Danny noted we had time to run several safe out patterns and watch to see if KC made any defensive adjustments after almost getting burned by JT up the middle. If no adjustments were made we'd come back with "roll right halfback deep".

We ran two short passes that got us to our 15 yard line; first and ten.

Here it comes. 14 seconds left in the game.

Danny huddles the team and calls "roll right halfback deep". Still no defensive adjustments by King City. The middle of the field should be wide open. It was. Just as the first time we ran the play JT was wide open. This time no whistle! JT caught the perfectly thrown pass in full stride and galloped 80 yards untouched for the touchdown! JT was accompanied the entire 80 yards by all his hysterical sideline teammates. When he crossed the goal line JT was engulfed by the Carmel mob behind the roped off endzone. The place was a mad house.

Luckily Coach Lawitzke kept his cool. He quickly got to our players and some of the mob and got them off the field before we got a penalty. Lawitzke can be most persuasive at times like that.

Order was finally restored. Both teams got lined up for the extra-point. The heart broken King City *Mustangs* made only a feeble attempt to block the extra point kick by Terry Bishop. It was right down the middle. The scoreboard now screamed at us: **CHS: 19-King City: 13.** The hands on the clock showed 8 seconds to play.

Again our crowd went into hysteria. "We won! We won! Game's over. We won!"

Again Lawitzke went into action. Showing surprising agility for a two-hundred thirty pounder he wildly jumped up and down waving his arms at the crowd: **"SIT DOWN!! SIT DOWN!! THE GAME IS NOT OVER!! WE STILL HAVE EIGHT SECONDS TO PLAY!"**

It didn't do a lot of good. The crowd ignored him.

The players and the head coach couldn't very well ignore the big guy when he got in our faces and shouted: **"LISTEN! QUIET DOWN. WE STILL HAVE EIGHT SECONDS. WE HAVE SOME DEFENSE TO PLAY. DEFENSE COME HERE!"**

So You Wanna Be a Legend. So Did I.

After our kick-off King City threw one long incomplete pass, called a time out, threw one more long incomplete pass. Game over!

The Spirit which Is Exclusively Ours still reigned supreme!

Jim Kelsey at the *Rinky-Dink* had "coffee on the house" all the next week. Coach Dick Lawitzke was even able to talk Kelsey out of a hamburger. It is great to be a winner. The *Padres* continued to roll undefeated through the remaining four games of the season. We climaxed the undefeated Mission Trails Athletic League season with a convincing 33-20 win over bitter cross-Peninsula rival Pacific Grove.

From that day on "roll right half back deep" was not called that again. The play was called *"King City Special"* to commerate the two times it was run against King City in the Championship game.

The "King City Special" won a few more games for CHS the next two years. Two more good CHS quarterbacks, Al Nishimura and Jay Lang, used the play when in tight spots.

No matter how many quarterbacks would take snaps for Carmel High in the future none would ever compare to Danny Holman. No touchdown pass would ever be quite as dramatic as the strike Danny Holman threw to JT Thomas with 14 seconds left in the critical King City game of 1962.

DANNY HOLMAN'S RESUME

Upon graduating from Carmel High School in 1963 Danny Holman attended Monterey Peninsula College from 1963-1965. The following quote is from *The Carmel Pine Cone/CV Outlook* newspaper, "Holman and O.J. Simpson were the only two Northern Californians named as Junior College All-American by J.C.Gridwire in 1965.

Holman attended San Jose State from 1965-1967. He threw for a school record 19 completions in a narrow loss to Stanford in his first game for San Jose State.

Holman's landmark college performance was on Oct. 15,1966 when he led SJS to a 24-0 upset win over Cal. It marked the first football win over the Bears from the then Pac-8 Conference.

Holman was recognized as Sports Illustrated's *Player of the Week* and was described by the magazine as having 'a buggy whip for an arm.'

After his senior season, Danny was selected to play in the East-West Shrine Game. Danny did not take a snap in that game; he was behind UCLA's Gary Beban, that year's Heisman Trophy winner who played the whole game."

Holman is a member of both Monterey Peninsula College's *Football Hall of Fame* and San Jose State's *Football Hall of Fame*

Danny Holman was the Pittsburg *Steelers'* 8th round draft choice in the 1967 NFL Draft. He was with the *Steelers* one year."

Danny Holman died in his Carmel home in July 1996 from a heart attack. Danny died alone. He was 51 years old.

JT Thomas was killed in Vietnam shortly after graduating from Carmel High School. He died a true American hero.

Many Changes
The *Padres* Roll on.

My first four years at Carmel High seemed to fly by, each year faster than the one before. I established myself as a "dyed in the wool" true Carmel High *Padre*. I was proud to be *Coach Hicks*. I found a home.

My wife Joan, our three children, Susie, Mike and Steve and I were recognized all over Carmel. We took our nightly walks down quaint Ocean Avenue. Sometimes we walked all the way down to Carmel Beach; our kids loved running through the surf.

We felt the need to belong to a church as most of our friends did. We joined Carmel Presbyterian Church mainly because Dick Lawitzke and his family attended.

Dick quit as my assistant football coach shortly after the 1963 school year. He was appointed as head Carmel High Basketball Coach. Basketball was always Dick's true love. There were no hard feelings when he resigned as assistant football coach. I told him he would be missed. He was an outstanding line coach. Much of our past success was attributed to Dick.

Replacing Dick was Jason Harbert who proved to be an outstanding line coach in his own right. Jason and his wife, Lois, and his kids, Kathi, Mike, Lori, and John soon became our dear friends. Jason and family belonged to Carmel Presbyterian also.

Shortly after joining Carmel Presbyterian I was asked to start a high school youth group. I knew most of the students who went to Carmel Presbyterian so it was easy to get a group of them to come on Sunday evenings for brief meetings. We were a close knit social group. There were lots of Sunday evening parties at the church and we had one memorable long weekend ski trip that Jason helped me chaperone.

Another Seed Planted

While on that ski trip to Yosemite National Park Jason and I had a few late night discussions on football and life in general. Jason talked a lot about his growing family. Lois was due to give birth to child number five in the near future. Jason grew up in a religious family. His dad was a preacher so Jason knew a lot about God. He talked freely to me about God on that ski trip. I did not feel uncomfortable as he talked; I did not say much. I did mention hearing All America Don Moomaw talk about Fellowship of Christian Athletes. Jason said it would be fun to start a FCA group at CHS. We never did though.

I thought often about that trip and our late night conversations. It just seemed to be natural for us to talk about religion; the fact that we were coaches did not seem to make much difference. I guessed since Don Moomaw, a great football player, and Jason Harbert, a high school football coach, could talk about God it must be ok for me as well.

The Importance of Loyalty

A new football tradition was started in 1963-*The Jamboree*. It was a great way to open the season. The Carmel JV team played one half of a game against the Pacific

So You Wanna Be a Legend. So Did I.

Grove JV team. Whatever the score was at the end of their half was where the two varsity teams started. Any scores by either varsity team were added to that team's JV team score. At the end of the varsity's full half whichever team had the highest cumulative score was the winner of The Jamboree. This format was an excellent way to build total team loyalty. The varsity depended on the JVs to get a good lead. The JVs rooted for the varsity to maintain the lead.

In the first Jamboree the CHS *Padrecitos* ran up a great lead for the CHS Varsity; CHS JV 33- Pacific Grove JV 7. At that point the two varsity teams came on the field and took up where the two JV teams left off. It so happened that our Varsity took over the ball on our own 40 yard line. Quarterback Al Nishimura hurried his team on to the field before I even got to the bench. I looked up just as Nish hit a streaking Rich de Lorenzon for a long gain. I knew at that point that CHS still had some offensive weapons even though the MTAL coaches had picked us to finish third behind King City and Hollister. At the time it looked like a pretty safe bet; we lost a bunch of good football players the past year including Danny Holman.

Our Varsity won our half of the Jamboree 13-7. Our over all score was CHS 46, Pacific Grove 14. Our JVs looked very strong. Our fans were disappointed in our Varsity. We only scored 13 points. Our fans were spoiled. What they did not understand was that the Pacific Grove Varsity had a strong team. They had a punishing fullback named Bob Roberts who gave us fits in the last League game of the season.

The Carmel grapevine got back to me on Monday that Coach Jason Harbert was not the coach that Dick Lawitzke had been. Some detractors were saying that our offensive and defensive lines were missing Lawitzke's motivation and skillful coaching I realized I needed to address that with our players and address it soon. Jason and I had discussed the issue during our prep period. I met with the players before we began practice. We decided that it was best if Jason was absent from the meeting. We wanted the players to speak freely.

It was my habit of gathering the team in a semi-circle in the endzone before each Monday's practice. We usually discussed the pros and cons of the game the previous week. This Monday we had much more important things to discuss than our glorified scrimmage Friday night.

I was well worked up by the time all the players were present. When I walked down the steps to the field they knew I was ticked; most of them knew why.

The team knew me well enough to know that I am not a yeller or a screamer but I can get intense at times. This was one of those times. I did not pull any punches with them. I told them that I was disappointed in some of the adult fans we had, possibly some of their parents. I was disappointed because they didn't have to guts to come to me with their complaints about Coach Harbert.

I asked them if they, the team, had any gripes about Coach Harbert or anything about his coaching techniques. I knew most of our kids well enough to expect some complaints if they had any. They were honest kids and would speak up. None of them had any negative comments about Coach Harbert. They all voiced favorable opinions. One even said he appreciated Coach Harbert pushing him in practices. The kid said he knew he would tend to loaf if Coach didn't "kick his butt" at times.

I ended our meeting by emphasizing loyalty. All good teams must have total team loyalty. We are a "family". If any one has anything against one of his teammates or one of the coaches, go to that one and air the complaint. If reconciliation is not achieved, then come to the coaches to talk it out. But never talk about one another behind their backs. Keep all disagreements in the family.

We agreed. We would stick together no matter what.

Coach Harbert returned to practice shortly after we had completed our warm up and stretching routine. When he took his linemen to the designated area for their drill sessions I noticed they all surrounded Jason and spoke to him briefly. A few got in some pats on the back and handshakes before they got down to business.

Our immediate business at hand was to get prepared for our opening non-league game with a tough San Francisco Bay Area team, Liberty High School.

We played well, as well as we could have expected for our first game. We lost 20-14. We were in the game all the way. We came away from the game disappointed to open with a loss but realistic enough to understand the positive aspects of the game.

We did score twice on a couple of well executed offensive drives. Defensively, we made Liberty earn their 20 points. They were big, strong and experienced; that told the whole story.

Their coaches were very complimentary after the game. They said that for them the game had been much like a mid-season game. They had to do some things that they hoped they wouldn't have to do so early in the season. They thanked us for giving them a tough test, for making them extend themselves.

On the long bus trip home, Coach Harbert told me he had been disloyal to me during the game. He pointed out one particular play in the third quarter. The score was tied at the time 14-14. CHS had the ball 2nd and 8 and we were on our own 10 yard line. I sent in a sweep right. Quarterback Al Nishimura handed the ball off to Ralph Juarez our best running back. Ralph ran parallel to the line of scrimmage several yards as sweeps require. Ralph could not find room to turn up-field for positive yardage. The Liberty defense made Ralph continue to run parallel to the line of scrimmage. He was tackled for a 2 yard loss. third and 10. Not a smart play called by me.

Coach Harbert told me that as soon as he saw the sweep being run he said loudly, "No! Dumb play! Hicks, why did you call a sweep down there?" Jason said that within earshot of some of the players. He immediately knew he should not have criticized me in front of the kids.

On the ride home Jason told me he was sorry and that he should not have said what he did. I told him I forgave him. I did agree with him that it was a bad call on my part. I appreciated Coach Harbert being up-front with me. Many of the players seated nearby heard our conversation and realized that loyalty was being played out between the coaches. A good lesson for them to observe. Disloyalty was never much of a problem between players, coaches, parents and townspeople while I was at CHS. That problem would hit me in the face much farther down the line. Big time!

The "Harbert" controversy was put to rest as we got into our season. Everybody likes a winner. The *Padres* rolled through the MTAL season undefeated again. Al Nishimura proved an adequate replacement for Danny Holman.

Coach Jason Harbert put together another strong defense.

So You Wanna Be a Legend. So Did I.

Newcomers to the CHS Varsity were strong defensive replacements for Kelley, Harris, and Whittaker; John Tracy, Dave Preve, Tom Poulous, and 220 pound Grant Pollock more than filled the void. All four were juniors. After the opening loss to tough Liberty High School the *Padres* encountered only three closely contested games.

Hollister High caught us on a down week after the Liberty battle. We jumped off to a 13-0 lead the first half, then hit a lack luster second half but we held on to win 13-6.

Al Nishimura, Ralph Juarez and Phil Zobel provided the only offensive spark we had all evening. I felt though that our new offensive strategies were beginning to jell even though we only had one good offensive half. During the previous summer I had read several good books on offensive football. I knew that Danny Holman could never be replaced and that the offense we had built around him would have to be radically changed. Those changes were slowly incorporated into our offensive scheme of things beginning with the Jamboree and the Liberty game. Most of the changes were taken from a book written by my friend Max Spillsbury, head coach at Northern Arizona College at Flagstaff, Arizona. The book was titled Slot T Football.

Football coaches are the greatest copy cats going. I learned early in my coaching career to be a discerning copier. What I copied had to fit into my philosophy of coaching. I tried to never make a change for change's sake. Some of the changes I made were much different from what I inherited from Coach Mosolf. I felt that I had earned my right to incorporate my ideas into our system. Very few even noticed nor cared about the changes being made, as long as we won.

The biggest change I made centered around our starting quarterback, Al Nishimura. The talk at *The Rinky Dink* all summer had been "who would replace Holman?" It soon became pretty obvious that Al "Nish the fish" Nishimura would be the guy. Al was a "Military brat" who had moved to Carmel two years previous with his military family. Al quickly established himself as one of the premier swimmers in Northern California, thus the nickname "Nish the fish". He would soon prove himself to be a good quarterback as well.

Coach Spilsbury in his book Slot T Football ran much of his successful college offense with a split end joined by a halfback who lined up in the slot between the split end and the offensive tackle. This alignment allowed for more offensive diversity.

THE SLOT-T FORMATION

```
E             T G (C) G T E
              B    QB

                 FB   HB
```

Spilsbury and other college coaches copied the "Lonesome End" concept which The United States Military Academy made popular during the late 1950's. The *Army* as their team was called, went to extremes with their split end. He was called the "Lonesome End" because he never came to the huddle. He stayed almost on the sideline and got his plays from hand signals from the quarterback. Most coaches did not split an end out that far.

Spilsbury's theory was that by taking an end, a kid maybe not too big but who could run and catch, by splitting him away from the rest of the offense you could be hidden out there. The defense would have to assign someone to cover him and thus weaken a section of the defense. That made sense to me. I felt we had the perfect kid to hide at split end. Richard de Lorenzo was not strong or big enough to play in close were he had to block a big defensive tackle. He had very good speed and was a great receiver. Someone from the defense had to go out there and cover him. In theory Rich was blocking someone from the defense on every play.

By our third game of the season our kids had pretty well gotten the hang of the split end offense. Quarterback Nishimura loved it. His passing options were increased. Rich de Lorenzo loved it. He caught short passes, quick slant-in passes, and medium across the middle passes. Our slotbacks loved it; reverses were possibilities, quick and long passes were options. There were lots of possibilities.

What de Lorenzo really loved were the sweeps to his side. By being split away from the defensive end and tackle he could be sneaky and block back down the line of scrimmage and catch the defensive end unaware. The defensive tackles and ends tended to forget that Rich was out there. A few times Rich forgot that he could not clip the man he was to block. He had to make sure that his head was in front of the man he was blocking. I was willing to risk a few clipping penalties to watch Ralph Juarez and Phil Zobel go for good yardage on the sweeps to the split end side.

We soon had the most potent offense in the League; we ran up 41 points against Gilroy, 25 against San Lorenzo, 19 against Live Oak, and 28 against Gonzales. King City and Pacific Grove two very tough teams held us to 20 and 14 points respectively. We won both those games in the only two close games we had since we lost to Liberty the first game of the season.

The King City game again was close and provided some excitement. We won 20-13. We played in King City; after our dramatic win the previous year King City was fired up for us. I'll let guard Tom Poulos give his first-hand recap of the game:

"Those KC players were totally intimidating. Big, rough looking guys. We got the kickoff and immediately Randy Mapstead was knocked out of the game. I think they hit him so hard it broke his face mask. My fault. I missed the block. I never understood why I was put back there. I was always afraid the ball might actually come to me and I would have to catch it and run. Our first play was some fancy screen you had cooked up. We totally blew it and lost yardage. So much for an early statement. We also lost Fluegge (fullback Marlin Fluegge) early. We were nervous and intimidated and getting picked off one by one. On a trap play where I pulled, their defensive left end hit me with an upper cut under my face mask, cut me badly, and I think broke my nose. Knocked my contact lens off and I blacked out in the huddle and had no clue what the next play was going to be. On that drive we went down to make the first touchdown without a functioning left guard. As we lined up for the kickoff, the guy next to me told me to get off the field and get fixed. Apparently I did not look so good. One of the song leaders, Barbara Bruce, gave me a mirror to fix my contact but looked at me like I was from Mars. At half time I saw why. My nice white uniform had blood all over it. Someone stuffed something up my nose to stop the bleeding and Harbert sent me back in. Some time in the second quarter it turned around. We found a weak spot in the middle and made big yards. I knew then we could do it by running that play right/left all night. They also never rushed their linebackers on pass plays so Nish had all day to throw. They should have blitzed…they probably would have nailed Nish at least a few times. On pass plays I actually had no one to block and would drift back to protect Nish's left flank. They basically gave us the passing game. They played tough but not smart. Nish was cool. I remember he changed a play at the line but it wasn't an audible. He simply said to forget the play he had called and to run this pass play…might have been the "KC special". He saw something was wide open. Not sure everyone believed him or got the message. All that counted was the receiver got the message and no one on the line got caught for being down field. This might have been the big pass play that resulted in a touchdown to Juarez near the end of the game. I'm really not sure. I also suspect we were much better at half time adjustments (good coaches) than other teams. You calmly questioned the linemen about weak links and what they were giving us and so you modified plays to take advantage. I think we actually made up some new blocking schemes at halftime. We owned KC the second half. They were tired and frustrated while we were playing like wounded bears. The defense you coaches cooked up shut them down. These guys ran a single wing (even in 1963 this was arcaic) and the goal was to stop Macklin which Pollock et al did well. Macklin was a really fast black player and I think they put white tape on his arms so even when he did not have the ball it still looked like he had the ball. I wasn't at all tired at the end of the game. We could have gone for another half. To beat those monsters in their own backyard was a real highlight."

When the season ended and CHS was the undisputed MTAL Champion, Coach Harbert and I were pleased with the season. Coach Harbert was no longer a question mark on our program. He proved many times during the season that he was a first-class line coach. On paper we would seem to be even tougher next year. We had a wealth of talent coming back. We could dominate the league in 1964.

The big question always is, "Who will be your quarterback?" From our many advisors down at the *Rinky Dink* that question was a no brainer. Jay Lang had proven to be a quality quarterback for the JVs. He was smart, he was a campus leader and he had a more than adequate arm. And what I really liked, Jay could run with the football.

The 1964 Padres
The Best Ever?

Somebody once said, "Statistics are for losers." Well, be that as it may, I truly wish I had appointed Art Black as our official statistician for the football season of 1964.

Art was a scholarly looking kid with thick black-rim glasses. He loved athletics and was equipment manager for several of our teams. He was a straight A student. Dan Yurkovich once made the statement about Art that "as he walks to class he is mentally calculating the square root of his steps." Art was a bright kid. Art was just the kid who could have provided the 1964 CHS *Padres* with the necessary figures to verify that they stood alone among the many fine CHS football teams.

I never before or since coached a more balanced team. We had it all. We had a great offense. We had a great defense. Our kicking game was near collegiate level. We had excellent over-all speed. We had a better than average bench, kids who could come in and replace a starter without losing team efficiency.

There wasn't a team in the MTAL who belonged on the same field with us. We averaged 24 points per game to our opponents 7. Our offense scored a season total of 211 points; our defense gave up a total of 63 points.

We had the best high school backfield I have ever witnessed. Ralph Juarez was an outstanding running back. Ralph was 5'9" tall and 175 poinds. Charlie Eyster, a "Military brat" who transfeered to CHS, was 5'11" tall, 185pounds and the fastest player on the team. Eyster never played football before the '64 season. John Tolan, a speedy and hard running fullback was 5'11" tall, 180 pounds. Any one of those three was capable of going the distance on any play; often they did. Sadly, I never saw individual statistics for them. Our leader and quarterback Jay Lang had an outstanding season as well. Again no statistics. I read recently that Jay threw 15 touchdown passes. I cannot verify that. I do know that he beautifully complimented the outstanding running attack we had.

Line Coach Jason Harbert had "a stable full of ponies" as he liked to say. Our center Grant Pollock was our largest lineman; he was 6'1" tall and weighed in the neighborhood of 220 pounds. Grant was tough and strong with good foot speed. To Grant's right and left were guards Dave Preve and Tom Poulos. Dave was 5'11" and 180 pounds and quick. Tom was a bit shorter at 5'10" and hit the scales at 170 pounds. He too was a quick, tough guard.

Our tackles did not look like typical tackles. Bill Stowers, probably our best lineman, was 6'1" and 180 pounds; Fred Gehring was a "squirt" at 5'10" and 175 pounds. But, man could he block! There was not an offensive team in the league that compared to ours. Nor was there a defensive team in the league to compare with us. How in the world then did we lose to King City AT HOME 2-6?

After winning the Jamboree rather easily we went up to The Bay Area to play strong Liberty High School in our opening game. The score was tied 6-6 going into the fourth quarter. Ralph Juarez opened the quarter with a beautiful 62 yard punt return for a touchdown. We won 13-6.

Our new Slot T offense got untracked the next week when we went to Gilroy and beat them 25-13. We felt we could have scored a few more in the second half but we played a number of reserves. Gilroy made the game look closer than it really was when they scored as the clock ran out to end the game.

Next on the slate: King City at CHS's Bardarson Field! As I think about that game I am glad we did not have Art Black keeping statistics. I get physically sick just thinking about it-2-6- impossible! Our offense ran up and down the field all day long. We probably had over two-hundred yards rushing; Juarez, Eyster, and Tolan ran at will against the King City defense, EXCEPT when we got near the King City 10 yard line.

Jay Lang completed passes whenever he wanted; EXCEPT when we got near the King City 10 yard line. Our offense must have been inside the King City 20 yard line five or six times. Each time my thinking was that we'd push it across for a touchdown. Time after time we had third and short yardage. Time after time we came up fourth and short yardage. Time after time we turned the ball over to King City on downs.

If only I had gone for a field goal just two of those times! Ralph Juarez was a decent field goal kicker. He was good from the 30 yard line fairly consistantly in practice. Two field goals and we win 8-6. But no. I was greedy. I wanted to go for the touchdown. I just knew our outstanding offense could pick up those fourth and short yards situations. But we didn't. The King City defense always found some way to stop us short of the first down. I don't know how many times King City took over the ball inside their 20 yard line. Our defense stopped them every time. Again statistics would show that the King City offense was completely shut-down. I wouldn't have been surprised if statistics showed King City had negative yards for the entire game.

I can't say too much about our tough and aggressive defensive unit, defensive ends Ron Bucher and Pete Conway were in the King City backfield all day. Big George Buck stuffed the KC single wing offense every time they ran it his way. Two-way performers Bill Stowers and Fred Gehring were simply outstanding. Our "midget" defensive backs Mikey Paul and Dennis Clark were all over the field, either knocking down passes or making vicious tackles on King City ball carriers on or behind the line of scrimmage. Linebacker Rod Sibley was like a wild man on a rampage up and down and behind the line of scrimmage. Ron Berry the best high school punter I have seen put the KC offense deep in their terrority several times with his 60 yard punts. I have often wondered what would have happened had we not gotten a safety for 2 points early in the game.

Defensively we completely dominated King City right from the opening kickoff. Our defense pushed them backward each offensive series they had. In the first quarter after Ron Berry boomed a punt that died on the King City five yard line, we swarmed the King City ball carrier behind his goal line for a safety, our early 2 points.

I believe a sense of over-confidence swept over us. I know it did with me.

Time after time King City punted to us from deep within their own territory. Surely Ralph Juarez would return a punt for good yardage; which he did several times. Surely he would break one for a touchdown. He didn't.

Again I got greedy. If I had called for our defense to try to block a punt instead of wanting the thrill of watching Juarez do his thing for a touchdown, who knows what might have happened?

If nothing else that humbling 2-6 defeat made our kids mad. They came out to practice on Monday determined to prove to our remaining foes just how good CHS really was. We still had San Lorenzo Valley, Live Oak, Gonzales, big Hollister, and cross-Peninsula rival Pacific Grove to play. And play them we did! When all was said and done a total of 38 points was scored against us by those five teams; they scored an average of eight points per game. Our offense was unstoppable. In those five games we scored 159 points for an average of 32 points per game. We won those last five games by an average score of 32-8

I would be surprised if any CHS *Padre* football team was as dominant as the 1964 *Padres,* EXCEPT for the King City game!

World-Wide Notoriety

There were 2 young men on that 1964 *Padre* football team who brought a large degree of notoriety to Carmel, California. I would be surprised if any other CHS football team could say they included youngsters who generated the world wide public awareness that Rusty Beardsley and Jim Amos generated.

The Beardsley Family

Rusty's brother, Mike Beardsley, was a member of the 1963 *Padre* football team. Both Rusty and Mike were tough, well disciplined football players. Both were offensive linemen. Both contributed greatly to the success of the Carmel High School football program. Rusty and Mike lived in a military family which consisted of a mom and dad and 20 siblings! Imagine dinner-time around that table! The Beardsley family was introduced to America via the 1969 released movie "Yours, Mine and Ours" which starred Lucille Ball, Henry Fonda and Van Johnson. The movie had its West Coast premiere in 1969 at the Del Monte Theatre on The Monterey Peninsula.

Later Mrs. Helen Beardsley wrote the book which detailed the marriage and the combined family's unique life. The book is titled: <u>Who Gets The Drumstick</u>?

I first heard about this special and unique family when Mike Beardsley gave a *Speech to Inform* in my Speech Class. The speech would have fit into the category of a *Speech to Entertain* just well. I remember that the students in class were totally absorbed in the details Mike revealed about living in a family which encompassed twenty two family members, and a strict Military family to boot! Tight discipline was a must.

Chief Warrant Officer-4 Beardsley, a thirty year Naval enlisted-officer brought ten children into the marriage with three boys and seven girls. Mike and Rusty were numbers one and two age-wise. Mrs Helen Beardsley had eight children to contribute to the family; she had four boys and four girls.

For you mathematicians reading this you have probably figured out that for the total children to add up to twenty, CWO-4 Beardsley and Helen must have had two children of their own; which was the case.

I often wondered what Roll Call in the mornings at the Beardsley family was like. This is what Rusty had to say, "No roll call. Everyone had assigned seating so it was easy to tell who was missing. Unless we were really sick we did not miss meals as there was nothing in between, so we were all ready to eat at the appointed time."

Rusty continued: "We did everything in teams. We helped cook breakfast, which was one of my jobs, made the lunches for school; fixed and prepared different aspects for each meal such as; making the salads, setting the table, clearing the table after the meal, washing the dishes and utensils.

"At breakfast Dad would read the day's various assignments which included making powdered milk for the day, cleaning bathrooms, vacuuming, washing the windows, and so on. We were well organized and disciplined."

That discipline carried over to the football field for Mike and Rusty.

CWO-4 Beardsley is "still alive and kicking at 93."

Mrs. Beardsley "passed away about 10 years ago."

So You Wanna Be a Legend. So Did I.

James F. Amos

General James F. Amos, USMC
31st Assistant Commandant of the Marine Corps

Nickname	Tamer
Allegiance	United States of America
Service/branch	United States Marine Corps
Years of service	1970-present
Rank	General
Commands held	Assistant Commandant of the Marine Corps Marine Corps Combat Development Command Deputy Commandant, Combat Development and Integration II Marine Expeditionary Force 3rd Marine Aircraft Wing Marine Aircraft Group 31 VMFA-312
Battles/wars	Iraq War
Awards	Distinguished Service Medal Defense Superior Service Medal Legion of Merit (2) Bronze Star

LT GEN James F. Amos, USMC

THE SECOND HIGHTST RANKING UNITED STATES MARINE
Semper Fidelis

I struggle to find the words to convey my feelings about Jim Amos. As a Carmel High School *Padre* football team member, Jim Amos was *semper fidelis;* always faithful.

Jim told me, referring to the CHS team he was on, "It was a team with a heart for winning; and it worked." Jim Amos had that heart for winning and he shared it with others. Jim was a leader who led by example. He was not at all boisterous. Jim was always available to do a job that needed being done. Coach Harbert knew that Jim Amos could step in and aid the team when needed. Even in high school Jim was *semper fidelis*.

Jim Amos was one of those kids who kept the team loose. On bus rides to away games Jim could be counted on to bring some laughter when the atmosphere was tense. He had a way about him that could bring his teammates to a full realization of what the game before us was really all about; the *Padre* spirit was in control. Everything was ok.

Lt. Gen. Jim Amos thank you for your faithfulness to America.

BARE-FOOT AND BRA-LESS
The Beginning of the End

As I reflect on my first four years (1960-1963) at Carmel High School, I see that the disturbing changes occured subtly. They were first noticable in the topics my Speech students seemed to hone in on. In the *Debate* units the students wanted to debate the school's policy on dress codes; should the students be allowed to bring Bibles to school? Should prayer be allowed in school?

Sometimes the debates got pretty heated. Students seemed fairly well divided on the issues. They soon became much more out-spoken than the students before them. I saw this as good. My Speech classes were much more lively and animated as the days and months crept by.

There were some changes I did not see as good. The "behind the bush smokers" were an annoyance to me. Their attitude flew in the face of every moral value that was instilled in me. I don't recall ever seeing a student hunkered down and smoking among the growth of bushes just off school grounds until sometime during my third year at CHS. That is not to say that students did not smoke until 1961. I know they did. They just weren't as flagrant.

The behind the bush smokers increased over the next few years. There were just a few initially. By 1964 there were maybe seven or eight smoking in the bushes before school.

As I drove by on my way to the parking lot they would often smile and wave, "Hey, Coach Hicks," knowing that they could get to me. And they did. What could I do about it? They were smoking off school property so they were legal.

As long as my football players were not smoking I did not get too charged up about it. They knew what was expected of CHS athletes. Each of the CHS coaches were in agreement that our athletes should hold themselves several steps above those who smoked and drank. We were not naive; we knew all our athletes were not lily-white. We also knew that they knew that if they were ever caught, the punishment could involve dismissal from the team or teams they participated with. We seldom had an occasion to kick a kid off for breaking training rules. Our athletes had respect for authority. At first.

That respect for authority began to crumble on December 3, 1964. It was on that date that a student at the University of California in Berkley made national headlines by defying the University authorities with his powerful verbal protest of most things the University of California stood for.

The student's name was Mario Savo and his student followers numbered in the thousands. After the media got through broadcasting Savo and his tirade worldwide his followers numbered in the millions. Savo christened his movement the FSM, Free Speech Movement. Campuses across America quickly followed suit, all under the guise of "free speech".

It wasn't long before the University of California unrest filtered its way throughout California. Carmel High School felt the effects almost immediately, subtly at first, then more and more classroom behavior problems, and more students feeling free to speak disrespectfully to teachers.

First it was free speech. Soon it became "free just about everything." The bumper-sticker that made its appearance on some students' cars said it all, "Defy Authority".

A nice, attractive girl in one of my Speech classes boldly walked into class one day barefoot and bra-less, noticeably bra-less.

Warren Edwards the Principal of Carmel High School told me that there was nothing that could be done about student dress. The Carmel School Board had given an edict to that effect.

I knew then that they had won.

GOING HOME

My wife Joan and I stayed up late several nights after our three children were put to bed; we discussed what to us seemed an important issue. Should we stay here in Carmel where things seemed to be getting less and less family-friendly? Did we want to raise our children in an environment where smoking marijuana might someday be morally acceptable? Where students were becoming more and more brazen in their moral behavior and in their lack of respect for authority?

I remember grieving at the thought of leaving Carmel High School. I could not imagine a more enjoyable place to teach and coach. The teachers I worked with were great. The students I lived with daily were "my kids." I loved them.

But I loved my wife and children more. I had to think about their future. We needed to go somewhere where this attitude of disrespect was not so pervasive.

With that thought in mind I called my cousin Dr. Paul Hicks in Prescott, Arizona. Paul's father, my uncle Dr. Taylor Hicks, Sr. was a prominent citizen of Prescott. He recently stepped down as Mayor of Prescott. He was on the Prescott

School Board for many years. In short Dr. Taylor Hicks had pull. I asked Paul to speak with his father. He would know if there were any openings for a football coach and Speech teacher at Prescott High School.

I had a degree of pull in Prescott, Arizona as well. I spent much of my childhood in Prescott visiting my dad's family. My dad had grown up in Prescott. I was still a legend to some in Prescott!

The call to my cousin Paul brought an almost immediate response. He talked with his dad, Dr. Taylor Hicks. Yes, there were openings at Prescott High School. The football coach, "Red" Ettinger recently resigned. A speech teacher also recently resigned. Was Lady Luck in my corner or what??

After six wonderful years in beautiful Carmel-by-the-Sea my family and I were going home, home to Prescott, Arizona; home to Arizona.

Though I've been to many place
That are beautiful and rare,
Amalfi Drive, Sorrento, and Capri
There's a certain spot I know of
That is quite beyond compare
And I miss that little town beside the sea.

Buzz Rainer
Little Town Beside the Sea
last stanza

CHAPTER 6

**Prescott High School
Prescott, Arizona
1965-1971**

*Bondservants, obey in all things your
masters according to the flesh,
not with eyeservice, as man pleasers,
but in sincerity of heart, fearing God.
Colossians 3:22*

**Thumb Butte
Picture credit. Marsha Hicks**

It seems like the Prescott, Arizona School Board does things by-the-book. My position with Carmel High School was agreed upon with a handshake and a verbal response. A formal interview was in store for me at Prescott.

I sent in a resume to the Superintendant of Prescott schools, Mr. Abia Judd.

Several days later I had a phone call from Mr. Judd informing me that an interview night for all the open positions in the Prescott school system was scheduled for an evening during Easter Break.

During my conversation with Mr. Judd he informed me that he and Dr. Taylor Hicks, Sr. were close friends. They knew each other for years and worked together on the Prescott School Board when Dr. Hicks was its President. I knew my Uncle Taylor would have pull.

Mr. Judd ended the conversation by telling me that if I was serious about applying for the Head Football Coaching job that I needed to write a letter to him indicating that I would be at the interview night. He would get back with me to let me know the time I was scheduled to be interviewed. That all seemed pretty formal to me. A simple "Yes, I will be there," seemed more than adequate.

Joan and I loaded our three kids in our Volkswagon camper and drove to Prescott arriving on the first day of Easter break. My cousin Paul and his wife Grace had a room for us in their apartnment. We planned to spend the entire Easter Week in Prescott with them. My interview was scheduled for the first Monday after Easter, the first day back to school for PHS.

I was certain that by the end of our stay in Prescott when my family and I were driving back to Carmel, we would be excited about my new position as Prescott High School's new Head Football Coach.

Wrong! Lady Luck would let me down.

Arizona's Legend
No Big Deal

I arrived at the Prescott School District's main office well before my scheduled interview time of 8:45 p.m. A secretary greeted me and told me that the interviews for the football position would begin shortly; the Board was finishing interviewing for a few elementary teaching openings. She indicated I should have a seat and they would be with me soon.

I had to wait approximately five minutes until an elderly gentleman opened the meeting room door to escort a young lady out. He pleasantly thanked her for her time and said they would have a decision for her within the next day or so. He then smiled at me and introduced himself as Mr. Abia Judd, Superintendent of Schools. We shook hands. Mr. Judd said it would be just a few minutes more before they were ready for me.

At 8:46 p.m. exactly according to the large wallclock Mr. Judd opened the door and invited me into the Meeting Room. These guys were punctual!

Mr. Judd got the interview started by introducing me to each member of the School Board. All I got from each of them was a smile and a nod of the head. No handshakes. No chit-chat. No "How was your trip Hadley?" They were all business.

The President of the school board was seated in the middle of a large semi-circular table; four men were seated on either side of him. The name plate in front of the President read, Reverend Fred James. President.

So You Wanna Be a Legend. So Did I.

I was seated at a table facing the School Board. I felt like I was on trial. Come to think of it, I guess I actually was. Reverend James got the questioning started by asking, "Mr. Hicks tell us about your brief tenure at Carmel High School."

I was rather taken back by two aspects of the question: Why "Mr." Hicks? Why not "Coach" Hicks? After all I was there applying for a job as a football coach. They knew I was a coach. Why not address me as one? These guys were too formal.

The second aspect of the question that kind of got to me was what I felt was emphasis on the word "brief". My brief tenure at Carmel High School. I was at Carmel High School for six years. I was head football coach for four of those years. I won two unofficial league championships. I tied for a third. In my book that wasn't a "brief" tenure. That was pretty darn impressive if you ask me.

I gathered my thoughts after a brief pause and told them about my love for Carmel High, the fine students-athletes and the quality faculty. I proudly told them that my win-loss record as Varsity Coach was 30-2 in League play. I told them about the spirit and pride that was generated. I did not mention that I backed into that enviable position when I took over for Coach Mosolf, the "father" of that "spirit which was exclusively ours".

I struggled with another question one of the board members asked, "Mr. Hicks, why are you leaving Carmel High School?"

I answered it as honestly as I could. I talked about my moral values. I did not approve of student drinking and smoking. My football players were guided by my strict code of conduct, my dress code specifically. I said I wanted to get away from the long-haired beatniks who were slowly creeping into the Carmel culture. I told them I felt Prescott would be a more moral environment to raise my family.

I really did not know how my answer to that question was received by the School Board. I hoped that Reverend James would see from what I said that I was pretty religious.

The last question of the night was from Reverend James, "Mr. Hicks, are you a strict disciplinarian?"

I again answered honestly. With a tone of humility I said, "With the wonderful kids I had the honor of working with at Carmel High School I did not have to be a strict disciplinarian." I told them the few times I had an inkling of a problem I got on it quickly. I credited my assistant coaches for being a big help in this area. I re-emphasized my strict dress code. I sensed that was not quite the answer they wanted.

Reverend James thanked me for my time and told me they would get back with me before we left for Carmel. I politely thanked them for their time and got up and left.

As Mr. Judd escorted me to the door he told me that if I wanted he would be glad to give me a tour of Prescott High School the next morning. I accepted his offer. Mr. Judd seemed like the nicest one of the bunch.

As I was saying "good-bye" and "thank you" to Mr. Judd I noticed an elderly man who was waiting to be interviewed next. We had a chance to introduce each other as Mr. Judd went back in the meeting room.

His name was Roger Hightower. We exchanged pleasantries for a brief time. He told me he had seen me play in high school several times. He seemed to know all about me.

Coach Hightower was an assistant for Coach Mutt Ford at Mesa High School, Mesa, Arizona. Coach Ford was one of the oldest Arizona coaches in terms of length of time coaching. He was highly respected throughout Arizona. I realized that Coach Ford's recommendation of Roger Hightower would pull a lot of weight.

I knew Roger Hightower was a strong contender for the Prescott High football job. I felt however that Hightower was too old. I felt that the Prescott School Board would go with the younger "Mr. Hicks." Wrong.

Superintendent of Schools Mr. Judd and I met the next morning for a tour of Prescott High School. But first Mr. Judd invited me into his office for a cup of coffee and a chance to visit. I had the feeling as soon as I sat down in Mr. Judd's office that I was not the Board's choice for Head Football Coach.

As I sipped my coffee (Mr. Judd was Mormon; he did not drink coffee.) Mr. Judd tried to gently tell me that the Board had chosen Roger Hightower. They felt his experience under Coach Mutt Ford at Mesa High School would be what Prescott High needed at the present time. Mr. Judd told me that Roger Hightower presented credentials which showed him to be a strong disciplinarian

The Board felt, Mr. Judd informed me, that my Carmel High School experience was too perfect, that I did not have to face problems many school districts had to confront. Many of my athletes at Carmel High came from home environments which fostered self-discipline and respect for authority. They were certainly right about that.

The Prescott School District was a much more diverse district with more ethnic minorities and more lower income families. Mr. Judd said these factors caused problems in the recent past. Thus a more experienced, older Roger Hightower was chosen.

Mr. Judd did make me feel somewhat better when he told me that Roger Hightower and I were the only two out of quite a few applicants who had been called to interview. Mr. Judd said, too, that he had a several other opportunities he wanted me to consider. We would talk as we looked the Prescott High Campus over.

The Prescott School District's offices were a short walk across the practice football field from the high school's campus. As we walked Mr. Judd told me what he had in mind for me if I was interested. I was interested.

Mr. Wayne Chapman Prescott High's Speech Teacher for a number of years, had just resigned. A Speech-Debate position was open. That very much interested me.

As we entered the main building of Prescott High School many students and teachers were milling around before school started for the day. One of those teachers brought a huge smile to my face! Les Fenderson! (B)

What a pleasant surprise to find that my Bisbee, Arizona friend was a teacher at Prescott High School. I had not seen Les in probably 15 years. We recognized each other immediately. After a few Bisbee punches and a brief visit Les had to get to his class. Mr. Judd and I continued our tour of the PHS campus.

While we walked I asked Mr. Judd if there was any chance I could be involved in the football program, possibly as Coach Hightower's assistant or JV coach. Mr. Judd replied, "Mr. Hightower is going to bring two assistants with him. That was another plus for Mr. Hightower; one of his assistants is from Mesa High School, Mr. Joe Pico has several years with Mr. Ford. The other assistant is a recent graduate of Missouri Valley College. He hasn't been affirmed yet so I'd better not tell you his name."

I couldn't believe how formal Mr. Judd was. He still had not called Roger Hightower "Coach", nor did he refer to Joe Pico as "Coach". He was afraid to use the guy's name from Missouri for fear word would get back to Missouri that I knew he was being considered as a coach at Prescott, Arizona. Weird.

Mr. Judd had more on his mind. He threw this at me: "Mr. Fenderson is head JV Football Coach and needs an assistant. I was hoping you would like that. The Board felt that since both of you have Bisbee ties you two would work together well.

Mr. Fenderson is also Varsity Baseball Coach. He would like to have you help him with that. Mr. Hicks we would like to have you with us. Please seriously consider these two coaching positions and get back with me as soon as possible."

It was still "Mr. Hicks." Wonder if he knows my first name?

I told Mr. Judd right then and there that I would be more than glad to work with Les Fenderson. I knew we could have fun together. Boy could we! (B)

It was not yet a done deal as Mr. Judd had to get the Board's final approval on me as an assistant. He would get back with me in a week or so. It was clear to me that the Prescott School Board called all the shots. I was glad that Carmel School Board allowed our high school principal, Warren Edwards some leeway in making his own decisions. I couldn't imagine Edwards going to the Carmel School Board to ask them if we could put a bunch of chickens on Chuck Moody's desk!

These guys didn't seem to have much fun. They were too strict. Yet, as I looked around at the students I saw that day I didn't see any long-haired beatniks. That was encouraging.

Joan and I had lots of time to talk on the way back to Carmel. Susie, Mike, and Steve could entertain themselves in the back of our Volkswagon camper so we didn't have too many interruptions. I had not signed a contract with the Prescott School District. I could still legally back out. The question was could I morally back out? All kinds of second-thoughts were running through my mind. In the final analysis we both knew that we should leave Carmel. The permissive way of life exhibited throughout California and Carmel in particular was not the way we wanted to raise our children.

As we were traveling and talking it suddenly hit me! Maybe those strict, formal Prescott Board of Education folks had it right. Maybe a strict formality was the way to go. Maybe if the beatniks do get as far as Prescott, Arizona they won't have as much influence as they seemed to be having in Carmel. Maybe.

"The Lord's trying to tell us something. I don't know what."

My dad drove to Carmel in his Ford pickup to help us with our move to Prescott. Joan and our three kids flew to Toronto, Canada after we packed our belongings to spend a week or so with Mr. and Mrs. Fallis, Joan's parents; at least until I found a place to live.

As dad and I drove down California Highway #1 towing our over loaded VW camper behind his Ford pickup, I was reminded of a similar trip my mother and I took just about 10 years earlier. On that trip I was headed to Arizona State University after my U.S. Army stint; *Momma's Chicken Wings* were fresh on my mind.

This trip I was headed to Prescott High School with six successful teaching-coaching years were behind me; Carmel High School was fresh on my mind.

As dad and I neared Los Angeles we noticed a tremendously large red-glow in the sky. The glow was noticable for many miles outside Los Angeles. We both assumed that it must be a huge oil fire of some sort. Since dad and I were discussing our move to his former home town of Prescott, Arizona we did not have the radio on. Dad's truck radio was worthless anyway, nothing but static.

The closer we got to Los Angeles the more spectacular the glow became. We could see flames shooting upwards for miles around. Dad and I were a bit worried though the highway we were on would not take us close to the flames. We also noticed that the traffic on the highway gradually got heavier the closer we got to Los Angeles. Heavy traffic at 11:00 p.m. did seem strange.

Dad noticed our gas gage was pushing close to empty. That concerned us as we had to leave the highway to find a gas station. The exit we took off the highway led to several gas stations we could see nearby. The first one we came to had a long line of cars all waiting to fill up. We drove to the next gas station; same thing. We decided we better get in line as we didn't have gas enough to go too much farther.

The first thing we noticed as we drove into the gas station was that every car we could see into was packed with black people. Now that was strange. Why were all these black people lined up and traveling somewhere this time of night? Dad and I seemed to be out of place. We were the only white people we could see in any of the cars. What was going on?

For a minute I think I may have had an idea of how my Pulaski *Cub* teammate Ernie King felt at times. He was a black among a bunch of mostly white people. I got up enough nerve to go to the car in front of us. I wanted to know what was going on. Their car window was rolled down so I could see the black man who was driving. He looked very scared and concerned. When I walked up to him he seemed startled to see me. I tried to be as polite as I could when I asked him what had caused the fire. What exactly was going on? As he turned to look at me I could see that he had tears in his eyes. He was crying.

All he said before he rolled the window up was, "The Lord is trying to tell us something. I don't know what."

After traveling many miles bumper-to-bumper going towards Arizona, dad and I pulled off the highway to gas-up and eat breakfast. The first thing I did after ordering was to buy a newspaper to find out what in the world was going on. Dad and I discussed all sorts of possible reasons for the fires and the large exodus of black people.

The newspaper told us what was going on. The newspaper dated August 12, 1965 was full of news about racial unrest. Watts, California a suburb of Los Angeles was burning, hundreds had been killed, thousands injured, and thousands more arrested.

It seemed to have started when a white policeman in Watts arrested a black woman for driving while drunk. Other blacks soon got involved and a riot broke out. It was quickly out of hand. White businesses and white business owners were targeted. Soon many police enforcements were called to the scene.

The few fire trucks available at first were not enough to keep the fires from spreading. Many businesses and homes for miles around were engulfed by fire.

Thousands of inhabitants were fleeing for their lives. The paper said the Watts riots were the worst riots ever in America.

I didn't really understand why the big fuss. Why did the black people carry their grudge to such extremes? So they were angry with the police. Why not just duke-it out with them? Why get so many others involved? I guess I just did not understand the whole of it. But truth be known, I didn't get too excited about the whole deal because I couldn't see that it would ever affect my family or me.

As I read about the riots in the papers the next few days I kept wondering if that black guy ever found out what it was that the Lord was trying to tell him.

THE PRESCOTT HIGH SCHOOL *BADGERS*

From a wimpy, pudgy, grinning, out of shape *Padre* to a vicious, mean looking *Badger,* I couldn't help but smile at the contrast. Those happy Carmel *Padres* were winners year in and year out. From what I understood about the Prescott High *Badgers*, they hadn't had a winning football team in quite a few years.

The future football fortunes of the *Badgers* were in the experienced hands of Coach Roger Hightower. It would be interesting for me to observe from the level of the PHS Junior Varsity team just how the players would relate to Hightower. In my opinion he was too old to relate to young high school kids. He did not seem very dynamic to me. He was low key and soft spoken. Could he get the players fired-up?

Coach Hightower certainly did not have much to rely on in terms of school spirit. After many years of losing seasons the PHS student body just did not have much to get excited about. Could Roger Hightower generate that much needed school spirit? I seriously doubted it.

My year on the JV with my Bisbee buddy Les Fenderson was highly enjoyable. Les and I got along great. Les was an outstanding football coach; we complemented each other well. Les was a get-in-their face, fire 'em up type of coach, much like Dick Lawitzke at Carmel High School. I was more the calm easy going type. I did not yell to make my point. Les Fenderson was the "bad cop" and I was the "good cop" to use a common cliche'.

At an assembly to introduce the football teams, Les had the shop classes build a make shift mobile animal cage like-trailer. He had our biggest JV player, Joe Flajnik, all 230 pounds of him get in the cage behind bars.

The cage was wheeled onto the gymnasium floor as the JV team was introduced. Fenderson had the whole team pulling the caged Joe Flajnik into view. Flajnik was growling and rattling the bars as he made his appearance. The student body loved it.

Coach Fenderson and I had a satisfying season. We finished 5-2-1. That one tie was a blunder on the part of our outstanding running back, Dennis Kendrick. I should say that the blunder was the fault of the Kingman High School maintenance department.

We were playing Kingman High JV on their poorly marked field. The Kingman High maintenance department carelessly had marked two goal lines about five yards apart.

As Dennis Kendrick ran all alone for a touchdown, he crossed the first goal line. Thinking he had scored, he dropped the ball and ran jubilantly back to our sideline. One of the Kingman players seeing Kendrick's error fell on the ball. Had Dennis crossed the correct goal line our JV team would have won the game. Instead it ended in a 7-7 tie.

Dennis Kendrick more than made up for his blunder in the years to come.

The 1965-1966 school year, my first at Prescott High, was the last year that any of us would be in the old buildings which housed generations of Prescott students. A beautiful new high school was built in north Prescott. Everyone was hoping that Coach Hightower would close out the history of football in the old school on a winning note. It was not to be.

Coach Roger Hightower and his coaching assistants Joe Pico and Wayne Howell ended their first season together as losers. I can't say that I was saddened to see that. The losing season merely verified in my mind that Coach Hightower was too old to generate a winning attitude in his players. Wayne Howell was the coach that Coach Hightower hired from Missouri Valley College. He was a knowledgable football coach. Howell would be a positive mainstay on the PHS Campus for many years.

Loyalty? What's That?

The 1966-1967 school year was the first year for Prescott High School to be in a brand new complex. Moving out of the old school buildings into a beautiful new environment seemed to generate new life into the Prescott High Student Body. The 1966 *Badgers* found that a completely new spirit and attitude was generated by the move to a new campus. It reminded me of the attitude the Carmel students had toward Carmel High. The result was not the same however.

The spirit of the student body did not filter down to the Varsity football team. They finished 3-7. Not a good start for the new chapter in Prescott High School's football history. The next season would see a dramatic turn around for the *Badgers*. Midway through the school year principal Joe Russo called me into his office. He informed me that Varsity assistant Joe Pico had resigned to take a position at Westwood High School in Tempe, Arizona.

Mr. Russo said that he was going to move my "tocus up to the Varsity." I knew what he meant; I was going to replace Pico on the Varsity. I just had no idea what "tocus" meant. Mr. Russo clearified the term for me. He said tocus was slang for "rear end" in some European language.

I was glad to be moving up to the Varsity. I realized that once again Lady Luck smiled on me. There was much more prestige for a varsity assistant than for a JV assistant. I would have a better chance to be Varsity Head Coach when Hightower retired. Wayne Howell would be my chief competition if he wanted Hightower's job as I did. I would miss working with Les Fenderson on the JV as we understood each other. Our Bisbee blood ran thick. Les said he understood completely why I wanted to move up to Varsity. He, too, felt Roger Hightower would be stepping down soon and one of his assistants at the time would replace him. Les had no such aspirations. He was content to remain Head JV football coach and Head Baseball Coach.

So You Wanna Be a Legend. So Did I.

One thing I really I liked about our new football facilities was that all the assistant coaches were in one locker-room. Head Coach Hightower had a much larger locker room at a far end of the gynmasium. Those of us in the assiatants' locker room included Les Fenderson and his new assistant Jack Orr. Wayne Howell and I were the Varsity assistants. Being distanced from Coach Hightower gave me plenty of opportunity to tell the others when I felt Hightower messed up.

Our 1967 Varsity season got off to a rousing start. We won our first four games. For the first time in years PHS was ranked in the top-10 Class AAA teams in the state. We were flying high. Then came our next game with perennial powerhouse St. Mary's High School of Phoenix.

The St. Mary's coach was a man named Ed Doherty. Talk about experience; Doherty had experience! He coached as an assistant at Notre Dame and head coach at Holy Cross and both the University of Arizona and Arizona State University.

What a feather in the *Badgers'* cap if we could defeat Coach Doherty's St. Mary's *Knights!* That would prove to our opponents that PHS football was for real!

Imagine my shock when Coach Hightower announced over the Monday morning KPHS- TV (more about KPHS-TV later) announcements that the *Badger* football team had been playing their hearts out. Coach Hightower felt they needed a day off! There would not be any football practice that Monday. Hightower said the day of rest for the *Badgers* would do them good.

I was in my homeroom period when the announcement was aired to all the classrooms. I let out a loud groan of disapproval. The students in my homeroom had no doubts about how I felt; not practicing the Monday before the St. Mary's game was stupid!

Soon after my first Period Speech Class started Coach Howell came into my room. The expression on his face said it all. He too was disappointed we would not practice that afternoon. What really bothered Coach Howell was that Roger Hightower told him the reason for cancelling practice that afternoon; an opportunity had come up for him to spend the afternoon practicing bugling elk. Coach Hightower was going to go elk hunting next weekend after the St. Mary's game and couldn't pass up the opportunity to practice bugling for elk.

Going bugling for elk the Monday of probably the most important game of the season! I had a hard time swallowing that. The students in my classes that day were among the first to hear how I felt. Soon teachers up and down the hall heard from me; Ray Wheiley, English teacher just a few doors away; Les Fenderson who taught science was down the hall. He just shook his head when I told him; Ed Villiborgi, American History got a taste of my disgust.

I had half a notation to go to principal Joe Russo to express my frustration or at least to Jim Topp, Vice-principal and Athletic Director. I kept my wits about me and did not say anything to the administrators. I did not want Coach Hightower knowing how upset at him I was. After all I had to work with the man.

The game against St. Mary's was on our beautiful new field. The stands on both sides of the stadium were full. The Arizona *Republic* called the game a toss-up and a key game for top ranking in the state.

It was a great game. It was nip and tuck right up to the last few minutes. With the score tied St. Mary's pulled it out with a well executed trick play; the old tackle eligible play. Our defense was completely fooled. By a simple shift in their line their tackle ended up on the end of the line thus becoming an eligible receiver. The tackle caught a short pass and went 40 yards untouched for the winning touchdown.

Our kids were terribly disappointed. They played well enough to win. Coach Ed Doherty's cunning and years of experience won it for St. Mary's. I had to admit one thing. Our kids were not at all hurt by the Monday off. They executed as well as they had all year and they were well rested. It was still my opinion that taking Monday off was not a good thing. I'll bet Ed Doherty at St. Mary's did not take Monday off.

The next Friday night against rival Flagstaff High School in Flagstaff our kids bounced back and beat the *Eagles* 20-14.

That weekend Roger Hightower bagged an elk.

After all was said and done Roger Hightower led PHS to a 7-3 season record, the best in many years for the *Badgers*. People were sensing a turn around for the football program. I wasn't so sure. In my mind Roger Hightower was still not the man to establish consistancy from year to year.

The Speech Team
Head Coach: Hadley Hicks

It wasn't exactly the Head Coach position I wanted but at least I was a head coach. Mr. Russo informed me in my initial meeting with him that I would be in charge of the Speech Team, a proud tradition at Prescott High Scool. By the time Russo finished explaining the job to me I could see that it was almost as time consuming as coaching an athletic team. I found out that the Speech Team required even more time practicing than a football or baseball team. True, there were no bruises, broken noses or sprained ankles but there were an abundance of bruised female egos. I hadn't been trained for that. I was certain I would never be chosen "Coach of the Year."

One of the students who was a three year participant on the Speech Team paid me a welcome visit at home one evening. His name was Ken Delp. Ken told me he heard I would be coaching the Speech Team in place of Mr. Wayne Chapman. Ken volunteered his help. He was appointed Assistant Coach to the Speech Team immediately! At no pay.

One of Ken's first suggestions was that as Sponsor I call a meeting of the "Speech Club" to begin planning for the annual "Readers' Theater."

Sponsor? Speech Club? Readers' Theater? What was all that about? I was prepared for the Speech Team and my Speech Classes, but Sponsor? Speech Club? Readers' Theater? Ken had some explaining to do for this new guy.

First Ken told me about the Speech Club. It was an official school club which met once a month, more often if need be. The purpose of the Speech Club was to drum up interest in the Speech Team and to have fund raisers for all the various activities we did during the year.

That *we* kind of got to me. That *do during the year* got to me as well. I was coaching JV Football. It was football season. I did not have time in the fall for any more activities. I would be coaching baseball in the spring. If anything baseball took up more time than football. When would I have time for a Speech Club?

Ken obviously wasn't worried about my time. I was the Sponsor of the Speech Club by default. I would find time. I would have to find time. I made a suggestion to Ken: How about if I have a cook-out on our deck and invite the Speech Club to come over for an organizational meeting?"

Ken was sitting in our living room. He took a peek out a window at our deck and politely said, "Mr. Hicks, there are over 40 members of the Speech Club right now. By the time we get the word out to the new kids in school we could have 50 or more. We usually have our meetings in the auditorium at school."

Oh. That kind of took care of that idea. Then I said, "Ok. Why not have a cook-out for just the officers of the Speech Club. I would like to get to know the officers. We could get organized before meeting with the whole Club." I thought that was a good idea.

Ken informed me the Speech Club had not elected officers yet.

Oh. Another idea shot.

Ken then told me what they usually do. Usually, they elect officers via a ballot distributed to Speech Club members in homerooms. That was the simplest way to elect officers Ken said. Ken would take care of getting the ballots to the homerooms. He and I would find an evening when we could get together to count them.

I agreed and then asked, "Ok. Clue me in. What is the Readers' Theater?"

Ken got a big smile on his face and said, "The Readers' Theater is the best thing we do all year. It is our number one fund raiser. We put on a Readers' Theater for the general public. We usually pack the auditorium." ...Long pause.....

"What is a Readers' Theater?"

I felt dumb asking the question. Ken looked at me like I was dumb. *"Any speech teacher should know what a Readers' Theater is."* That is what Ken did not say, but what I knew he was thinking.

Ken explained a Readers' Theater to me as patiently as he could:

- a Readers' Theater is when the Speech Club puts on an enjoyable evening of various *Interpretative* readings for the public.
- selected Speech Club members choose readings which would be entertaining and interesting to the public.
- the evening usually lasts an hour and a half and often includes up to ten readings of varying length.
- the Speech Club meets early in the school year to begin try outs for the readings.
- the Speech Club decided last year that this year the readings would be old fashioned melodramas**.** Ken was very excited about that. "That will be so much fun. All of us are really looking forward to doing the melodramas !"

I felt that one dumb question a night was one too many. I did not ask Ken what was on my mind at that point, *"A melodrama is a play. How do you make it a reading?"*

I would find out the answer to that soon enough. I too would be excited.

THE READERS' THEATER. WHAT A BLAST!

I found out quickly that this Readers' Theater was serious business.

At our first meeting of the Speech Club we had 45 students show up. I had no trouble at all getting that group to settle down. I took nominations for officers but was told quickly that the officers were pretty much already decided on.

Three veteran long time members of the Speech Team were chosen hands-down for the leadership of The Speech Club. Ken Delp was elected President, Lisa Parson was Vice-President, Jan Phillips was elected Treasurer. Things went up-hill from there. Three melodramas were chosen and parts for each were selected. A lot of practice time was involved. These practices were an eye opener for me. They were every bit as intense as a football or baseball practice. Ken Delp as student director was as demanding as most football coaches. The practices were usually after supper from 6:30 p.m. to 8:00 p.m.. I insisted on one and a half hours. I promised the parents I would not keep the students longer. Sometimes we practiced early Saturday mornings. We never practiced on Sunday. Some of the students went to church.

As the days and weeks flew by we could see it all coming together. Unlike the stage performance *Uncle Fred Flits By* which I co-directed for my student teaching experience, all the characters in a Readers' Theater line up in a row in front of the stage curtain.

On cue the characters read their lines standing where they are. There are few props and the characters act out their parts with a minimum of movement. Facial expression and vocal variations are the keys to effective interpretation.

The three melodramas the students chose were, *Switched at the Crossroads, Tillie the Teller,* and *The Miner's Daughter*. All three were presented to the public on opening night. The most popular by far was *Switched at the Crossroads*.

SWITCHED AT THE CROSSROADS OR...TRUTH WILL OUST
by John Healy

Switched at the Crossroads tells the age old story of the mortgage on the farm, the wicked villain *Sebastian Spitzmiller* played by Mike Kelly, the staunch hero *Barney McDougal* played by Bill Murie, virtuous heroine *Cymbeline* played by my favorite PHS comedienne Judy Shipley, the hard working farmer and his wife played by Wayne Everett and Debbie Williams, the comic maid played by Judy Crawford and the local sheriff *Mike Slade* played by Dave Halley.

There is a special twist in the convential format for melodramas: the hero turns out to be the villain and the villain is the hero after it is discovered that the two were "Switched at the Crossroads" as babies. *Cymbeline,* Judy Shipley, turns out to be a Secret Service Agent and the comic maid Judy Crawford turns out to be *Cymbeline's* outside contact.

There are few props in the reading. Judy Shipley as the heroine had on a child's knee length frilly dress with a huge pink bow in back. She had a large dinner plate size lollipop she was always licking.

Mike Slade, the sheriff, wore a black vest with a silver star. The hero/villian wore a reversable white/black hat. The villian/hero wore a reversable black/white hat. All other characters wore everyday school clothes.

At the climax when true identies were revealed *Cymbeline* turned her lollipop around to reveal a Secret Service badge and *Sheriff Slade* immediately arrested hero-turned-villian *Barney McDougal* who turned his hat around to show black as his true identity was made known.

My first attempt at a Readers' Theater presentation was a standing-ovation success. Some less than successful Speech Team activities were on the horizon.

SPEECH TEAM TROPHY TOURNAMENTS

Trophy Tournaments were where it was at! This was where the rubber meets the road. A Trophy Tournament. The competition was intense. The object was to win at any cost, especially for Prescott High School Speech Team members. PHS had a long and proud history of finishing first in most Trophy Tournaments. Mr. Wayne Chapman developed a no holds barred speech team juggernaut; the Speech Team members loved to compete. Other teams hated PHS.

The boys on the team were typical male competitors. They loved to mix it up. The girls however were something else! They could be vicious; throw them down and stomp on them if necessary.

Most speech tournament judges hated to get into a tussel with a female PHS speech team member who thought she had been given the short end of the stick by a judge. The judges always won but not before witnessing tears, feet stomping, and a female harangue; many judges lost their own composure during the tirade.

To be caught cheating was the ultimate sin for a PHS Speech Team member.

It was a common occurrence in a speech tournament for a team's entry to be caught cheating in some fashion; to trade places with a teammate was one of the most often attempted ploys. This happened if a team member was entered in a certain event and for some reason could not compete; one of his teammates would assume his name and enter in his place, a definate no-no.

Prescott High Speech Team members were above such things; win at all costs but win fairly. It was also very much against the State Speech Tournament Regulations for a student to enter a tournament using the same speech material used the year before. Should they do so and get caught not only was the guilty student disqualified for the entire tournament but the student's team was graded down heavily. The team would not be awarded a Trophy no matter how high up the team finished.

This happend to one of our Prescott High School girls my first year as Speech Team Coach. One of our best and most experienced female team members used a speech she had won tournaments with the previous year. One of the judges recognized the girl and her material from the year before and confronted me with his accusations. We talked to the girl at length. After harsh accusations from the judge she finally admitted she had cheated. Even though her team members were compassionate she had seriously let the team down. She knew it and the team knew it.

Several of her teammates came to me to tell me they were as guilty as she. They knew for several weeks that the speech she was working on was the one she won with the year before. They should have told her to not jeopardize her team by using the illegal material. They didn't. It was too late for regrets now.

When the team got home from Phoenix where the Trophy Tournament was held, we were greeted by a host of sad parents. Word got home before we did. Not much was said. It began to snow which further dampened the spirits of all of us.

Much later that night I was awakened by a phone call from the girl's father. The girl went for a walk in the snow and did not return when she was supposed to. The father told me how sad and disappointed he was in his daughter. He said he loved her so much and was very worried about her. He called the police to see if they couldn't find her. The girl was found by the Highway Patrol much later-safe but cold. She wandered down the highway is a semi-comatose state. The peer pressure she felt over her poor judgement was almost too much for her to endure. The young girl recovered but never again competed on the Speech Team. She learned the hard way that there can be serious consequences to breaking rules.

THE *GOLDEN BOYS.*
High School Baseball at its Best

Year in and year out, high school baseball in Arizona is among the best in America. Prescott High School under the leadership of Coach Les Fenderson always ranked among the best AAA teams in Arizona.

In 1969 possibly the best Arizona high school team was the Prescott High School *Golden Boys.* Dressed in their white pants with the gold stripe, blended with their gold stockings, their white shirts with *Prescott* in gold lettering, gold caps with a bright blue *P.* The *Golden Boys* were indeed a classy looking group.

Dennis Kendrick and Dick Bowles were the most feared 1-2 punch in the state. Kendrick was a speedy left-handed power hitter. He was always a threat to drag-bunt so the third baseman had to play in towards home plate. The shortstop and secondbase had to play deep as Kendrick could "hit 'em where they ain't." The first baseman did not dare play in close for fear he would catch a Kendrick line drive shot in his face.

After graduating from Prescott High, Dennis went on and had a fine career for the nationally ranked Arizona State *Sun Devils* coached by Hall of Fame Coach Jim Brock.

Dick Bowles was also a left-hander with tremendous homerun power. He too could run; not as fast as Kendrick but he was no slouch on the base paths. Some of Bowles' blasts bounced off the Prescott National Guard Armory which was located well over 400 feet from home plate in right field.

This brings up the much discussed Prescott High *home-field advantage.* High school baseball coaches all over the state lost sleep trying to solve the dilemma of PHS's right field ground rule!

The *Badgers'* played all their home games in The Prescott City Park. The City Park diamond was originally designed to be a softball diamond. In fact, all summer long the field was used for a softball diamond. Many state and national tournament softball games were played at City Park each summer.

During the Arizona high school baseball season, the PHS *Badgers* have the only field in the state where a simple infield pop-up becomes a possible game deciding home run. The right field fence is permanently situated 135 feet from home plate. And I mean permanently! When the City Park was built in the 1900's a beautiful granite wall was constructed to circle the entire park area. Granite and cement seats were built into the wall from deep center field to right field and down the right field foul line. At the junction where the wall down the right field foul line ends was a unique and ornate granite and cement grandstand. Probably 300 fans could be seated directly behind home plate in these stands. Most regulars at the games brought padded cushions to sit on.

The structure was constructed at one time for rodeo grounds. The seats which accommodated the rodeo fans stretched almost a city block across deep center field to where right field merged with the right field foul line some 135 feet from home plate.

When softball became popular, a sturdy wire fence was built from about 325 feet in left field and encircled the entire playing area all the way around to the granite and cement stands.

The home field coach traditionally has the right to designate the ground rules which govern the playing field. Coach Les Fenderson was the home field coach. Les dictated that any ball landing on the fly 135 feet from home plate, in the right field area behind the fence, into the granite and cement seats was a home run and not a "ground rule double" as less win-oriented coaches would have designated; but a home run!

I was all for it. What fun to watch visiting teams try to get their right handed batters to "just poke" the ball to right field.

Anything in the air they reasoned would be a home run. Usually the result of a right handed batter trying to unnaturally poke the ball to right field resulted in a weak pop up to the right fielder for an easy out. At best a poke resulted in a grounder to either the second baseman or the first baseman.

Coach Fenderson wisely coached his players to swing naturally. We had a lot of right field home runs by right handed hitters. A few were of the pop-up variety which always brought sheepish grins from the hitter as he rounded the bases.

Dennis Kendrick and Dick Bowles, both left handers hit numerous home runs to right field. Most of their home runs were the result of tremendous blasts, not dinky little pop ups like some visitors were glad to get. Kendrick and Bowles are both in the Prescott High School Baseball Hall of Fame.

John Denny.
Future National League *Cy Young* Winner.

The 1969 PHS Junior Varsity baseball team had a young freshman pitcher who, as a freshman, showed great potential. JV Coach Jerry Nelson told Coach Fendeson many times that his best Junior Varsity pitcher was a tall, skinny 6'1" kid named John Denny. Sometime about mid-season Coach Fenderson had an oppertunity to watch Denny pitch for the JV team. The next week John Denny was called up to the Varsity. John went on to break every PHS pitching record including the number of strike outs in one game; he struck out 19 Flagstaff *Eagles* in one game his senior year.

John did not waste any time after graduating from Prescott High School. He spent two years playing Junior College baseball and then signed with The St. Louis *Cardinals* National League Baseball team. After several seasons with St. Louis minor league affiliates Denny was called up to their Major League team in 1976. He replaced the great Hall of Fame pitcher Bob Gibson in the *Cardinal* starting rotation when Gibson retired. Denny led the *Cardinals* to a National League Championship in 1976 with a team leading Earned Run Average (ERA) of 2.32

John spent some time with the Cleveland *Indians* and the Philidelphia *Phillies*. It was with the *Phillies* in 1983 that he was the National League's coveted *Cy Young* winner for the best pitcher in the league. His won-loss record was a League leading 19-6. John Denny retired from baseball in 1988 after 12 seasons in the Major Leagues.

Denny is in the Prescott High Baseball Hall of Fame.

John's older brother Gary Denny was an All-America softball fast-pitch pitcher. He was one of the best softball pitchers in the Western United States. Gary was often recruited and paid to pitch for softball teams in tournaments around the country.

Another freshman Prescott High *Badger* with a PHS Baseball Hall of Fame career was a small middle infielder named Bobby Manriquez. Bobby could play either second base or short stop equally well. He was quick and possessed just unbelievable baseball instincts. Bobby was always in the right place at the right time; he had a knack for judging ground balls. I don't ever remember him ever being handcuffed by a bad-hop. From the moment Bobby stepped into the *Badger* starting lineup as a freshman he was the coach-on-the-field. His teammates, even those a grade or two above him, respected Bobby's abilities and his leadership. He was not a rah-rah vocal leader. He led by example and sometimes a timely word of advice given quietly and privately. Often during batting practice I observed Bobby demonstrate to a teammate a hitting technique the teammate should try. Usually the teammate benefited from Bobby's coaching. Bobby Manriquez was in my opinion a young man who would have made an outstanding high school baseball coach. Bobby Manriquez was one of the finest all-around baseball players I had the privilege to coach, high school or college.

Bobby was a three year starter for the PHS Varsity Football Team as a quarterback and defensive half back.

So You Wanna Be a Legend. So Did I.

MIKE AND STEVE HICKS
Getting Started Early

Mike and Steve, my two sons got their first taste of competitive baseball during our family's summer camping trips to Montana, the first being the summer of 1965 before moving to Prescott. We camped just outside of Bonner, Montana several miles outside Missoula, the capitol of Montana.

I attended graduate school at the University of Montana in Missoula. My class schedule was always arranged so that I was out of class by noon. That gave me many hours of daylight to fish the Black Foot River. Our good friends Al and Evelyn Holbrook owned a home in Bonner, Montana near the deserted Boy Scout Campground where we camped. Our camp was literally on the bank of the Black Foot River. Susie, Mike and Steve became proficient with the fishing rod and reel.

Al and Evelyn put us in touch with the people who ran the Bonner Little League. The teams in the league were sponsored by the Bonner Lumber Mill, the community's main industry. The Bonner Little League team was named the Bonner *Toothpicks*. Their Babe Ruth League team for older kids was named the Bonner *2 x 4's*

Mike and Steve played several summers with the *Toothpicks*. They had fun, met a lot of nice kids and had some playmates besides Al and Evelyn Holbrook's three, Vonnie, Jerri, and Doug.

While Mike and Steve were becoming baseball enthusiasts Susie was becoming a horse lover riding horses with Vonnie and Jerri. What a great way for the Hicks family to spend a summer's vacation!

It was after we moved to Prescott in the summer of 1965 that Mike and Steve really became absorbed in baseball. Prescott at that time was "The Little League Capitol of Arizona." As soon as Prescott boys learned to walk they were given a baseball glove and cleats. Youngsters and their dads were devastated if the son did not get placed on a Little League team. There were such a large number of Little League teams available that it was rare for a kid who wanted to play to not get that opportunity.

Doug Williams, a fellow PHS Faculty Member, and I coached the *Mays and Heap* team which Mike, Steve and Jimmy Williams, Doug's son, were on. Both Mike and Steve became good Little League baseball players. The competition was competitive. I don't recall that we ever won a league championship but we were always near the top of the league.

Mike was lefthanded so he was always the first baseman. Steve was a good fielder and had a strong arm so he was always short stop and pitcher. Both hit well for Little Leaguers. During the PHS Varsity baseball seasons Mike and Steve were bat boys for the *Badgers*. Mike even had a four stitch scar on his chin to prove it. He stood too close to Rocky Krumbholz while Rocky was beside the batting cage getting loose with his bat. Both boys loved hanging around the the big kids. They took their bat boy jobs seriously.

Coach Fenderson was good to Mike and Steve. He looked for little jobs for them to do which made them feel even more important. A few times Les let both boys go on a trip to Phoenix with the team. That was special to Mike and Steve, especially the pre- and post-game meals which they got to eat sitting with the players. Baseball was to be an important part of the Hicks family for many years.

KPHS-TV

Prescott High School was one of the few high schools in Arizona to have its own self-contained TV station and studio. It was a first class arrangement with the best equipment money could buy. Bill Lea, husband of Prescott High English teacher Luanne Lea, was the PHS Television Technician. Bill ran KPHS-TV with an iron fist! What Bill said regarding the studio was the way it was. Bill's insistence on doing things the right way, which was his way, led to daily conflicts with Mrs. Ethel Tyson, the Director of KPHS-TV.

My three Speech Classes were in the same room where the daily KPHS-TV News programs were produced; the KPHS-TV daily news program was held first period. My three Speech Classes came immediately after KPHS-TV finished with the news for the day. Due to the timing, I was the victim of Bill Lea's venting! Almost daily when I came to the room Bill would give me the latest on *Hollywood,* Bill's derogatory name for Mrs. Tyson.

Ethyl Tyson was the Drama Coach for PHS as well as KPHS-TV Director; she was the expert on all things theatrical.

Mrs. Tyson let Bill Lea know in no uncertain terms that his technical crew was to be totally under her direction; she would direct the lighting; she would direct the camera angles; she would direct and place the sound-booms. In other words Bill Lea was to watch *Hollywood* and keep his mouth shut, which Bill Lea was not about to do.

Bill was always harping on me to take over the KPHS-TV Production class. He said that *Hollywood* was driving him nuts. Bill Lea finally got his wish. It seems that *Hollywood* was as sick of Bill Lea as Bill was of her. She resigned from the KPHS-TV Production Class, maintaining that her talents were much more suited for "the intellectual climate she could generate on the stage." Bill Lea, she said was "too common."

Principal Joe Russo accepted Mrs. Tyson's resignation. Bill Lea was overjoyed. My arm was twisted and I became Prescott High's KPHS-TV Production teacher. The class was designed to give the students a feel for Television Production. Bill Lea had a group of students each year who were interested in learning how to work with television cameras and all the electrical equipment needed to produce television programs.

Some of PHS's more intellectual technically minded students were in Bill Lea's Technical class. Year in and year out they were great kids; Bill Lea was pretty tight with each of them. Not "a short-circuit" among them as Bill was known to say.

Each year I had 15-20 of PHS's more socially outgoing students who loved to be visible to others, who were, to put it bluntly, hams and ad-libbers!

I enjoyed my time with KPHS-TV more than any other assignment I had at PHS. I fit in well with them. They were a "hoot" as the saying goes.

"Good morning from KPHS
Here is your news"

With that opening we were off and running. The daily ten minute PHS TV news was on the air!

The class worked out the morning's format the last period the previous day. They had an agenda to be loosely followed within the PHS's Administration's ten minute time limit. It was always amazing to me how much fun we could have in that ten minute boundry.

Usually the program would include not only the daily announcements which were a necessary function of PHS's existence, but various interviews with faculty, coaches and student-athletes.

We tried to work in as many "Specials" as we could. That was where the real fun came in. Some examples:

"The Leader of the Pack," a parody of the popular song of the same title.

As the sound track of the song began "The Leader of the Pack", Lon Yaeger peddled on-camera on a very small tricycle. Lon had his T-shirt sleeve rolled up to hold a package of "cigarettes." He looked like the hoodlum he was depicting.

Off-camera a trio of girls consisting of Mary Young, Lisi Powers and Bonnie Bohning were singing the sad laments of "The Leader of the Pack" as he rode in circles to finally meet his fate in a serious tricycle crash.

"The Lemon Sisters" was a spoof of the Lennon Sisters popularized on the Lawrence Welk Program. As the three "Lemon Sisters," Penny Price, Lisa Parson, and Dori Zabriski pantomimed singing in sinc to a medley of the original Lennon Sisters' songs many bubbles floated up and all around the singers.

Unnoticed by the viewing audience was one of Bill Lea's techinical crew, Paul Newman, lying flat on his back out of camera-view blowing bubbles upward to lend a touch of uniqueness to the special. That bit of camera ad-libbing was well received. We could hear classes up and down the outside hallway loudly laughing.

Danny Brambilla one of Bill Lea's camera men thought it would add class to the special if he zoomed down and in on Paul Newman on his back blowing bubbles. Unknown to Newman, the entire school saw that he was the source of the bubbles. It brought the house down.

"The Fractured Faculty Four" may have been our all-time favorite. It was the only special that had many requests for encores.

"The Fractured Faculty Four" consisted of Math teacher Jack Orr, Coach Wayne Howell, Coach Les Fenderson, and History teacher Dean McIntosh. The moment the four popular teachers were introduced to the students a roar of approval reverberated throughout the school.

Each teacher was dressed in a somewhat similiar attire. They each had a derby hat of some sort, a loud tie loosely tied, and Levi's with the cuffs rolled up. Les Fenderson had a shirt which had a conspicious bulge that popped a gap between two unbuttoned buttons to reveal his well endowed stomach. They were indeed a humorous sight.

These four practiced for their TV debut for several evenings before their moment of fame was realized. They were going to pantomime singing the popular Barber Shop Quartet song, *Down By The Old Mill Stream.*

Their practices went so well that it was decided that since they knew the words, instead of pantomiming the song, they would actually sing it. It was great!

Believe it or not they actually harmonized in places. Dean McIntosh had the necessary barber shop quartet bass part. He did several lines solo. The other three had a hard time keeping straight faces.

At the final stanza as the song ended Wayne Howell tossed his derby hat in air and caught it right side up on his head. Wayne had to practice that many times before he got it right.

What I have not mentioned is that this was all filmed. We could practice until it was performed to our liking. Howell must have tossed his derby in the air a couple of dozen times before the hat hit right-side up on his head. Bill Lea got it on film.

The students especially liked the fact that the four teachers were in their respective classrooms when the special was aired. They got standing ovations from their classes at various times during the performance.

I enjoyed practicing for those KPHS-TV Specials much more than I did practicing football. I was not cut out to be just an assistant football coach

JUST AN ASSISTANT COACH

My six years in Prescott were difficult years for me in one respect. I was not a head coach in either football or baseball. Head Speech Team Coach did not count. My dreams of being head coach at Arizona State University were being eroded with each passing season. Frank Kush was putting ASU on the football map big time!

His winning record and exciting teams were winning acclaim nationwide. Frank Kush was a household name not only throughout Arizona but around the country. Hadley Hicks was a household name in a few homes in Prescott, Arizona. Most of those households were Hicks family.

I was just an assistant coach, and, as I would find our later, not a very good one.

My search for significance was going nowhere fast. I knew my family loved me but that did not fill the void in my life since my days as a Bisbee High School Arizona Legend. Maybe the Head Football job at Flagstaff High School would fill that void. Wrong!

WAS I NUTS OR WHAT?

Shortly after the PHS baseball season of 1971, I read that long time football coach John Ply resigned at Flagstaff High School, 60 miles north of Prescott. Without discussing the possibility of getting Ply's job with my family I applied for it immediately. The job application process for Flagstaff High School was much simpler than for Prescott High School. The article in a Phoenix newspaper that reported Ply resigned gave the name Roy Smith, Flagstaff High Athletic Director as the one to whom applications should be sent. I met Mr. Smith when I played in The Arizona All-

So You Wanna Be a Legend. So Did I.

Star Football Game in the summer of 1952. (I won't bore you again with my statistics in that game.) Mr. Smith was one of the coaches for the AA All-Star Team.

I called Mr. Smith from my downstairs fly-tying room one morning while Joan was getting the kids ready for school. Mr. Smith, of course, knew that I was at Prescott High School as Prescott and Flagstaff played each other every year. The two schools had been serious rivals for many years.

Mr. Smith said they would be glad to accept my application. I was to send a resume' as soon as possible. I did so that same evening when I got home from school. Joan was supportive of my desire to be a head coach again.

I had a phone call from Mr. Smith two days later. He asked me if I could come up for an official interview with Mr. Don Clark, Assistant Superintendent of Schools.

If I understood Mr. Smith correctly they were not taking any more applicants. I got the idea that if I wanted the job it was mine. Mr. Smith indicated that the Flagstaff High School football program was in pretty bad shape. Not too many coaches were interested. He was honest with me. He said that if I took the job it would be a definite challange.

Leaving Prescott High for Flagstaff High? I had to be nuts!

I visited with Mr. Abia Judd, Superintendent of Prescott School District as soon as I found out that I had a good chance to get the Flagstaff High job.

I wanted some indication from Mr. Judd that I would be given a good shot at the Prescott High Head Coach position when Coach Hightower retired. If he had assured me of that I believe I would have stayed at Prescott High School. Mr. Judd was nice as always but he said that without speaking with the School Board he could not assure me I would be a strong contender. Mr. Judd was still "a company man" right up to the end. He went by the book.

Shortly after word got out that my family and I were moving to Flagstaff my cousin Taylor Hicks, Jr. decided to give us a farewell party. Taylor and his lovely wife Marsha invited many of our Prescott friends to their house for what one might call a "Hadley Roast."

The guests had been asked to each bring a going away gag gift for both Joan and me. The ones to Joan were all sincere and meaningful. Not so the gifts to me.

My gifts ranged from a toy bullwhip to control the Flagstaff thugs in my classes, to a loaf of bread for "the hard times". The gift that brought the most laughs was what Coach Wayne Howell gave me-a construction worker's hard hat.

Howell wrote a long note on construction paper outlining the type of protection the hard hat would provide: it would protect my head from bottles and rocks the disgruntled Flag High fans would be pelting me with each time PHS beat the *Eagles*; it would protect me from the clubs wielded by parents wanting to get rid of me; it would protect my head from the falling debris in the ancient, in-need-of-repair Flagstaff High School buildings; and lastly the hard hat would protect me in case I had to break up a gang fight on the FHS campus.

In the course of the evening amid much laughter was a comment by my cousin Paul saying he doubted that I'd have enough guts to wear the hard hat. I'd probably be too proud to admit I needed the protection.

That really got my goat! A challenge had been issued. I bet those who were man enough to meet the challenge that I would wear the hard hat next fall when Flagstaff High played Prescott High. The game was in Prescott, a big advantage to Prescott. Even so I was just cocky enough that I said we would beat Prescott High with me wearing the hard hat.

The bet was on. An official paper stipulating the terms of the bet was drawn up and signed by all those willing to put forth the required $50 individual fee. What the signees did not consider was that the total amount was prohibitive for me to pay should I lose the bet, thus guaranteeing that I would indeed have to wear the hard hat.

The outcome of the game was not a factor in the bet. The big issue was me wearing the hard hat during the game. Oh, I would wear it alright!

Even though Flagstaff is not very far from Prescott as the crow flies, it was still very difficult to leave. It was especially tough on our three kids. Susie was going into junior high and had many close friends among her classmates. Mike and Steve, ages 11 and 10 respectively, were going to miss their baseball buddies. Joan and I had been through this before. We could handle it. But there were difficult times ahead for us.

PART TWO

*Yet when I surveyed all that my hands had done
and what I had toiled to achieve,
everything was meaningless, a chasing after the wind;
nothing was gained under the sun.*

Ecclesiastes 2:11

CHAPTER ONE

Flagstaff High School
Flagstaff, Arizona
1971-1979

*Jesus answered and said to him,
"Most assuredly, I say to you,
unless one is born again, he cannot
see the kingdom of God."*
John 3:3

San Francisco Peaks
Sam Borozon, NAU

THE PROPHECY OF THE HARD HAT

What Coach Howell did not realize at the time, was that the wording of his message with the hard hat would be prophetic. Some difficult times were ahead for me. My search for significance would flounder.

Flagstaff *Eagle* Football

Flagstaff Schools' Assistant Superintendent Don Clark told me I could bring one assistant coach with me from Prescott just as long as he was a Physical Education instructor. My good friend Benny Bishop and I often discussed the possibility of someday working together. Benny was the Gymnastics Coach at Prescott and a Physical Education instructor. We came to Prescott High School the same year. Benny and his wife Judy, their two kids Timmi and Todd and the Hicks crew were almost inseperatable while in Prescott. Benny and I went on many fishing trips together, our two families camped together many times and Susie baby-sat Timmi and Todd on occasion. We were two closely knit families. Benny came with me to Flagstaff High as head Junior Varsity Football Coach, head Gymnastics Coach, and PE instructor. Benny would have a positive impact on FHS over the years.

I got into hot water with the Flagstaff School Board almost immediately after signing my contract. I spoke out of turn to Paul Sweitzer, Sports Editor for the *Arizona Daily Sun*, Flagstaff's newspaper by announcing that my number one football assistant was Ken McElyea. Ken was a Flagstaff Junior High Football Coach and PE instructor. More importantly Ken was my football teammate at Bisbee High School. We were both former *Pumas*. Bisbee blood ran thick in both of us. I was way out of line by announcing to Paul Sweitzer and thus to all of Northern Arizona who my assistant coach was without first getting School Board approval. Oh well, live and learn.

The number two assistant coach I was allowed to have was also a Flagstaff Junior High Football Coach, Jim Clements. I interviewed Jim and liked his philosophy. He impressed me as a knowledgable football man. Jim's major football coaching area was defense, and Ken and I were more geared to offense so Jim Clements would be an asset.

Both Ken McElyea and Jim Clements knew the Flagstaff *Eagle* personnel. They worked with most of the kids at the Junior High and watched them for several years at FHS. FHS played in the tough Arizona AAA League; we were the smallest school in terms of student numbers. FHS was a AA school playing in a AAA league. The Phoenix schools dominated the league. Somebody somewhere told me about a revolutionary high school football defense called "The Radar Defense." I wasn't a defensive football coach and didn't know much about that side of the ball. The title of the defense intrigued me.

I purchased the book <u>The Radar Defense for Winning Football</u> by Jules Yakapovich and was immediately impressed with the man's philosophy. It sounded like just the type of change the *Eagles* needed. It was designed for smaller defensive personnel who were standing up at an angle to their offensive opponents. They were drilled over and over again about avoiding the offensive linemen's block. Quickness was the key. Avoid the block and never take on a bigger offensive lineman one on one. With that defensive philosophy settled, my new coaching staff and I got busy planning for the 1971 football season. Before I had ever met any of the players Ken and Jim went over the returning prospects name by name. Before deciding on what offensive schemes we would use I had to have some idea of the various attributes we would have to work with: size? speed? toughness? coachability?

So You Wanna Be a Legend. So Did I.

I liked what my coaches said about a couple of black kids who had good speed. Jerry Nichols and Frank McCain had a year of Varsity competition under their belt. Both would be seniors and both would more than likely be starters for us. Two other blacks had a world of potential according to Coach McElyea. Robert Joyce was a 6'2", 200 pound end with good speed who would be a fine split end and he was strong enough to be a tight end. Donnie Joe Hickman, a junior, was undisciplined but talented.

Donnie Joe was 6'2", 240 pounds, the biggest and the fastest kid in school. McElyea said that as a freshman Hickman could stand flat footed, take one step and dunk a basketball. He said that Donnie Joe could be tough and aggressive when he wanted to be. Hickman just might be our fullback if he wanted to be. In other words Donnie Joe Hickman as a junior was lazy!

I never worked with black athletes before. To be perfectly honest I was concerned. I heard all the typical racist stereotypical, "All blacks were lazy." Not so. "All blacks are just looking for trouble." Not so. "All blacks are ignorant." Not so. The many blacks I was honored to work with during my years at Flagstaff High School were, for the most part, good kids. Like any other group of kids we had our good ones and we had our bad ones.

Coaches McElyea and Clements presented a rosy picture of what we had as offensive and defensive linemen. They were especially high on Mike Kohlbeck, a 210 pounder who went both ways as a tackle. The coaches said Kohlbeck could play for any team in our league. Others who weighed in close to or over 200 pounds were David Gonzales, Richard Navarro, Randy Rhoten, Dan Dowell, Randy Alcott, Vince Lopez and Doug Walter. In addition we would have any number of athletes weighing in at 165-180 pounds. Coach McElyea and Coach Clements said we could put up a defensive team that man for man could play with the big schools in our league. Depth would be our big draw back. Key injuries could kill us.

The Radar Defense looked better and better as we evaluated defensive personnel. We didn't have the depth needed and we were not as big as the teams we'd be up against. We had to rely on quickness and toughness.

Our offensive backfield looked like we had a pretty potent attack. Quarterbacks Jerry Hansen and Nick Lynn gave us good athleticism at that position. Both were potentially good leaders. Both could pass the football. Neither had had previous Varsity experience. How fast would they catch on to our offense? That was the big question going in to the opening game. Bruce Evans was a shoe-in for the fullback spot according to McElyea. He was a tough runner who liked to grind it out for tough yards. Bruce could run well when in the open and was an excellent blocker. Bruce was a solid 185 pounder. Unless there were some surprises among our new kids, Jerry Nichols and Frank McCain would be our starting running backs. Both were also good pass receivers. Big Donnie Joe Hickman was a big question mark going in to the season. Would he come through when the going was tough? Could he handle the discipline we would require?

I had a good idea of my main offensive people. On paper the FHS *Eagles* had speed. I liked that; my offensive philosophy had never been smash mouth, grind it out football. I liked trick plays; I liked to score quickly and often; I didn't have the patience to slowly move the ball down the field. I wanted a wide-open passing and running game, one that kept the opponents off-balance.

I stumbled across just such an offense while I was at Prescott High School. While reading my monthly copy of *Scholastic Coach* magazine I read an article by Glenn "Tiger" Ellison which briefly summarized the offense he had developed. I was so taken by the article and its exciting depiction of his offense that I ordered a copy of Ellison's book. Run and Shoot Football became my football bible for a number of years. Sadly for me, when I first read the book I was just an assistant coach at Prescott High. I could not adapt any of the concepts while being just an assistant coach to Head Coach Roger Hightower. Prescott High had a quarterback who fit the Run and Shoot offense to a T; Bobby Manriquez would have been perfect for it. But I was just an assistant coach. What did I know?

Both McElyea and Clements liked the Run and Shoot offensive philosophy when I went over it with them on the chalk board. The offensive formation for the Run and Shoot was similiar to the formation Max Spilsbury used with his *Slot T* formation; one end was split well away from the rest of his linemen. He was "hidden" as Spilsbury explained. A weak-blocking kid to be covered by a defensive player when the split-end was spread out, in essense "blocking" that defensive player.

The difference with the Run and Shoot was that both ends were split away from the other linemen and two running backs were were split out, but not as far as the ends.

It looked like this:

```
E................T   G   (C)   G   T................E
         B              QB              B

                        FB
```

This formation gave the offensive team many options; it could effectively run the ball to one side or the other or pass the ball to one of the split ends or to one of the backs split out.

On the snap the quarterback sprinted to one side or the other with the ball. Would he pass the ball? Keep it and run? Maybe hand the ball off to the fullback? Quite a few offensive options confronted the defense. Each defensive counter-movement could be recognized by the offensive personnel and adjustments made. It was not as complicated as it appeared to be. At least not on paper.

McElyea and Clements had only one concern and it was a big one. They both were not sure that we had a quarterback who could handle the "run" part of the offense. Both were inexperienced. Could they pick up the fine points of the Run and Shoot? In summer workouts two kids stood out as good passers. Jerry Hanson and Nick Lynn were both better than average passers. Could they throw on the run? If not we had to make some adjustments. As "Tiger" Ellison explained it in his book, the quarterback was the key to the whole thing. The q.b. had to be able to immediately read particular defensive movements on the snap of the ball. If the linebacker did one thing, the q.b. would have a counter-move. It was all based on the quarterback recognizing and reacting to the defense.

So You Wanna Be a Legend. So Did I.

We felt confident that by the time official practice began we coaches would know both the new *The Radar Defense* and the new *Run and Shoot* offense. All three of us had confidence our kids could pick up the changes being made in the FHS Football Program. The coaching changes as well as the philosophy changes would present challanges to all of us. We felt we were up to it.

By *Arizona Interscholastic Athletic Association* rules teams would be allowed one week of "helmets and shorts only" practices. No pads, no contact, conditioning and teaching only. That rule was a god-send for the *Eagles*. Coaches McElyea and Clements and I planned three tough practices per day (school had not started). We would find out quickly who wanted to play football *The Eagle Way*. When I first brought up the three practices per day concept McElyea did not think the kids would buy it. Ken had been a part of Flagstaff High Football for a few years. He said Coach Ply never practiced more than twice per day; sometimes only once per day.

Coach Clements and I felt we had to do something different and challenging. We had to make it tough. Clements said that we should have the first of three practices per day early in the morning at 6:00 a.m.. I was all for it. McElyea gulped. Clements furthermore said that if any were late for the 6:00 a.m. sharp starting time we should give them extra running at the end of practice. I agreed. McElyea said the whole team would be late. They had never had discipline before.

Coach McElyea was wrong. When Student Manager Johnny Sandoval took roll at 6:00 a.m. sharp the first day not a single soul was absent; even Big Donnie Joe Hickman was there, barely moving but he was there. Some of his buddies in "The Hood" had roused him out of bed at 5:30 a.m. That conditioning week was grueling. We worked 30 minutes daily installing our new offense and defense. After that we had various conditioning stations set up, each station manned by a coach. Our JV coaches were involved. Coach Benny Bishop and his assistant JV Coach Eddie Garcia plus 25 potential JV football players were on hand.

We had five stations scattered around our practice field through which the 37 Varsity players and the 25 JV players rotated. The players had to run from one station to another when Manager Johnny Sandoval blew his whistle. The only rest the players got was when the coach at the station gave them a brief breather from the "up-downs", the "quick feet drill" or whatever drill the particular station called for. Each station was five minutes of a quick, intense workout; the Varsity and JV players went through all five stations one after the other followed by a five minute water break. We ended each practice with four-100 yard "bear crawls".

The players were separated Varsity and JV. Then they were separated by positions. The Varsity went first. All the linemen lined up on the goal line on their hands and knees. On the verbal signal to "go" they had to bear crawl as quick as they could 100 yards to the next goal line. They were on their hands and feet the entire 100 yards. They could not stand up and run. After the linemen had gotten 50 yards down the field the backs and ends started out. Backs and ends smaller and quicker than the linemen, were told if they could catch and pass one of the linemen before the 100 yard mark they, the back or end, could have that much more time to rest before they had to start back. The entire Varsity and JV teams bear crawled up and back, up and back for a total of four-100 yard bear crawls. It took some time but every player, Varsity and JV, was able to do the four laps daily. The one who had the most difficulty? Donnie Joe Hickman, the largest player on the field.

Coach McElyea took Hickman to be his special project during that week of conditioning. McElyea was running the entire last few laps with Donnie Joe yelling in his ear encouaging him. Donnie Joe was the last player each day to finish. All the Varsity and all the JVs had finished long before Donnie Joe. But finish he did.

I made it a point to go to Donnie Joe daily as he was trudging into the locker room to congratulate him. I told him numerous time how great he could be if he made up his mind to do so. Donnie Joe became a very good football player for FHS. He was our kick-off and extra-point man his junior and senior years. Donnie Joe got a lot of time at fullback his junior year and was our starter his senior year. He became an outstanding player for The Southern California *Trojans* and various professional teams in his football career. He made up his mind to make himself the best he could be. Donnie Joe was not a quitter.

By the end of the first week of practice I could see we had a concern that presented me with a challange I had not anticipated; players' parents on the field! I should clarify that. It was only one parent who was a problem though several parents took the liberty to stand on the sideline to watch our every move.

One parent was literally standing behind our offensive huddle when we worked on our new offense. Dr. Dave Smith was our team physician. He had a son, Britt Smith, who was to be one of our toughest kids in a few years. The first few days when Dr. Smith stood overly close to our huddles I overlooked it. He was our team physician.

However, he over-stepped his bounds when he criticized me in front of the players as we were practicing our kicking game toward the end of a day's practice. As Coach McElyea and I were positioning our punt team personnel Dr. Smith butted in. He said, "Coach Hicks. You line up your punter way too close to the line of scrimmage. He will get his punts blocked. Get him back deeper."

I almost lost my cool. I turned around to Dr. Smith and quietly said to him, "Dr. Smith, I don't tell you how to perform your appendectomies. Don't you ever again tell me in front of the players what I should do with my football team."

As soon as the words were out of my mouth I felt bad. I could have been much more diplomatic.

Dr. Smith was already on his way to stand with some of his buddies on the sideline; I did not say anything more to him. I doubted if anyone heard what I said. I don't even think Coach Mc heard me and he was standing nearby when the exchange took place. Two other physicians were standing on the sideline that day. Both were from Bisbee, Arizona and I considered both to be my good friends. Both within days of each other called me to tell me they thought I may have alienated Dr. Smith to the point that he was going to resign as *Eagles'* team physician.

The first to call was Dr. George Hershey.(B) George was an outstanding football and track performer for Bisbee High several years after I graduated. He had been in Flagstaff for several years, long enough to have a pretty good grasp of the "good o' boy" network that Coach John Ply had drawn to him over the years. Dr. Dave Smith was one of Ply's closest supporters. They were poker buddies. When Dr. Smith

So You Wanna Be a Legend. So Did I.

was heard to say he couldn't work with "that arrogant Hicks," Dr. Hershey sensed aggitation. Smith would not be team physician much longer.

The second physician to call was Dr. George Yard. George Yard was one of Bisbee's and now Flagstaff's all time great personalities.(B) Yard was much older than both Hershey and me. I remember watching George Yard play football for the Bisbee *Pumas* when I was in grade school. He was one of my schoolboy heroes. Dr. Yard's message was different than Hershey's. He was more subtle. Yard did not mention Dr. Smith by name. He merely said that maybe I should get Dr. Hershey as FHS team physician. I did and I never regretted it. What this episode with Dr. Smith showed me was that the road I had to travel as Head Football Coach at Flagstaff High School would be bumpy. Parental involvement could become troublesome.

Our first game of the 1971 season was against Coconino High School, Flagstaff High's cross-town rival. Coconino was relatively new to Flagstaff. They fielded a varsity football team only since 1968. CHS beat Flag High each year since.

A bitter rivalry existed between the two schools, so much so that it was suggested that I have someone patrol the shopping center parking lot which was on a hill over looking our FHS practice field. CHS could easily have someone up there with spyglasses charting our practices. I had a hard time believing that. Yet, I couldn't help but sneak quick glances over my shoulder to the shopping center parking lot during practices. I was getting paranoid.

As game day drew closer and closer I could sense the tension building, not only among our players but throughout our student body. The entire west side of Flagstaff wanted a win over Coconino, its first ever win over the east side school.

It would be tough. The pressure was on FHS. New coaches, new offense, new defense, new philosophy were hurdles we had to overcome in a short period of time. The *Eagles* had a great week of practice. The enthusiasm and spirit on the team was sky-high. We cut back our daily practice time to 1 hour 30 minutes. We eased up on our intense conditioning. The *Eagles* were ready.

FHS principal Paul Schreiber told me he sensed the student body was very excited about the new school year. There were not any fights and teacher classroom complaints were almost nil. It was a smooth beginning to a new year.

Mr. Shreiber made one other positive comment. He told me that Superintendent Dave Williams and Athletic Director Roy Smith didn't see any of the new coaches going into the practice field storage shed for a quick smoke during practice sessions. Over the years they had often seen smoke billowing out the door of the shed as the team was practicing.

My thought was, *"If the Superintendent and the Assistant Superintendend did not like coaches smoking during practice time, why didn't they tell the coaches to stop?"*

I verbally expressed that question to Mr. Schreiber. He merely shrugged his shoulders.

GAME DAY. FINALLY!

The City Championship was on the line! The new kids on the block, the Coconino High *Panthers* were the reigning champs. Could they successfully defend their championship? On paper they could.

Paul Sweitzer, Sports Editor of the *Arizona Daily Sun,* was having a field day interviewing the coaches, the players and taking pictures at practices of both teams. He went out on a limb and predicted early in the week that Flagstaff High with a new attitude and spirit would win. Paul was impressed with the way the *Eagles* had adapted to the new coaches and the new systems of offense and defense. By the end of the week however, Paul gave the *Panthers* a slight edge due to their history under Coach Bill Epperson of having Flag High's number. Another factor in Paul Sweitzer's mind that tilted the game in favor of CHS was the fact that the game was being played on Coconino's home field.

Flagstaff High did not have a home football field. All FHS home games were played on Coconino's beautiful new field when the *Panthers* were playing out of town.

If the *Panthers* were playing at home that week, FHS played on Northern Arizona University's field. Not a good setup for the *Eagles*. We were the football team without a home field. We felt like the neglected kids in town

The article in the *Daily Sun* by Paul Sweitzer giving the favorite's role to Coconino High was prominently posted on our locker room bulletin board. It was just more fuel for the fire. By game time our kids were pumped. Some of the black kids were jiving around which I did not like until Coach McElyea and Coach Clements told me that was the way black kids got loose. If they had been quiet that would have been bad.

The white kids on the other hand were quiet, going about their business. They weren't at all bothered by the jiving. Quiet was their way to get ready.

Our honorary captians for the game as selected by their teammates were fullback Bruce Evans, halfback Jerry Nichols and tackle Mike Kohlbeck. The three were consistant leaders in our practices; they had the honor of being team leaders for our first win of the season. Coconino won the coin toss and elected to receive. That was the only win they had all night.

Jay Reavis was an excellent punter but only a so-so kick off man. Jay was projected to be our kick off man but Donnie Joe Hickman came on strong the last few weeks. His kick offs were consistantly high and to the five yard line. Donnie Joe won the job. Donnie Joe's opening kick off was taken on the goal line by Coconino running back Brad Thieme; Thieme returned the ball to the CHS 35 yard line. Pretty good field position for the *Panthers* to take over.

CHS ran three running plays and came up fourth and five. They had to punt. Jerry Nichols caught the punt on our 25 yard line. Behind a beautifully set up wall of blockers Nichols returned the ball 75 yards untouched for our first touchdown of the game; and of the year!

Hickman's extra point kick made it FHS: 7-CHS: 0. The FHS crowd was loud to say the least! I hadn't heard that much pandemonium since Carmel High's last second win over King City in 1965.

Our second touchdown came in the third quarter. Quarterback Jerry Hansen hit wide receiver Felton Burr from 18 yards out. Hickman's second extra point kick was good. FHS: 14-CHS: 0

That was how the game ended. 14-0 FHS! What a way to begin the year! What a way to begin a resurgence in Flagstaff High School football!

When the final gun sounded it looked like the entire FHS student body and half the city of Flagstaff was on the field! It took us most of an hour to get to our bus and begin the joyful trip over the hill to our side of town.

As the trip home began so also began a chant, "PARTY! PARTY! PARTY!" I did not like that at all. When the bus pulled in to our school parking lot we were greeted by a host of students, parents and young kids wanting to greet the victors. I quieted down the players before I let driver Tuffy Rice open the bus door. I told them again how proud I was of them, just what this win meant to us. It was big! I also gave them one of my lectures on "drinking and smoking." I cautioned the kids on the consequences of alcohol, not the least of which was possible dismissal from the team if caught.

I wondered just how much good my talk did. McElyea and Clements both told me that student drinking had gotten worse over the past several years. It was the thing to do after athletic events, win or lose. It was the thing to do on weekends-period. They said there was not much we could do about it; just hope that none of our players got caught.

DON'T DO AS WE DO
Do As We Say

Jim and Holly Clements invited all the FHS coaches, wives, some faculty members and other team-insiders to their home for a party of our own. There, of course, was plenty of beer. I remember thinking *"What hypocrites!"*

But, hey, we were adults. The players weren't. It was easy to o.k. our drinking. Students could not handle alcohol until they were older. Adults could. I was disappointed to see how many of the coaches and faculty who were at the party did drink. There were few of us who did not. Joan and I stuck with Pepsi since wine was not available. Judy and Benny Bishop were drinking soft drinks, as were George and Brenda Hershey. It seemed to me that most all the others were going at it pretty well.

From what I could see coming to Flagstaff, drinking was much more accepted among the faculty and students of FHS than it had been in Prescott or Carmel. My mother's lifelong struggle with alcoholism made me frightened of what the effects of alcohol could do if one overdid it.

Besides speaking out against it to my players, what else could I do? Yeah, I could strongly discipline them if they got caught, but what more could I do to help curb some of the drinking? Often as I mulled that concern over in my self-absorbed mind I was reminded of Don Moomaw and his talk about FCA, the Fellowship of Christian

Athletics. Those thoughts did not stay around long however; something else more pressing at the time always got me back to thinking about what was really important, like winning the next football game.

When Coach McElyea, Coach Clements and I reviewed the films of our 14-0 win we saw a lot of good things the *Eagles* did. We were especially impressed with how well our defense adapted to our newly installed *Radar Defense* We watched in awe how many times John Zanzucchi, our tough 145 pound defensive tackle, avoided the block of the 220 pound offensive tackle Coconino had opposite him. We also liked our defensive pursuit. On every CHS running play we had a bunch of white *Eagle* jerseys surrounding the ball carrier. When our defensive personnel avoided blocks, that left them free to go get the guy with the ball. Tackle Mike Kohlbek was all over the field. He wasn't blocked effectively all night, nor was linebacker Lee Haines. Coconino High School could not solve our Radar Defense. They had a dismal 102 yards rushing, only 34 the entire second half. Coach Clements and the entire defense got an A for a job well done.

Our offense was another matter. Our Run and Shoot offense did not do as good a job with the *run* part we would have liked. Bruce Evans, Donnie Joe Hickman, Jerry Nichols and Frank McCain each picked up good yardage at times. We were just too inconsistant. Our offensive linemen needed a lot more work on staying with their blocks and not quitting until the whistle blows the play dead. We had a net 224 yards rushing; we felt we should have done better.

I made some pre-season adjustments in the Run and Shoot Offense as I felt our personnel were not quite suited for the total package. Instead of two split ends we had one tight end, Robert Joyce. We flip-flopped him from one side to the other as needed. Felton Burr and John Kolek split time at wide recever; we filp-flopped them to the opposite end from Joyce. Our quarterbacks were able to adapt to the reading of defensive keys and they did well with the sprint out passing attack the Run and Shoot required. Quarterback Jerry Hansen did a decent job with the *shoot* part. He had a couple of nice completions to Robert Joyce and one to Jerry Nichols on a quick look-in. There were times when I thought Jerry Hansen looked unsure of himself. I wrote that off to inexperience.

All things considered we coaches felt we could win some games this year. We were scheduled to play some of Arizona's year in and year out best teams. Realistically we had no business being on the same field with some of them. Upsets do happen; we knew going into each game that we possibly could win IF we played error free and IF we got some breaks here and there.

We had good press all that week after our big win over Coconino. Teams would no longer overlook the Flag High *Eagles*. The year before FHS went 1-9. Every game but the *Eagles'* 14-13 upset win over Brophy Prep. had been a "'laugher". Not so this year. Word got out pretty fast that FHS was for real.

Our second game of the season was against always tough Cortez High School in Phoenix. The 1-0 *Eagles* were going to be given a lesson in humility. We were pretty cocky going into the game. We were not too cocky after the game.

When we drove into the Cortez High stadium parking lot the players got off the bus and as high school players all over America do, they went out to inspect the field. I went to the Cortez locker room and looked up the head coach as I did every time I was the visiting coach. I knew we were in trouble as soon as I walked into his office. There in the middle of his desk in plain view was <u>The Radar Defense For Winning Football</u> by Jules Yakapovich! The Cortez coach had done his homework. Our defense would be put to the test tonight.

And tested they were. Cortez pounded the ball down our throats all night and won 38-0. That was the bad news; the good news was that we found our quarterback for the next 2 years.

By the middle of the first quarter, starting quarterback Jerry Hansen was not up to the task. He was sacked the first two times he tried to pass through no fault of his. Our offensive line was like sieve; we were completely over-powered by the bigger and faster Cortez *Colts*. Jerry looked very uncertain. He just couldn't get it together. I put in junior Nick Lynn and our offense came alive. We didn't score but I could sense a degree of desire that had not been there since the game began. Nick had a confident presense which seemed to permeate the offense. They broke the huddle with a sharpness which had been lacking. We were losing to a much better team but Nick seemed to lift the team to a new level of desire. We lost but we lost with our heads held high.

Nick had a grasp for the game which was rare for a high school kid. He had a maturity football-wise which Coach Clements put his finger on when we discussed our quarterback situation after the game.

Jim Clements knew that Nick's father, Brad Lynn once played and coached at Notre Dame University. Brad infused his son with a knowledge and love for the game that was just beginning to surface. Nick was on his way to being a very fine quarterback.

I had an opportunity to meet Brad Lynn shortly after Nick's debut in the Cortez game. I found Brad to be a soft spoken unassuming man. He had much coaching experience but in the two years I coached his son, Nick, Brad never once was critical of anything I did.

He said he would not ever be one to give me advice as he was going to stay in the background and let Nick be Nick. I told Brad I would love to have him on the field as a volunteer coach. Brad said that would possibly cause Nick some undue pressure. He was probably right.

Brad Lynn did his coaching of his son at home. Nick's football maturity was nourished at an early age by dinner table conversations. Brad and Nick had many lengthy football talks which gave Nick a knowledge of the finer points of football that most boys never get. One of those "finer points" was revealed when the *Eagles* played Sunnyslope High School in a driving rainstorm. Going into the game I told Nick that the field would be very slippery. Our passing game may not be there.

Nick had a great night passing! He threw for three touchdowns in a 33-12 win. In the locker room after the game I shook Nick's hand to congratulate him on an outstanding performance in adverse conditions. When I pulled my hand away from his mud coated hand I felt something odd.

I looked closely and noticed that each of Nick's fingers on his right hand were wrapped with a muddy piece of tape. The tape was needed to hold the thumbtack Nick had taped to each finger. The points on the tacks were filed down to just barely protrude through the tape; the tacks aided Nick's grip on the football greatly.

Great idea! Highly illegal. Wonder where he learned that trick? Could that be why Notre Dame quarterbacks always did well in the rain?

Brad stayed in the background unlike Jerry Hansen's father, Northern Arizona University Professor, Dr. Hansen. I had several intense discussions with Dr. Hansen as to why Jerry was not our starting quarterback. My reasons were not good enough for him. He made phone calls to Coach McElyea and Coach Clements expressing his thoughts about the "unfair" treatment Jerry was getting.

Parental pressure. It would only get worse.

THE HARD HAT GAME

I'll bet he will! I'll bet he won't! Coach Hicks wouldn't be dumb enough to wear a construction hard hat during the game!

My Bisbee buddy Coach Les Fenderson told me the chatter up and down the halls of Prescott High School was about the hard hat; not so much about who would win and who would lose the game.

Somehow word about the bet I had with some of the pillars of the community about whether or not I would wear the hard hat had gotten around. It was even well known about the derogatory comments Coach Howell made about FHS and our fans. I made sure the *Eagles* heard about that; fuel for the fire.

On Wednesday the week of the game my good friend in Prescott Rio Zaro Sports Editor of the *Prescott Courier* newspaper called me for a pre-game interview Rio's first question was, "Hadley, are you going to wear the hard hat? Howell says there is no way you will."

"Rio, you tell Howell that I would go naked just to see those guys fork out that money. They agreed to give me over $100 if I wear the hard hat. Of course, I am going to wear it."

Coach Howell's retort to my comment as reported in *The Courier* was, "He won't wear the hard hat! I'll see to that."

I knew Wayne Howell well enough to know that he would devise some drastic measure to try to keep me from wearing the hard hat. He himself might try to rip it off of my head or he might try to highjack it before the game. No telling what a tight wad like Howell would do. He stood to lose the money he contributed to the pot, no telling how much.

When game night came I believed I devised a fool-proof plan to protect the hard hat from any trickery Coach Howell might have planned. When our team bus pulled into the Prescott High parking lot we noticed an unusually large number of kids hanging around. I remember thinking, "*Oh, oh, Howell has a bounty on the hard hat.*"

I knew where the bus would be parked. It was a good walk to the back of the PHS Fieldhouse where our locker room was. I knew this. I knew, too, that Wayne Howell had those kids hanging around for a purpose.

I had a plan in place: As we got off the bus I had Manager Johnny Sandoval surrounded by some of our biggest players. Johnny was carrying one of Dr. George Hershey's old black medical bags. The medical bag was tied to a piece of rope attached

So You Wanna Be a Legend. So Did I.

to Johnny's wrist. Johnny's bodyguards had been instructed to be vocal about keeping the crowd of kids away. Johnny and the medical bag got through the gang of kids to our dressing room unmolested.

After the *Eagles* dressed and were ready for pre-game warm up the Specialty Teams went out: the kickers, centers, passers, and backs. No Manager Johnny and the black bag. When the Specialty Team players were warmed up and the rest of the team came on the field, Manager Johnny came with them. He still had the black medical bag tied to his wrist. There were still four *Eagles* surrounding him. I assigned four of our players who were slightly injured and would not be suited up to guard Johnny and the black bag. The four, Jim Bert, Billy Tinnin, Steve Pittard and Vernon Parker wore their White *Eagle* game jerseys; they did a good job looking menacing. There were still a good sized group of kids eyeing the black bag.

When the captains from both FHS and PHS met at the 50 yard line for the flip of the coin, I still had not put on the hard hat. PHS won the toss and would receive. Just before our team ran on the field to kick off I had the team huddle around me for a last minute word of encouragement. When the 11 players on the kickoff team broke the huddle to run on the field, all eyes were on Coach Hicks. Would he now have on the Hard Hat? Nope! Maybe he chickened out.

My good friend Prescott High English teacher Ray Wherley who was in on the bet told me after the game that the most tense moment on the Prescott side of the field was at that moment; just as both teams were getting ready for the kickoff. Still no hard hat. Just as the Head Linesman was getting ready to blow his whistle to officially start the game, I calmly walked over to our ball bag which had been left unguarded the whole time. I dumped out the dozen or so footballs, got the hard hat which had been securely hidden at the bottom of the bag and smugly put it on.

I won the bet and got all my money. Eventually.

As if the hard hat episode wasn't excitement enough, the game was even better. In my book the hard hat game ranks right up there with the game Danny Holman won for Carmel High with his last second 80 yard TD pass to to JT Thomas to beat King City.

This game was won by FHS due to the predictablity of PHS Coach Roger Hightower.

I worked with Coach Hightower for five years as his assistant. There were some things Hightower did the same way game after game, year after year; he never varied.

In our practices the week before we went to Prescott we worked hard on a play that would win the game for us. It was a play we would run on fourth down when we were punting.

Every time an opponent punted to Prescott High, Coach Hightower gave the punt return team the "return right" signal. Every time. It was always "return right". Never "return left". I was banking on Hightower giving "return right" when we punted. What Hightower did on "return right" was have their right defensive end crash hard and make sure the punter punted the ball. The rest of the Prescott team took a step into the punting team's line; then sprinted hard to the left and went down the left sideline to form a wall of blockers for the return man.

Every time-crash the right end hard to make sure the punter kicked the ball; the rest of the team set up a wall to the left. Every time.

I felt certain Hightower would not change for this game. But I wasn't sure. I took no chances and put in "Fake Punt, Screen Right, Screen Left."

Here is what we did. Jay Reavis was our punter and a good athlete. He drilled all week when we practiced punting that he was to get the center's snap and immediately glance to his left from were the PHS right defensive end *may* be coming in hard. I was banking on Hightower not changing. BUT if he did, if he had called "return left" instead of "return right," we were prepared. Our punting team drilled to form a screen to BOTH the right and the left sides.

On the snap of the ball our left guard, left tackle, and our left end faded out to our left to form a screen for a short pass from punter Reavis to our left blocking back if the Prescott right defensive end crashed in hard on Jay.

If Coach Hightower got cute with us and tried to switch up and run "return left," our right guard, right tackle and our right end on the snap of the ball would fade out to our right to form a screen for a short pass to our right blocking back from punter Reavis who was thoroughly drilled to determine from which side Prescott rushed their end.

No matter which side Coach Hightower ran his punt return we had it set up so that our punting team run a screen pass away from the PHS players going down the opposite side. Our back catching the short screen pass from punter Jay Reavis should have clear sailing down the opposite sideline from where most of the PHS team was headed.

On the drawing-board the play looked like a winner. Whatever Coach Hightower did on a fourth down punting situation by PHS we felt we could gamble and catch the *Badgers* off guard. It was definitely a gamble but that is what makes football fun. Gamble. Win some lose some.

The "Fake Punt. Screen right, Screen left" was one of those plays that had to be run at exactly the right time. The right time may or may not come up during a particular game. For the *Eagles* that night the right time came up. It was at the start of the fourth quarter. The score at the time was PHS: 14-FHS: 12. We seemed to have momentum on our side. We started a drive on our own 20 yard line after a PHS punt. We had moved the ball in four plays to our own 45 yard line. We came up third and six. If we did not make a first down we would be in a possible punt situation.

With third and six, I sent in "Roll right. Joyce ten and out." Robert Joyce our big tight end was to run a ten yard out pattern. If he caught the ball for a first down he would be able to get out of bounds to kill the clock. If he did not catch it, we were in a fourth and long situation. We would have a right time for the "Fake Punt. Screen right; Screen left." Maybe.

I had a big decision to make. Coach Mc was squatting near me. I leaned over and asked him, "If we come up short on forth down, should I call Fake Punt?"

Coach McElyea said, "Sure. Why not? Go for it." As he said that he had a look on his face that I couldn't read. Almost like, *Go for it. It is no skin off my nose if we don't make it.*

I didn't have the time to mull over his response. I did that later. Now I had to decide.

We came up short. Prescott High's fine defensive back Duke Flores had done a good job defending Joyce all night long. Duke made a great defensive play on our third and six pass to Joyce. He put a vicious hit on Robert just as quarterback Nick Lynn's pass got there. Joyce could not hold on to the ball. Fourth and six coming up.

I turned to Jay Reavis our punter and said, "Fake punt." There was no hesitation. I patted him on the rear and in he sprinted. Jay was drilled well in practices. He quickly huddled the punt team and gave the play. "Fake Punt" was all he had to say. The team knew what to do. If we could at least pick up a first down here with six yards to go maybe we could go in and score. We had a shot at winning the game right here. If Prescott Coach Hightower had Jack Orr, a PHS spotter, in the pressbox with binoculars it would look to Orr like Reavis had called "punt." He would likely phone down the Hightower, "They're punting." Hightower would likely give the return right signal.

It couldn't have worked any better. We were lucky. PHS's tough defensive right end Don Welch came crashing in just as Coach Hightower had him do on every punt the last several years. The rest of the PHS punt return team peeled off and sprinted down their left sideline just as they had done numerous times in the past.

Eagle punter Jay Reavis got center Vince Lopez's perfect snap of the ball. He quickly glanced and saw Prescott's defensive right end Don Welch flying in at him. Jay took one quick step as though to punt; then avoiding Welch's uncontrolled rush, Jay dumped off a short pass to Bruce Evans our left side blocking back.

With most of the PHS punt return team headed to our right, Bruce had clear sailing down the left sideline to the Prescott High five where he was finally tackled. On the tackle, ball carrier Bruce Evans fumbled into the end zone where Robert Joyce our defensive end recovered it. Touchdown! Final score: FHS: 18-PHS: 14.

When the gun sounded to end the game I immediately took off the hard hat.

The *Eagles* went on from the big hard hat victory to win three out of our last four games of the season. We beat Sunnyslope 33-12; Glendale 32-0; Paradise Valley 18-6. We lost to Washington 0-14. When all was said and done, we had a successful season. We finished 5-5 which was much better than some had predicted. At the AA North Conference coaches' meeting, Flagstaff High's Frank McCain and Mike Kohlbeck were named to the All Conference football team by a vote of the Conference coaches. Jerry Nichols and Bruce Evans received honorable mention.

We achieved FHS's best record in five years. We had 14 varsity veterans returning for the 1973 season; plus some very tough kids off of JV Coaches Benny Bishop and Eddie Garcia's four wins-three loses team; things were looking up for the *Eagles*.

FEELING THE *PULSE*
FHS Faculty Room

I felt pretty good about my first season as Head Football Coach at Flagstaff High School. I had put a winning team on the field. The morale of the team was good. Many of the players came up to me after the season to thank me for restoring a positive environment to the football program. Most of the students I was in contact with on a daily basis showed me the utmost of respect. It was always a smile and a "Good morning, Coach." I got very few surly looks. I could tell that most of the students liked me.

Why then did I have such an uneasy feeling about Flagstaff High School in general? For some reason I did not feel that I fit in, that I was an "outsider." One could usually feel the "pulse" of a high school by observing the school's faculty room. The feeling in the FHS Faculty Room was so much different than what I felt in the Carmel High School Faculty Room or the Prescott High Faculty Room. The feeling of camaraderie that was so welcoming to me as a new faculty member in both those schools was sorely missing at FHS. Oh, they would smile and say "hello" when I went into the room. Some even commented about the Friday night's football game. Something was missing. I just sensed it. I became aware after a few weeks that the faculty that were in the FHS Faculty Room were the same ones day after day. There did not seem to be the varying influx of faculty in and out that I was used to. One other thing I soon noticed; very few of the women teachers went in the Faculty Room. It seemed to be a men's only clique.

Those who frequented the Faculty Room the most were male teachers who had been at FHS for many years. Former Head Football Coach John Ply was a mainstay. He was one of the most popular teachers at FHS. Gil Corona FHS Baseball Coach and Business teacher, had been at Flag High for quite a few years; as had Fred Anderson Head Basketball Coach and Driver Training teacher.

Sometimes those three were the only ones in the Faculty Room when I went in. Other times there were a few others of the same ilk. I didn't go in very often. I was obviously an outsider and I felt it.

I found that the majority of the FHS Faculty pretty much stuck to their own classrooms during their free time or two or three of them would congregate in a class room near their own.

The FHS Faculty was fractured. "Cliquish" is not the right word. The Faculty were not at all snobbish. They just hung out in their own comfort groups.

Terry Davis' classroom seemed to be the place for the History Department to meet. Doug Baker, Dick Kuhn and sometimes Bruce Parker got together with Terry and discussed a wide spectrum of current events all the way from the latest Viet Nam news to the fight at the homecoming dance. They were all great guys. I enjoyed my all too infrequent visits with them.

In my eight years at FHS I never felt that I quite fit in. I am sure that a lot of that was my own self-absorption with the fact that I was Head Football Coach. Period. I had no other extra-curricular activities such as Speech Team or baseball coach. My total focus was on being the best football coach possible. Everything else was secondary.

I was told by Athletic Director Roy Smith when I had my initial interview for the football job that I could also be Head Baseball Coach when Gil Corona retired which was to be in a year or so.

Corona retired at the end of my first year. Eddie Garcia, a Crafts teacher, got the job. I didn't ask Roy Smith if I had been considered and he never brought up the subject.

Content With Mediocrity

The first few years I was employed by the Flagstaff School District I became aware that the Administration as well as some long time teachers were content with mediocrity. They had been doing things their way so long that any new concept was ignored. Why bother? Things had gone along pretty well for years. Why change?

One example of this attitude I saw was the pitiful excuse for a Coaches' Locker Room which was adjacent to the pitiful excuse for the Varsity Team's Locker Room. The two areas were in need of much renovation. They had obviously been in disrepair for years.

When Athletic Director Roy Smith gave me a tour of the FHS Athletic Facilities I was appalled by the murky, foul smelling dungeon-like area the male athletes and coaches had to use. A screened off area for the coaches and shelves of athletic equipment was all that separated the athletes from the coaches. Both coaches and athletes had to use the same toilets and showers. The whole place looked to me like it should have been condemned years ago.

When I discussed this with Mr. Smith I asked him if money had been a problem for not getting the area renovated. He said that money was not the problem. He said they had just put it off, they had just not gotten around to it. "Someday" he said.

It was into this most unpleasant premises that Al Norton had to come each morning. Al was a Native American Hopi Indian. He was the head custodian for the men's locker facilities.

Many mornings I found Al on his knees scrubbing out the men's urinals and commodes. A filthy job which Al always did with a smile and a, "Good morning, Coach Hicks." I had utmost respect for Al Norton. It was sad that he had to work in those conditions. The FHS School District had been negligent in my opinion.

Smooth Sailing
Until the Phone Rang

In the summer of 1972 after my first year of teaching-coaching at Flagstaff High School my wife Joan and I purchased two and a half acres of beautiful pine woods just outside the Flagstaff City limits. My good Bisbee buddy Dr. George Yard, who owned the property, gave us a "deal we couldn't afford to turn down" as he put it. We bought the land at "fair Bisbee-market value."

Joan and I were excited. We always wanted to live in the pines. We got busy looking for affordable housing to build on our new homestead. We never owned a home before. We always rented. Owning my own home in the pines would give me status in Flagstaff. I felt. I knew I would gain more significance, feel better about myself. I had resigned myself to the fact that for some reason I was destined to be just a high school coach. Being head coach at Arizona State University was not very realistic; head coach at Flagstaff High School was to be my lot in life.

I worked to be the best high school coach in Arizona. I would find my significance in that.

Joan was good at budgets and money matters. I wasn't. I put all that stuff into her hands. I had other things to worry about, like having another winning season which was coming up soon. I was on my way. My future looked bright with a new home being built, a great family and a prominent position as Head Football Coach at Flag High. How lucky could I get!

Sometime in late July I started getting regular phone calls from a Mrs. Eva Vandevier. Mrs. Vandevier was the mother of Mark Vandevier one of our returning football players. Mark was a starting linebacker for us in 1971. The gist of all her calls were centered around Mrs. Vandevier's insistance that I make sure that Mark makes All-State the coming football season. Mark and Mrs. Vandevier had their sights set on a stellar season for Mark, one that would get Mark a full-ride scholarship to Arizona State University. Of course I could not guarantee that Mark would get a scholarship to ASU much less that he would make All-State. Mrs. Vandevier would not hear any of that. I was told pointedly that if I "used" Mark correctly his toughness would do the rest Mark Vandevier was a tough kid. He had decent size; about 6"1' and 210 pounds; he was strong and quick. Mark played offensive guard and defensive linebacker. He had been a starter as a junior.

Toughness was not a problem for Mark. His big negative was his lack of discipline. Mark at times was like a loose cannon on the field. He got it in his head that instead of what defensive coach Jim Clements wanted his linebacker to do in a certain situation, Mark Vandevier did something radically different, often to the detriment of the team.

I tried to gently explain all this to Mrs. Vandevier. The more I tried to explain the more insistant she became that Mark would make All State. If I wasn't zeroed in on her wishes when the season started, if I didn't promote Mark for state honors to the newspapers at the beginning of the season Mrs. Vandevier would not hesitate to transfer Mark to Winslow High School 30 miles east of Flagstaff.

Winslow High was coached by Coach Emil Nassar a long time, very successful football coach. Mrs. Vandevier made it plain that she and Coach Nassar were friends and he would treat Mark right. Nassar would get Mark a scholarship to ASU. Eva Vandevier did not seem to understand that a coach cannot "get" a football player a scholarship. He can recommend only. I never realized that one woman, one mother, could be so insistant, so obnoxious. Her phone calls went on daily well into the start of the season. I even had several calls after midnight. She was a real pain, and she got worse!

The *Eagles'* "Stand-Around Defense".

Great things were expected from the *Eagles* as the 1972 season got underway. We had an experienced team returning, we had veterans starting in most positions both offensively and defensively.

As Head Coach I received rave reviews from the press state wide. To quote one source, "Hicks has infused the power of positive thinking into football at Flagstaff High and the results are already beginning to show. His dressing room is plastered with slogans

So You Wanna Be a Legend. So Did I.

that forbid negativism--many of them words of wisdom by the late Vince Lombardi--and his attitude was best summed up in his first talk to his players last May.

'You must learn never to accept defeat,' he told them quite bluntly. He sounded like a man who meant what he said. He's gone on to prove he's that kind of man."

The Hicks led Flagstaff High *Eagles* opened the 1972 season with a 6-19 loss to Coconino High School, followed the next week by a 14-38 stomping by St. Mary's High School. We opened what was forecast as a promising season for Flag High by going 0-2 right out of the gate. The Flagstaff High faithful led by Mrs. Vandevier and others were getting restless. Our "stand up" Radar Defense was getting raked over the coals around town. The defense was beginning to be refered to as the "Hicks stand around defense."

Even though Dr. Dave Smith was no longer our team physician he still managed to attend a number of our practices. He always attracted a crowd when he came to practice. Dr. Smith and his buddies grouped together on the sidelines and analyzed our practices. I could tell when they were making sarcastic remarks as the laughter could be heard, especially during our defensive practice segments. I knew our "stand around defense" was up for scrutiny. I got a little upset when Coach Ken McElyea often managed to chit-chat with Dr. Smith and his buddies during our practices. He seemed to fit right in.

We lost the last game of the season to Prescott High School 18-20 in a driving snowstorm. We scored with seconds remaining to make the score FHS: 18-PHS: 20. Our attempt to go for two points to tie the game was stopped just short of the goal line. Lady Luck was not with me that time. Our season record was a mediocre four wins-six losses.

Several weeks after the season ended I got word from the *Arizona Interscholastic Athletic Association* (AIA) that we had to forfeit our four wins. Timothy Blackwater one of our tough Native American kids was never cleared to play by the AIA. When our team took physical examinations at the beginning of practice that season Dr. Hershey, our team physician, informed me that Timothy did not have a birth certificate. In checking with our Athletic Director Roy Smith I was told that is pretty common with the kids off the Reservation. The AIA would accept a valid Census Number from *The Bureau of Indian Affairs* (BIA) for athletic eligibility purposes in lieu of a birth certificate.

Mrs. Eileen Manzer our FHS Front Office Receptionist called the BIA to report the Blackwater problem. The BIA told Mrs. Mazer that they would find Timothy's Census Number "by the end of the week." In the meantime Timothy was cleared to practice with us but he could not suit up for any of the games. Week after week went by. No Census Number. Timothy was at every practice. He scrimmaged with us. He worked his tail off knowing that he could not play until the BIA sent his Census Number. Timothy was at every home game sitting on our bench but not in uniform. He did not go on away games.

By season's end the BIA had still not sent a Census Number for Timothy. Mrs. Manzer called them each week. No results. The BIA just never got the job done. A fine young man was forced to sit out a whole football season and not suit up or play in a game. The AIA said FHS would have to forfeit our four wins due to Timothy's practicing with us. I had not understood that aspect of the situation. I knew he could not play in a game but had no idea he could not practice either. The AIA was adamant. We would forfeit. As Head Coach I should have known the rule.

I decided to award Timothy Blackwater a football letter even though he had not played in a single game. We knew by the time the Football Banquet rolled around that the *Eagles* had to forfeit our four wins. It was widely publicized. Still it was unanimously approved by the team to award Timothy his letter at the Awards Banquet.

My job at the Banquet was to call each member of our Varsity Football Team to the podium to receive his letter.

I was a bit uneasy about calling Timothy to come up in front of all the team and their parents. Timothy did not have his parents there. He sat with his buddies and their parents. Native American kids are overly shy about being singled out in front of a group. When I called Timothy's name I told the assembled crowd about Timothy's struggle all season with the BIA. The BIA's lack of assistance in getting Timothy his Census Number was frustrating to all of us. Timothy received extended applause as he approached the podium to receive his award. He was very sober. He did not appear nervous at all.

I made some complimentary remarks about Timothy's commitment to the *Eagles*. I thanked him sincerely for that commitment. Timothy accepted the award, shook my hand and took several steps away from the podium. He paused, got a slight grin on his face and returned to the podium.

He leaned into the microphone and spoke very quietly, "When Custer.....ride away to Little Big-Horn....he told BIA not to do anything until he come back."

That brought the house down! Timothy received another long applause after that remark, a great one-liner!

The forfeitures landed right on my lap. As Head Coach I was responsible. As President Harry Truman was famous for saying, "The buck stops here."

Officially our four wins were wiped out. Unofficially we all knew we had won those four games. Much luster had come off of *Eagle* Head Football Coach Hadley Hicks.

Mark Vandevier did not make All-State. He walked-on at Arizona State. Our outstanding Quarterback Nick Lynn went to the United States Air Force Academy where he continued his football-Air Force career. Donnie Joe Hickman got a full-ride scholarship to the University of Southern California. He played in three Rose Bowls with the *Trojans*. Donnie Joe's professional career included stints with the Washington *Redskins,* and the Detriot *Lions*.

Mrs. Vandevier cranked up the telephone. It had not been a good season. Things would get worse.

"Get rid of Hicks"

As I walked into school one morning in mid-December Mrs. Eileen Manzer, Receptionist/Secretary to Principal Paul Schreiber, had an upsetting message for me. She said that I was to go immediately to Superintendent Dave Williams' office. "It is important," was all Mrs. Manzer said.

The Superintendent's Office was on the same piece of property as FHS so I did not have far to walk but far enough to fill my head with all kinds of drastic possibilities for the meeting. The over-riding ramification in my mind was, "*I am being fired...losing season. We are going to lose our home in the pines.*"

Sitting around Superintenent Williams' large oval meeting table were the Superintendent, Assistant Superintendent Don Clark, High School Principal Paul Schreiber, and Athletic Director Roy Smith. The meeting was obviously important.

Without any preliminary remarks Mr. Williams got right to the point. He held up a typed letter and said, "Coach Hicks, some prominant people in Flagstaff have signed a petition for your removal as Head Football Coach. I will read the allegations; I want you to respond to them."

So that was it. A signed petition for my my removal as Head Football Coach. I had a dreadful sinking feeling in my stomach. I was almost panic-stricken. I sat in disbelief as Mr. Williams read the brief letter.

When he had finished reading the letter I was speechless. I was absorbed by the thought of losing our newly purchased piece of land out in the pines. I sat with my head bowed for what seemed to be an eternity. I don't ever remember being so shocked or so scared in all my life. The four men before me held my future in their hands.

Mr. Williams was the first to speak. He said, "What do you say to those allegations?"

My thoughts were beginning to clear. I was getting angry. I said, "Besides Eva Vandevier who else signed that thing?"

Each of the four seemed a bit startled at my mention of Mrs. Vandevier. Mr. Williams said it did not matter who signed the petition; they just wanted to know how I answered what was alleged.

I was getting pretty hot by this time. I told my four judges and jury all about Mrs. Vandevier bugging me for the past several months. I said I knew she instigated the petition because Mark had not received any recognition and would never make All State. None of the four men acknowledged that Mrs. Vandevier was behind the petition nor did they say she wasn't.

I was on a roll. I continued by saying that I could get most of the football team to sign a counter-petition to keep me. Besides that I knew I could get a good number of parents and *Eagle* fans to sign the counter-petition as well.

As far as the allegations were concerned I told them I would not give them credence by answering them. They were all "a bunch of crap," my exact words.

Mr. Williams thanked me for my time and excused me by saying they would get back with me in a week or so. I couldn't believe what I had just gone through! Mr. Williams was the only one of the four administrators who spoke during the entire inquisition. None of them seemed to have any compassion for what I was going through. None of them offered any encouragement. Their silence seemed to indicate the petition held some validity.

The next few weeks seemed to creep by. I expected to be called back to Mr. Williams' office any day. I expected the worse. My competative spirit drove me during those difficult times. I vowed to work all the harder for the 1973 season even though I might not be around. I didn't tell anybody about the petition. I don't think I even told my wife.

The football season of 1972 had be the most difficult time of my coaching career. It was not the losses that were so difficult to swallow nor was it the *Eagle* team. Those kids were great. They never gave up and never developed a negative attitude. On paper we were losers. In my heart and mind we were winners. What was so difficult for me was the supposed parental unrest among those who sided with the petition signers. I carried the questions of how many and who signed the petition into the winter months. In my mind most of the community wanted me gone.

Shortly after Christmas I drummed up the courage to talk to Principal Paul Schreiber. He was the only administrator whom I felt was compassionate enough to understand my anxiety over the unresolved issue of the petiton. I had real concerns. Was the issue going to be carried over to the 1973 season? Was I going to be around to coach next fall? Would I be put on some kind of probation? Would my family and I be able to live in our new home in the woods?

Mr. Schreiber was rather taken back by my questions. He apologized sincerely for not getting back to me. He thought Superintendent Williams had told me. The petition was being dropped by the administration. Only six of Mrs. Vandevier's friends and relatives had actually signed it, not enough to get too excited about. Mr. Schreiber told me that I had the full support of the Flagstaff District Administration.

My questions: *If the number of signers was "not enough to get excited about" why did Superintendent Williams make such a big deal out of it? Why in the world didn't Superintendent Williams get back to me to put my worries to rest?* I wish I had the guts to ask Mr. Schreiber those questions. I was too relieved to hear him say what he said. I was just glad to drop it.

DONNIE JOE HICKMAN
Proved Them Wrong

When Donnie Joe finished his senior football season at FHS he stood 6"3' tall and weighed 275 pounds. He was still one of the fastest kids in school. Donnie Joe's offensive statistics were not overly impressive. It was obvious to me that if Donnie Joe was going to play college football he would do so as an offensive lineman.

I had several serious discussions with Donnie Joe regarding his future. I told Donnie Joe that there was no doubt in my mind that he could play Division I football. He could play with the best. He was bright enough to get a degree from a major university with football as his vehicle. Donnie Joe did not think so. He wanted to stay home in Flagstaff and go to Northern Arizona University. I told Donnie Joe that in my opinion that would be a big mistake. If Donnie Joe stayed in Flagstaff, there would be peer pressure on him to play the "big man." He knew what I meant. There would be many familiar avenues for Donnie to go down with his buddies which could lead to trouble.

Donnie Joe said he just did not think he could play football in a Division I school. If he wanted to get a college degree via football it would have to be at Northern Arizona University. Nobody else would want him.

One evening I received a surprising phone call from a coach who seemed very interested in Donnie Joe. The call was from John McKay, Head Football Coach at the University of Southern California. Coach McKay had looked over the list of players I recommended to him and he said he was interested in Donnie Joe Hickman. Coach McKay told me he was going to fly one of his assistant coaches to Flagstaff at a convenient time for us to visit with his assistant. We set a date for the Southern Cal assistant coach, Donnie Joe and me to get together.

When I called Donnie Joe about the phone call and the upcoming visit from a coach from the University of Southern California *Trojans,* he did not believe me. I had to talk to Donnie's mother to tell her before Donnie Joe believed me. The next day the news was all over school. Donnie Joe was being recruited by Southen Cal! An SC coach was coming to Flagstaff to talk to Donnie Joe!

One of the most surprised teachers at FHS was History Teacher Bruce Parker. Bruce approached me during the day and asked me if I had indeed recommended Donnie Joe to USC? When I assured him I had recommended Donnie Joe, Bruce was incredulous. He said, "Hadley, there is no way Donnie Joe can make it at Southren Cal. Donnie Joe is not disciplined nor motivated academically not to mention his lack of the football skills needed at that level."

Bruce Parker would eat his words.

The Southern Cal assistant coach liked what he saw when he met with Donnie Joe, so much so that he flew Donnie Joe to Los Angeles to meet Coach John McKay and the rest of the *Trojan* football staff. During Donnie Joe's weekend visit he was put in a pick-up basketball game with a number of SC football players including the famous O. J. Simpson. The basketball court the pick-up game was played on was an outdoor cement court directly outside the Southern Cal football office. Intently watching the game through an office window as Donnie Joe got bounced around by the football players was Coach McKay and some of his staff. They were impressed with the way Donnie Joe handled himself. He more than held his own.

Donnie Joe returned to Flagstaff with a "Letter of Intent" he and his dad and mom had to sign for Donnie Joe to be accepted as a scholarshiped football player at the University of Southern California. They all three signed the letter and the rest is history.

When Bruce Parker heard that Donnie Joe had signed with Southern Cal his comment to me was, "Hadley, Donnie Joe will be back here before Christmas." Bruce Parker was right. Donnie Joe was back before Christmas. Coach John McKay had given his Southern California *Trojans* a Christmas break before they got back to business of preparing for Ohio State in the 1974 *Rose Bowl.* Flagstaff High's Donnie Joe Hickman would play in the *Rose Bowl.* Bruce Parker wasn't the only skeptic who doubted Donnie Joe Hickman's academic and athletic abilities. Mrs. Mary Lavin also doubted. Mrs. Lavin, FHS English teacher and my former Speech Teacher at Arizona State University, was frightened to death one day shortly before Christmas vacation. Her classroom door suddenly opened and standing before her with a huge grin on his face was Mrs. Lavin's most troublesome former student, Donnie Joe Hickman. Mrs. Lavin was genuinely afraid of Donnie Joe when she had him in class his senior year. Without a word Donnie Joe walked over to Mrs. Lavin, gave her a big hug and apologized to her for all the trouble he had caused her. Mrs. Lavin said Donnie Joe Hickman gave her the best Christmas present she had in many years.

A New Beginning

When Cocohino High School was opened in 1968 the Flagstaff School District was split in half. We had two schools AA size instead of one AAA size school. For some unknown reason FHS stayed in the AAA League North even though we were AA sized. It made no sense. After Mr. Schreiber gave me a new lease on life in January 1973, I spent much time that summer analyzing the football program. We had one more year in the AAA North Conference. What changes did I need to make?

One change I had to make was to replace Coach McElyea. He and I had come to an agreement. He could no longer support much of what I stood for. He and Dr. Smith seemed to be on the same page there. I had the gut-feeling that Ken McElyea wanted to get off what he and Dr. Smith saw as a "sinking ship." We agreed that it would be best if he resigned, which he did.

Coach McElyea was replaced by one of McElyea's fellow Junior High teachers, Rick Smith. Rick was destined for many outstanding years as a football coach at FHS.

Fast Forward to the 1980's

As I was writing this section for my book and mulling over changes I initiated for the football program in 1973, something I read way back in the 1980's was brought back to me; it hit me hard back then. I had read the book titled, <u>Winning. It's How You Play the Game</u> written by Baylor University Head Football Coach Grant Teaff. This book was written in the early 1980's.

Coach Teaff said some things which made me realize that not only were changes made in our FHS Football Program back in 1973, but changes were forthcoming in Head Football Coach Hadley Hicks personally which were long overdue.

Now as I begin to write about our 1973 season and beyond I feel it would be appropriate to consider Coach Grant Teaff's words that impacted me back in 1983. Coach Teaff wrote a section in his book called, "Loyalty Makes a Difference". This section was an eye opener for me. The following are several quotes from that section:

"Coaches, as well as players, have played a special part in my life. I have learned much more from them than I have taught.

Coaches come in two categories, those who are working to become head coaches, and those who are committed to growing where they are planted. It is great that in coaching we can fall into either category and do what we love to do--work with young people in their total development."

Ouch! That hurt! I couldn't help but reflect back on my "commitment to growing where I was planted." Had I been committed to growing where I was planted when I was "just an assistant coach" in Prescott High School under Head Coach Roger Hightower? Absolutely not! My total commitment and focus was on working to make ME recognized as the one who should be the Head Coach! It was all about *me*.

I was a lousey assistant coach; I did not support Coach Hightower. I was critical of him behind his back. As I reflect on this I am better able to understand Coach McElyea's attitude.

Again to quote Grant Teaff in referring to his assistant coaches, *"These men have invested their lives with me at Baylor."*

I did not invest anything with Coach Hightower much less my life! I am very thankful that I had the opportunity to visit with Coach Hightower and with sincerity of motive ask him to forgive me for my disloyalty to him and his football program. Roger graciously shook my hand and said he forgave me.

My former Bisbee *Puma* teammate Ken McElyea had not been a loyal assistant coach, yet neither had I been loyal to Coach Hightower. Should I then harbor ill feelings towards Ken McElyea? Of course not. Several other assistant coaches I had in the ensuing years exhibited traits of disloyalty which caused me anxiety. Should I harbor ill feelings towards them. Of course not. These men had *"been planted"* with me. I pray they all grew from that experience.

WAS FCA THE ANSWER?

I don't know why it was but ever since I left Carmel High School and its permissive leanings, I had the feeling our high school youth were fast becoming more and more rebellious.

The Beatniks of Carmel appeared at Prescott High School as Hippies. Their life styles and appearances were the same: pot smoking, long hair, "go to hell attitude" towards authority figures.

That same attitude was present when I got to Flagstaff High and it was becoming even more prevalent with each new year. Some of our good athletes were taking that road. As Head Football Coach I had to do something.

But what? I had a tough dress/conduct code. My football players knew I did not want them wearing long hair; to their ears was the limit. I did not allow earrings. I still held to Bobby Winkles' "yes sir, no sir" respect for authority attitude.

The former Arizona State *Sun Devil* baseball coach was still a household name in Arizona. When I laid out my dress code I always referenced Bobby Winkles. Forcing rules on the athletes did not seem to be the answer. Each year I found it more and more difficult to make the players toe-the-line. I even rethought the "Lettermen's Oath of Conduct" that I tried one year at Carmel High. That failed miserably.

I wasn't about to subject myself to ridicule again. It seemed like each time I got in one of those pensive moods I was hit with the same thought: *Don Moomaw....Fellowship of Christian Athletes...Christ-like living...FCA...high schools all over California...*

It was always the same. Bits and pieces of Don Moomaw's speech at that football clinic at St. Mary's College in Moraga, California came back to me. The brief reminders would override whatever else I was trying to get a handle on at the moment.

Finally I gave in. I wrote The Fellowship of Christian Athletes headquarters in Kansas City, Missouri and got information on how to start what they called a *Huddle Group*. I was sent all I needed to get started, including a packet of lessons for the first few meetings.

It was strongly recommended that when we started a Huddle Group that we have the students pay a Membership Fee. By becoming a member of The National FCA Association they would receive a monthly magazine with articles and stories of well known Christian athletes, college and professional athletes. Plus, the FCA Huddle Leader would receive monthly lesson outlines for weekly meetings.

Since I was going to attempt to get a FCA Huddle Group started by myself I decided not to push the membership aspect of it. If I was able to recruit ten or so interested athletes, I may look into membership status for the FHS FCA Huddle sometime in the future. As I looked over the information I was initially sent by FCA I could see that it might be just what FHS athletes needed to help steer them away from the declining moral life style which seemed to be so attractive to our young people. It was sure worth a try.

I advertised around school several weeks in advance of FCA's initial meeting: it was mentioned in the classrooms in each day's announcements; I had several Cheerleader made posters displayed in the halls; I pushed it hard to my football team. All FHS knew a new school club was on the horizon.

Mr. Charlie Morgan, Vice Principal gave us permission to hold FCA meetings in my classroom on Monday evenings. He suggested that since FCA was a religious organization that I ask each student's parents to sign a permission slip allowing their son to attend. I did so and was surprised at the response. Over ten permission-slips were turned in the evening of our first meeting and several more showed up without permisson slips which they said they would turn in next meeting. I was enouraged by the first turnout.

For the most part our first meeting was more social than religious. I had not thought to ask parents to help with treats. I bought cookies, donuts and pop and that seemed to do the trick. I asked for volunteers to have their parents donate some treats for the next meeting which we agreed would be the following week.

I could see from the material that the National FCA Office sent that it wouldn't be too tough teaching the first several lessons. The Teacher's Guide was outlined so well that all I had to do was read the lessons ahead of time. The Teacher's Guide suggested that for starters we should explain the difference between The Old Testament and The New Testament. That was a good place for me to start. I had no clue. I told the kids that I was going to learn as much if not more than most of them. My Bible knowledge was very skimpy. By reading the lessons ahead of time I hoped to not appear too ignorant.

I was pleased that two Biblically informed new comers to FHS had shown up the first night. They had been in FCA at the school they attended previously. Robin and Keith Baker were the sons of new FHS basketball coach Doug Baker. Neither Robin nor Keith were shy about speaking out. They got me off the hook several times that night. I asked the group questions the Teacher's Guide suggested I ask. I wasn't too sure of exactly how to explain the answers. Robin and Keith came to my rescue. We had some good discussions.

All in all I felt pretty good about the start FCA had. The kids seemed interested in religious topics. Some besides Robin and Keith were familiar with Biblical teaching

So You Wanna Be a Legend. So Did I.

and they asked good questions. Some of the questions I could answer; those I couldn't Robin and Keith Baker could.

New Church in Town.
Victory Chapel "Rabble-Rousers".

A favorite discussion topic at some of our FCA meetings was good natured talk about the various churches the guys attended. Some laughed about the way the Catholics said the same prayers over and over. Some said the Methodists always got out earlier than the other churches and beat everyone to the Pizza Hut. The Presbyterians were known for having an off-key choir made up mostly of old men and old women. The Baptist Church on the hill had a new pastor who did nothing but scream at the people.

One night Bill Phillips, a junior football player, brought a copy of the evening's *Daily Sun* to the meeting to show us a front page picture and article about a new church in Flagstaff. The picture showed several policemen ushering some young men into a squad car. The caption under the picture told of these young men illegally distributing religious material on street corners in Flagstaff. They were called "rabble-rousers". They accosted people on the streets and forced them to take religious material saying, "You are going to hell if you don't read this!"

The accompanying article went into detail about the church and its religious philosophy. I was interested in reading the article because it mentioned Prescott, Arizona. According to the article the church had its start in Prescott under the leadership of a Pastor Wayman Mitchell.

I really sat up and took notice when I read that one of Mitchell's assistants, a young man named Ron Burrell, was an assistant pastor at this new church in Flagstaff. Ron Burrell! Holy cow! I knew Ron from my days at Prescott High School! Ron Burrell was one of the long-haired, dope smoking hippies who as far as I could recall, was kicked out of Prescott High School. What is he doing as an assistant pastor at this new church?

The article in *The Daily Sun* quoted the church's head pastor, a guy named Jack Harris, as saying this new church, Victory Chapel, was going to turn Flagstaff, Arizona upside-down for Jesus Christ!

They would do that alright. In the process they would destroy many families and individual lives. I was to find this out firsthand.

"How come no Mormon guys come to FCA?"

Flagstaff, Arizona had one of Arizona's largest populations of Mormons. A large percentage of FHS students were Mormons. They added to the school environment in many positive ways.

We always had some good tough Mormons on our football teams. Just a few on my first team in 1971 were Randy Rhoton, Jerry Hansen, Paul Thurber, and Dan Dowell. There may have been others that I wasn't aware of. Most of the Mormon kids were good students. They were active in school activities. Many held class offices. They seldom caused trouble in their classes. They were for the most part model students.

The question posed by one of our FCA Huddle members after the second or third meeting was a good one, "How come no Mormons guys come to FCA?" I could not answer that. One of the Bakers, Robin or Keith, said, "Because they are not Christian." That response certainly opened up a can of worms! Much give and take took place for almost a half hour. Danny Cox one of our fine football players finally suggested that we get one of the Mormon *Elders* to come to a meeting and answer our questions.

The Mormons in FHS were given an hour of release time once per week to attend a class on Mormonism held off campus. The Mormon Elder who taught the class was a very nice guy. He was at all of our school events and was known by all the students, Mormon and non-Mormon.

Danny Cox volunteered to ask the Mormon Elder to come to a meeting. Some of our FCA kids did not think the Mormon Elder would come. "They are very strict about not going to another religion's stuff," was the comment made. Danny said he could talk the Elder into coming.

He did. The Elder came to our next meeting.

Mormonism 101

It was a most interesting meeting. I was especially interested. I had dated Mormon girls when I was in high school. My good friend Coach Max Spilsbury former great football coach at Northeran Arizona University, was a Mormon; I wanted to attend BYU, the Mormon University when Coach Spilsbury was considered for the Head Football job there. I always admired the Mormon's emphasis on family and I liked the Mormon students I had in class at FHS. Yes, I was very interested in what the meeting would reveal.

The classroom was packed. A few parents had come as well as a few more students than I expected. Coach Doug Baker, FHS Basketball Coach was there which pleased me. He was a Christian and could no doubt answer some questions which might come up. Robin and Keith Baker did not seem to mind their dad being present. In fact, they sat by him.

The Mormon Elder seemed glad to be there too. He joked and kidded with several of the FCA kids. He seemed right at home.

I got right to the point, "Why don't any of the Mormon students come to our Fellowship of Christian Athletes meetings?"

His answer seemed reasonable to me.

He said, "We Mormons feel that it is very important that Mormon children learn early to worship Jesus Christ with their family. We have many Church functions which involve the entire family. Our high school age kids just do not have time to attend other religious activities. We don't tell them they can't, they just make that choice. Their families are very important to them."

At that point Coach Doug Baker spoke up, "Who do Mormons say Jesus Christ is?" The Elder did not hesitate to answer.

The Elder quoted several Mormon books: "Jesus was begotten by a sexual relationship between Mary and God the Father who has a body."

"It was the personage of the Father who begat the body of Jesus."

"Jesus was begotten, conceived and born in the normal and natural course of events, for he is the Son of God, and that designation means what it says."

The Elder said further, "Jesus Christ is an important member of the Godhead."

The Elder continued saying that Mormons are Christians who believe the Bible is the Word of God as are three other books: The Pearl of Great Price, Doctrine and Covenants and The Book of Mormon.

The Book of Mormon rang a bell with me. That was the book that my Arizona State *Sun Devil* teammate, John Allen gave me when we were talking about religion after football practice one day. All I could remember about it was that it was a boring book about some obscure Indian tribes in America.

Coach Baker and the Elder got into it pretty good. Neither of them got angry but they both felt strongly about their personal beliefs.

Coach Baker said that Christians believe that the Bible is the true and inspired Word of God. The Elder said that Mormons believe that, too; "as far as the Bible is interpreted," he added. I could not follow that logic.

As the meeting came to a close it was pretty obvious to me that Mormons would probably not be attending our FCA meetings. And that was o.k.

The Mormons were Christians just as we were, only a different *brand* of Christian. FCA had gotten off to a good start even without Mormons. By the end of the 1973-1974 school year, the Flagstaff High School *Fellowship of Christian Athletes* had begun to establish themselves as an active School Club; we would only get stronger in the following years.

SUSIE

For our daughter Susie the 1973-'74 school year brought her both good news and bad news. The good news was that Susie was entering FHS as a sophomore. She and her friends were finally going to taste the exciting life they had only heard about. They would have many more cute boys to flirt with than at the Junior High. The Junior High boys were so immature. The bad news was that Susie was "Coach Hicks' daughter." The cute boys were hesitant to date the Head Football Coach's daughter. I was also a Speech and English teacher. My classroom was at the head of Sophomore Wing; all sophomores had to walk past my classroom sometime during the school day. That was a huge embarassment for Susie. The really bad news for Susie Hicks was that she could not wear make-up as she had at the Junior High School.

For the past four years at the Junior High School, Susie would leave her house devoid of make-up as per "Dad's rules." On the way to the Junior High Susie always stopped at Susie Smith's house. The two would then spend time applying mascara, lipstick, rouge and whatever else it took for them to be beautiful. Susie could go all day without laying eyes on her parents. The make-up was easy enough to get off before she went home for the evening.

Now all that freedom was ruined. Susie had to walk past my classroom several times each day. She was always with a group of giggling girls. Susie would not look at me nor would she speak to me.

I made it my priority to speak to her. Sometimes I would go out of my way to stand in front of the group Susie was with and tell all of them, "Good morning girls." They were always friendly and giggley to me except Susie. Susie did not speak to me her entire sophomore year. All I'd get from her were a few *grunts*. Never "Good morning, Dad"; never "Have a good day, Dad." Always just *grunts*.

1973 Football.

Last Year in AAA

The old adage *It is not the size of the dog in the fight; it is the size of the fight in the dog* was applicable to the 1973 Flagstaff High School *Eagles!*

Our season's record was three wins-seven losses. Very poor. There were some good points however. We opened with a decisive 22-6 win over our bitter rival Coconino High School. Our speedy running back Steve Larson led the way with over 100 yards rushing. He scored two touchdowns on long runs. Tackle Brian Dierker tackled a Coconino High ball carrier in his own end zone for a two point safety. Fullback Kit Mills finished off our scoring with a five yard blast up the middle. The *Eagles* had bragging rights in Flagstaff for another year.

We defeated AAA Sunnyslope High School 35-14 on their home field.

We beat AAA Prescott High School 14-0 in Prescott.

We played well in a couple of close losses to AAA teams; 7-9 to Apollo High; 13-15 to Brophy High.

We lost badly to five AAA powers: Sunnyslope, Marcus de Niza, Moon Valley, Paradise Valley and Washington.

We ended the season with the satisfying 14-0 win over my old school, AAA Prescott High.

I was satisfied with that win for two very personal reasons: Robert Lee Smith stunned the PHS *Badgers* early in the first quarter when he went 65 yards on a reverse play which I stole from Coach Roger Hightower when I was his assistant. Two of our toughest kids, Mike Yard and Britt Smith, provided key blocks for Robert Lee on that run.

Mike, like his father, Dr. George Yard former Bisbee High *Puma,* was an intense competitor. Mike was small for a guard by AAA standards but was very quick and an excellent blocker. He weighed maybe 160 pounds at the most.

Britt Smith, like Mike Yard, was not very big, weighing in the neighborhood of 170 pounds. Britt was also quick and an excellent blocker. He was the son of former FHS team physician, Dr. David Smith.

Those two, Mike Yard and Britt Smith, gave us two of the best blocking guards I was privileged to coach.

That win was satisfying to me because our Stand-Up Radar Defense had its grand finale with a shut-out. We used the defense off and on all season, mostly as a change-up to our regular basic defense. Coach Rick Smith our defensive coach would use it just enough to show it to opposing coaches. By using the Radar defense in certain situations and in some games more than in others, the opponents had to use practice time preparing for it.

The Radar Defense had served its purpose. It kept some teams off balance and gave our sideline skeptics some fun belittling our "stand around defense."

Our seniors went out winners in more ways than just the last win. They set the tone for following FHS teams. Their season-long desire to be the best they could was evident. Their attitude in spite of some tough losses remained upbeat.

I still get irritated when I think back about all these great kids playing year after year against teams much larger and more physical. It seemed to me our Flagstaff Public School Administration really blew it by not pushing harder and sooner to get FHS down to AA ranking where we belonged. Many great kids were cheated by the FHS Administration's contentment with mediocrity and lack of aggressive leadership.

CHAPTER TWO

The Death of The Legend
Flagstaff, Arizona
October, 1974

Therefore if anyone is in Christ he is a new creation; old things have passed away; behold all things have become new.
2 Corinthians 5:17

Little did I realize when Gary Milton introduced himself to me in mid-August of 1974 that he would have such a huge impact on my life. Gary had come into my classroom as I was preparing for pre-season football practice which was just a few weeks away.

He introduced himself and apologized for just walking in unannounced. He said he wanted to meet me for some time. Gary was getting a degree from Northern Arizona University in Physical Education. His purpose for wanting to meet me was two-fold.

First; he wanted to ask if he could possibly find a spot on the football staff where he could volunteer to assist in coaching. He explained that he always wanted to help coach high school football. After playing in high school and a brief fling at college ball, football was in his blood. Gary's main area of interest was coaching quarterbacks and receivers. Our Junior Varsity team was coached by my good friend Benny Bishop and Jim Sims, a Flagstaff Junior High School counselor. I knew that neither of them felt overly confident coaching the quarterbacks and receivers. Gary might be just the ticket.

After visiting with Gary for a brief time I knew that he would be a welcome addition to our staff. He just had a spirit about him that I couldn't help but be attracted to. His enthusiasm for coaching was evident. I knew we would hit it off well.

Gary's second reason for approaching me was to ask if he could help with the Fellowship of Christian Athletes. He read in the Flagstaff *Daily Sun* that I was the sponsor of FCA. Gary explained that he was a Christian and had the same desire I did to help kids cope with the peer pressure which was so prevalant. He volunteered to help any way he could, even teach a Bible study if needed.

I jumped at that suggestion. I told Gary I was not well versed in the Bible. I would appreciate any help he could offer. His eyes lit up. I could tell Gary was eager to get started.

Gary made a statement which kind of took me back as we shook hands in parting. He said, "Coach Hicks, I appreciate you letting me be involved with you and your football staff. I am anxious to meet Coaches Bishop and Sims. Please tell them I will gladly assist in any way possible. Coach, I can hardly wait until our first FCA meeting! We'll tell them about Jesus!"

I thought to myself, *"Oh,oh, I hope Milton isn't one of those weird Victory Chapel types."*

Gary told me he went to First Baptist Church so I knew he did not go to Victory Chapel. First Baptist was one of the more normal churches in Flagstaff. I just hoped Gary Milton was not a street corner rabble-rouser like the Victory Chapel folks.

END OF THE SUMMER FISHING TRIP
A Near Tragedy

My two sons, Mike and Steve, and Steve's buddy Greg and I ended the summer by taking a fishing trip to Chevelon Lake, our favorite Arizona fishing spot.

My family and I went to Chevelon Lake a number of times and we usually took our canoe. This time since we were only going to fish Chevelon River we did not have to paddle across the lake. We would be camping Friday and Saturday and coming home Sunday, so we went light. We each carried our sleeping bags and personal gear on our backs. We had two ice chests with sodas, hot dogs, and snacks well iced down. Steve and Greg carried one chest while Mike and I had the other.

We had to negotiate a pretty steep decline to get to the bottom of the hill which bordered Chevelon River. The trip down would normally take maybe an hour. Not a bad hike for three pretty much in shape kids and me.

I was surprised that Mike was having trouble keeping up. He had to have me stop several times while he got his breath. Steve and Greg beat Mike and me down to the bottom by a good 15 minutes.

I got on Mike for not being in shape. "Come on, Mike. You start Freshman Football next week. You should be in better shape than this."

When we got to the bottom and found where Steve and Greg began to set up camp Mike and I unloaded our gear. Mike was very sluggish.

Steve and Greg did not even wait to eat. They were off to catch fish. I fixed a sandwich and offered to fix Mike one but he was already asleep on his sleeping bag. He was a tired kid. I wrote it off to being out of shape.

When I returned from an hour or so of fishing Mike was still sleeping. I had to shake him several times to get him awake. I made him drink a Pepsi and eat a sandwich; that got him pretty much awake and ready to join Steve, Greg and me on the river.

We fished until almost dark, went back to camp, got a fire going and enjoyed an evening of eating and shooting the bull. We all four had a good night's sleep. Mike was rejuvenated the next morning and had a good two days fishing.

We hiked out Sunday morning, got home early Sunday afternoon and had a good night's sleep. We were ready for the first day of football practice on Monday; Mike would be playing ninth grade football and Steve eighth grade football.

I was pumped for the Flagstaff High *Eagles'* first season in AA North competition.

THE HADLEY HICKS FAMILY
Would Never Be the Same

I remembered it like it was yesterday. I was mid-way through our first practice; I had just blown my whistle to start a new drill for our Varsity and Junior Varsity teams.

I heard Dr. George Hershey calling me from behind the wire fence which bordered the street running in front of our practice field. George was motioning to me to come to him. I knew something was wrong as soon as I saw the urgency in George's actions.

George's first words, "We had to take Mike to the emergency room. He was near passing out as he was getting ready for practice. Had, Mike has diabetes."

I could hear my wife, Joan, and a nurse talking when I walked into Mike's room. Mike was in a bed surrounded by a white curtain. The first thing I noticed when I parted the curtain was the hanging IV bottle dripping fluid into Mike's arm through a long tube. Mike looked alert. He was intently looking and listening to the nurse. When Mike saw me coming through the curtain he immediately burst into uncontrolled sobs. I hugged him as best as I could and cried with him. All I could think to say was, "Mike you'll be o.k., you'll be o.k."

Joan was crying too and had been for the better part of an hour. When I came in the room, I interruped the nurse just as she was preparing to instruct Mike on how to give himself insulin shots. Just as she again began her instructions she was interrupted once more. When the curtain parted this time I was very surprised to see former *Eagle* football player Paul Thurber walk in. Without any preliminaries Paul boldly said, "I am a diabetic. May I help?" I can't begin to tell you how much Paul and his gentle instructions to Mike helped him. The nurse was kind enough to let Paul do much of the instructing. She even prepared a shot for Paul to inject in himself after Paul convinced her that his second shot for the day was due.

Mike watched with much interest; he would be giving himself shots for the rest of his life.

Dr. Hershey came into the room shortly after Paul and the nurse had left. Besides further instructions on diabetic care, George told Joan and me that we had been very lucky.

If Mike had gone into a diabetic coma at the bottom of Chevelon Canyon just a few days before, he would probably be dead now. A tragedy had been averted when I made Mike eat a sandwich and drink a Pepsi. Pretty lucky.

Mike was in the hospital overnight. He came home the next morning and missed one day of school. He recovered quickly. Dr. Hershey told us that Mike should not practice football for a few weeks to make sure the diabetes was under control. Mike was a big ham. He enjoyed his new celebrity status as a diabetic. He was the center of attention when he showed his classmates how he had to give himself shots of insulin twice a day.

By the end of his second full week of missing football practice he was chomping at the bit to get on the field with his buddies. Dr. Hershey gave Mike a good check up and okayed him for full speed ahead.

It took Mike awhile to catch up with the rest of his team but when he did he got to play in several end of the season games.

He did well. He improved to the point where he became one of Flag High's all-time great receivers.

Meanwhile the FHS Varsity football team was playing its first AA North Conference schedule. It was not what we expected; we finished six wins- four losses. Still it was a winning season.

Oddly enough, it was two of our losses which motivated us for a successful season the following year 1975

We went to Tucson the second game of the '74 season to play AAA powerhouse Salpointe High School.

I had a pretty heated discussion with our Athletic Director Roy Smith for scheduling Salpointe High. First of all we had a five hour drive to Tucson for the game; secondly, Salpointe was one of the favorites to win the AAA State Championship. We had no business playing them.

Roy just shrugged it off and said it would give us good experience for our AA games.

Salpointe was all they were built up to be. Still, our physically out-manned kids played them tough. We matched them touchdown for touchdown until the fourth quarter when Salpointe scored a touchdown plus two points on the extra-point to win by eight. We lost 12-20 and had what some called a "moral victory." Salpointe was favored by the Tucson media from 18 to 24 points.

Quarterback David Diaz and running back Kenny Gill both had above average games. Diaz had the Salpointe defense off balance a good portion of the game. His sprint-out passing was tough to defend. Kenny Gill had 90 yards rusing.

The Salpointe coach was complimentary about both Diaz and Gill after the game. The coach was especially complimentary about the *Eagles'* competative spirit.

Our last game of the season was probably the poorest game FHS played all year. I have to take much of the blame for that.

I was too easy on the team at practices all week. We soundly defeated a good Kingman team 17-0 the week before. It was a hard hitting game. We came out of that game beat-up, bruises and sprains, nothing serious. But, I felt we should go easy leading up to our last game against Coconino High.

We had fun in practice on the Monday before. We had relay races; we had a brief "two-below" game; the linemen-ends against the backs; I had the cheerleaders and pom-pon girls bring the team refreshments at the end of practice. The team was in much too good a mood when we left the practice field. We never did get them prepared for the tough game with our bitter rival Coconino High.

They thoroughly trounced us 27-7.

And, while I am taking the blame for team losses I must mention the first game we played that year. We scheduled an *easy* opener. We were going up to Page, Arizona to play Page High School. Page was a B conference team and were moving up to A. Flag High was dropping down from AAA to AA. Common sense said we should have little trouble dealing with a team moving up a notch from Class B to play in a Class A league. After all we were moving down a notch from a AAA leaguer to a AA league after playing the big boys for years.

Again we were not prepared.

I didn't bother to get a scouting report on Page High. Page High had two backs who could have played for anybody, running back Ron Beckwith and quarterback Max Hamblin. Hamblin ran the veer-option attack to perfection. We had never seen it before. A scouting report would have greatly helped though I doubt if we could have stopped their offense. Those two kids ran up and down the field all night long.

Page High humiliated the *Eagles* 26-0.

While six wins against four losses was not a horrible record it was still not good enough for the "Hicks Haters." There was still a segment out there who would like to see me gone. Or at least so I thought. Mrs.Vandevier hung up the phone but I had an idea she and her followers were still around and active. I had no reason to feel that way; no reason not to feel that way either. My self-esteem was pretty near rock bottom. 1975 just had to be better!

It Is So Simple; Yet...

Gary Milton and I got FCA started the second week of school. We had several freshmen who were interested in attending our meetings. I was excited that my son Mike and some of his buddies were among those interested.

After I announced to the Varsity and JV teams we would begin to have FCA meetings, my new Assistant Varsity Coach Ernie Thornburg cornered Assistant Coach Rick Smith and asked some questions about FCA.Ernie never heard of FCA before nor had he heard of religion being talked about at football team meetings. He was rather skeptical of it. When Rick told me later of Ernie's questions I got Ernie aside and told him he was more than welcome to come to our first FCA meeting to see what it was all about. I invited Rick Smith to come to a meeting the year before but he never did. Rick told me he was Jewish and wouldn't be comfortable talking about Christian religion though he didn't seem to mind that Gary Milton and I did. Ernie Thornburg never did attend an FCA meeting.

At our first FCA meeting of 1974 held in Dr. George Hershey's home. Gary Milton taught a lesson on *God's Sovereignty*. The lesson was part of the pack of materials the National FCA Headquarters in Kansas City had sent to me. I was more than glad to let Gary teach that lesson. I had no clue about God's sovereignty nor did I know what "sovereignty" meant. Before the meeting Gary had asked if I would mind if he used my son Mike's recent diabetic problem as an example of God's sovereignty. I had no problem with that. Gary asked if Mike would be embarassed to be singled out in front of his peers. I said Mike would not mind. In fact he would be more than glad to answer personal questions if there were any.

Dr. Hershey would also be in attendance. He might be able to answer questions regarding diabetes any of the kids would ask.

It was an interesting lesson. I opened by telling the group about our fishing trip down to Chevelon Creek. I told them how Mike had gotten so exhausted hauling the ice chest down the steep hill, how he went to sleep immediately upon arriving at the bottom and how hard it was to wake him up.

The guys all laughed and kidded Mike about being out of shape. Mike, of course, ate it up. He was like his dad in that respect. He loved attention.

When Gary took over the lesson he got my attention immediately when he made the point that God had planned that whole trip; that God was in control of the whole thing.

God could have let Mike die while in a diabetic coma at the bottom of Chevelon Creek. Instead God allowed Coach Hicks to get Mike to eat a sandwich and drink a Pepsi. God had a plan for Mike's life.

Gary also made the point that God had allowed Mike to get diabetes for a reason. That certainly arroused some questions! Why would God allow something bad to happen to Mike; or anybody for that matter?

Good questions. That was what the lesson was all about. The next half hour Gary Milton held our attention with an excellent teaching on God's sovereignty. I know I learned a lot and I am sure most of the guys did as well. I had no problems at all with what Gary taught that night. Ever since my grade school days at St. Patrick's Grade School in Bisbee, Arizona I was a believer in God.(B) Those nuns and priests instilled in me a fear of God that had been with me ever since.

Gary Milton was active in *Campus Crusade for Christ* at Northern Arizona University in Flagstaff. He knew some of NAU's Christian athletes. Gary asked me if he could invite one of them to come to one of our next FCA meetings. We both thought our FCA'ers would be impressed with a NAU *Lumberjack* talking about God.

In mid-October of 1974 Gary brought a young NAU athlete named Robert Fowler to an FCA meeting we held at Eddie Babbitt's house. Robert Fowler was the NAU *Lumberjack's* starting fullback. He was a big, good looking athlete. Gary introduced him as a lay preacher in a Baptist Church in Dallas, Texas.

Before the meeting officially started Eddie Babbitt's mother served us several different kinds of refreshments. The guys, including Robert Fowler, chowed down pretty well. There was lots of joking around, laughing and talking football; Robert was right in the middle of it all. He seemed very much at home. I could tell that our guys really liked Robert. He had a captive audience for his talk.

I heard a lot of Bible talks in my day, both before that night in October of 1974 and since that night. I have never had a talk impact me as profoundly as the talk that Robert Fowler gave!

Robert's Biblical text was *John 14:1 and :6*

> (1:) "Let not your hearts be troubled; you believe in God, believe also in Me.
>
> (6:) Jesus said to him, "I am the way, the truth, and the life. No one comes to the father except through Me."

Robert talked for 30 minutes on these two verses. I honestly cannot recall all that he said. I remember only a few key points which hit home to me.

The first point was the latter part of verse 1 when he quoted Jesus as saying *"You believe in God, believe also in Me."*

I believed in God ever since my grade school days at St. Patrick's Grade School in Bisbee, Arizona. I knew God had always wanted me to be good. For the most part of all my life I had been as good as most people. I was pretty much a "straight-arrow". I did not drink or smoke much. I drank wine at times and I smoked a pipe when I went camping and sometimes out in the garage. I never smoked a pipe in public where some of my students might see me. But I was good.

Robert set us up for the *kill*. He knew most of us did indeed believe in God. He described all of us pretty well. Good people. God believers.

Robert then asked us what Jesus meant when He added, *"….believe also in Me."*

Not many of the guys volunteered answers to that.

Robert then asked, "Do you believe in Jesus?" We all shook our heads "Yes". "Believe what about Jesus?" Robert asked. An awkward silence followed that question.

Robert proceeded to talk about *faith in Jesus;* we should believe by faith what Jesus says about Himself.

Robert concluded his talk by emphasizing *verse 6, "I am the way, the truth, the life. No one comes to the Father except through Me."*

You could have heard a pin drop in that room. Robert made it clear that Jesus is the way to get to Heaven because Jesus is the truth about God and Jesus is the life of God. Jesus is exclusively the only way to get to Heaven, to the Father, to God. Robert explained it all very simply. It all depended on *faith in Jesus.*

Robert then prayed a simple prayer. He prayed that God's Holy Spirit would speak to each of us; that we would be convicted to respond to what The Holy Spirit was laying on our hearts; no raising of hands, just a private moment in the stillness of our hearts where we would hear what the Holy Spirit was saying to us.Then Robert prayed that we would each individually respond to The Holy Spirit.

Robert gave each of us a tract, a religious pamphlet put out by *Campus Crusade for Christ* titled, "How to Be Sure You Are a Christian."

When the meeting was over most of the guys stayed around, ate some more and talked with Robert and Gary. I thanked Robert for his talk and excused myself. I had much to think about.

I remember to this day when I left Eddie Babbitt's guest house and stood by my car.

It was one of those beautiful Flagstaff evenings. I remember looking up to the bright star-studded sky and being overwhelmed by what I just heard.

The only thought I had that I can verblize now or could ever verbalize was: *So that is the difference between Santa Clause and Jesus. It is all about faith in Jesus!*

I know that sounds childish; it makes no sense. But that was my thought. It made sense to me. Jesus Christ is real.

On the way home to my house in the pine forest I mulled over another point that Robert Fowler talked about, John 14:1 the very first words, *"Let not your heart be toubled."*

Robert emphasized what Jesus told his disciples: we have no reason to worry about anything. Jesus is in control. Jesus, God is in control of my future. He is in control of Mike's diabetes.

The religious tract Robert gave us made it all so very clear to me. I was alone in bed when I read the tract. When I finished reading the tract I realized that I was not a Christian. All this time, all my adult life, I believed in God but had never believed in Jesus. I never by faith trusted Jesus as my Lord and Savior. I never confessed to Him that I was a sinner. I did so that night and had a peaceful night's sleep. It was all so simple, yet so very, very profound.

GOD'S SECRET SERVICE

The next day Gary came up to me as we were waiting on the practice field for all our players to get dressed. He told me that he knew when I left the meeting so quickly that I had a lot on my mind. I told Gary pointedly that I had not been a Christian; for most of my 41 years I had believed in God, yet I never trusted by faith in Jesus. I was not a Christian. I understood that God's way was the best way for us to live and that maybe FCA was the answer to society's moral decline. I now knew that it was *Jesus* Who was the answer, not FCA. It was all so simple.

I wish I could say that my transformation was accompanied by a God generated excitement. It wasn't at all. There were no fireworks going off, no tears of joy. There was just a tremedous peace in my mind knowing that "all was well with my soul."

Gary always talked about being "bold" for Jesus. Now I knew what he meant. I vowed to be bold!

I would let my students know that I was a solid believer in Jesus. I immediately joined "God's Secret Service." I became an *undercover agent* in God's Secret Service. One of the first things I did was to buy an FCA beltbuckel. It was like cowboy rodeo beltbuckles, large, round, silver and gold with the FCA logo boldly standing out. People who saw my belt buckle would know for sure I was a Christian. Then just to make sure people knew I put a Christian *fish* on the trunk of my car. What boldness!

SUMMER FCA CAMPS

The school year of 1975-1976 was overflowing with God's sovereignty and grace for the Hicks family. My wife Joan, our sons Mike and Steve committed their lives to Jesus Christ at 1975 Summer FCA Camps; daughter Susie did the same at a Josh McDowell Rally at Northern Arizona University in the Spring of 1976.

Joan and I went to a FCA Coaches' Conference in Granby, Colorado in the summer of 1975. What a great time we had!

The FCA Coaches Conferences are highly organized and "couple-friendly." When the coaches are attending talks by well-known college and professional Christian athletes and coaches, the ladies are attending talks and Bible studies by well known Christian women. There were times during the days for individual and couple freetime. These were times for solitude, prayer, or walks in the beautiful Colorado forest with our wives. They were special times.

The *FCA Huddles* were also special times. Each person attending the FCA Conference was assigned to a Huddle. The male coaches were in separate Huddles from the women. Each Huddle was comprised of no more than ten individuals. The men Huddles were organized around a series of competative athletic events; flag football, basketball and softball games. The ladies played volleyball, softball and soccer. On the last day of the Conference an assembly was held to present awards to the winning Huddles based on cumulative won-loss records. These Huddles were a blessing for me. I became close to a number of men in my Huddle during the brief time we had together.

I was in the same Huddle as Ken Hatfield, a well known and highly successful college football coach. Ken, over his long coaching career, coached at Clemson University, Rice University, and the University of Arkansas. He was National Collegiate Athletic Association (NCAA) "Coach of the Year" at the United States Air Force Academy. As a 42 year old coach I was still in fairly good shape. I could still compete. What a joy it was to compete athletically with and against men who loved the Lord and played to glorify Him rather than themselves! Ken Hatfield was just such a man. In one of our Huddle football games, Ken was one-on-one with the ball carrier. He was preparing to make the "tackle" (grab the guy's flag) when the ball carrier gave Ken a pretty vicious straight-arm which flattened Ken. Ken jumped to his feet and chased the ball carrier to the end of the play. Both teams thought Ken was angry since he was screaming and yelling as he chased the ball carrier. He was made to look bad by an opponent, and no athlete likes that.

Ken ran up to the ball carrier, grabbed him by his arm and shouted in the guy's face, "**Do you have any eligibility left? Man, I have a scholarship to the University of Arkansas for you!**" Great fun!

The Closing General Assembly on the last evening we were all together was an inspirational and meaningful time. There was lots of singing and laughter led by Ray Hildebrand, one of FCA's most popular conference personalties. An "open-mic" time was provided for any who had a testimony or a praise on how the Lord touched them during the three-day Conference. Quite a few told how they had been converted to Christ during the Conference. Many of those talks reminded me of my conversion at the Flagstaff FCA Meeting at Eddie Babbitt's house.

As Joan and I drove back to Flagstaff over the beautiful Colorado *Rockies* we had time to talk and reflect on our experiences at our first FCA National Coaches' Conference.

We made several stops at viewpoints along the way. At the first stop Joan and I saw a young coach whom we both saw at the Conference. He was all alone and was glad to see us. He recognized us as Conference attendees. We struck up a conversation with him and were immediately drawn to him by his friendliness and eagerness to talk.

The three of us sat down on a bench and reviewed our individual experiences at the Conference. He told us in great detail how he "met Christ" at the Conference.

He was over-joyed by his "new beginning" as he called it. He said he could hardly wait to get back home to share his happiness with his family.

As he spoke I noticed tears in Joan's eyes. We said our good-bys to him, hugged and went on down the road. Joan seemed very quiet as we drove along. I finally asked her what she was thinking.

She was hesitant to tell me at first. Finally she told me that she too had experienced a "new beginning" at the Conference. She said that after one of the women's meetings she went back to our room and in the quiet of the room she prayed to receive Christ's forgiveness for her sins.

Joan's confession opened the door for me to talk about my faith in Christ realization that I experienced at Eddie Babbitt's house the past October.

I don't know why it took me so long to tell Joan I become a Christian. I guess it was just that I was more comfortable being in God's Secret Service. I was still too focused on my feelings; I had a hard time talking about the change in me. That reluctance would slowly vanish as I grew in Christ.

When Joan and I drove to Granby, Colorado for the FCA Coaches' Conference we left our three kids at home alone, Susie was in charge. She was a high school senior and felt qualified to handle Mike, a sophomore, and Steve, a freshman. She did a good job, as far as we knew.

Mike and Steve were excited about going to an FCA Boys' Conference in San Diego, California shortly after Joan and I got home. They were going to San Diego in Walt and Marge McDonald's travel trailer. Randy McDonald, Walt and Marg's youngest son was one of Mike's best buddies. Randy was a sophomore with Mike; he too was looking forward to the FCA Conference as well as the opening of football practice soon after they got back from San Diego. I learned months later that Mike, Steve and Randy had made professions of faith in Christ at the San Diego FCA Boys' Conference. The three of them had also joined God's Secret Service. God showered his Grace on His Secret Service personnel just as abundantly as He did on all His children.

"Yeah...and we won the fight too!"

Our second game of the 1975 season was one of those football games all coaches and players dream about! AAA powerhouse Salpointe High School from the Tucson, Arizona desert had to come up to the rarified air of 7,000 foot Flagstaff, Arizona. One of our *Eagle* fans tacked a hand painted sign to a tree near the Salpointe locker room which read:

"Welcome to Flagstaff, Arizona. Elevation 7,000 feet above sea level"

I am not prepared to say that the psychological ploy had any effect on Salpointe. I can say that the FHS *Eagle* offense and defense had a huge effect on them!

We more than redeemed ourselves from the previous year's loss to Salpointe down in Tucson. Salpointe did not dominated that 1974 game. They won it but not without a fight.

The *Eagles* totally dominated the 1975 game; including the fight! The fight occurred in the fourth quarter when our quarterback Danny Anderson was tackled out of bounds near the Salpointe bench. As Danny was getting up one of the Salpointe coaches kicked him. Unfortunately for that coach, big Joe Joyce was standing nearby. Joe was 6'4" tall and a solid 215 pounds. Before the coach could hide behind his players Joe Joyce plowed into him and was on top ready to pound the guy into oblivion.

Luckily for the coach, cooler heads prevailed. Several of our *Eagle* players got hold of Joe and dragged him away before the coach was injured. Surprisingly none of the Salpointe players tried to intervene. They either saw the rest of our *Eagle* team running to the fight or the Salpointe players did not like the coach. Salpointe was penalized 15 yards for unsportsmanlike conduct. Both teams were warned and the game continued.

While at our after game coaches' party at Coach Rick Smith's house, I had a phone-call from a sports reporter from one of the Tucson newspapers. He previously talked to the Salpointe head coach who gave the reporter his version of Flag High's 20-7 upset win. The Salpointe coach blamed the loss on the rain which fell on both sides of the field and did not have any effect on the outcome at all. The coach said that we scored on a few lucky plays. One lucky play he sited was a 35 yard run by our quarterback Danny Anderson on a "broken-play."

When the reporter asked me about the "broken-play" I told him that was not a broken-play. It was an option-play that Danny Anderson read correctly; he had out run the Salpointe team to the goal line. The reporter asked about the muddy field that caused Salpointe to abandon their vaunted running game and "go to a passing attack which they were not used to." I told the reporter that the field was not muddy, wet maybe, but not muddy. I told him that our running game had torn apart the Salpointe defense for over 200 yards. We had no trouble running on the wet field. Plus, I said Salpointe had to pass because our defense completely cut off their running game.

The reporter was incredulous that AA Flagstaff High School won the game. He had a hard time believing that we won the game legitimately. His last question was, "And I hear Flagstaff started a fight." I was pretty irritated by this time. I replied, "Yeah, and we won the fight too!" And I hung up on him.

Salpointe opened the game by running their first play 65 yards to our 10 yard line. Joe Joyce set the tone for the night for FHS. He came from across the field and knocked the Salpointe ball carrier not only out of bounds but ten more yards into the track. I believe that Joe Joyce's aggressiveness did much to inspire us for the rest of the game. Joe's tackle was one of the most vicious, legal tackles I ever saw.

Salpointe took two more plays to score. With less than two minutes into the game the score was Salpointe 7-0 over the yet to run a play Flag High *Eagles*. I am glad my players could not read my mind at that point: *Is this going to be a blowout? That was too easy.*

FHS quarterback Danny Anderson's leadership was textbook caliber. His play calling totally confused the Salpointe defense all night long. He had our seldom used option-series down pat. Danny's fakes to fullback Mark Chipperfield going up the middle drew the Salpointe linebackers to Chipperfield. Danny either give the ball to halfback Kenny Gill off-tackle or keep it himself around the end for sizeable gains

Danny's quick passes off the fake to fullback Chipperfield thrown to ends Rick Horton or Joe Joyce were our big play threats. Joyce scored from 15 yards out in the first quarter and Horton caught one in the third quarter for a key 25 yard gain. Horton's catch led to Kenny Gill's 25 yard romp untouched into the endzone. In the meantime the *Eagle* defense did not take the night off. Time after time the huge Salpointe offense was stymied by Coach Rick Smith's varied defense. Linebacker Jim Rice, one of Flagstaff High School's all-time best, and defensive ends Joyce and Randy Ryan led the defense in what was perhaps our "shining moment", our best all-around performance of the season.

Our smallest defensive starter 160-pound noseguard Manuel Loya was past their center and into the Salpointe backfield more times than we could count. When Salpointe passed, Loya was in their quarterback's face so quickly that any pass pattern they had was completely destroyed before it got going.

The 1975 FHS *Eagles* were perhaps the most balanced team I had the privilege to coach at Flag High. Offensively we scored an average of 18.4 points per game to our opponents' 8.1 points per game. Field goal kicker Hank Lopez was a threat from 50 yards out. He set a school record of 51 yards in our 23-6 win over Holbrook. In our 3-7 loss to AA North Champions Snowflake, Hank got us on the board with a field goal of 40 yards.

The *Eagles* ended the season with a most satisfying 22-6 win over cross-town rival Coconino *Panthers*. Our seniors went out in grand style.

Oh! I almost forgot. Those pesky Page High School guys. They stuck it to us again in the first game of the season. Ron Beckwith and Max Hamblin were still around. They led Page High to a come from behind 19-17 win. With the clock showing one minute and 54 seconds to go and the *Eagles* in front 17-13 quarterback Max Hamblin took Page High 60 yards for the winning touchdown.

Defensive Coach Rick Smith and I kept our defense in a "prevent defense." We thought that if our linebackers and defensive backs played deeper than usual, Hamblin could not complete any long passes.

In a gutty performance Hamblin completed several short passes to receivers who stepped out of bounds to stop the clock. Beckwith had two beautiful ten yard runs in the last minute drive. The clock showed ten seconds left when Beckwith crashed across the goal line from 3 yards out. Page: 19-FHS: 17. As the Head Coach I should have taken our defense out of the prevent defense for that final drive by Page. If Page was to win make them beat us at our best. The prevent defense was not our best. Some of our fans in the stands let me know as I walked off the field that we should not have been in the prevent defense. Live and learn.

I know if I ever had to come up with a mythical "All-Opponent Team," Ron Beckwith and Max Hamblin from Page High School would be on it. Maybe they'd even be co-captains!

Thanks, Josh

In the fall of 1976 shortly after our daughter Susie graduated from Flag High she and her good friend and classmate Lori Bliss attended an evangelistic rally featuring well-known Christian author and speaker Josh McDowell. Josh McDowell was well known for his best seller <u>Evidence That Demands a Verdict</u> which presents historical evidence for the Christian faith. Northern Arizona University at Flagstaff had an active *Campus Crusade for Christ* chapter which drew many NAU students to McDowell's two-night rally. Susie and Lori both enrolled in NAU as freshmen a few weeks earlier and decided to go hear Josh McDowell out of curiosity.

In all of Josh McDowell's lectures he made it very clear that he was speaking to college students world wide for only one purpose: to glorify and magnify Jesus Christ and not to win an argument. The evidence he presented was not for proving the Word of God but simply for providing a basis for faith. McDowell was a persuasive speaker who related to college-age students. Susie Hicks and Lori Bliss came away from Josh's lectures as new believers in Jesus Christ. Their lives would never be the same again.

FOOTBALL 1976.
Finally! Split 'em Both!

I was excited for the 1976 football season to get underway for several reasons. My son Mike was a junior. He would probably, barring injuries, be a starting wide receiver. Mike played in a few Varsity games as a sophomore and did well.

Mike adapted to his diabetic routine of giving himself insulin shots and laying off the donuts. He got stronger which greatly helped his endurance and his speed.

I knew from his earliest grade school days that Mike could catch a football. He had what coaches call "soft" hands. When good receivers catch a football there is a unique sound that emanates from the ball hitting the hands. It is a "soft" sound. Mike had that gift.

Mike could catch a football with the best of them. He had enough speed to run good pass patterns. He had a knack for getting open. I had little doubts he would be one of our starting wide receivers.

I was excited also because a new kid had moved to town. His dad was a professor at Northern Arizona University. The family was from Oklahoma and were die-hard Oklahoma *Sooner* football fans. Mark Gaither was an answer to prayer. Literally. I prayed that we would get a good quarterback in school because I could sense that we would be able to split both of our ends out and run the true *Run and Shoot* offense. Mark Gaither could do what a good *Run and Shoot* has to do-pass on the run.

Rick Horton was the other one I felt could be a starting wide receiver. He was a tough kid who could catch well. He had enough speed to be dangerous. He played quite a bit the year before.

I spent a lot of time during the summer diagramming our offense; both our passing offense and our running offense.

For the first time I wanted to try out the *silent signal* aspect of the Run and Shoot offense. I never quite felt confident in my ability to teach it well, nor did I feel confident that the personnel we had could adequately adapt to it. I felt we could do it this year. The "silent signal" system was a complex series of hand signals between the center, the quarterback, and the wide receivers; the rest of the team had to be alert for them as well.

The silent signal was a spin-off from a Run and Shoot series called *The Gangster Pass* series. When "Gangster pass" was called the quarterback and receivers had options. When the ball was snapped nobody knew who the pass was going to; the quarterback had a number of options depending on what the defense did.

I used parts of this scheme over the years but never all of it. This year we would use all of it. The quarterback was trained to look at both wide receivers when he came to the line of scrimmage.

The receivers developed a sign between them and the quarterback as to what pass pattern they would run, depending of course on where the defender was positioned.

If the quarterback saw a silent signal from a wide receiver, he had to decide to either throw the receiver a pass or to ignore the silent signal. If the quarterback ignored the signal he went ahead with the play called in the huddle. However, if the quarterback thought the silent signal was a possible successful pass, the quarterback before saying a word at the line of scrimmage would lightly tap the center in the area the quarterback placed his hands to receive the ball-in the center's crotch area. On feeling the light tap from the quarterback the center was trained to snap the ball immediately, no questions asked! But, and this was the tough part, the linemen had to be anticipating the silent signal on every play. Should the silent signal be given and the quarterback signal the center to snap the ball, the linemen had to react quickly to the ball being snapped; they had to pass block not knowing where the ball was being thrown.

Though the system could be pretty complex our kids had great fun with it. They incorporated all kinds of weird signals. Some of the signals were real signals and some were fake signals. Our wide receivers often looked like "hand-talkers" to a deaf quarterback. It got to the point where the coaches did not even know which were real signals and which were just the receivers hamming it up. The important thing was that the receiver and the quarterback knew which was which; the defense didn't. The players adapted so well that they soon got to where they could throw the silent signal pass at any time to either side.

Mark Gaither soon developed into an outstanding run and shoot quarterback. I do not have any statistics from 1976 but I know that Mark had an excellent completion average. He was a bright kid with a good head for football. He was a leader the others respected and listened to. Mark was also a leader in our Flagstaff High FCA *Huddle*.

When Mark graduated his family moved back to Oklahoma. I always thought he could have played college football. I lost track of him and do not know if he ever played after leaving FHS.

"I LOVE YOU, WILLARD REEVES."

Flag High School's game with Coconino High in 1976 was one the *Eagles* would like to forget. At our FCA meetings prior to the Coconino game we had Bible studies on *First Corinthians 13*, the well known *Love* chapter. During the meeting the week before we were to play CHS we discussed how Jesus would play against a bitter rival like Coconino High. There was no love lost between the two schools. Just how would a loving Jesus handle that? Gary Milton and I both said that we thought that Jesus would go all out to win the game. He would be aggressive, tough but loving.

One of our guys said, "Oh come on coach. How could Jesus show Coconino love while playing to win?"

Good question. We discussed that awhile. Gary Milton came up with this example, "Suppose Willard Reeves (Coconino High's great running back) was coming around the end and Jesus had to tackle him. Jesus would tackle Reeves as hard as he could. But after he tackled him Jesus would help Reeves up and tell him He loved him."

Our kids thought that was a good idea; a way to show Coconino High how Christians played football. Willard Reeves was one of Arizona's best high school running backs that year. We decided that each time one of our *Eagles* tackled Reeves they would say to him, "I love you Willard Reeves." Our guys thought it would be cool when several *Eagles* gang-tackled him to say in chorus, "We love you Willard Reeves." Coconino clobbered us that year. Willard Reeves ran wild. He probably had over 200 yards by himself. As one of our players said after the game: "We didn't get to tell Willard that we loved him very much, did we Coach?" Willard had a great career at Northern Arizona University. He went on to play several seasons with the Green Bay *Packers*. Willard Reeves was a good one. He would no doubt make my mythical "All Opponent Team".

A CHURCH THAT TEACHES FROM THE BIBLE
That's Different.

Gary Milton and I became close through our involvement together with FCA.

We both loved fishing and camping. We had some great times fishing during the day and talking about the Lord around the campfire at night. Gary was influential in getting me to realize that my enlistment in God's Secret Service was about due to expire. He was unaware that as we discussed the Lord and Christianity in general that I began to realize some Biblical deficiencies in the church Joan and I attended for several years.

Reverend Kendall, the minister at The Federated Church in Flagstaff where my family and I attended from day one in Flagstaff, was a good guy. I really liked him. He enjoyed sports and could discuss football intelligently. Reverend Kendall's son Matt was a regular at our FCA Huddle meetings. He was a starter at defensive back his junior-senior years at FHS. Matt was an all-around good kid; He was personable and very popular.

One evening at FCA after we had discussed *John 14:6* where Jesus said, *"I am the way, and the truth and the life. No one comes to the Father except through me."* Matt came up to Gary and me and made what I thought was an insightful comment. Matt said, "Here I have grown up with a minister father and have attended church all my life. I have never heard that before. I need to really think that through."

Reverand Kendall made an insightful comment to me one Sunday that made me really think things through also. After Joan and I came back from our summer FCA

Coaches' Conference I approached Reverand Kendall at church one Sunday to tell him about the great time we had. I said something about what "a blessing it had been to be fellowshiping with men and women who truly loved Jesus." I thought Reverend Kendall would be excited for Joan and me. Instead he looked at me rather quizzically and only made one comment, "I'm glad you had a good time." Shortly thereafter both Joan and I decided we needed to find another church; one that taught the Bible like they did at FCA Conferences.

I was interested in the church Gary and Nancy Milton attended.

Gary talked to me about Flagstaff's First Baptist Church and their Pastor Al Parmenter. Gary invited me to visit "First B" several times; he was not "pushy" about it. He just said, "If you and Joan ever want to visit us, just let me know."

Joan and I went with Gary and Nancy one Sunday. I knew immediately that was the church we needed to attend. Pastor Parmenter preached directly from the Bible. He didn't preach about the Bible. He preached *from* the Bible. Quite a difference from what we were used to.

The music at First Baptist was great. Instead of a choir in colorful robes they had a praise team with several guitars, tambourines, drummer, trumpet, and several good singers.

Their music was worshipful and upbeat. Not at all sleep inducing like a lot of choirs were. The praise team was comprised of mostly Northern Arizona University students. They had an excitement about them that added much to the over-all environment. Jesus Christ was exaulted and glorified in every aspect of First B's service. I came away feeling refreshed. I had a true worship experience, the first since the FCA services in Granby, Colorado.

I found a home. Joan was not so sure. She said the First B service was, "o.k." She was not as excited as I was.

The Rabble-rousers
Louder than Ever

One Saturday evening Joan told me she was going to go to church the next day with Susie's close friend, Carol Lynn. Susie went to Salt Lake City for a few months to work with a Christian organization that witnessed to Mormons. Carol wanted someone to go with her to Victory Chapel, the street-corner rabble-rousers. Carol and Joan were good friends so Carol had asked Joan to go with her. Joan was a bit reluctant to tell me she was not going to First B with me; she knew too about Victory Chapel's reputation in Flagstaff. That didn't seem to bother her a bit. She knew some of the young people who attended Victory Chapel and said they were nice and as normal as most other Christians.

I didn't at all like the idea of Joan going to Victory Chapel. I was worried that some of my friends would see her. Worse yet, I didn't want any of my players or their parents seeing her. My reputation in Flagstaff was on shaky ground as it was. My wife being involved with the Victory Chapel weirdos would not make it any better. Joan went with Carol Lynn the next morning and came home very emotional about her experience there. She informed me that she and Carol were going back that evening. I made two huge mistakes that day. The first one was letting Joan go to Victory Chapel Sunday morning. The second mistake was letting her go back in the evening. Two huge mistakes I would regret the rest of my life!

CHAPTER THREE

I Messed Up !
Flagstaff, Arizona
1979-1985

*"But if he does not make them
void after he has heard them,
then he shall bear her guilt."*
Numbers 30:15

Joan became a regular at Victory Chapel. We first tried to compromise. She went with me to First Baptist in the mornings and I went with her to Victory Chapel in the evenings. That didn't work. Joan broke out crying in the middle of the service at First Baptist. I tried to console her but that did no good. She had get up and walk out to wait in the car. That was embarassing for me. Her only reason for the tears and walking out was that First Baptist was not preaching "truth." She said that Pastor Jack Harris at Victory Chapel was the only pastor in Flagstaff who preached the truth. Victory Chapel was the only church she could go to and feel comfortable. Joan was emotional about it.

The Victory Chapel services were lively to say the least. The music was a raucous, hand-clapping clamor which I am sure bothered the neighbors. They had few musicians, maybe a drummer, a trumpet player and the piano player. They did have loud-speakers. The people were few in number but made up for it in noise. To me it was not at all worshipful.

Jack Harris was the one who preached most of the times I went with Joan. His sermons seemed to go on and on and on. His messages were all the same. He spent most of his time giving his testimony, how sinful and evil he had been before he was saved.

He told the people how the other churches in Flagstaff hated Victory Chapel. They were the only church which preached the truth, the only true Christian church in town. Often during his preaching he would break out in a lively bit of "tongues." It was all a bunch of mumbo-jumbo which immediately got the people following suit. It was emotional and frenzied, never was an intrepreter present as Scripture says must be the case. I often thought, *you phonies!*

When Pastor Harris realized that Joan Hicks' husband did not come to church with her regularly he wanted to know why. At one of the evening services I attended with Joan he invited Joan and me to have coffee with him and his wife after the service.

I wasn't too eager to go but Joan insisted. We met Pastor Harris and his wife, Patty at *Denny's*. I recognized Patty immediately and she me. I was Patty's Home Room teacher at Prescott High School. I did enjoy the time talking about "old times" at Prescott High with Patty. I liked her. She seemed like a nice girl. I did not enjoy at all the time Jack Harris took asking me questions about my less than adequate Christian life. He asked first if I had ever gone to a Pentecostal church before. He insinuated that since I had not and was not familiar with the Pentecostal teaching that my headship of Joan may be lacking. I did not understand at that time just what he was getting at. I did not understand the husband's role as spiritual head of his home. I would soon learn the hard way.

Joan and I went out with Pastor Harris and Patty a few more times. Each time I felt that Jack Harris was pressuring me to go to Victory Chapel. I got the feeling he would count it as a coup to get the Flag High Head Varsity Football Coach to join his church. I did not at all appreciate the way Jack Harris cut down the other churches in Flagstaff including First Baptist. None of them believed in speaking in tongues nor being "baptized in the Spirit," thus they were not Christians according to him. Harris often said that in his sermons. He pounded home the point that other churches were not serving God like Victory Chapel. They were the only church in town that believed in all the gifts of the Spirit. Being "baptized with the Holy Spirit" was another requirement and Victory Chapel was the only church in Flagstaff that practiced that.

It did not take long for the people at First Baptist Church to realize that Joan and I were on different wave lengths spiritually. They were kind and understanding and made me feel welcome at First B. They did not in any way criticize Joan for going to Victory Chapel nor did any give me harsh instructions to "dump" her. I knew quite a few of the First B congregation and the ones I did not know, I soon got to know. I attended a Wednesday night Bible study in Cole Durham's class on *The King of the Home* which dealt with the husband's role as spiritual head of his home. The teaching went right over my head; I failed miserably as the spiritual head of my home.

Soon Joan and I called off the compromise of splitting time between two churches. She couldn't bring herself to attend First B with me, so she quit coming saying that she knew God wanted her at Victory Chapel. I quit bugging her about it and I continued going most Sunday evenings with her. I didn't know what else to do. I initially told her that I would support her involvement with Victory Chapel. Big mistake.

FOOTBALL 1977
"Hicks to Hicks to Hicks for Six."

Mike's senior year at Flagstaff High School was such a joy for me. Coaches told me for years that it is too difficult to coach your own son. I did not find that to be the case. Mike was the best receiver on the team and he proved to be one of the best in Arizona that year. It was not difficult at all to coach one so talented even if he was my son.

My son Steve was our starting quarterback as a junior and had the Run and Shoot offense down pat. His grasp of the Gangster pass series was beautiful to watch.

If the Gangster pass is run correctly by all the backs and the receivers, it is nearly impossible to stop. That was a big "IF." These were young high school kids and they all make mistakes. When the Gangster was called no one including the coaches knew who would end up with the ball. A split end may get a quick pass from a silent signal, a slot back may get a quick pass if the linebacker blitzed, a wide receiver may get a long one if the silent signal was ignored or a slot back going in motion may get a swing-pass if the quarterback can't find any other open receivers. Lastly, if none of these options were open the quarterback may keep the ball and run. It all depended on what the defense did.

Many times the next two seasons when we found ourselves in a difficult situation, say third and five deep in our own territory, the Gangster would bail us out. Usually it was dangerous to pass in that situation for fear of an interception.

At times I huddled on the sideline with Larry Gray, who had come up to the Varsity from the JVs in 1976 and we made suggestions what to call. One of us would usually end up looking at the other one and saying, "Gangster."

In those two seasons I do not ever remember a Gangster pass being intercepted. I am sure one was somewhere along the way but I don't remember it.

Again, I do not have statistics on those two years.

I believe that Coconino won the AA North as they had an outstanding football player named Ray Smith who ran all over us just as Willard Reeves did a few years before.. Ray went to Northern Arizona University and was an All Big Sky Conference defensive back. He was one tough kid! He later coached at Kingman High School.

I remember several highlights of the 1977 season:

I was proud of my son Mike. He was a unanimous choice for Arizona Class AA All-State as a wide receiver. He was selected to play in the All-Star football game between Arizona All-Stars and Utah All-Stars. The passing combo of Steve Hicks to Mike Hicks, according to many in the media, was the most prolific in Northern Arizona. Paul Sweitzer, Sports Editor of the *Flagstaff Daily Sun* newspaper coined the phrase, "Hicks to Hicks to Hicks for Six." The Hicks trio was responsible for a number of FHS touchdowns that year. Again, no statistics.

Paul Sweitzer wrote one last article about the Hicks brothers in 1994. The headline to the article read: *Former Flag High Athletes Complete One More Pass.*

Paul's article detailed Mike's need of a kidney due to his diabetic enduced kidney failure. The article made reference to Steve "completing another pass to his brother. Steve donated a kidney to Mike." Steve's kidney lasted Mike 9 years before Mike had to go on home-dialysis.

Upon graduation from FHS Mike was offered a walk-on scholarship to Northern Arizona University. Our feeling was that Mike would probably sit the bench at NAU and maybe get to play his senior year, if then. Mike was not a big kid when he graduated. He was 5" 11' and 165 pounds. We decided Mike should go to a smaller school where he could play right off the bat. Former Arizona high school coach Les Unruh was coaching at a small Christian college in Kansas. Les heard about Mike and recruited him to Sterling College in Sterling, Kansas, the best thing that ever happened to Mike.

God was still in control of Mike's life! God is sovereign.

Another highlight of the 1977 football season was working with Larry Gray as the FHS Assistant Varsity Football Coach.

Larry came to Flag High in August of 1976 as an assistant to Jim Sims on our JV football team. He was a popular senior guidance counselor.

Early in the winter of 1976 I let Ernie Thornburg go as Varsity Football Assistant. Word got back to me that Ernie was critical of my involvement with FCA. Ernie did not think that religion should be mixed with football.

Ernie and I talked about this. I told him how much my relationship with Jesus Christ meant to me. I told Ernie that I did not push "religion" on the team. The team knew most of the players were enjoying their involvement with FCA. None of the team minded at all that we prayed before and after games. They looked forward to the occasional Christian guest speakers we had before games. Erine and I just did not see eye-to-eye on the issue. Rather than having him disgruntled and complaining to others, including players, about me, Ernie and I decided to agree to disagree. It would be best if I let him go.

I replaced Ernie with Larry Gray. I heard nothing but good things about Larry from Jim Sims, Head JV Coach, and some of the students. Larry was a good fit. He had no problems with my committment to Christ nor my involvement with FCA. Plus, Larry and I were on the same page football wise. Larry's coaching of the offensive linemen and receivers added tremendously to the success of our Run and Shoot offense, and to quarterback Steve Hicks' development as an outstanding quarterback. Larry possessed the one key ingredient that all good assistant coaches must possess. I have mentioned it before. It was something I did not possess when I was an assistant to Coach Roger Hightower at Prescott High. Loyalty!

Never for one minute did I ever doubt that Larry Gray was 100% loyal to me and my headship of the football program. Often Larry and I got together during lunch and went over various aspects of our offensive schemes. If Larry did not like something I suggested, he would not hesitate to tell me. If I disagreed with him and did my own thing, Larry supported it.

I am grateful to Larry Gray for the impact he made on me, my two sons and the rest of the team. His enthusiasm, hard work, his love for the players and his loyalty was such a blessing to me.

Let Larry tell you in his own words just what his being involved with FCA meant to him:

"On the bigger picture, my most cherished memory is being introduced to the FCA and how that changed my life and has influenced the lives of Shelly and our sons. I will never forget Steve Hicks pacing outside the locker room at Holbrook after the Hadley Hicks led Eagles beat Holbrook to secure a playoff spot saying, 'Is that all there is? Isn't there more to this than that?'

He was right, he knew it and taught it to me. Praise be to God!! The huge build up didn't match the joy of victory, life went on for both teams; it wasn't the REAL game we were to play."

I praise God that He "planted" Larry at Flagstaff High School when He did.

So You Wanna Be a Legend. So Did I.

FLAGSTAFF HIGH FCA'S LAST STAND

1978-'79 was to be my last year of involvement with FCA at Flag High. Our FCA Huddle died a slow year long death brought about by Gary Milton and me standing firm on our stance against Rock Music. It seemed like most of our Huddle meetings that year revolved around the pros and cons of Rock Music. The discussions often got heated. Most of the athletes were die-hard Rock Music advocates. A few agreed with Gary and me that Rock Music was satanic.

The issue came to a head early in the winter of 1979. Gary and I invited Dan Slayton, a gifted musician and former Flag High football player, to one of our FCA meetings. At that time Dan was a lay youth pastor at First Baptist Church. Dan's presentation to our Huddle meeting that night was an excellent expose of satanic Rock Music.

It was clear that Dan was not saying all Rock Music was satanic. His point was that non-satanic Rock Music could subtly lead the unwitting listener right into the lap of satanic induced Rock Music. Dan Slayton played a tape of "Lead Zepplin," a popular Rock Music group which contained "back-masking", a technique whereby satanic dialogue was clearly revealed when the music was played backwards. The evidence Dan presented was convicting. It left little doubt to those with open minds that Rock Music could be a huge stumbling block to Christians desiring a healthy walk with the Lord. Those with closed minds stumbled. Attendance at our weekly FCA Huddle meetings slowly dwindled from that point on.

Gary and I knew that we were faithful over the years to present the Gospel of Jesus Christ at our Huddle meetings. We were not discouraged to see the FCA Huddle die out; disappointed but not discouraged. We would be blessed someday when God would reveal the fruits of our efforts.

One Sunday in 1982 Gary and I did received a special blessing at a baptism during our regular First Baptist Church Service. Gary and I seldom sat together during church; this particular Sunday however we were seated together. God wanted us to share in the blessing He planned for us. Included in the ones being baptized that day was a young girl who looked familiar to Gary and me. We couldn't place her until Pastor Parmenter asked her to give her salvation testimony as he did with all candidates for baptism.

The girl told how she became a Christian while attending Flagstaff High School Fellowship of Christian Athletes meetings her senior year. Gary and I both got choked up on hearing her testimony. This young girl was in the first group of FHS girls we encouraged to come to FCA Huddle meetings. She went into The United States Navy shortly after graduating from Flag High. In her testimony she gave Jesus Christ credit for walking with her through some difficult times while she served in the Navy. Gary and I both silently praised God for using FCA and the two of us as His earthly assistants. God is faithful.

MARRIED SINGLES

As the days and months went on, Joan and I grew farther and farther apart. She was involved with Victory Chapel her every waking moment. I tolerated it. If she wasn't going to church which it seems she did almost every night, she would spend the morning hours with some of her friends going "to prayer." When she wasn't at prayer, she was with her new friends going door to door witnessing and handing out tracts. They talked about their various witnessing opportunities frequently. I remember hearing Joan and one of her Victory Chapel friends, Kathy, laughing about how some workers on a building almost fell off a ladder when Joan and Kathy shouted to each other as they were going their separate ways, "PRAISE GOD!" I didn't feel that was the best way to witness for Christ.

I continued to go to church with Joan most Sunday evenings. I listened to Jack Harris and others rail away endlessly about the same topics Sunday after Sunday.

One night it hit me! I realized that Jack Harris was doing exactly what I did with my football teams. He was brainwashing them! The music each service primed his people for the harangue which followed. By the time Jack got to the microphone the audience was pumped! They were ready to accept anything Harris said. When he was finished, the alter call was the grand finale. If people had been "saved" last week and had backslidden during the week, Harris got them saved again. If they had been a bit hesitant about witnessing during the week, he made it pretty clear that maybe they needed another dose of "the Holy Spirit's power." If they were not quite proficient at speaking in tongues they needed more practice during the weekday meetings at church. They would soon learn. They had to be in church every time the door was opened; if not "God could not use them."

I did the same thing with my football teams. The band and cheerleaders got the student body and the teams primed. They were ready to go come game time. My speeches during the week at practices were geared to progressively bring the teams to a fever's pitch on game day. The locker room slogans I posted were to get their minds focused on the up-coming game. The team we played was not worthy to be on the same field with us. We were the Flagstaff High School *Eagles!* We were better prepared, better conditioned, and had more desire. We would win! Now get out there and do it!

It was sheer brainwashing based on pure emotion.

I couldn't convince Joan that what she was experiencing at Victory Chapel was not true Christianity. We did nothing but argue. She wouldn't listen to me and I wouldn't listen to her. We sometimes went for days without speaking to each other unless absolutely necessary. Joan's total focus was on Victory Chapel and the people who became her close companions. She was with them day and night. The Victory Chapel people were her mentors.

I had my mentors as well. Gary Milton and Pastor Al Parmenter provided much spiritual growth for me during these difficult times. Gary's friendship and concern for my marriage were such an encouragement to me. He was there for me at all times. Several times when he knew that I need a picker-upper he would come out to the house early in the morning, rouse me out of bed and make me go with him to cut wood.

Gary helped clear my mind of negative thoughts. Pastor Al Parmenter was such a good preacher. I looked forward eagerly to his sermons each Sunday mornings.

His teachings Sunday evenings were up-lifting as well. I am so thankful that God "planted" me in First Baptist at this time in my life.

The daily radio ministries of J. Vernon McGee, John MacArthur, and Chuck Smith probably did more for my spiritual growth during this time than anything else.

I got up early each morning, fixed my coffee and turned on the radio. McGee, MacArthur, and Smith came on one right after the other weekday mornings. Joan got irritated at these three great teachers. I didn't have earphones so she could not help but hear some of what was said.

I used the information they gave me as ammunition to battle Victory Chapel doctrine. Often I confronted Joan with something one of those three said. I know now that was not good. It only turned Joan off and alienated her more. In other words I was vindictive and not at all loving as I should have been.

During one of our arguments Joan told me she doubted that I was a Christian because I did not speak in tongues nor raise my hand when I worshipped God. Besides that, I probably wasn't saved because I did not read from The King James Version of The Bible! She told me that Pastor Harris told her that and that they were praying for me. Joan concluded by telling me that I was not her spiritual head because I was not a Christian. Her pastor was. That did it! I called Jack Harris and told him I wanted to speak with him. I went down to his office as soon as I possibly could. His office was in the back of the Victory Chapel sanctuary which was a large bare former storage shed. The first thing I noticed as I walked into his office was, I did not see a Bible anywhere. I found that strange for a pastor not to have a Bible on his desk. I gave him the benefit of the doubt. Maybe he had one in his desk drawer.

I confronted Harris immediately. "Where in Scripture does it say one has to speak in tongues to be a Christian? Where does it say I have to raise my hands when I worship? Where in Scripture does it say I have to use The King James Version of The Bible? How can you say that you are Joan's spiritual head? Show me that in the Bible!"

We argued back and forth for over an hour. As I walked out I pointed my finger in his face and told him he would have to face God someday for the families he had wrecked with his false teachings.

From that point on I seldom went back to Victory Chapel. I went to a few potluck dinners at some of Joan's friends' homes plus several at our house that I attended. I did go to several weddings I was not happy with. The first wedding I attended at Victory Chapel was an eye-opener for me. Joan's good Victory Chapel friend Nancy had asked me to "give her away" at her wedding as her father was not available for some reason. I agreed to do her a favor and walk her down the aisle.

The Mexican-American young man Nancy was marrying came out of Catholicism and his entire extended family attended the ceremony held at Victory Chapel. I never witnessed such a travesty in all my life! Jack Harris spent over an hour belittling the Catholic religion. Several members of the wedding party got up and gave testimonies on how God delivered them from the Catholic Church. Harris made it pretty obvious that Catholics were doomed for hell if they did not "come out of her", a phrase from the *Book of Revelation* Harris said meant come out of the

Catholic Church. Mid-way through Harris' insulting treatment of his Catholic guests, the groom's elderly grandmother got up and aided by two of her grandsons walked out directly in front of Jack Harris as he continued his harangue. Shortly after the grandmother walked out, most of the groom's family followed her example. By the time Harris finished, most of the groom's Catholic family and friends had left. I was very embarrassed for that family.

Jack Harris did nothing to aid the cause of Christ that day.

FOOTBALL 1978
The Best Ever?

To compare one good team to another good team is like comparing two good friends. I hate to do that. The Flagstaff *Eagles* of 1978 were up there among the best I ever coached. We lost in overtime to Gilbert High School by one yard in the semi-finals of the State Playoffs. Regulation tie games were decided by letting each team run a series of downs from the 50 yard line. The team that made the deepest penetration in their series of downs was the winner. Gilbert won by one yard! Gilbert went on to beat Tollison for the State AA Championship.

We lost two regular season games: Canyon del Oro of Tucson beat us 7-6; Coconino High beat us 21-19 in a thriller. We averaged 20.1 points per game to our opponents 9.1 points per game.

What made the 1978 team stand out in my mind was the poise we maintained in some challanging games. We came back strong after two tough defeats. We were down 7-14 at half time to Kingman and came back to win 21-14. Here is how Coach Larry Gray remembers that game: "At Kingman we were behind at half time; Hicks to young Nagle (Todd) with a bomb at the end of the second quarter fired up the *Eagles* and we took them apart in the second half. Great lesson for me, never give up. A game can change on one play."

The Canyon del Oro game was a classic. It was brother vs brother. FHS Coach Rick Smith was pitted against his brother Bubba Smith, the CDO coach. CDO was the defending State AA Champion and came to Flagstaff undefeated.

Early in the first quarter FHS quarterback Steve Hicks brought the *Eagles* to the line of scrimmage and noticed the CDO right defensive back out of position while talking to his safety man. The defensive back was slow getting back to cover the FHS wide receiver, John Pappas. Steve did not hesitate. Without saying a word he tapped center Kenny Macias lightly. Macias automatically snapped the ball to Steve. Before the CDO defense could react, Steve hit Pappas with a quick pass. Pappas had good speed and he outran the CDO defense for a 50 yard touchdown. The silent signal at its best.

The extra point was wide. FHS: 6-CDO: 0. Late in the first quarter a Hernandez 15 yard field goal attempt was partially blocked. No good. In the second quarter we had a good drive down to the CDO five yard line. On fourth down Steve called, "Gangster pass right." Our receiver was wide open in the end zone. Steve hit him in his hands chest high. He dropped it! We led at half time 6-0; could have been 16-0.

So You Wanna Be a Legend. So Did I.

Coach Rick Smith designed a special defense for his brother's bread and butter play, an off-tackle power play that had been effective for CDO the past several years. The special defense had completely shut down CDO until late in the fourth quarter. With three minutes left in the game CDO got the ball deep in their own territory. Slowly, yard by yard, the CDO offense began to move the ball. They made adjustments and were now able to run against our special defense. Both Coach Smith and I were slow to counter what CDO was doing. We were helpless to stop their drive. CDO scored with 40 seconds left in the game and won 7-6.

Merry Christmas to Bubba from brother Rick, Coach Hicks and the Eagles!

Then there was the yearly battle with Coconino, the last regular game of the season. This year the Coconino game decided the AA North Champions. For the past two seasons Flag High played all our home games in Northern Arizona University's beautiful new Sky Dome, home of the NAU *Lumberjacks*. Our kids loved playing in the Dome. The locker room facilities were beautiful, the artificial turf which covered the field was a pleasant change from grass. My only complaint was the noise! Even a small crowd made the calling of audibles (plays called at the line of scrimmage) very difficult. When both Flagstaff High School and Coconino High School football fans jammed both sides of the 15,000 capacity Dome, the place was a mad-house!

I taught a simplified audible system ever since my Carmel High School days. Our quarterbacks came out of the huddle to the line of scrimmage and with a series of commands either tell the team to go ahead with the play called in the huddle, or he canceled the play by shouting a "live" color. Then the quarterback would shout code words indicating the play to be run. Of course, the quarterback had to incorporate fake calls along with his live calls. It was a simple and effective system that high school players had no trouble learning.

With the noise in the Sky Dome our team sometimes had problems hearing the quarterback's audibles. It was especially tough for our wide receivers so far away from the quarterback. Our silent signal system was a tremendous asset in the Dome.

Coach Larry Gray and I worked up a different blocking scheme for Coconino. Coconino Coach Bill Epperson was a good football coach. The past several years he devised a defensive technique that did much to cut down on the effectiveness of our trapping game. We had run inside and off-tackle traps (where a guard pulls and blocks on the other side of the center) as a change up from our "bread and butter" Green Bay *Packer* sweeps.

In the 1977 game Epperson's defense seriously stymied our traps by shooting a linebacker through the gap left by our pulling guard. They were able to stop the play before it got started. Our traps and sweeps were soon so ineffective we relied on running plays we felt uncomfortable with. What Coach Gray and I came up with for the 1978 game was instead of the guards pulling on traps and sweeps we would have both our tackles pull. Coach Gray and I felt that our two starting tackles, Phil Passalacqua and Chuck Potee were quick enough to get the job done. Epperson's shooting line backers would be thrown off stride by not having the guards pull to trap. It worked beautifully.

Our two fast running backs, Eric Stingley and Greg Turner, both picked up good yardage with sweeps and traps. They both scored a touchdown apiece in the first half. We led at half time 13-7.

The *Eagles* had two turnovers in the third quarter, one which allowed Coconino to score a touchdown and another which stopped a drive of ours on the CHS 10 yard line.

With the score 14-13 in favor of Coconino at the start of the fourth quarter FHS put together another nice drive. We went from our own 40 yard line to the Coconino 20 yard line. On second and three quarterback Steve Hicks called "Sprint right, wingback delay." It worked perfectly. Steve sprinted to his right, right wingback Greg Turner delayed at the line of scrimmage allowing our receivers on the left side to run deep patterns thus clearing out the left side of the defensive backfield. Steve pulled up on his sprint to the right and threw left across field to a wide open Greg Turner. Turner scored. Our extra point try was no good. Score FHS: 19-CHS: 14.

Unfortunately Steve Hicks was not the only good quarterback on the field that night. Coconino's Tim Salem was no slouch as a quarterback. Salem led the CHS *Panthers* to a go-ahead touchdown with less that 2 minutes left in the game. Score: CHS: 21-FHS: 19. Coach Bill Epperson showed why he was such a good football coach. He instructed his kick-off man to kick the ball along to ground. Epperson did not want Stingley or Turner to get a sizeable return. It worked perfectly. The ball bounced through the end zone. We took over on our own 20 yard line. We had 80 yards to go to win the game with 50 seconds left. Time to go to our seldom used "two minute offense." Steve did a beautiful job of moving us down field. He hit several short patterns allowing the receiver to step out of bounds. Time was running out on us. With 30 seconds left and the ball on our own 40 yard line I called our last time out. Coach Gray and I talked the strategy over. We felt Coconino would be expecting another short pass to get our receiver out of bounds to stop the clock. I called another, "Sprint right. Wingback delay". We had our fieldgoal team ready should the play be stopped short. It was almost a brilliant call. Greg Turner was wide open when he made the reception. One of Coconino's defensive backs recovered in time to trip Turner on the CHS 15 yard line.

The field goal team hustled on the field. No time outs. The clock showed ten seconds left. *Eagles* down by two points; 19-21. Ray Hernandez' field goal attempt from the CHS 15 yard line was partially blocked which threw the angle of the kick off just enough to make it miss by inches. The *Eagles* lost a heartbreaker.

When the game ended I walked to meet Coach Epperson and the CHS coaches to congratulate them on a great game. The CHS coaches showed a lot of class. They told me that we should have won. We completely out played the *Panthers* offensively. Had it not been for a couple of FHS turn overs we would have won handily.

I was proud of our kids. We did not get down on ourselves when we made mistakes. We hung in there and had a chance to win. God just had other plans. I encouraged our kids to come back to practice on Monday ready to "get after it" again. We had one more game to play.

So You Wanna Be a Legend. So Did I.

For the first time two teams from AA North would go to the State Play Offs. We would know on Monday who we played next Friday night. We still had a chance to play for the State AA Championship as did Coconino High.

A "Fine Line" Between Victory and Defeat

The Gilbert High School *Tigers,* coached by Dan Dunn, were year in and year out one of the strongest AA teams in Arizona. This year was no exception. The *Tigers* were our opponents in the Semi-Finals of the State Play Offs. Gilbert High School was the home team. They had a home field advantage that proved God had a sense of humor. At the end of regulation play the score was tied 13-13. The tie is the result of God's sense of humor. The two teams went into overtime where Gilbert won by a "fine line" and one yard!

I was told by the head linesman before the game that Gilbert High School had a home field rule on the north end zone that was a bit different. It seems that when the Gilbert football field was being built years ago an electrical line from a light pole had been strung in a weird fashion. The electrical line went from one light pole on a straight line just above the north goal posts to the next light pole. The home field rule stipulated that should the football ever hit the electrical line either on a field goal try or on an extra point try the ball was ruled out of play. The kick was no good. The head linesman said that a kick had never hit the electrical line as far as he knew. He said the electrical line was hung too high. Oh yeah?

The *Eagles* scored their second touchdown in the fourth quarter to tie the game 13-13. The extra point could put the *Eagles* ahead 14-13 with just minutes to play.

Ray Hernandez's extra point kick was right down the middle, BUT high. It hit the electrical line. No good. Game tied due to a "fine line."

We went into overtime. Arizona Interscholastic Association rules said that in case of an overtime game each team had a series of downs from the 50 yard line. The team that penetrated deepest past the 50 yard line won.

On the coin toss to determine who got the ball first, Gilbert won and wisely chose to have the ball second. By letting Flag High have the ball first, Gilbert High would know how far FHS had advanced the ball and would know what they had to do to advance the ball deeper.

I have second guessed myself over what happened next many, many times:

We practiced all week on several plays that we not run all season. Two of them involved our tough fullback Chris Britt. Chris's nickname was "The RIb" because he was so skinny. Chris was one of the toughest blocking backs I ever had.

On our sprint out passes Chris's job as fullback was to block the defensive end to the side Steve, our quarterback, was sprinting. Chris would just destroy the defensive end no matter how big he was. Chris had a key block to make on our Green Bay sweeps. He seldom failed. I put in a quick screen pass to Chris off of a fake sprint out pass. Chris faked a block on the defensive end and then slipped out in the flat beyond the line of scrimmage. Steve hit Chris with the pass. In practices it worked like a charm. Chris was fast enough to pick up big yardage. But Chris besides being very skinny weighed at the most 135 pounds. I was very hesitant to have him carry the football. It was o.k. for Chris to hit them, I just didn't want them hitting Chris.

Another play we put in especially for this game was a quick trap to Chris right up the middle. Our fullback seldom carried the ball. A quick fullback-trap could fool the defense. Then the last surprise play I had in the back of my mind was to tell Steve Hicks to call Gangster pass; instead of him passing the ball, Steve would sprint out faking the pass, getting the defensive backs in full coverage and then he would keep the ball and run himself. I saw that play as a sure big gainer. Steve could run well. I never asked him too run as I feared injury to him. He was our only proven quarterback.

In the overtime God showed me a real weakness I had as a head football coach. I had little patience. I wanted to go for the big play too quickley. I was a big play coach. I was not a methodical, five yard at a time coach. FHS had the ball first in the over-time. We picked up ten yards on our first play, a sweep. On our second play I called a pass play to Todd Nagel our right split end.

All fourth quarter Todd told me that on any run to his side the defensive back came flying up to stop the run. Todd said a fake run to his side would leave him open for a long pass. I called, "Gangster pass. Hit him deep." In my haste I did not tell Steve which side to run Gangster nor did I tell him who to throw to. I just said, "Gangster pass. Hit him deep."

As soon as I saw Steve sprinting left instead of right I knew that I had blown it. The pass was intercepted. We penetrated ten yards.

Gilbert only had to gain 11 yards and they would be in the State Finals the next week. On Gilbert's first play they gained six yards. They gained five on the next play. Gilbert won in overtime 11 yards to 10 yards. I lost my last high school football game by a "fine line" and 1 yard.

CHAPTER FOUR

God Hates Divorce
Flagstaff, Arizona
1976-1983

For the Lord God of Israel says
that He hates divorce, for it covers
one's garment with violence"
Malachi 2:16

THERE WAS LIFE AFTER FOOTBALL AND TEACHING

Going into the Gilbert High playoff game I had a pretty good idea 1978-1979 would be my last year as Flagstaff High School's Head Football Coach and Speech Teacher. There was no doubt in my mind that my search for significance seriously hindered my marriage. Perhaps I could salvage the marriage if I got out of teaching and coaching. I would be able to spend more time with Joan and hopefully we could reconcile our differences. Shortly after the 1979 football season ended I resigned.

I planned to go fulltime with Franklin Life Insuranced Company. I was making decent money with them after being parttime for eight years while teaching and coaching at Flagstaff High.

When I announced my retirement from Flagstaff High School I had a long private discussion with Principal Bill Williams, a Bisbee High School buddy who was named Flagstaff High Principal several years earlier.

I was very frank with Bill. I told him why I was leaving education for life insurance, it wasn't just the money. In my nine years at Flagstaff High School I was never once awarded for my contributions. Never once was I made to feel important by the Flagstaff Public School Administration. For that matter I don't recall any teacher recognized or rewarded for their dedication to the students of Flagstaff, except of course for the yearly mandatory "Teacher of the Year" award in the FHS year book, *Kinlani*. Every once in awhile an administrator would pat me on the back for a good game. That was pretty much all I ever received, a pat on the back. I told Bill that I got more "thanks" from some parents than I did from the Administration of Flag High School.

Teachers by and large were not made to feel appreciated. I contrasted that with Franklin Life Insurance. I received several nice tokens of appreciation for my work with Franklin Life. Included were several vacation trips to nice hotels at beautiful resort areas. I did not expect school districts to match such lavish treatment, but maybe nice "Five Year" pins, recognition plaques or certificates for outstanding teaching-something to let the teachers know they had significance in the school district. Education had a long way to go to catch up with the business world.

Just Fuel for the Fire

With my retirement from coaching and teaching I was honestly hoping Joan and I could somehow reconstruct our rapidly deteriorating marriage. I hoped to have weekend dates with her. Weekends for years had been consumed with football and my coaching companions; that's where I got my significance. Joan's significance was found in Victory Chapel. Joan's total life was steeped in Victory Chapel and its activities "for Jesus."

It wasn't long after I quit teaching and coaching that it became obvious to me that Joan had little desire to spend time with me. It wasn't until years later that I realized that Joan needed significance just as I did. Now she had it. She was no longer "Coach Hicks' wife." She had an identity of her own. She belonged to Victory Chapel, Pastor Harris and the people there. She was one of theirs.

Victory Chapel's cultish hold on their people became obvious to me. Joan was not the only one held captive by the legalistic demands on Victory Chapel people. There were many examples. I will mention two:

I sat by a big good looking young man at one of the Victory Chapel pot-luck meals I attended with Joan. He told me he had come to Northern Arizona University to study pre-veterinary medicine. He planned to be a veterinarian someday. When I quizzed him further he told me he dropped out of school after attending Victory Chapel for several months. Pastor Harris told him that in order for him to serve Jesus he should drop out of school and serve Jesus at Victory Chapel. He quit school and got a job at Babbitt Lumber Company. He handed out tracts on weekends.

Another young man, married with several children was saved at a Victory Chapel outreach in Winslow, Arizona. The young man had worked for the railroad line that ran through Flagstsff and Winslow. He was offered a promotion that Pastor Harris told him he could not accept. The promotion would require the young man and his family to move to Kingman, Arizona. Harris told him that he was saved at Victory Chapel and should stay and serve Jesus at Victory Chapel.

Both of these examples were young men who made a decent salary. The railroad paid well, Babbitt Lumber Company paid well. Victory Chapel would benefit from their giving since an offering was taken every time the doors of Victory Chapel were opened. Sometimes an offering was taken twice in one of their long services. There was speculation as to where all that money went. It was said that much of it was funneled down to Wayman Mitchell in Prescott, Arizona. He founded the first Victory Chapel church.

Joan just could not support my working with Franklin Life Insurance Company. She told me more than once that Franklin Life's emphasis on "The Good Life" and its desire to make money was sinful. She said, "The Lord is coming back soon and money will be worthless. You should be spending your time getting people saved."

Franklin Life Insurance Company proved to be more ammunition for Joan to emphasize my pagan life style. My involvement with Franklin Life was more fuel for the fire. Things did not get better. They got worse.

Joan and I took one last trip together. We went to see Mike play a football game at Sterling College. Very little conversation took place going out or coming back.

On the way home I had a lot of time to think. I fell in love with Sterling College. Its Christian environment and the students and faculty were friendly.

Mike introduced me to Clair Gleason the Athletic Director and Baseball Coach of Sterling College. Mr. Gleason and I hit it off immediately. When he found out I had been a high school coach for 21 years and was now selling life insurance he told me I should put in an application at Sterling College. Mr. Gleason said, "You never know, we may need some coaching help. You would enjoy coaching at Sterling College."

Shortly after Joan and I returned home to Flagstaff and after I had prayed about it, I approached Joan with the possibility of trying to save our marriage by moving to Sterling, Kansas. We could get a new start.

I was very serious. We could move to Sterling, I could sell for Franklin Life there and possibly work part time coaching at Sterling College. She would not hear of it! She said God wanted her in Flagstaff and at Victory Chapel. Joan reemphasized to me that I was not her spiritual head. I pushed that point once again: "Where in Scripture does it say that a wife is not to be under the authority of her husband?" Joan's answer was always the same, "I just know He wants me at Victory Chapel." Nothing I said or read her in the Bible could persuade her otherwise. Until I started going to Victory Chapel and "got saved" I had no authority over her.

I told Joan if she wouldn't come with me I would move to Sterling, Kansas without her. At the time I was dead serious. I even sent Mr. Gleason my resume'. I did not understand the legal ramifications should I indeed move and not take my wife. I felt I should have legal advice.

During this hectic time in my life I was meeting with a teacher friend, Lee Brooks and a couple of Flag High students for Bible study and prayer in Lee's classroom during lunch period. One of the students, Catherine Patton, worked part time for a Christian lawyer, Cameron Sechrist. I decided to seek the lawyer's advice. I met Cameron Sechrist via Catherine and had several informal meetings with him over coffee. He had had some run-ins with Victory Chapel and was well aware of the hold they exercised over their people. Cameron was the first one I ever heard call Victory Chapel a "cult." Cameron advised me to not move away from my wife. I would incur many legal situations if I did; as her husband I was still legally responsible for her. I would have to pay some degree of support.

As a Christian, Cameron could not advise divorce. His suggestion was that I continue to live with Joan and do all I could to love her unconditionally, which was hard to do. I found it difficult to continue to love Joan when that love was not returned. She showed much more love for Victory Chapel people than for me.

I don't know if Joan contacted a lawyer of her own or if her "lawyer" was Victory Chapel pastors Jack Harris and his new assistant pastor Conrad Orosco. At any rate

Joan was getting advice from somewhere. She informed me that she was going to court to force me to move out of the house!

I called Cameron Sechrist immediately. Cameron's first question was to ask me where I had my Franklin Life Office. I told him my office was in my house. I could not afford to get an office in downtown Flagstaff. By this time I developed a small Franklin Life District Agency comprised of five part time agents under my leadership. The agency sold enough AP (annualized premium) to legally claim my office and my car as "business expenditures". When Victory Chapel pushed the issue they were told by the court that they could not force me to vacate my office. Joan's alternative was for her to move out. Harris and Orosco encouraged that, as I am sure did her many friends at Victory Chapel. I made it clear to Joan that I was not forcing her to move out. I told her that she was welcome to come and go as she had been doing for several years. It seemed to me that she had had a convenient set up. She had been sleeping in Susie's bedroom and our paths seldom crossed. Joan was gone most of the day at her part time job as a dental hygienist and she was either at church or with Victory Chapel people until after midnight most nights.

I came home one day and found that Joan had moved out. All her personal belongings were out of Susie' bedroom and closet. No note. No forwarding address. I did not worry about her whereabouts. She had plenty of friends at Victory Chapel.

GOD WAS BLESSING A MESS

During these very stressful and emotional times while the Hicks household was being destroyed by Satan's tactics our three children were beginning families of their own: Susie had married a young man named Dennis McDonald, a guy who was a student at Flagstaff High School whom I "prevented from playing football because he didn't like the coach". Or so he would tell you if he was asked. I heard Dennis telling an off-color joke in the hall at FHS one day. I took him to the principal's office for discipline and Dennis was suspended from school for a day. The following football season Dennis, who was a promising lineman, did not go out because he hated the coach. Dennis did not think it was fair that I had reported him for telling a dirty joke his mother had told him. Or so he said. Dennis and I became friends over the years. He said he married Susie to get even with me.

Dennis went to First Baptist while I was attending. He was one of the group I was with who attended the "Tuesday Morning Backsliders' Breakfast" Bible study held at Choi's Restaurant in down town Flagstaff. Dennis proved to be a blessing for Susie while she struggled with her mother and dad's trauma.

Mike was an outstanding wide receiver for the Sterling College *Warriors*. He was one of the Kansas Collegiate Athletic League's (KCAC) best receivers during his four years of participation. Mike had the misfortune of playing for Sterling College during some lean years for the *Warriors*. They finished on or near the bottom of the KCAC each year. Mike was one of the popular kids on campus during his tenure at Sterling College. He was elected Student Body Vice President his junior year. He made many friends and was loved by all who knew him. Mike married his Sterling College sweetheart, Jean Strott, shortly after his graduation.

So You Wanna Be a Legend. So Did I.

Jean was a blessing for Mike; she aided Mike through a number of serious health problems during their marriage.

Steve enrolled at Prescott's Yavapai Junior College where he was on a baseball scholarship. During an inter-squad game in the fall Steve was beaned in the head by a pitched baseball. He spent several days in the Prescott Hospital. During his stay in the hospital God made it clear to Steve that he should go to Sterling College with his brother Mike. Praise God Steve was listening! Steve enrolled in Sterling College in time for the *Warrior's* baseball season. He made an immediate impact. Steve was starting shortstop and was in SC's pitching rotation his first year. Steve was a three year All KCAC Conference Baseball Team selection. In my opinion Steve's greatest baseball achievement during his four years of baseball at SC was his record as a hitter. Steve struck out a mere six times in his four years! I tell people that I struck out that many times in double headers. I believe Steve could have had a good shot at professional baseball. He had all "the tools" as the saying goes. God had other plans for Steve.

Steve was a four year starter at quarterback for the *Warriors*. His pinpoint passing and his strong arm got him several "feelers" from professional scouts. Steve's plans for his life did not include professional football or professional baseball.

Steve, like his brother Mike, found his life's companion at Sterling College. Steve married a Kansas girl, Lori Carroll. Steve and Lori served God as missionaries in Caracas, Venezuela for 17 years. Steve has been elected to Sterling College's Athletic Hall of Fame for both his football and his baseball achievements.

I praise God that He provided companions for our three children as Joan and I were in the process of destroying our marriage.

GOD HOLDS THE HUSBAND RESPONSIBLE

I become good friends with Dave Holland a young man who previously went to Victory Chapel and had since "seen the light." Dave and Joan struck up a friendship before Dave realized that Victory Chapel preached heresy. He left the fellowship. Dave often sympathized with me over Joan's emotional attachment to Victory Chapel. I received a call from Dave one day that threw a whole new light on my thinking about Joan and her involvement in Victory Chapel. Dave called to tell me to read in the Old Testament Book of *Numbers 30: 13-15*. There I would find what God had to say about vows, especially vows made by a wife. I was hit right between my eyes when I considered *Numbers 30:13-15*: *"Every vow and every binding oath to afflict her soul, her husband may confirm it, or her husband may make it void. (14) Now if her husband makes no response whatever to her from day to day, then he confirms all her vows or all the agreements that bind her; he confirms them, because he made no response to her on the day he heard them. (15) But if he does make them void after he has heard them, then he shall bear her guilt."*

I remember so well the day Joan and I traveled to Prescott on Franklin Life business. Joan was going to spend some time with Hicks relatives while I attended to my business obligations. On the way down Joan and I had an indepth discussion about her involvement with Victory Chapel. I made it clear to Joan that I did not agree at all with Victory Chapel's doctrine and that I wished she would attend church with me at First Baptist Church. But, and here is where *Numbers 30:15* comes in,

I said if Joan really had her heart set on attending Victory Chapel I would support her. This conversation occured shortly after Joan had become seriously involved with Victory Chapel. It was not until many months later when our relationship began to unravel that I fought her bitterly over her total dependence on Victory Chapel. It was much too late at that point. I had not been the Godly spiritual leader of my wife that God demands. I must *bear her guilt.*

How I prayed and wept over that revelation! I prayed that God in his mercy and grace would allow me a second chance to be the spiritual leader in my home. That was my prayer for many months. During this time First Baptist Church Pastor Parmenter and my lawyer Cameron Sechrist both advised me to file for legal separation. They both insisted I not file for divorce. I filed for legal separation and months later the case came to court. The law in Arizona at that time stipulated that both parties in a legal separation case must sign an agreement that both agree to the legal separation. If both do not sign the case is automatically terminated in divorce. I had signed on the advice of my lawyer Cameron Sechrist. Joan did not sign. I assumed it was on the advice of her lawyer or Victory Chapel. Possibly both. The divorce became final.

Flagstaff Frozen Yogurt and Nancy

I had seen Nancy Stecker in church several times. I thought she was one of the many Northern Arizona University students who attended First Baptist. I met her one Sunday evening when Pastor Al Parmenter and I were talking outside the church before the evening service. Nancy had two beautiful red haired children with her. Pastor Al introduced me to her, Nancy in turn introduced both Al and me to her children, Kristin and Anthony. They were both elementary school age.

Nancy was the Administrative Supervisor of the new Walgreen's Warehouse being built in Flagstaff. She and her two children were recently transferred to Flagstaff from Denver, Colorado. Nancy's two children, Kristin and Anthony, took a liking to me. I was the only adult at First Baptist Church who kidded around with them. When they came to church one Sunday evening, Kristin leading Anthony, spotted me sitting alone. Kristin told Anthony, "Go sit by that guy." The two kids became my buddies at evening church. Sometimes they would sit with me by themselves, sometimes Nancy would sit with us.

Ever since Joan moved out of our house I would eat breakfast out. One of my favorite places to eat was The Flagstaff Frozen Yogurt Shop. I could eat a large cup of delicious frozen yogurt while I prospected for insurance business. The Flagstaff Frozen Yogurt Shop was a popular hangout for young couples just getting started in life. Franklin Life offered a good insuance program for newlyweds. I picked up a few clients at the Yogurt Shop, some of them former Flagstaff High School students. I was still "Coach Hicks" to them.

The owner of Flagstaff Frozen Yogurt Shop was Jack Delang whom I got to know through First Baptist Church. Jack was involved with Campus Crusade for Christ. I worked on a couple Campus Crusade committees with Jack.

One Saturday morning as Jack Delang and I were enjoying a cup of yogurt Nancy Stecker and her Walgreen's co-employee Joyce came in. They sat at a table near Jack and me. We struck up conversation. During the conversation one thing led to another and Jack said he was going to sell the yogurt shop. He and his wife were going to Yuma, Arizona to open another shop. He wondered if we knew anybody who would like to buy the lucrative business. We discussed what buying the business would entail. It sounded interesting to me. I said as much to Jack.

My insurance business had gone downhill ever since Joan and I had been separated. I was not as motivated as I initially was. I was hoping business would pick back up once I got my feet under me. It hadn't.

I met Nancy in the yogurt shop a week or so later and she indicated she might be interested in buying the business if the terms were right. Nancy had recently been divorced; her move to Flagstaff from Denver had been difficult, especially for her two children. They were often on their own in getting ready for school in the mornings as Nancy's Walgreen's job sometimes demanded that she be at work before the kids were up and ready for school. She would like to find something that would give her more time with Kristin and Anthony. The yogurt shop sounded good to her.

We met with Jack Delang several times over the next few months to talk over the possibility of a partnership purchase. Nancy and I would be business partners if we could work out the arrangements. The partnership would be perfect for both of us. I would open and close the shop which would allow Nancy to be home for her kids before they went to school and she would be home when they got off from school. Nancy would be the "brains" behind the business venture. She worked for Walgreen's for a number of years and was an experienced bookkeeper.

I was a former jock who knew nothing about business. I was a people person. I enjoyed meeting and talking with people. I would enjoy serving people yogurt and gabbing with them. Nancy would handle the business end.

The Delang family owned the "Flagstaff Frozen Yogurt Shop" outright. It was not one of the common yogurt shop franchises. The recipes for the various flavors of yogurt were recipes owned by the Delang family. Many agreed that the Delang recipes were the best. They made their profits by buying and selling yogurt shop locations. With the purchase of the yogurt shops came their secret recipes. Each location was carefully scrutinized for "walk-in traffic." The Flagstaff location was perfect: a few blocks from Northern Arizona University and in the middle of many Flagstaff businesses which drew lunch time traffic. It was a "money maker" as Jack Delang told us.

Soon Nancy and I were co owners of "The Flagstaff Frozen Yogurt Shop". It turned out to be quite an interesting venture to say the least. The Yogurt Shop's office was behind the serving area. The wall separating the office from the customers had a one-way mirror; we could see the customers come in but they could not see into our office. Nancy liked that. She could sit in the office working on the books while I waited on customers; nobody could see her. She was not a people person. Several months into our partnership Nancy discovered that the books just did not add up. The figures we had received from Jack Delang just did not match what Nancy's figures indicated. We were doing as well customer wise as Jack had done. We just did not have the money to show for it. We felt that we were doing something wrong. We would figure it out in time.

During this abrupt transition from life insurance to yogurt shop co-owner I had been woefully negligent in my walk with Jesus Christ. I was still going to First Baptist Church. I was still having fellowship with the Tuesday Morning Backsliders' Breakfast Bible study at Choi's Restaurant. Most mornings before going to the Yogurt Shop, I listened to J.Vernon McGee, John MacArthur and Chuck Smith on the radio. Sometimes I listened to them as I got the Yogurt Shop ready for the day. I hung a whiteboard on one wall of the shop where I wrote a Scriptuer verse each morning. The Scripture verse often draw customer comments; some would lead to discussions of various aspects of Christianity. The discussions often led to good witnessing opportunities. I was negligent was in my prayer life and was not seeking the Lord's direction for my life. This Yogurt Shop involvement had been strictly on my own, no direction from the Lord. I was in constant prayer during my six year struggle to save my marriage. Since the divorce I had fallen back into self reliance and self focus. I did not depend on the Lord as faithfully as I had done. I thought I could do it myself.

When I got serious about prayer again was when I felt Nancy and I were becoming more than partners in the Yogurt Shop. I was strongly attracted to Nancy and Kristin and Anthony. They were searching for stability in their family. The kids needed a father figure who would be there for them. Was I to be that person? Were Nancy, Kristin and Anthony God's answer to my prayer for a second chance to be the spiritual head of my family? I prayed for God's leading.

I had gotten pretty well acquainted with the two kids. They were hired as our weekend help. They both got proficient at odd jobs around the shop. The job they both enjoyed was keeping the topping display area filled with the various kinds of toppings; the toppings made for great snacks even without the yogurt.

Nancy told me that both Kristin and Anthony had made professions of faith in Christ through the guidance of their grandmother. I didn't learn about Nancy's salvation until later.

One Sunday during Morning Worship Service Pastor Al Parmenter announced that First Baptist was going to have an old fashioned "tent reivival" minus the tent. The revival was conducted by a team of Christians led by two Canadian brothers. They were scheduled for four revival services at First Baptist: on a Friday night, a Saturday night and Sunday morning and night. One of the brothers did the preaching and the other led in the music. Special meetings for the women were led by one of the women singers. "Uncle Bill," one of the musicians held special meetings for the children. There was something for everyone. Nancy, Kristin and Anthony and I went Friday night more out of curiosity than anything. We had never been to a revival before. The preaching was good. Both Nancy and I liked it. Kristin and Anthony said that Uncle Bill was very good. They both wanted to come back on Saturday. The brother who led the music played an accordion and led us in hymns and praise songs. Nancy said the accordion music was "hokey". I liked it. It was different.

We went again Saturday evening. It was pretty much the same thing except this time the men had a men-only meeting. The women met with the lady singer. Uncle Bill ministered to the children.

In our men-only meeting we were encouraged to share from our hearts any prayer concerns we may have. My concerns of course centered around my relationship with Nancy. My divorce had been finalized for several months. Was that too soon to ask Nancy to marry me? I was hesitant to share that with the men. I was sitting next to my buddy Gary Milton. Gary and I had been through much together: the slow break up of my marriage, FCA for several years, my salvation, fishing trips where Gary taught me much about Jesus as we sat around the camp fire. Gary knew me better than most people at that time. He sensed my uneasiness. Gary nudged me and whispered my nickname, "Speak up, Hickory". I felt as though the Holy Spirit had nudged me but I knew the Holy Spirit would not call me "Hickory". I felt convicted to pray for God's leading in the matter of asking Nancy to marry me. I had prayed that prayer several times the past weeks. Never so fervently though as I did at Gary's nudging. I had spoken the prayer so most of the men in First Baptist had heard me. No longer was it a concern only between God and me.

After the group prayer time we were divided into groups and encouraged to share and discuss our concerns with the group we were with. It was in this group time where someone brought up the point that God had a "perfect will" and a "permissive will". A concept I had never considered before. I understood that God's perfect will was not to divorce. Divorce is always a sin. God's permissive will would allow divorce due to "hardness of heart". If there was true repentance for the sin, divorce was not the unpardonable sin. I felt a peace come over me when our men's group was dismissed to return to the church sanctuary for the closing praise time. I still was not sure how I should approach Nancy or if I should.

When the ladies came back to the Sanctuary I noticed a number of them had been crying. Nancy was one of them. When I asked her what was wrong Nancy just shook her head. She did not want to talk about it.

Later that night after Nancy put the kids to bed we sat around around her kitchen table as we often did. Only this time Nancy was uncommonly quiet. I held her hand and asked her what the problem was. For the longest time she just sat with her head down, not saying a word. Suddenly she broke into sobs. When she finally got control of herself, she told me she had "accepted Jesus as her Savior". It was my turn to get quiet. I couldn't speak for a few minutes. I was surprised. I had assumed that all these months that I had known her that she was already a Christian. Nancy told me before that when she was a child growing up her father had read the Bible every morning at the breakfast table. Nancy and her three sisters and younger brother went to a Methodist Church with her dad and mom for as long as Nancy could remember. A lot of seeds had been planted by Nancy's dad and mom.

The Holy Spirit waited until Nancy was a mother of two and attending a "hokey" revival to make Jesus real to her.

Nancy didn't mess around with God's Secret Service as I did. She joined God's A-Team immediately. One of Nancy's first acts of faith was to tell and show a Catholic Walgreen's friend the fallacy of the friend's beliefs. Nancy did so with such love and sincerity that the friend was in tears begging Nancy to tell her more. Nancy did not have the head knowledge at that time to dispute Catholicism Biblically. She had just enough heart knowledge to tell her friend the Gospel of Jesus Christ. As a follow-up to Nancy's loving concern for her friend, Nancy asked Patty, from First Baptist to lead her Walgreen's friend in the sinner's prayer. Nancy felt that a more mature Christian was needed for that.

I took Nancy's salvation and subsequent hunger for Biblical knowledge as an indication that God was allowing Nancy, Kristin and Anthony to be my second chance opportunity to be the spiritual head of my family. Because of my repentance, the finished work of Christ on the cross paved the way for God's grace, mercy, and forgiveness to cover my sin of divorce.

NANCY WAS A HARD SELL

I had some interesting times courting Nancy. She was a challenge to say the least. I lost track of how many times I asked her to marry me. I tried to convince her that even though both of us had failed in our only marriage we could make a go of it the second time. We were both Chistians, we were both doing our best to be obedient to Him.

Nancy was a hard sell. Even a sly twist at a Chinese dinner did not sway her.

We had a date for Chinese food at our favorite Chinese restaurant in Flagstaff. I had an idea that was unique. Nancy would be impressed. That afternoon I went to the Safeway grocery store and bought a bag of Chinese fortune cookies. I carefully took a pair of tweezers and removed the small fortune slip from inside one of the fortune cookies. I then inserted into the cookie another slip on which I had written, "For the 100th time, will you marry me?" Then to put the finishing touch on my clever idea. I went to the Chinese restaruant and talked to one of their Chinese waitresses. I asked the waitress if she would mind doing me a favor; when I came back in just an hour or so would she be sure that the lady I came in with got the fortune cookie I had prepared? I told the waitress that I had a special surprise for the lady. The waitress was all for it. She thought it would be a good idea. I gave the special fortune cookie to the waitress and left.

The Chinese waitress was not at all a good actress. As soon as Nancy and I walked in the restaurant my chosen waitress was all giggles. She seated us and all through the ordering process she giggled and looked at Nancy excitedly. Then the big moment came: after a delicious Chinese meal when the waitress brought me the check and two Chinese fortune cookies she was still giggling. She pointed to one of the fortune cookies and said, "This is the one for the lady!" Nancy knew something was up. I just shrugged my shoulders and made some comment about that "crazy waitress." Nancy opened her fortune cookie, read the message, squeezed my hand and said, "That's sweet." She was impressed. She still said, "No."

I finally hit the jackpot when I took Nancy to my favorite Flagstaff steak house. Mormon Lake Lodge is situated on the shore of Mormon Lake 20 miles outside of Flagstaff among beautiful Ponderosa pine trees. It was beginning to snow when we got to the Lodge. It was a quiet, still evening with just a slight breeze stirring through the pines, a beautiful Flagstaff winter evening.

Nancy ordered grilled rainbow trout. I had my usual t-bone steak, medium-well with a side of onion rings which we shared. After a shared dessert of deep-dish apple pie and ice cream we sat for an hour more just "dining" as Nancy calls it. We relaxed and talked about the yogurt shop, our families, our struggles and whatever else was on our minds.

We had no trouble talking with each other. It was a special evening When we left to get to the car we found several inches of snow on the ground and slight flurries still coming down. We were holding hands as we walked across a road to the car; we stopped in the middle of the road, embraced and kissed. I said, "Nancy, let's get married." She began to cry, shaking her head "yes". We hugged and kissed again to seal the engagement.

I Married *Shirley Temple!*

Months later Nancy and I were married on the side of a mountain behind Nancy's mother's home in Albuquerque, New Mexico. Nancy's father died a year before.

I was so blessed to have my 80 year old father, Dr. Hadley H. Hicks along with brother Bill and his wife, Linda, my sister Quila, and my son Mike and his wife Jean attend the wedding.

Nancy's immediate family all attended: sister Lucy played the flute as Nancy walked up a path to the rock where I was standing. Lucy's husband Bob Springer took pictures, sister Barbara and husband Randy Fuller were there. Barbara prepared a delicious Mexican dinner for all the relatives and guests who attended, sister Becky and husband Greg Barton came all the way from Boston, Massachuttes; younger brother George "Brad" Bradley was there. He was in Engineering School at the University of New Mexico in Albuquerque. Nancy' mother Norma Bradley was a gracious host. Her house was beautifully decorated; it sat high on a mountain overlooking Albuquerque. What a beautiful view!

Nancy and I initially wanted First Baptist Church Pastor Al Parmenter to perform the wedding. Al felt he would stir up a hornets' nest if he did so as several of the First Baptist congregation told Al they did not think Nancy and I should marry. My divorce had been final for only six months. They thought that it was too soon for us to marry. My good friend and business consultant Pastor Don Carpenter filled in for Al. Don attended First Baptist and knew all the details of my divorce. He knew the few who opposed the wedding, he understood Pastor Al's hesitance to marry us. Don was more than glad to perform the wedding.

The wedding ceremony was so meaningful to Nancy and me. To begin with we had found the perfect ringset in a Christian book store in Flagstaff. Both rings were stamped with identical symbols of a dove representing The Holy Spirit. Not only was our marriage to be a commitment to each other but the doves were evidence of our marriage's commitment to God. Nancy and I spent time separately writing our vows to God and to each other. Nancy cried through part of her reading of the vows. She sang a part of them too, which embarrassed me a little. I was not used to someone singing to me.

The part of the ceremony which I remember so vividly was when Nancy came out of the house and began her walk up the path to the large flat rock I was on. She was beautiful! She looked so young and vibrant. Nancy was sixteen years younger than I was but she looked much younger than that. As she walked towards me I thought, *She looks so young! Good grief! I am marrying Shirley Temple!*

Kristin was walking arm in arm on one side of Nancy, Anthony was walking arm in arm on the other. The walk with their mother up the path to me was their way of saying they were walking with her on her new journey. As Nancy was walking towards me I noticed that my son Mike had tears in his eyes. I could imagine the thoughts going through his mind. He was saddened; he was remembering the many good times we had together as family, his mother, Joan, Susie, Steve and me. He was sad that Joan and I were no longer husband and wife. He hated the divorce. He knew it was sin. Yet he was letting me know he loved me and that he understood. Mike knew that Joan would always be his mother. I would always be his dad. He could never call Nancy "Mom". Yet, Mike would grow to love Nancy, Kristin and Anthony. They would become family to him. We would all be there for him when he needed us in the years to come.

Nancy and I spent our honeymoon in beautiful Ouray, Colorado. We had a wonderful week nestled in the *Swiss Alps of America* as the Colorado Chamber of Commerce literature called the area. We loved it; we would return one day.

We returned to earth all too soon. Kristin and Anthony were waiting anxiously for us. They were left in care of Patty, the high school senior daughter of another Walgreen's friend.

Our Yogurt Shop was left in the capable hands of Lisa, a Northern Arizona University student in whom Nancy and I had complete confidence. Lisa was with us from day one of our ownership of the Yogurt Shop. She knew the ropes.

Don and Roxie Jacobson, a couple from First Baptist, aided Lisa with the bookkeeping aspect of the business in our absence.

We quickly got back into the routine of managing the popular Yogurt Shop.

I drove my car to the shop early in the morning, usually about 5:00 a.m. I put all the yogurt machines together, filled them with the flavors of the day, tidied up the customer area, then search the Bible for a meaningful verse of the day. Nancy got breakfast for Kristin and Anthony and got them off to school. Then she had an hour of quiet time with the Lord before driving her car to join me for the day in the Yogurt Shop.

Our First Jesus' Birthday Party

Our first Christmas together was special. Kristin and Anthony went to Denver to spend the Christmas holidays with their father. We did not want to spend Christmas alone so Nancy got the idea of having a Christmas party for Jesus. We invited my daughter Susie and her husband Dennis to celebrate with us. Nancy had prepared a great roasted ham with all the trimmings. Her showcase touch was a beautiful Boston cream pie she had made to be served as Jesus' Birthday Cake. The Boston cream pie was a two-layered vanilla cream filled chocolate covered cake. Nancy placed the cake on a table off to the side of our large dinner table. In the middle of dinner and conversation Dennis' eyes started to bug out. He stuttered something and pointed to the Jesus' Birthday Cake. We all looked to where Dennis was pointing. The top layer of the cake was slowly sliding off toward the floor! It was out of reach of any of us. All we could do was watch the beautiful creation slide off the table and plop on the floor. After a moment's silence we started laughing. There was not much else we could do. It was a funny sight to watch. I scooped up what was on the floor, placed it as best I could on top of the part still standing. It looked almost as good as before the accident. It tasted great.

That Jesus' Birthday Party was the first in a long line of traditonal Hicks family Jesus' Birthday Parties. Over the years Nancy added a number of meaningful ideas to worship Jesus on His special day. As our family grew, as spouces and children were involved, Nancy added a beautiful Christmas wreath which had holders for candles.

The candles symbolized the Biblical participants in God's miracle of His Son's birth: the angel who announced His birth, the shepherds, Joseph, and Mary His mother. The Jesus Candle was the tallest candle in the Christmas wreath. The youngest child at the Party that year got to light the Jesus Candle, often with help from dad. Nancy chose the Scripture to be read as each symbolic candle was lit. Grandkids were eager to light the candles. Older grandkids read the scriptures.

The highlight of each Jesus' Birthday Party was the "giving of gifts to Jesus."

Each person at the Party gave Jesus a gift. It had to be something we struggled with that we wanted Jesus to take from us. I remember so well when our grandson, Michael, Mike and Jean's boy, was small and just becoming a TV addict, he gave Jesus "his Ninja Turtles". Michael was hooked on the Ninja Turtles; he wanted Jesus to take them away from him. Michael's mom and dad said he did pretty well the rest of that year. Michael seldom tried to take the Ninja Turtles away from Jesus.

At each year's party the adults would give Jesus gifts which symbolized difficult segments of their lives, their finances, their relationship with their children, difficulties in their marriages. This gift-giving to Jesus part of the Jesus' Birthday Party often got personal and emotional. Tears were frequently shed. The one time that was especially emotional for all of us was when Mike, our son, who was struggling with diabetes more and more each year, gave Jesus his "health". It was difficult for Mike to confess his concerns. He was so choked up he could barely be heard telling us he wanted to give Jesus his health. For just a moment we could all see into his heart. There was silence all around the table. I finally broke the tension by asking Mike if his allergies were acting up. Mike laughed, blew his nose and we went on.

The gifts to Jesus were recorded on paper, usually by Michael, and were read back the next year. It was interesting to hear the confessions of those who had been Indian-givers during the year.

That first Jesus' Birthday Party when Nancy's Boston Cream Pie slid on the floor was a fun way to begin a tradition which continues to this day.

Our Failed Business Venture

We had an ideal arrangement for the first six months after our wedding. Shortly after Christmas Nancy discovered a discrepancy in her figures from the figures we were given by the previous owners. Briefly what the discrepancy showed was that we were spending money we did not have. To make a long story short Nancy and I had a several months' wrangle with Jack Delang and his family. I had contacted Mike Flournoy, a Flagstaff lawyer, who told us that Nancy and I had legal grounds to pursue the matter.

As Christians Nancy and I did not want a legal battle with other Christians. We finally came to a mutual agreement with the Delangs. Nancy and I sold the Yogurt Shop for a loss which put a hefty debt load on us.

During the time Nancy and I were going through all the Yogurt Shop hassle my good friend Bob Young paid us a visit. Bob and I worked together for a number of years in the life insurance business. Bob was my Franklin Life District Manager; he worked out of Phoenix. Before getting into life insurance Bob was a highly successful football coach at Maryvale High School in Phoenix. He won several state championships. Bob got out of Franklin Life and returned to football as Head Football Coach at his alma mater, Sioux Falls College in Sioux Falls, South Dakota. When Bob visited Nancy and me he was on a recruiting trip to Arizona and was on his way back home to Sioux Falls.

It is interesting and amazing how God works to allow loose ends to be tied up. Bob Young, a strong evangelical Christian, for whom I had the highest regard, just happened to drop in for a visit. Nancy and I were at loose ends as to what to do if we had to sell the Yogurt Shop. Bob and I stayed up half the night discussing what Nancy and I might consider.

Nancy and I discussed the possibility of going into the Christian Marriage Counseling arena. After all, who better to counsel hurting married couples than ones who had been through a divorce, who knew the pain, who knew now how to look to God for answers?

I sought Bob's advice. The advice Bob gave was advice I never thought I would ever consider. Bob suggested that I get back into coaching football as his assistant at Sioux Falls College! I told Nancy I would never coach again! Bob informed me that The North American Baptist Seminary was just down the street from Sioux Falls College. I could coach and work towards a degree in Christian Counseling! What a deal! God is so good.

Nancy and I prayed about the opportunity. Should we leave Flagstaff? Should I get back into coaching? What could I do in Flagstaff if we lost the Yogurt Shop and if I didn't go to Sioux Falls?

When Bob got back to Sioux Falls College he talked to the college President Owen Hallen. The two of them worked up a proposal for me. If I could come up within the next few weeks there might be a position available immediately. Sioux Falls College needed a director of retention. It was spring in Sioux Falls and they needed to boost student retention during Summer School hoping for a good percentage of returning students in the fall. Director of Retention? What in the world is a Director of Retention?

Bob Young came to my rescue. He explained the function of a Director of Retention was to evaluate the various departments as to their "friendliness" to the students enrolled currently. Were the departments meeting the needs of the students within the departments? The Director of Retention was expected to survey students in the departments to see what complaints they had and if their expectations were being met? Bob said it was pretty simple. I would survey the students, then confer with my immediate supervisor after tabulating the results of the survey. He would take it from there. It sounded pretty simple.

So You Wanna Be a Legend. So Did I.

Nancy and I felt God was urging us to leave Flagstaff. We needed to get a fresh start somewhere else. But Sioux Falls, South Dakota? We had to look on a map to find South Dakota, much less Sioux Falls, South Dakota! We decided to go for it. We both had complete trust in God. He would work out the details. And there were some details to work out!

It was mid-March. Both kids were in school. Should we take them out of school and enroll them for two months in a new school? The Yogurt Shop had not been sold. How could we sell it when we were going to South Dakota?

So here is what God had us do: Anthony and I left for Sioux Falls College leaving Nancy and Kristin in Flagstaff to wrap up loose ends. Bob Young said Anthony and I could live in an apartment in the Campus Married Housing until we found a house to buy or rent. We would get Anthony enrolled in a grade school adjacent to the college.

Nancy and Kristin had the difficult job. Nancy continued to work the Yogurt Shop until it sold, while at the same time trying to sell our house. Kristin walked several blocks to the Yogurt Shop after school let out in the afternoon. She helped Nancy with the management of the Shop until evening help arrived. Usually Nancy had one of the Northern Arizona University students close the Shop at the 11:00 p.m. closing time. When a student was not available Nancy and Kristin closed, which meant they didn't get home until after midnight. We kept a sleeping bag in the back office area. Kristin could get a few hours sleep until Nancy needed her help closing. It made for a long day for both of them.

Anthony and I got to know each other pretty well in our small married housing apartment. The biggest problem the two of us had was cleaning the dishes after we ate meals. I made it a rule that we only used one dish, one knife, one fork, one spoon and one glass apiece. Each of us was responsible to wash his own dish and utensils after every meal. I cleaned the pots and pans. If one of us did not wash his dish and utensils after a meal he had to eat off a dirty dish next meal, with dirty utensils. We would not wash each other's dish and utensils. Anthony was usually in such a rush to go outside and play that he seldom washed his dish or his utensils. They got pretty grubby after a few days of no washing. He soon learned.

Anthony enjoyed being the "new kid in school". He had a number of new friends to mess around with.

Most evenings I drove all over Sioux Falls looking for a nice home Nancy, the kids and I could move into. Nothing seemed to be in our price range. God again got involved. One evening I was enjoying a walk down the block where married housing was located. It was a pleasant walk and I walked down that block several times in the past. I spoke on a few occasions to a gentleman I recognized as a Sioux Falls College employee. He was often in his front yard or on his porch enjoying the spring weather. One night I stopped to shoot the breeze with him and found he was moving out of Sioux Falls to take a position at another college in another state. I asked him if he was going to sell the house he was presently in or did he rent it? He said he was calling a realtor the next morning to put the house on the market to sell. As we talked it became apparent he was in a hurry to sell. He told me the price. It was quite a bit lower than other houses I looked at in Sioux Falls. It was in our price range. The man gave me a tour of the house, it was small. Two bedrooms, one bathroom. The basement was furnished and would make another bedroom, if needed. It was a nice, clean house; only a short walk to my office. A perfect location! I told him then and there that I would take it. We shook hands on the deal; we would get the paperwork done in the morning.

Not long after we signed on the house in Sioux Falls our home in Flagstaff and the Yogurt Shop both sold within days of each other. God at work again!

Even though we sold the Yogurt Shop we still had a heavy debt to pay off. We weren't out of the woods yet financially. God took care of that problem before we left Sioux Falls in less than a year.

Nancy was excited that I found a nice home close to the college. One of our dreams was to have a Bible study in our home with college students. Being so close to campus made that a definite possibility.

CHAPTER FIVE

> Sioux Falls College
> Sioux Falls, South Dakota
> 1986-1987

> *But those who wait on the Lord*
> *Shall renew their strength;*
> *They shall mount up with wings*
> *like eagles,*
> *They shall run and not be weary,*
> *They shall walk and not faint.*
> Isaiah 40:31

Coach Bob Young
Driving "Miss Henrietta"

Coach Bob Young is the epitome of a true Christian servant leader. I praise God for allowing me special times with Bob over the years.

When Nancy and I decided to accept Bob's offer to coach with him at Sioux Falls College he volunteered to help us move from Flagstaff, Arizona to Sioux Falls, South Dakota. Bob was going to be in Phoenix anyway so he said he might as well return to Sioux Falls via Flagstaff; he volunteered to drive a load of our belongings back to Sioux Falls for us. It turned out to be quite a trip, maybe more than he counted on!

Bob ended up driving a large U-Haul moving van, towing his private vehicle behind.

Not only did he have to help us pack the U-Haul van in Flagstaff but he had to make a stop in Albuquerque, New Mexico on the way to Sioux Falls. Nancy's mother lives in Albuquerque and was giving her piano to our daughter Kristin. Since Bob had to go through Albuquerque on his way home to Sioux Falls he said it was no problem making an overnight stop to load a piano in an already well packed moving van.

Nancy saw Bob's stop in Albuquerque as an opportunity for him to bring *Henrietta Hen* to Sioux Falls. "Henrietta Hen" was the name I gave to a large, cumbersome, ugly, ceramic, adobe colored chicken shaped dry-arrangement monstrosity that was a family heirloom. Nancy loved it. Nancy's mother had adorned Henrietta with a bunch of dried cattails placed through a hole in the beast's neck, a failed attempt to beautify Henrietta.

There was no room in the van for Henrietta except on the passenger's seat next to Bob. Henrietta was so large and bulky that everytime Bob used the van's brakes he held out his right arm to keep Henrietta from crashing to the floor; a big pain in the neck for Bob. Henrietta did provide company for Bob on the long drive to Sioux Falls. He had several long uninterrupted conversations with Henrietta. He said he even sang to her at times.

My one regret about my coaching relationship with Bob Young is that I did not know him sooner in my coaching career. Had Bob and I been friends earlier I am certain that I would have been a more Christ-conscious coach.

Bob's wife, Diane expressed my thoughts well when she wrote recently regarding Bob: "He accomplishes more than anyone I know and touches more lives than you can imagine. His FCA coaches ministry has become a passion along with everyting else he does at church and USF." Sioux Falls College is now "University of Sioux Falls."

Bob's total focus is on Jesus Christ. Yes, he coaches to win, but only to win as Christ would. Bob makes it clear to his assistant coaches and his players that his commitment to Christ will not be compromised. I am certain that every coach who ever coached with Bob Young and every player who ever played for Bob Young has the highest regard for him. When all is said and done, we come away from our time with Bob Young knowing we have been in the presence of coaching greatness. Bob's relationships with his coaches and his players lasts a lifetime. Again in the words of Diane Young, "I don't know of another profession where the relationships continue for a lifetime. Bob and I love to see what the players do with their lives and we love to see their families. It is not all about wins and losses!"

My first coaching experience with Bob was in the summer of 1979 when I was chosen along with Bob to coach the North Arizona High School All Star Football Team. We played the Southern Arizona High School All Stars. I spent an enjoyable seven days with Bob and a group of Arizona's best high school football players on the University of Arizona's campus in Tucson, Arizona. I learned then just how important Bob's relationship with Christ was to to him. Bob led in prayer either before or after practices. He led brief Bible devotionals for those who wanted to attend. Bob even led in prayer after our North Arizona All Stars lost a close, hard fought game to the South Arizona All Stars. Bob's prayer included thanking the Lord for the time all of us spent together that week. He prayed the Lord would bless each of us as we went our separate ways.

That first coaching experience with Bob led to a loss. My first college coaching experience with him led to a losing season. We finished with three wins and seven losses in 1986. Bob's comments on our three win-seven loss season reflect the character of Coach Bob Young, "It (1986) was a special year in so many ways. God meets our needs in more ways than we ever know at the time. As I look down the roster there were many key freshmen and sophomores who came into our program that certainly served as a basis for our 10-0 season in 1988. Having you and Nancy at USF that year was probably the greatest blessing. I certainly cherish our relationship and know it is all because of our common love for our Lord and Savior, Jesus Christ."

So You Wanna Be a Legend. So Did I.

Coach Bob Young, Mrs. Diane Young, daughter Milisa Garrow, Chad and AJ Garrow

Bob Young led the University of Sioux Falls to three National NAIA Football Championships; the first in 1996 and two more in 2006 and 2008.

Bob retired as Head Football Coach in 2009. Bob's 22 season record was an impressive 172 wins-69 losses-3 ties. The winning Christ-centered football program developed by Coach Young is the foundation for The University of Sioux Falls' perennial place among the Nation's NAIA football powers.

The University of Sioux Falls' *Cougar* football teams play their home games on "Bob Young Field," a fitting tribute to an outstanding man who exemplifies Christlikeness. A man whom I am proud to call a friend and a brother in Christ.

NORTH AMERICAN BAPTIST SEMINARY
Trouble Right Off the Bat.

My career as a seminary student lasted two days. I found out rather quickly that I was going to be at odds with the professor teaching my Christian Marriage Counseling Class. The guy was a dyed in the wool liberal.

The professor encouraged discussions. I like discussions in a class of any kind. He started the second lesson by talking about married couples who have issues over finances. The discussion generated a lot of give and take. Most of the class was comprised of married males. Many said their wives had to work to make ends meet. I could buy that. The professor could buy that as well. When he really got to me was when he said if a couple had goals that required the wife to work, whether or not they had children at home, then it was wise for her to work. He said even if the couple could make it on only one income it was o.k. for the wife to bring in a second income.

I could not totally agree with the professor. I said that I did not agree that the wife should be working if the couple had children at home. Babysitters could not take the place of a mom at home. The professor rather smugly reminded me that the *Proverbs 31* wife worked to earn an income for her family. She had children at home yet she still worked. The professor, of course, quoted verses from *Proverbs 31* describing work the wife did to earn money and clothing for the family.

My contention was the the *Proverbs 31* wife did her work *from* her home, not *away* from her home. She was a stay at home mom who worked from her home. The professor's retort was to ask me if I had ever taken Hebrew or Greek. When I told him I had not he said, "If you were knowledgeable in the original language *Proverbs* was written in you would quickly change you views." End of argument. Case closed.

As I left class that day another student came up to me and said he agreed with me and that the professor was one of the Seminary's most outspoken liberals. His pompus attitude never left room for much disagreement. That professor was the one from whom I would have to take most of my Christian Marriage Counseling classes. We would never hit it off I could tell. After class the next day I dropped it. No sense wasting my money or my time.

Nancy unofficially got into the counseling business quickly after arriving at Sioux Falls College. She didn't have to take a seminary class to do so. I met a lady in the office where I worked who was nice. She and I hit it off immediately. When she found out I was going to enroll in North American Baptist Seminary to study Christian Marriage Counseling she became immediately interested. She began to confide in me regarding some family issues she was struggling with. I told her that Nancy would a good one for her to visit. Nancy and I agreed that when and if we ever got into counseling that we would never counsel the opposite sex. I invited the lady to lunch the next day so she could meet and talk to Nancy. The two of them hit it off immediately. They met a few more times during the next months before the lady and her family moved out of town. Nancy got a nice note of thanks from her soon after the lady moved. She indicated that Nancy helped her cope with several issues. What pleased Nancy was that the lady told her she was closer to Jesus than she had ever been before.

Sioux Falls College was a Christian liberal arts college affiliated with the American Baptist Church and it required that all students attend Chapel Services each Wednesday morning. Faculty and staff were encouraged to attend as well. A week after I dropped my Christian Marriage Counseling class at the Seminary I attended a Chapel Service which encouraged me. Campus Pastor Keith Anderson spoke on "Walking in The Spirit." Some of the points he hit on struck a chord with me. For his Scripture source Pastor Anderson used *Galatians 5:16: I say then: Walk in the Spirit, and you shall not fulfill the lust of the flesh.* Pastor Anderson explained that *walk* in verse sixteen refers to a believer's everyday habitual lifestyle, his progress in submitting to the Spirit's control and his obedience to the simple commands of Scripture. A cross-reference to *Galatians 5:16* pointed to *Galatians 6:1-2.* This one really got to me: *Galatians 6:1-2: Brethren, if a man is overtaken in any trespass, you who are spiritual restore such a one in a spirit of gentleness, considering yourself lest you also be tempted. (2) Bear one another's burdens, and so fulfill the law of Christ.*

As a Christian counselor who is walking in the Spirit my response to another's sinful life style should be with an awareness that I too am a sinner. I should direct my efforts to restore such a one with a spirit of gentleness as Christ would do. My lifestyle should be one that makes it easier for another to approach me without fear of being harshly condemned for whatever sinful issues he may have.

I came away from that Chapel Service confident that I did not need a seminary degree to be an effective Christian marriage counselor. If I lived day to day submitting to the Holy Spirit's leading God would lead others to me. I did not need to "hang out a shingle" to advertise my desire to help people with their sinful issues.

As God tells me in *Galatians 6:2*, I am to, *"Bear one another's burdens, and so fulfill the law of Christ."* The "law of Christ" refers to the new commandment Jesus gave his disciples as He was leaving them to go back the His Father. In *John 13:34* Jesus told them, *"A new commandment I give to you, that you also love one another; as I have loved you, that you also love one another."* My job was to love all people. God would take care of the rest.

CHRISTMAS
Away from Home and Family

The first church Nancy, Kristin, Anthony and I attended regularly as a family was a small Christian and Missionary Alliance Church in Sioux Falls. We were captivated by the friendly, loving people we met during the brief time we attended.

Pastor Mike was a young dynamic preacher who, with his wife and family were active in all aspects of the CMA Church they led. Pastor Mike encouraged his flock to meet often to "break bread" together as Jesus encouraged us to do.

That Christmas in Sioux Falls was our first Christmas away from family. Our two kids were with their father again. Nancy and I were alone except for the new family of believers we had met at The Christian and Missionary Alliance Church. Pastor Mike and his family invited Nancy and me to share with them at his home in celebrating Jesus birthday. I believe Pastor Mike knew we were alone.

It was a wonderful time of worship, fellowship and celebration of our Savior's birth. We enjoyed laughter, food, and most of all worship focused around the events of Jesus' birth. Nancy and I are so thankful to Pastor Mike for showing us the love of Christ at that special time. Pastor Mike and his congregation at Sioux Falls Christian and Missionary Alliance Church were a special gift from God to Nancy and me.

SHARING THE WORD WITH COLLEGE STUDENTS

Nancy and I were blessed to be able to have a Bible study in our home for married college students and a few singles, usually 11 or 12 total in attendance. Our purpose was to show couples what a premium God places on marriage. We strived to reveal to them the mistakes Nancy and I made hoping to teach them what a Godly marriage looked like. One older couple who attended had been married for over 20 years; they had many ups and downs in their marriage. They gave God total credit for keeping their marriage intact all those years. I used John MacArthur's study on *The Fulfilled Family* as the basis for the lessons. We had excellent response to the teachings and the older couple proved to be a welcome additional resource to MacArthur's teachings. Nancy and I found this college age Bible study to be enjoyable, rewarding and what we felt was encouraging to the students. We hoped to continue teaching Bible studies to college students for many more years. With God's blessings we did but not at Sioux Falls College.

REPLACED BY A SCULPTURED SIOUX FALLS COLLEGE *COUGAR*

The most anticipated improvements for Sioux Falls College was the soon-to-be constructed "Stewart Wellness and Athletic Center." It was obviously an expensive project, one that would necessitate the usual budget cuts associated with huge college construction endeavours. I was one of those cuts. My immediate college authority was Dr. Neil Eddy. It was his unenviable duty to inform me of the Administration's decision to cut the Retention Director and Assistant Football Coach's positions. My positions were to be terminated in a few months when the school year ended.

Neil Eddy and I were on friendly terms. We hit it off with each other from the moment we met. We played tennis several times together. Neil usually won so he was sorry to have to let me go. Neil called me into his office to tell me the bad news. His sincerity was comforting to me; I saw sadness in his eyes. He was tearful as he told me I was being let go. He knew I was newly married with two young elementary school age children. Neil knew this would be a big blow to us. Where would we go to find other employment? Where could we go? I had no idea, but God had an idea. A great idea!

Even though this was a stressful time for my family and me, I was able to find humor in the situation. One of the "spin-offs" to building the new Stewart Wellness and Athletic Center was that the Sioux Falls administration bought the idea of placing a bigger than life sculptured cougar in a prominent setting near the proposed Wellness Center. I read in the school newspaper what the cost of the sculptured Sioux Falls *Cougar* was. The cost of purchasing this stone replica of the College's mascot was almost dollar for dollar what my salary had been. I was being replaced by a schulptured *Cougar*!

My dear friend and brother in Christ Jack Brintnal gave me a great illustration of how God works in our lives. Jack said God uses our lives as a giant chessboard. He moves the pieces from square to square at His pleasure. God's moves aided by our obedience to Him always lead to "checkmate" of any moves by God's opponent, Satan. This illustration of God using our lives of obedience was apparent to Nancy and me as we saw how God orchestrated our getting out of heavy debt from our Yogurt Shop fiasco. The first thing God did was put the book, Master Your Money by Ron Blue in our hands. Nancy and I both read and studied the book. Ron Blue promised that if God's steps to financial freedom were followed faithfully, we could be out of debt within three years. We prayed and did all we could with the income we had to be obedient to God's word regarding being wise stewards of His money. God rewarded our obedience and we were out of debt before we moved from Sioux Falls. God is good.

I could see God's hand clearly as he moved Nancy and me from a place we dearly loved, Sioux Falls College, to an even more perfect place for us, Sterling College in Sterling, Kansas. My search for significance was put on the fast track by God!

CHAPTER SIX

Sterling College
Sterling, Kansas
1987-To the Present

For I know the thoughts that I
think towards you, says the Lord,
thoughts of peace and not of evil, to
give you a future and a hope.
Jeremiah 29:11

COOPER HALL

ANOTHER GREAT MOVE BY GOD

A month before I was let go at Sioux Falls College, Nancy and I planned a summer trip to Sterling College to visit with our two sons and their families: Mike, Jean and Michael, age six months; Steve, Lori and Joanna, age one year. Mike was the Head Football Coach at Inman High School a small community thirty miles east of Sterling. He got the Head Football job at Inman High School upon his graduation from Sterling College in 1985. Steve graduated from Sterling College in 1986 and was working in the College Financial Office.

Nancy and I were to stay with Steve, Lori and baby Joanna in their small house directly across the street from the Sterling College Campus. As Nancy and I were planning our trip to Sterling College, God gave me another nudge to encourage me to bring my resume' in case there were coaching opportunities for me.

I was saddened to hear from my son Steve that Clair Gleason, the Sterling College Athletic Director whom I met on an earlier trip to Sterling College, passed away in the fall of 1986. I hoped to visit with Coach Gleason as he once suggested that maybe someday I could land a coaching position at SC.

I did get a chance to meet Coach Lonnie Kruse who took Coach Gleason's place as Athletic Director. Coach Kruse was encouraging about the possibility of getting Coach Gleason's position as Head Baseball Coach if I were interested. He said that Coach Gary White, Head Football Coach might have an assistant football coaching position available as well. I told Coach Kruse that I had little baseball coaching experience, but that I played college baseball and one season of professional baseball. I would love to coach baseball on the college level. Before I left Coach Kruse's office he called the President of Sterling College, Dr. Robert Veitch and arranged for me to meet with him the next day. Coach Kruse told me that President Veitch was eager to get the baseball coaching position filled.

I was proud when Coach Kruse told me what a positive impact both Mike and Steve made on Sterling College. Besides both being outstanding athletes they both popular and active on campus.

President Veitch confirmed Coach Kruse's assessment of Mike and Steve when I met with him the next day. He said that Sterling College would be proud to have Mike and Steve's father on the Sterling College *Warrior* athletic staff. I was humbled and proud. My interview with President Veitch reminded me of my Carmel High School interview way back in 1957. It consisted of a few minutes of informal visiting, a handshake and I had a job. God is good.

Nancy and I had a lot to talk about on our trip back to Sioux Falls. We had the car to ourselves. Our two kids, Kristin and Anthony went to Denver, Colorado to spend the summer with their father, David. We wondered how the two of them would react to another move in less than a year's time.

The day after Nancy and I returned to our small home in Sioux Falls, I received a phone call from Mrs. Guy'lene Dwyer the Administrator of Sterling College's Academic Opportunity Center. Mrs. Dwyer told me that President Veitch suggested to her that I be hired to fill a need in the Academic Opportunity Center as a male to work with the male students who came to the Center for Career Counseling. Mrs. Dwyer knew both Mike and Steve. She told me their careers at Sterling College were all the recommendation I needed to be hired.

I had one visit to Sterling College and came away with three jobs: Head Baseball Coach, assistant Football Coach, and Career Counselor. God doesn't mess around!

Our brief time in Sioux Falls was a meaningful time for Nancy, Kristin, Anthony and me. We learned much about each other in that time. The four of us had to be flexible and considerate; we had one bathroom to share. That was probably the biggest single adjustment to make. In order for the daily routine to get started on time each of us had an allotted time to get in and out of the bathroom. Nancy was first as she had to get breakfast ready. I was second, Kristin third, and Anthony fourth. He enjoyed his extra sleeping time. We had family devotions at 6:45 a.m. followed by breakfast at 7:00 a.m. Those times were set in stone. Nobody was allowed to miss devotions except for sickness. I don't ever remember that happening.

The family devotions were important to Nancy and me. Kristin and Anthony often rolled their eyes at something I read or said. They both kept an eye on the clock to make sure I didn't go over my allotted time. They were hungry and usually bored with the devotions. Nevertheless we stuck with it; family devotions every day. No exceptions. Nancy and I saw a number of times over the years the validity of God's Word. He said in *Isaiah 55:11: So shall My word that goes forth from My mouth; It shall not return to Me void, but it shall accomplish what I please, and it shall prosper the thing for which I sent it.* Our family devotions brought forth fruit as our kids grew to became teenagers. We saw God's faithfulness during some very difficult times.

God used our brief time in Sioux Falls to give us the beginning of a firm foundation upon which to build a Godly family, a family that strives to glorify God and His Son, Jesus Christ.

SETTLING DOWN IN FLY-OVER COUNTRY

On a good day when Sterling College is in session the population of Sterling, Kansas swells to 2,600. The population doesn't fluctuate much from one year to another.

When Nancy and I arrived in Sterling with a loaded moving van, we had to spend several nights sleeping in an empty room in the basement of Campbell Hall, a men's dormitory across the street from Steve and Lori's home. During the days we were with Joe Henry, Sterling's realtor of choice, looking for a home to buy. The housing market in Sterling depends to a great degree upon the number of Sterling College personnel coming and leaving on any given year. Realtor Joe Henry showed us three homes. The first two were nice homes, the third was perfect. We loved it immediately. It would be our home for ten years. The home was in an ideal location, directly behind the City Library one- half block off of Broadway, the main street in Sterling. We were within walking distance of anywhere in Sterling. It is said that any place in Sterling is within walking distance of anywhere else in Sterling.

The house Joe sold us was the home Coach Clair Gleason was living in at the time of his death. Coach Gleason and his family had lived in the house for many years.

I found it humorous that most of the do-it-yourself projects around Coach Gleason's home were adequately completed with athletic tape.

Sterling, Kansas is noted for the popular movie of the 1950's *Picnic*, which starred Henry Fonda and Kim Novak; and was filmed mostly in Sterling. Sterling Lake, a beautiful lake on the south edge of Sterling was a focal point in the movie. I remembered seeing the movie when I was going to Arizona State University. Little did I know that I would live there one day.

Sterling College *Warrior* Football 1987

"Give the Ball to Bennett"

Early one morning a few days after we moved into our new home the doorbell rang; our first visitors. Who in the world would be ringing our doorbell at this early hour? I was greeted by three sweaty young men in shorts and T-shirts. The spokesman for the group introduced himself and his buddies, "Coach Hicks, I am Jeff Bennett; this is Mike Brannon, and this is Ray Langley. We are Sterling College football players. We are just out running and we wanted to stop by and welcome you to Sterling. We are looking forward to playing for you."

I invited the three in to meet Nancy who was cooking breakfast. They thanked me but declined saying they were too sweaty and had to get their running in for the morning. With that welcome and a handshake from each they ran on up the road. The impromptu meeting made a positive impression on me. I would be working with these three young athletes closely as the Sterling College football team's Offensive Coordinator. I was to be part of a fine Sterling College football team which was called the best in the past seven years.

Several weeks before football practices were to begin, Head Coach Gary White and I got together to discuss philosophy; he wanted to find out my strengths and weaknesses. I let him know right up front that I had very little experience coaching college football. My brief time at Sioux Falls College under Coach Bob Young was beneficial for me in that I realized that football on the college level was quite a bit more complex than on the high school level. With Coach Young I was on a "watch and learn" mode. Had I been with him longer I would have been much more able to coach the college game. I was still steeped in the big play concept that I developed during my high school coaching days. Coach Young was analytical of the various defenses he confronted. His offense was geared accordingly.

My offenses were designed to be run irregardless of the defense. Some plays could be run against certain defenses, others could not. My style was more "hit and miss". I was too simplistic.

I believe Coach Gary White was much like me. His offense was similiar to my philosophy. What made him a successful coach at Sterling College was that his offense was geared to the tremendous talents of Jeff Bennett. His whole offense revolved around Jeff. Jeff was such a threat that opposing coaches designed their defenses with one thought in mind: "Stop Bennett." They knew that if they could effectively slow down Jeff Bennett, Sterling College did not have enough other offensive weapons to mount much of a threat. My philosophy fit in very well. Coach White appointed me Offensive Coordinator though he called most of the offensive plays. That was no problem for me; Coach White and I often briefly consulted prior to the plays being sent in. He saw the value of allowing me to install some of my silent signal passing and Gangster Pass concepts. With just a few added wrinkles to the SC offense, the opponents could not totally focus on the running ability of Jeff Bennett. Quarterback Mike Brannon's passing could not be ignored. He caught on well to the few silent signal and Gangster concepts we put in.

A number of times during the season when the Sterling College *Warriors* were in a tough spot I was reminded of how Coach Larry Gray and I reacted at Flagstaff High School; we'd look at each other and the call was often "Gangster pass." Only at Sterling College, Coach White and I would look at each other and the call was "Give the ball to Bennett." More often than not Jeff would get us out of trouble. He was a great running back.

My first two years of coaching on the college level were real eye-openers for me! I always thought that if one could coach successfuly on the high school level the adjustment to college would not be too difficult. After all, the quality of the players would be better and therefore coaching them should be easier than coaching the less gifted and less mature high school kids. My brief time as an assistant at Sioux Falls College and as an assistant at Sterling College made me realize I was a long ways from being a qualified head college coach.

Coach White had several former players with a fifth year of college before graduating: those he utilized as graduate assistant coaches. These were eager and enthused young men who did the job Coach White assigned them to the best of their ability; however it takes a graduate assistant many years before he is qualified to handle head coaching responsibilities.

Warrior Football
Hadley Hicks, Head Coach
What?
1988-1990

Sterling College President Dr. Robert Veitch paid a surprise visit to my office in the Academic Opportunity Center one cold January day in 1988. The purpose of his visit was to tell me that Head Football Coach Gary White resigned. Dr. Veitch wanted me to consider taking Coach White's place on an interim basis. We discussed what "interim" meant. Dr. Veitch made it clear that he wanted me to keep the Head Baseball position. If after my first season as Head Football Coach I wanted to keep that job, and the Board of Trustees agreed, it was mine. I was of course flattered that Dr.Veitch offered me the head job. I explained to Dr. Veitch that Nancy and I would pray and discuss what this change would mean to our family. I told Dr.Veitch that at this point in my life my family was my most important consideration. I wasn't sure we wanted the stress and pressure that the head football position would involve. There would be plenty of both for an inexperienced college coach like me.

After Nancy and I prayed about the offer for several days I went back to Dr. Veitch and told him I would take the job as interim head football coach for the 1988 season; the Board of Trustees would have a year to begin a search for a permanent head coach. Dr. Veitch was sure the agreement would be agreeable with the Board of Trustees.

I don't know if the Board of Trustees ever agreed or not. I do know that the powers that be on the Sterling College faculty were highly upset that Dr. Veitch had not consulted with them about my appointment. They felt that the faculty should always be consulted when one of their own was chosen for such a prominent position as Sterling College Head

Football Coach. They were probably right. I am sure they were doubly upset when my one year interim position as Head Football Coach turned into a two year ordeal.

My first season, 1988, as Head Football Coach was one I would like to forget! It was fraught with disappointment. I knew going into the season that we had many obstacles to overcome. We graduated Jeff Bennett, one of the best running backs in Sterling College history and one of the best in America in 1987. Jeff had been selected as an NAIA All American. Jeff followed in his dad's footsteps. Curt Bennett had been an All American back at Sterling College back in the late 1950's

We lost an outstanding quarterback as well. Many felt Mike Brannon should have been selected to the All KCAC Team. We did not win the conference championship and usually the quarterback from the conference champion is selected as All Conference. I thought Mike Brannon was the best quarterback in the KCAC in 1987.

We graduated a number of good linemen to compound our woes for 1988. All Conference Linemen Jeff Washerlesky and Steve Harrell would be hard to replace.

The offensive linemen returning were too few and too little. Rick Stallings and Vince Walker were our only experienced linemen. They both had decent size. Vince Walker was 235 pounds and Rick Stallings was maybe 225 pounds. They were all we had. We filled in around them but we did not have enough size or experience to match our opponents.

The best blocker on our offensive line was center Chris Loven. Chris seldom missed a blocking assignment. His blocking technique was nearly perfect. Chris had one problem: he weighed 165 pounds. Chris had as much heart as any player on our team. After games he was exhausted and so frustrated that he could not get the job done against his much heavier opponents. Had Chris been a 200 pounder he would have made a good college center.

Shortly after I was appointed Head Football Coach I began to tackle the difficult task of planning for the upcoming 1989 baseball season and preparing the recruiting necessities for the 1988 football season. I appointed Rick Ashley to be our Recruiting Coordinator. Rick was Coach Gary White's defensive coordinator and was an enthusiastic young man. He seemed like the perfect one to be Recruiting Coordinator; he was outgoing, pleasant, hard working, and easy to talk to. He was a born salesman. Rick could sell Sterling College to prospective recruits.

I knew Rick for quite a few years. He played at Sterling College with my two sons, Mike and Steve. Rick and Steve were especially close. Both had been assistant residence directors in Kilbourne Hall, one of the two men's dormitories. Steve brought Rick home to Flagstaff, Arizona over one Christmas break. During Rick's stay with us in Flagstaff I grew to love the guy. We became close over the years. There was one big problem with my appointment of Rick Ashley as Recruiting Coordinator.

Rick was also Defensive Coordinator and his recruiting emphasis was focused on defensive players. I would regret my dependence on Rick for recruiting.

We had a pitiful 1988 sason. The *Warriors* struggled through a dishearting 0-10 season. Officially we won one game by forfeit. That wasn't much consolation, kind of like kissing your sister. I made many mistakes that year. Possibly my biggest was trying to do things the way Coach White had done them. I was talked into ignoring completely what I had learned about organizing practices; instead I attempted to organize things as Coach White had. I ignored the old coaching adage "do what you do best." As a result the first early morning practices were poorly organized. Coach White did things much differently than I had ever done. I was not Coach White and could therefore not run things the way he did. I lost credibility with the assistant coaches right off the bat. I never regained credibility with them the entire season. The fact that we were losing did not help.

Dr. Veitch dropped a bomb on me when I visited with him at the end of the season. He informed me that he had resigned and due to the urgency of his resignation the Board of Trustees could not take the time to be involved with a football coach search because the Presidential search took priority. The Board of Trustees had too much on their plate to be concerned about finding a football coach.

Dr. Veitch informed me that my one year agreement to be Head Football Coach would have to be extended into the 1989 season. He was candid with me explaining that the Board of Trustees was faced with a major dilemma that was tied in with his resignation; the College was at the brink of closing its doors. Sterling College had been spending money it did not have! The Board of Trustees, the Faculty Advisory Board, and any others who knew what was going on behind the scenes were in near-panic mode.

Though I was somewhat aware of all that was going on administratively, I had other problems to deal with. I still had a baseball team to coach and recruiting was my big concern. I again had to depend on Rick Ashley to organize the entire off-season task of recruiting. The job was too much for one man. Rick was pretty much on his own as I had my hands full with the upcoming 1989 baseball season. Rick and I met several times that winter to discuss how best to handle the recruiting for the 1989 football season. I tried to impress on him that we needed to shore up our offense. To have a successful season the *Warriors* had to be balanced between offense and defense. Coach Ashley's recruiting correspondance was carried on primarily with defensive recruit possibilities. He recruited a number of good defensive players but few offensive players.

In looking back at the 1988 and 1989 seasons I found that God was put on the shelf by me during my difficulties. I again became so self-absorbed that I spent little time seeking God's wisdom. My prayer time had been limited. I had been there before and as I slowly got back in the groove God began to show me that His ways are better than my ways.

The 1989 season was a blessing in disguise for me. Our 2-7 win-loss record did not appear to be much of a blessing; it was though. God gave me a wake-up call to remind me He had taken me through the struggles with assistant coaches before. I am a slow learner.

I picked up a former SC *Warrior* football player as an assistant coach; Brad Starnes was a teammate of my two sons Mike and Steve. Brad would prove to be a positive asset to me. Brad Starnes teamed with veteran SC player, Pierce McIntosh to form an excellent offensive coaching staff. Bryce Kristofferson, a quarterback from the 1988 team and Vince Walker offensive guard from 1988 were graduate assistants who helped us.

Defensive Coordinator Rick Ashley and I put together a good defensive coaching staff: Bo Frondorf another former *Warrior* teammate of Mike and Steve's was Rick's defensive back coach, Mal McCluskey former *Warrior* All KCAC linebacker coached the linebackers.

A big mistake that God showed me I made as Head Coach was that I didn't confront Coach Rick Ashley immediately after the 1988 season about his lack of recruiting support. I had flashbacks to my days with Coaches Ken McElyea and Ernie Thornburg at Flagstaff

High School in Flagstaff, Arizona. Coaches McElyea and Thornburg had been disloyal; I confronted them and they resigned. The problem was solved. With Coach Ashley the problem was never resolved. His lack of support became more and more evident as the season progressed and the loses mounted. One particular incident weighs heavily on my mind. Toward the end of one of our early season practices I was at one end of the field with our offensive personnel. The defensive personnel were at the other end. Coach Ashley gave his players a water break. To get to the water source the defensive players had to run past where our offensive players were running through offensive drills. As Coach Ashley and his defensive players ran by us I heard one of the defensive players shout an obscene comment to another player. Coach Ashley was well within hearing range of the comment. As Coach Ashley ran by I said, "Coach, get on him! You heard what he said!" Coach Ashley replied to me disrespectfully, "You're the Head Coach. You get on him."

Yes, I should have gotten on the player. More importantly I should have called Coach Ashley on the carpet immediately after practice. I didn't. I never addressed it.

I had enough coaching experience to be well aware that the conflict between Coach Ashley and me was flowing over to the other coaches and the players. Soon it became a wedge between the offensive team and the defensive team. It was obvious that our defensive team was much stronger than our offensive team. The offensive team could not maintain any consistancy in games; we were usually "three and out" as the saying goes. We'd run three plays, not get a first down and we'd have to punt. The defensive team was on the field way too much. The chatter among the defensive players soon became demeaning towards the offense. Their defensive meetings became a "rag on the offense" time. A good head coach would not have allowed that to continue. God made it evident to me that my significance would not be found as a head college football coach.

I was appreciative of Coach Bo Frondorf as he worked closely with Coach Ashley. Coach Bo was open in his discussions with me. He offered me advice which would help the entire team not just one segment of the team. One suggestion Coach Bo made was that we spend more time in practices with our Speciality Teams. Bo was our Specialty Teams Coach and he recognized that our kicking game was the only consistant bright spot. We needed to spend more practice time fine tuning that part of our team.

Coach Bo's advice paid dividends. Punter-kicker Jay Hollis was the *Warrior's* Most Valuable Player that year. He punted a bunch! I am sure it was rare for a punter-kicker to be a team's Most Valuable Player. Without a doubt Jay Hollis was our most valuable player in 1989. His high, booming punts constantly kept the opponents backed up deep in their own territory. It was common for an opponent to drive down the field 70-80 yards against our defense to score a touchdown. Our defense got plenty tired. Jay's kickoffs were also high and deep. He kicked 60 yard field goals in practice at times. O.k., so if he had such a strong kicking leg why wasn't he at a larger school? Why was he at little NAIA Sterling College?

At one time Jay Hollis was recruited out of his California high school to attend the University of Southern California by Southern Cal *Trojan* Coach Ted Tollner. Before Jay could enroll at Southern Cal, Coach Tollner was fired and replaced by Coach Larry Smith. Smith was not interested in Jay Hollis. Jay then enrolled in Los Angeles City College; while at LACC Jay heard about Sterling College. After a series of letters and phone calls Jay Hollis came to Sterling College for a recruiting visit. He brought his buddy

Jo Jo Corral with him. Jo Jo was a pleasant surprise. He was a big 240 pound offensive lineman. Both Jay and Jo Jo thoroughly enjoyed their visit to Sterling College.

They were taken to a Sterling College *Warrior* basketball game their first night in town. They could not believe how friendly the SC students were to them. Jay said that many students came up to the two Southern California boys and made them feel welcome.

Jay said that they'd go to a game in Los Angeles and the only ones who would speak were the ones they came to the game with.

Jo Jo stayed at Sterling College and after two good seasons of football he graduated. Jo Jo was a fixture around Sterling and Rice County for several years as he served as a Patrolman in the Sheriff's Department.

Jay Hollis earned Most Valuable Player and All Conference football in 1988. He was Most Valuable Player and All Conference in baseball in 1989, then with one year of eligibility remaining he went back to California. Jay was looking for bigger and better things. He heard that Hall of Fame Coach George Allen was fired by the National Football League Washington *Redskins* and that Allen was immediately hired by Cal Poly University in Southern California. Jay contacted Coach Allen. Allen was interested in Jay. Jay went to Cal Poly for the 1991 season. Coach Allen died before he coached a game at Cal Poly. I never heard from Jay Hollis again.

BUILDING A FOUNDATION
Sterling College Baseball
1987-1997

When Dr. Veitch hired me as Head Baseball Coach at Sterling College in Sterling, Kansas, in May of 1987, I became a pain in the neck almost immediately.

I am not the brightest guy in the world, and I had never coached baseball before, except for a brief, unimpressive, three year stint on the high school level. However, I was bright enough to know that there were major problems with the Sterling College baseball field. To begin with our outfield did not have a fence! We were probably the only National Association of Intercollegiate Athletics (NAIA) college baseball field in the country without a fence. I battled our administration, our maintenance department, and our athletic department for ten years trying to get them to let us put up an attractive portable fence. It never happened during my reign.

During my first season as Assistant Football Coach I was oblivious to another major flaw I encountered in my baseball program. Not only did the baseball team not have a fence, we did not have a full-sized field! Our SC football team laid claim to our entire outfield area for much of the school year. Our outfield was the football team's practice field. It had been for decades.

I was able to relate horror stories of outfielders trying to catch ground balls and fly balls on the mutilated surface the baseball team had to share with the football team. "Back each other up" was a baseball cliche I firmly embed in the minds of our Sterling College outfielders.

I called a meeting of our baseball team after the 1987 football season ended. That meeting was my first real introduction to all the problems the baseball program tolerated. I found that Sterling College baseball was like what I found at Arizona State College when I enrolled there after my U.S. Army days; our Sterling College Administration did not put much emphasis on baseball. The baseball program was more like an intramural activity. Anybody who wanted to could go out for the team.

Unlike Arizona State College, Sterling College was a member of an organized and well established athletic conference; we were in the KCAC, the Kansas Collegiate Athletic Conference. One would think that peer-pressure would have made the Sterling College Administration want to keep up with the other KCAC baseball programs. Not so. Sterling College baseball was the "step-child" of the Sterling College Athletic Department. It was expected to field a representative team in the KCAC yet the Sterling College administration was not supportive of the baseball program. There was no such thing as a recruiting budget. I was told Coach Clair Gleason did his recruiting among the incoming freshman class each year. Recruiting trips for baseball were unheard of.

I had several meetings with President Veitch to discuss the baseball problem. Dr. Veitch, to his credit, made several promises to me that he made good; he promised that I could take our baseball team to the 1989 Christian College Baseball Tournament in Florida and he promised I could take a recruiting trip to Arizona, New Mexico, Oklahoma and Texas during the summer of 1989. I assured Dr. Veitch that the baseball team would hold several fundraisers in the fall to help defray the cost. These two trips Dr. Veitch permitted were the beginning of a resurgence in the Sterling College baseball program. "Sterling College Baseball" soon became a recognized name among several large high school districts in various states.

By the time I was on my pre-Christmas recruiting swing through the southwest states I took on the difficult task of being both Head Football and Head Baseball Coach. I made recruiting visits for both programs. I spent hours in high schools talking with coaches and athletes of both sports. It was necessary for me at times to visit with prospective Sterling College recruits in their homes. I enjoyed that part of the recruiting process. One such visit paid Sterling College huge dividends for our football program.

I visited with James Silman and his mom and dad in their El Paso, Texas home one evening. James' high school football coach recommended James to me when I visited with the coach earlier in the day in his office. When first meeting a coach I made it clear up front that Sterling College was a Christian college. I was looking for athletes who would fit in a Christian college environment. James Silman's football coach said James and his family were Christians; he felt James would be a good fit. James was not available to meet with me at the time I was at his school so I made arrangements to meet with James at his home that evening.

James' father, CW-4 James Silman and his family were stationed at Fort Bliss in El Paso, Texas. Silman was a career U.S. Army man. CW-4 James Silman and his wife, Margaret, were hospitable and friendly people. They were obviously evangelical Christians. Mrs. Silman was excited about the possibility of James attending a Christian college. The Silmans liked what I told them about Sterling College. They were excited that James would have a chance to play football at a Christian college.

James was on campus in early September; ready for his freshman year. He had four good years at Sterling College. He was a four year starter at linebacker and was All-KCAC his senior year. James Silman was my first Sterling College football recruit and the only football recruit I was able to sign for the 1988 season.

I had much better results recruiting baseball players that winter. Mentioning the fact that the 1988 Sterling College baseball team was going to Coco, Florida for the Christian College Baseball Tournament was a big factor in drawing recruits to our program.

I started recruiting for baseball shortly after my family and I moved to Sterling from Sioux Falls. Well before the football season started in late August, I made many phone calls to high school baseball coaches in Arizona. I was able to get quite a few names of potential recruits. As soon as I mentioned the Christian College Baseball Tournament in Coco, Florida those Arizona boys perked up. Five good Arizona baseball players were on campus and registered by the time classes started in September: Vince Mendibles from my stomping grounds of Prescott, Arizona, Glenn Kopp from Phoenix, Arizona, Chet Brown from Coolidge, Arizona, Matt Caffaro and Nick Giacoma from Tucson. Those five fine baseball players laid the foundation for a number of others from Arizona who would do well at Sterling College in the ensuing years.

I was excited and eager to get started with baseball after the 1987 football season ended. My son Steve was slated to be one of my assistants; Steve graduated from SC in 1984 and was working in the Sterling College Business Office for the past three years. When I accepted the head baseball position Steve agreed to help me.

My second assistant was Larry Smith who just happened to be the Mayor of Sterling. Talk about getting things done, Larry knew everybody in town. One of the first things Larry did was get a portable batting cage constructed for free I might add. The next thing was to get tin roofs put over our two ancient cement slab dugouts. At least both teams could get under a roof when it rained.

Steve never got to assist me. God called Steve, his wife Lori, and baby daughter Joanna to be missionaries to Venezuela. I was proud of Steve but disappointed that he would not be around to help me coach. I had several talks with God about the situation and I told Steve that God told me He wanted Steve and family to stay in Sterling. Steve didn't buy that. He and his family went to Venezuela and spent 17 years in Christian ministry.

My oldest son, Mike told me that losing Steve was the best thing that happened to the Sterling College baseball program that year. Mike replaced Steve as my assistant coach for the 1988 season. Mike played one season of baseball for Coach Claire Gleason. He was a fine fielding left-handed first baseman. Mike played four years of high school baseball at Flagstaff High School. He proved to be an outstanding baseball coach as well as an outstanding football coach at Inman High School just a short disance from Sterling. Mike was in Inman for 23 years.

With Mayor Larry Smith and my son Mike as assistant coaches, I was ready to get the season underway. But, I still had a baseball field problem to contend with.

Sometime between the last football game of the season, usually early November, and the official start of baseball season in mid-February, our team attempted to put up old "Slats Roebuck." Slats was the name I coined for the ancient wooden snow fence we had to get up before our first game. Sometime in late November the half a dozen rolled up sections of Slats were hauled out from a corner outside and behind Gleason Gym. As Slats was being unrolled, broken, rotted slats had to be pulled out and discarded; to leave them in was to invite injury to outfielders running down fly balls.

Slats was ugly. Slats was dangerous. Slats was an embarrassment to the Sterling College baseball program. Slats Roebuck was named after our left fielder, Don Roebuck. Don hated Slats with a passion. He called that fence every name in the book. It was definitely a hazard. When being installed for the season, Slats would have to be wired to metal fence posts every 20 feet or so. Besides the danger of running into a rusty fence post, the odds of impaling one's self on a broken wooden slat was reasonably high.

I will say this for Don Roebuck; he learned how to play left field with the utmost of caution. Prior to Don's senior year he was voted "Fence Captain." This meant Don had to take charge of getting Slats set up as soon as possible before the first game. It was not an easy task getting the fenceposts pounded firmly into the frozen Kansas ground. No two fence posts were pounded in at the same depth. This caused Slats to buckle inward in places. The Fence Captain got to determine the distance of the fence from home plate. I had to pull rank on Don my first year. He wanted Slats 500 feet from home plate, at least in left field. He reasoned that the deeper the fence the less chance he had of being impaled if he should forget and go all out for a fly ball.

I can't let go of this discussion about how dangerous our outfield was without mentioning another major hazard, The Kilbourn Turnpike. Kilbourn Hall is a men's residence hall just beyond our right field. The Gleason Gym is in foul territory down our left field line. The Physical Education classes are held in Gleason Gym. It is a straight line from Kilbourn Hall to Gleason Gym. That straight line is the quickest distance between Kilbourne Hall and Gleason Gym. Sterling College men are both bright and resourceful. Thus, when they had to go to Gleason Gym for class they took the shortest, straightest route; over Slats, through right field, on through short left field behind shortstop, to Gleason Gym, and back. During the season I found that it was not unusual for a game to be held up while some freshman student wandered around in our outfield trying to get to Gleason Gym. By the time students were sophomores, they pretty much figured out the difference between a game and a practice. If the team was just practicing it didn't seem to matter to the students. To get to Gleason Gym they took the Kilbourn Turnpike willing to risk being hit by a batted or thrown ball and being called all sorts of unsavory names by our disgusted players. During games however, most Sterling College students were bright enough to stay off the Turnpike. They graciously used the sidewalk which went around the baseball field some 50 feet out of their way, parallel to right field and behind the football stadium. The Kilbourn Turnpike was a good six inches deep. Generations of Sterling College students had walked it. It was a revered landmark on our campus. When it rained, as it often did in the Spring, Kilbourn Turnpike resembled a picturesque little creek running the entire distance from right field to Gleason Gym.

So You Wanna Be a Legend. So Did I.

The Physical Education instructors were always glad to see a heavy rain. The Turnpike became a convenient water hazard for the golf classes to practice water shots If that wasn't bad enough, what really frosted me was when the golf classes practiced their short irons and chip shots on our newly planted grass infield.

I might make note here that the football team gave the Turnpike a wide berth. They practiced only in left and center field. Any football player caught near the Turnpike was automatically given 50 up-downs for endangering his physical well being.

The baseball field in reality was loaned to us by the SC Football Program. It remained that way for the next 12 years.

The most difficult and frustrating aspect of trying to put together a representative baseball team on a par with the other KCAC teams was the crucial task of recruiting. You can't imagine how tough it was to try to recruit some kid who played baseball for four high school years, several Little League years, on fields which put our's to shame. I felt I had a good recruiting interview if neither the recruit nor his parents asked any questions about our field. They invariably did. Baseball players are a rare breed. They take great pride in their home field. I will never know how many recruits we lost when I had to tell them that the football team practiced all fall in our outfield and that we did not have a permanent fence. I can only guess how many recruits and their parents suppressed expressions of dismay as they looked out my office window at our pitiful excuse for a college baseball field.

Sterling College Baseball Field
1987-1988
Recruit to This!?

"My Way of the Highway"

I was confronted by several disciplinary issues almost immediately in my first season as Head Coach of the Sterling College Baseball Team. The first proved to be relatively minor. I heard about Tony Pujol at the first meeting I had with the baseball team before my family and I moved to Sterling. I met with most of the returning team members when I came down one weekend from Sioux Falls. I wanted to get a feel for the pulse of the team. After I introduced myself to the team I had them introduce themselves. The 15 who were in attendance were returning for the 1988-1987 school year. When the introductions were over I asked if there were any returning players who were not at the meeting. Rob Kiepke, returning catcher kind of snickered and said, "Yeah. Pujol is not here." Most of the team joined in with chuckles and comments. As I quizzed the players further I found that Tony Pujol was the returning first baseman and best pitcher. He was the unofficial leader of the team. It seemed that Pujol came and went on his own schedule. I couldn't help but be reminded of Dave Graybill at Arizona State University. He did his own thing but he did what he did better than most. ASU Coach Mel Erickson pretty much gave Graybill free reign. Pujol would not have that privilege at Sterling College in 1988. Tony Pujol was one of the several Sterling College athletes from Florida. I told the team to be sure to let Pujol know that when I got on campus permanently I wanted to meet him. I wanted to find out if Tony wanted to go to Florida the next spring with the baseball team; if he did he had better come visit with me.

Tony Pujol came up to me at one of our first football practices and introduced himself.

It was a brief meeting. I told Tony that I had heard about his many baseball talents. I made it pretty clear that if he planned on using those talents he needed be at all our team meetings and practices. If he wasn't, I told him I would send him a postcard from Florida. Tony Pujol got the message. He did not miss a practice or a meeting for the next two years. Tony became one of Sterling College's finest baseball players.

The next disciplinary issue I was confronted with was one I was uncertain how handle. It was a spiritual matter which I ended up discussing with Sterling College Campus Pastor Dave Cornett. The issue involved one of our veteran players. He was believed to be living with his girlfriend in a trailer off campus. Several issues were involved: Sterling College was a Christian college. What the player was doing was flagrant sin. The player was violating college rules. He did not have permission to live off campus, much less with his girlfriend. The player could be denied graduation if the issue came to a head. He could be dismissed from college. When Pastor Dave Cornett and I discussed the issue it became clear that what the player was doing was sin and sin has consequences. I was to confront the player and if repentance was not evident the player would face the consequences. I confronted him in a one-on-one meeting. The young man did not seem to be repentant nor did it seem to bother him that he would be dismissed from the team if he chose to continue in his present sinful lifestyle. Mid-way through the season the player was dismissed from the team. All I needed to tell the team was that the player was dismissed for disciplinary reasons; they knew what those reasons were.

Pastor Cornett discussed the issue with the Administration of Sterling College. I never did find out what they decided to do about the player living off campus. I do know that he graduated in the spring.

The last major issue occurred in Coco, Florida during the team's seven day spring break trip to play in the Christian College Baseball Tournament. The second day we were in Coco the team had free time that afternoon. While browsing around downtown Coco playing tourist, one of our players "accidentally" walked out of a gift shop with an expensive pair of sunglasses. He was immediately arrested for shoplifting. He called me at the dormitory where the team was housed to tell me that he was calling from the Coco Jail. He explained that he returned the sun-glasses and if I came to pick him up and sign for his release, he would be released to my care. I took the jail's phone number and told the player I would see what I could do about getting a car to come get him.

My two assistant coaches, Mayor Larry Smith and my son, Mike, were not on the trip with me; I had to make the decision on my own. Really it was very simple. I told the team before we left Sterling that if any problems occurred on the trip the guilty party would be put on a Greyhound Bus and sent home.

I told the two Christian men who were administrators for the Christian College Tournament what the problem was. They said that they would take me to the jail and we would pick the culprit up and bring him back to the dorm.

I called the jail and told the officer who answered the phone to give the player a message. I would pick him up sometime the next day depending on our game time schedule. He would have to spend the night in a jail cell. I really felt sorry for the young man. He was a good kid. I knew though that he would benefit from his time alone in a jail cell. He had time to mull over his mistake. When we picked him up the next day he greeted me with a tearful hug. He promised me he would never do such a thing again. I told him all was forgiven and to think and pray about his actions as he took the long trip back to Sterling on a Greyhound Bus.

The Christian College Baseball Tournament

The Sterling College baseball team was blessed to be able to participate in the Christian College Baseball Tournament two years in a row, spring break in 1988 and 1989. What wonderful memories for those of us who got to make the trips. And what competition! Some of the nation's best NAIA teams were there. I was excited that we would have these great teams to play to get us ready for our KCAC season. If the truth were known, I was glad that no other KCAC team was entered so we could get a head start on them.

One of the coaching points I drilled into our team was that a good baseball team did not "wait for something to happen. They made something happen." Be aggressive, make something happen. This point bore fruit in the first game we played in the 1988 tournament.

Huntsville College, Huntsville, Alabama had a highly publicized catcher from the Dominican Republic. We watched in awe as the kid threw bullets to second base during their pre-game infield warm up. He was a big strong kid with a bigger ego. He was very cocky.

SC got off to a good start the first inning. We had several hits and scored one run. Don Roebuck our left fielder led off the game with a single. While he was on first base Don noticed that the catcher would dare him to try to steal second base. The catcher would catch the pitch, cock his hand behind his head and take two quick shuffle steps toward the pitcher staring at Don on first. He seemed to be saying:"Go ahead. Try me." The catcher nonchalantly tossed the ball back to the pitcher. Don also noticed that the second baseman did not bother to cover second when he saw that the runner was not going to steal. The second baseman turned and walked back to his position without looking towards the catcher.

Between innings Don came to me and said he thought we could pull a "delayed steal" against the cocky catcher and the unwary second baseman. I said if the opportunity arose again to "go for it." Don't wait for something to happen; make something happen. Sure enough. Don came up again in the third inning. This time with Jeff Bailey on second. Bailey doubled with two outs. Don singled Bailey to third.

With two outs Don Roebuck made something happen. On the first pitch Don took two weak shuffle steps toward second, obviously not a true attempt to steal. The cocky catcher quickly came out of his crouch daring Don to steal. When the catcher dropped his arm out of his throwing position Don took off for second. By the time the catcher and the second baseman realized that Don was running to second their timing was off. The catcher threw quickly to the second baseman who wasn't back to second in time to receive the throw. The ball sailed into centerfield. Jeff Bailey easily scored from third base, Don Roebuck slid into third. We had our second run thanks to Don Roebuck making something happen. That was our last run of the game. Huntsville beat us 6-2.

The Christian College Tournament was just what I needed as a rookie coach unfamiliar with my players. I told the team that we would use the games to experiment; I needed to know who could do what. Who could steal bases, who could execute a hit and run, who could hit to the opposite field and which pitcher could work as a reliever. The opportunities were endless.

I had a 25 man roster. We played seven games. Nobody complained because they didn't get a chance to play. Each pitcher got several innings of work and a couple players got to play at unfamiliar positions. Rob Kiepke, our regular catcher, played a couple innings at third base, Victor Rodriquez, regular third baseman, went to right field. Jeff Bailey, regular right fielder, sat the bench for an inning.

The umpires and opposing coaches were lenient when I wanted to make a switch. I talked to them prior to the game to explain what I wanted to do. As long as it didn't turn into a comedy of errors they didn't mind. I think other coaches may have done some experimenting also.

I got some mileage out of another idea I experimented with. When we went back on the field each half-inning instead of the first baseman throwing warm up grounders to the other infielders, I did something different. I assigned two players who were not in the game at the time to hit grounders to the infielders. One of these would be located on the third base side of the catcher and the other on the first base side. The one on the third base side would hit grounders to the first baseman and the second baseman; the one on the first base side would hit grounders to the third baseman and the shortstop.

Each player hitting grounders had another player with him to catch the balls thrown back from the infielders. So as not to delay the start of the inning each infielder got only three grounders.

Two more players were assigned to hit fly balls to the outfielders. The one on the right field side hit to the left fielder and center fielder; the one hitting from the left field side hit to the right fielder. They too only hit three fly balls to each outfielder.

So You Wanna Be a Legend. So Did I.

I did this for only a couple of games. It became too much of an organizational chore trying to figure out who would do what each inning. Players were on the go constantly either playing that inning or hitting warm-up flies and grounders. It was just too chaotic. I liked the idea and wanted to try it during the regular KCAC season. It would be easier during the regular season as the players would not be switching around as much. However the KCAC umpires wouldn't allow it.

The Sterling College *Warriors* won one game out of seven. We beat Kentucky Christian out of Grayson, Kentucky 5-3. We lost two one run games; Master's College of Santa Clarita, California beat us 4-3 and Central Methodist of Fayette, Missouri beat us 4-3. We were blown out by Geneva College of Beaver Falls, Pensylvania 10-1; Campbellsville, from Campbellsville, Kentucky thumped us pretty well 13-1.

I am grateful the the 1988 *Warrior* Baseball Team. Their hard work and commitment to what needed to be done to establish a solid foundation for my tenure as baseball coach was crucial.

I prayed that they found their time involved with SC Baseball was as spiritually uplifting for them as it was for me. We had Bible studies in the evenings while at Coco, Florida. Back at home I had early morning Bible study in the college cafeteria with several players and some of their buddies during the winter before baseball started. We had team devotionals after practice on Thursdays. I vowed that every student who ever played on a team that I coached would at some point hear the Gospel of Jesus Christ. To the best of my ability I kept that vow during the ten seasons I coached baseball at SC.

I was pleased with my first season as Head Baseball Coach. The *Warriors* had an over all record of 11 wins-19 loses. We finished a distant second in the KCAC to Friends University. We were 8-11. Our catcher and team co-captain Rob Kiepke was selected on the KCAC first All Conference Team. Left fielder Don Roebuck was a Second Team All Conference selection. Third baseman Victor Rodriquez was Honorable Mention All Conference. Tony Pujol played basketball in the winter of 1988 and never quite reached his potential during baseball season. He more than made up for it in 1989.

WHAT A DIFFERENCE A YEAR MAKES

I knew we would be good in 1989. I just did not know how good.

Again the Christian College Baseball Tournament, this time near Daytona Beach, Florida, was a great jumping off place for the *Warrtors'* 1989 season. We had ten returners from our good 1988 team. I knew what they could do. I had high hopes that Tony Pujol would reach his potential. He did. I had high hopes for Gustavo "Chuy" Dorado. Chuy was recruited to Sterling College in 1987 to play soccer. He never played baseball before except the usual grade school pick-up games. He asked me before the start of the 1988 season if he could come out. He did and was a contributing member of the team as a part time utility player.

This year, 1989, I felt that Chuy could find a spot somewhere as a starter. He had plenty of ability, but he was unorthodox. He did things differently, such as hitting triples on pitches over his head. He could steal bases sometimes without being told;

sometimes when he was on second with two outs he would steal third. But as I always told the team, "Make things happen." Chuy made things happen. I played Chuy a lot in the infield at all positions during the Christian College Tournament. He was a natural at fielding a ground ball and he had a strong and accurate arm. He was a good one. He drove me crazy but he was good; he made things happen.

I recruited a number of Arizona players again. I was anxious to see them in action. The son of one of my Bisbee, Arizona, high school classmates joined us. Derek Dabovich was a lanky shortstop with a world of talent. His dad was John Dabovich who was a year behind me at Bisbee High. Derek's uncle Chris Dabovich had been one of Bisbee High School's outstanding baseball players several years before me. Baseball ran in the family. Rob Felner from Tucson, Arizona would be in our starting pitching rotation. Rob was 6'3" tall and had a whip for an arm. He had a blazing fast ball. Chris Garzone, David Hightower, and returning infielder Vince Mendibles were all three from Prescott, Arizona. Chris was in our starting rotation and won several key games for us.

Arizona was well represented on the 1989 *Warriors*. Besides Dabovich, Felner, Hightower, Garzone and Mendibles, I had veterans Rob Kiepke catcher from Holbrook, Arizona, and Chet Brown from Coolidge, Arizona. Chet would make Honorable Mention All KCAC as an infielder.

Ed Smith from Northern California was perhaps our best all around pitcher. Ed was left handed and besides being a good pitcher, he was a valuable pinch hitter. Ed had power to right field. He hit Kilbourne Hall in one pinch hitting at bat that was a blast! It hit near a Kilbourn Hall third floor window on the fly, an estimated distance of well over 400 feet.

The Christian College Tournament experience we got in 1989 was even better than we had the year before. I wasn't trying so many players at different positions. With ten veterans as a nucleus I pretty much knew what to expect individually. The concern coming away from the tournament was putting all that talent together as a cohesive team for the rugged KCAC season.

1989
"Best in Years"

The "designated hitter" rule stipulated that a player could be designated to hit for the pitcher if a coach so desired. If a designated hitter was used the pitcher could not hit. The designated hitter was determined by the coach when he gave his starting line-up to the umpire before the game started and he had to hit in the order placed on the line-up card. The "dh", as the designated hitter was called, was made to order for our 1989 team.

Jay Hollis the refugee from the football team; Jeff Bailey, Ray Langley our starting fullback for the *Warrior* football team and Don Roebuch were all four good outfielders; only three could play in the outfield as starters. Jay Hollis became our every-day designated hitter. And what a dh he was! Jay Hollis was perhaps the most feared power hitter in the KCAC in 1989. He was usually in the number three position in our batting order. He had such power that the third basemen and the shortstops of the opposing teams played extra deep when Jay was at bat. Several times during the season Jay fooled everybody, including me, by laying down a drag bunt. The infielders were too deep to make a play on Jay. The few times he did that Jay got to first without a throw being made. He'd stand on first, look at his teammates and smile. I am sure the opponents thought Jay was a little cocky, but they respected him. There were times when he hit the ball so hard directly at one of the infielders that they either were unbalanced by the force of the hit or the ball ricocheted off their outstretched hand. One time Jay hit a shot to the right fielder so hard on one bounce that the right fielder was "hand-cuffed." He literally did not know for a second how to play the ball. He was startled to have a ball hit to him with such force. Jay was a line drive hitter. He had many doubles and triples but no home runs. His hits did not have elevation, just line drive shots.

Jay was used several times during the season as a closer, a pitcher who came in the last inning to save a game for us. Jay had an arm which matched the power of his bat. He threw in the low 90 mile per hour range with such power the batters were not about to "dig-in" on him; they hung loose in the batter's box. Batters often swung at bad pitches in self-defense. Jay did not have the best control.

Professional scouts who saw Jay Hollis play said he could play outfield on the professional level right then. I know that a few of them kept in touch with Jay when the season was over. Jay could have signed a professional contract I am certain. He hit .351 for the *Warriors*. He was unanamously selected as First Team KCAC Designated Hitter.

Nobody on our team could match Jay Hollis for sheer hitting and throwing power though Ray Langley came close. Ray was the *Warriors* starting centerfielder in 1987 the year before I took over as Head Baseball Coach. Ray was the starting fullback for the football team in 1987 and 1988. He sat out my first baseball season but came back for his senior season, my second. Ray was our clean-up hitter behind Jay Hollis who hit third. The Sterling College *Warriors* had a potent third and fourth hitting combination with those two.

Chuy Dorado was our lead off hitter. Chuy was always on base. He bunted for hits and had good speed to beat most of them out. He got base hits on pitches most hitters would take for called "ball". Every now and then Chuy would surprise everybody and get walked. With Chuy on first the possibility of a steal was always there.

With left fielder Don Roebuck batting second, the hit-and-run was a threat with Chuy on first. Don, besides being one of SC's better defensive outfielders, was a good singles hitter. A hit-and run execution between Roebuck and Dorado was a thing of beauty. Many times the two of them were on their own. They could hit-and-run when they thought the time was right. Those two made something happen.

With either Dorado or Roebuck on base, maybe both on base, Hollis and or Langley often knocked one or both in. If Hollis or Langley left a runner on base, first baseman Tony Pujol in the fifth spot accounted for a number of runs batted in.

Pujol led the '89 *Warriors* in homeruns with four.

Seniors Tony Pujol and catcher Rob Kiepke were our team leaders. Both by their never say "die" attitude and all-out hustle set the tone for the rest of the team.

Jeff Bailey hitting sixth was a power hitter who had many extra-base, run producing hits for us. Bailey had a strong and accurate throwing arm from right field. He threw out four runners trying to go first to third. In 1990, Jeff Bailey's senior year he had seven assists from right field to nail a runner at third or home. He was unanamously selected All KCAC Right Fielder in '90.

The seventh spot in our batting order was second baseman Chet Brown. Chet was a pleasant surprise. He came from Coolidge, Arizona as a highly rated shortstop. He was good but not as quick or sure handed as Chuy Dorado. Chet was a good hitter and had to play somewhere. He willingly converted to second base where he was selected All KCAC Honorable Mention. The eight and ninth spots in our batting order were veteran seniors Victor Rodriquez third base and catcher Rob Kiepke. Vince Mendibles and Derek Dabovich gave us excellent infield bench-strength.

One local newspaper called the 1989 *Warriors* "the best in years."

A GOOD PROBLEM TO HAVE

On the ride home from the Christian College Tournament I spent much of my waking moments jotting down thoughts that I had after seven days of ball games. The big problem as I saw it was that I had an abundance of skilled baseball players, but where to play them? I was afraid that there could be dissension in the ranks if players of equal abilities had to share playing time. Junior Roman Guerra a veteran second baseman was asked to share playing time with freshman Chet Brown who was being switched to second base from shortstop. That was tough for a junior to share with a freshman but Roman did so with class. Roman would get his reward the following year, 1990. Freshman Derek Dabovich a fine shortstop who might be better than Chuy Dorado with a year under his belt had be content to play only rarely; Chuy was solid at shortstop.

In retrospect I have to credit the Lord with our 1990 17-7 KCAC season record which was good for second place. He placed the right players in the right place at the right time.

Beginning in Florida and continuing throughout the season the *Warriors* were regularly involved in team Bible study and pre-game devotionals. God is faithful to His Word. He promises that His Word will not come back empty in Isaiah 55:11. God's Holy Spirit has a way of grabbing hold of hearers of the Word. The Holy Spirit sometimes grabs hold of a hearer immediately, sometimes He takes His time. But He will always give a hearer a choice to make at sometime in life.

I am certain that the Lord grabbed hold of Tony Pujol early in the 1989 season and led Tony to choose a close and personal relationship with Himself. Tony's leadership that year was a key for our team togetherness. I sensed a different attitude in Tony Pujol from the Tony Pujol of 1988.

There may be others that year who were grabbed by the Holy Spirit; I don't know for sure. The whole team responded to me and to each other in such a way that we overcame what could have been ego taxing situations. We had a number of potential prima donnas who were kept under wraps. A few surfaced in 1990.

I am thankful to the Lord that we had several different players each game step up to the plate and perform well. It could never be said with credibility that one player was getting preferential playing time over another player. Our pitching staff was led by Arizona recruit Rob Fellner and Ed Smith from Northern California. Both had

So You Wanna Be a Legend. So Did I.

identical 7-2 records. Ed Smith got into some hot water during the season. He was suspended for several games for an off-campus beer party he attended. He knew the rule said he would be suspended premanently for a second offense. His first suspension required that he sign a contract saying if it happened a second time he was gone. He toed the line the rest of the '90 season as far as I knew. Jay Hollis, Tony Pujol and freshman Chris Garzone filled out the pitching staff to give us strong pitching.

On the bus ride home from Florida Rob Kiepke and I discussed a hitting tip we picked up from Houston *Astros* great first baseman, Glenn Davis. It was a tip I found valuable to teach to my teams.

It was common for the Christian College Tournament to have Christian Major League players speak to the assembled teams at night sessions. These Christian Major Leagues shared their testimonies as well as their baseball knowledge. At one of the gab sessions after he spoke Glenn Davis was asked a question by Rob about hitting with a 3-2 count on the hitter. Davis' answer and demonstration made Rob Kiepke a much better hitter when he had 3 balls and 2 strikes on him. Glenn Davis verified my philosophy of "make something happen" when he told us that a 3-2 count on the hitter was the time the hitter had to make something happen. The hitter could not be passively particular about what pitch to hit. Davis advised that the hitter should widen his stance, take a short stride or no stride at all and swing aggressively at any pitch close to the strike zone. Davis' philosophy was that a batter should never be called out in a 3-2 situation. If the pitch was close enough for the umpire to call it a strike it was close enough for the hitter to swing at; a tip from a pro that would be valuable for *Warrior* teams in the future.

That 1989 Sterling College *Warrior* baseball team was a special team.

Not only were they a threat to win the KCAC but they were a team which had a great attitude. As I said there was not a prima donna on the team.

Glenn Davis, Houston Astros
SC Warriors Rob Kiepke, Tim Gipe, Roman Guerra

Former Prescott High School, Prescott, Arizona pitching ace John Denny was a 12 year Major League veteran. John's Major League career was spent with the St. Louis *Cardinals,* Cleveland *Indians* and the Philadelphia *Phillies.* With the *Phillies* John was the National Baseball League's best pitcher in 1983 earning him the coveted *Cy Young Award.*

John Denny, Philidelphia Phillies; his mother, Mrs. Dixie Denny 1983 Cy Young Award winner

There weren't many college baseball teams in the country who had former *Cy Young Award* winners as pitching coaches and who coached for free! The Sterling College *Warriors* were blessed to have John Denny for six seasons as our pitching coach. What an asset he was!

My friendship with John goes back to the mid-1960's when I coached at Prescott High School in Prescott, Arizona, John Denny's hometown. I had the pleasure of coaching John in both baseball and football at Prescott High. Besides being a great pitcher, John was a good and tough defensive halfback on the football team.

I followed John's Major League career closely. John had retired from baseball for several years when I heard his family and he were in Chesterfield, Missouri. John was enrolled at Missouri Baptist College getting a teaching degree.

I got in touch with John the winter of 1990 and talked him into coming to Sterling to visit Nancy and me. Sterling and Chesterfield, Missouri are only half a day's drive apart. John, his wife Pat and their three sons, John, Mark, and Christopher spent a weekend with us. To say John loved it in Sterling would be an understatement. I had little trouble talking John into coming up for several weeks during the 1990 season.

So You Wanna Be a Legend. So Did I.

I told John he could coach our pitchers for the first several weeks of our season. John was thrilled to get a chance to coach at a Christian college. John and I both knew God had His hand in our meeting after so many years.

The *Warriors* did not go back to Florida for the Christian College Baseball Tournament in 1990. Instead we went on a four day spring break trip to Northern Oklahoma where we played some good Oklahoma NAIA teams; NW Oklahoma State University, Oklahoma Baptist University and Mid-America Bible College twice. We swept Mid-America Bible and lost to both NW Oklahoma State University and Oklahoma Baptist. I felt pretty good about the way we played so early in the season. To come back to Sterling 2-2 was not bad.

I was not pleased about an attitude I sensed surfacing while in Oklahoma.

I had voluntary Bible studies in my motel room several evenings. Most of the team attended and we had good discussions. What bothered me were that three of the non-attenders displayed an aloofness towards me that was prevalant most of the trip.

It was not something I could put my finger on. Their wisecracks and flippancy became annoying to the point that I confronted them in a team meeting. I told them if they had anything to say about the way I was running things to get it out on the table. They just kind of smiled and shrugged their shoulders; no comments.

John Denny joined us the first week we got back from Oklahoma. Our players and John hit it off well immediately. John had a natural way about him that drew the players to him. The fact that he was a 12 year Major League baseball player and a *Cy Young Award* winner certainly did not hurt. I had a team dinner the night John arrived to introduce him. During the dinner John was peppered with questions. He loved it.

What the players loved were John's stories about his adventures as a Major League player. John's stories about the Philadelphia *Phillies'* strength and flexibility coach Gus Hoefling were so intriguing that John had to tell them in "chapters." He could tell Gus stories by the hour. Each time we had a team dinner John told some more Gus stories.

The following is just a synopsis of Gus Hoefling's life according to John Denny.

As a kid growing up in Iowa Gus became enthralled with kids' comic book stories about the hand-to-hand battles between American soldiers and Japanese soldiers during World War II. As Gus grew into a teenager his fanaciation with karate, kung fu, ju-jit-su and other Oriental hand-to-hand combat forms grew as well; so much so that Gus moved to Los Angeles, California to be near where the best karate schools were located. Gus became acquainted with kung fu masters who trained him extensively in the art of hand-to-hand combat. Gus was getting pretty cocky about this time. He heard about a man named Jimmy Woo who was considered the best martial arts master in America. Gus met Jimmy Woo and challanged Woo to a fight. Gus told John Denny that when Woo and Gus got inside the traditional nine foot circle to battle it out Gus had no doubts that he would win. The first thing Gus remembered was being thrown up against a wall outside the nine foot ring. Gus was mad. He cussed Woo and jumped back inside the nine foot ring. Gus was immediately thrown up against the other wall. Gus had met his master.

Gus and Jimmy Woo became close friends. Woo trained Gus for a few years. During that time Gus Hoefling was unbeatable, on a par with Jimmy Woo. He ran out of competition in America. Jimmy Woo told Gus that the best martial arts man in the world was in China. His name was Jung. Gus was going to China to meet and challange Jung. There was one problem in Gus's plans: The Mao Tse-tung Revolution of the 1940's- 1950's was tearing China apart. Visas were hard to get. Visitors were not welcome. Jimmy Woo somehow arranged to sneak Gus into China. Gus knew the name of the small village where Jung supposedly lived. Using an interpreter Gus asked among the villagers as to the whereabouts of Jung. Nobody was willing to tell Gus anything about Jung. Gus was so cocky he told all who would listen that he wanted to fight Jung.

Gus spent several days in the village giving demonstrations of his martial arts prowess.

Unknown to Gus, Jung was secretly watching Gus's every move. Jung was deciding whether or not to kill Gus. Jung suddenly one day presented himself to Gus. Gus said he was astonished at Jung's size who was 6'2" and over 220 pounds. Jung was a big man. He was impressed with Gus and his fighting style. He agreed to instruct Gus in the unique style he used for all his life. Jung's fighting style was a family technique developed over decades. The style originated in Mongolia where Jung's family was from.

Jung found Gus a willing student. Soon Gus was the best fighter in that region of China under Jung's tutelage. At one point, Gus told John Denny he was 91-0, undefeated. Gus became an expert at disabling opponents by dislocating their hips to the point that the opponents became immobile and unable to continue the fight.

Gus had a difficult time telling John about the fight that made him realize it was time for him to come back to America. Gus had one more fight in China. Gus's opponent was a man of tremendours courage. As they fought Gus had so disabled the man that he was crawling after Gus on his hands and knees refusing to give up. Gus knew that his opponent was helpless. Gus stepped outside the ring to indicate he did not want to finish the fight against his valiant but crippled opponent. When Gus stepped out of the ring Jung who had been overseeing the contest became livid with Gus. He had committed an unpardonable act! By stepping outside the nine foot circle before the opponent had quit or been knocked out Gus unknowingly indicated that the fight was unfinished. Gus's opponent now had the right to determine how the fight was to be completed. The opponent could choose the time of the return match and he could choose a weapon to use.

Gus's opponent chose to finish the fight after he had healed completely from his hip dislocation. Months later the fight was resumed. This time Gus's opponent choose the type of fight they would wage. The opponent chose to use a type of Chinese hatchet that was short but razor sharp. Gus and his opponent each had a hatchet.

When Gus Hoefling got to this point in the story, John Denny said that Gus became silent. Upon prodding by John, Gus only replied, "I won." Still John persisted: "Did you kill him?" Gus only replied, "I won."

Gus later served America in the Korean war. He was captured by the North Koreans and held captive in a small village. The villagers staked Gus to the ground spreadeagle. All during the day the male villagers urinated and spit on Gus while the women and children hit him with sticks and rocks. During the night two days into his captivity, Gus was able to escape. He made his way back to his U.S. Army unit. Gus got an Army bulldozer and drove it back to the village. He plowed the village pretty much out of existence. You didn't mess with Gus.

After the Korean War ended in 1953 Gus Hoefling became several professional football teams' strength and flexibility coach. John Denny knew that one of those teams was the Los Angeles *Rams*. I've check the records. Gus was not with the *Rams* until the 1960's. I hoped to find that Gus was with the *Rams* when I played against the them on July 30, 1955 while I was with the Fort Ord *Warriors*.

Gus was strength and flexibility coach for the Philadelphia *Phillies* when John Denny won the *Cy Young Award* in 1983. At that time John was the *Phillies* team chaplain as well as one of their best pitchers. John is a committed Christian. He told the *Warriors* at one of our team dinners that Gus would often come to the chapel services. He was open to the claims of Christ but John did not know if Gus ever trusted in Jesus. Gus was pretty steeped in Oriental religion

I found it interesting to Google "Gus Hoefling strength and flexibility coach." The website is full of information about Gus and his strength and flexibility program. There is one group picture of some of the Philadelphia *Phillies*. John Denny is in the picture. He is in the back row, last one on the right.

John's impact on the SC *Warriors* was felt at once; Gus Hoefling's impact was felt as well! John put the *Warriors* through a series of demanding exercises that Gus used when he was with the *Phillies*. His "John Denny Chinese torture program," as the players called it was unique and demanding. It was a 45 minute ordeal that John took the team through every other day each week. On the odd day John took them through an abbreviated form of the workout. The full 45 minutes every day would be too much.

To begin the workout the team stood with knees flexed, backs straight through most of the 45 minutes. The arms were out stretched, palms pointed to the front. Many different exercises were done with the arms extended, too many to try to explain. All the time they were standing with knees flexed, arms out stretched. Very demanding. At times the players got a chance to get on their backs, knees bent and do sit-ups. Other times they were on their stomachs doing "Marine push-ups": hands with palms and fingers pointed straight ahead, or palms and fingers pointed to the outside, or palms and fingers pointed straight in at each other. Very difficult push-ups. It was a demanding program for our players. The 45 minute segment, John told us, was just Gus Hoefling's warm up to his full program.

His full program involved among other fun things a five gallon barrel filled with rice. The players had to dig one-handed through the rice all the way to the bottom of the barrel. Very strenuous on the hands and arms. Then there was the rice-trough, a 60 foot long wooden trough filled with rice. The players had to run the length of the trough and back through rice up past their calves. John said only the strongest legs could make it down and back in the allotted time. The SC *Warriors* to a man were thankful that John Denny only took them through Gus Hoefling's warm up workout.

One year while he was with us John put on a pitching clinic for area coaches and we advertised that John would demonstrate his workout program using the

SC *Warriors*. I suggested that coaches who were interested in learning the workout program bring cameras and film it. We had maybe fifty attend and most of them brought cameras. John is a big ham. He loved it.

What impressed me as we opened the clinic with the coaches seated in the gym, was that John began the day with a heartfelt prayer. That could have been the only baseball clinic those coaches attended that was opened with prayer.

One cold day when we had to have baseball practice in the gym we were running through various 15 minute drill stations. John was in charge of the bunting station. I was in charge of a hitting into a net station across from John. I happened to look towards John during one of the 15 minute segments. John had all the players seated while he was talking to them. Later when I had time I asked John what was so important that he had to stop his bunting instruction time to just talk. John said that one of the players had asked him how he, John, became a Christian. John took most of the 15 minutes giving his testimony. Petty good reason to get off the bunting subject I'd say.

1990 Baseball
Good news; Bad news

Our 16-8 KCAC 1990 season was a good year for the *Warriors* record wise. We were tied for first with Friends University going into the final game of the season with Friends. We played them at their home field in Wichita, Kansas. We were ahead of Friends 5-4 going into the bottom of the 7th and last inning. Friends at bat with two outs got the tying run on second base. A high fly ball was hit to the outfield; an easy out. I was about to tell the manager to bag the bats when our outfielder dropped the ball.

The Friends runner on second with two outs took off running when the batter hit the ball. The runner scored the tying run; score 5-5. The batter was now on second base thanks to the dropped fly ball. The next hitter singled and drove in the winning run. Friends won the KCAC. Sterling College was second for the second year in a row.

The bad news during the 1990 season was my inability to stop the negative attitude which crept in during the spring break trip to Oklahoma. The same three players who had displayed a subtle disrespect for me continued it well into the regular season. One of the three especially was arrogantly disrespectful at times. During batting practice one day I made a comment that good hitters were often able to hit inside pitches to the opposite field. This particular player laughed out loud as though that was the most foolish thing he'd ever heard. I told him I had seen George Brett of the Kansas City *Royals* do it. The player snickered all the harder. What really brought out the bad attitude among those three was when I dismissed our most effective pitcher, Ed Smith from the team.

Ed violated the contract he signed earlier in front of Coach Lonnie Kruse, Athletic Director and me. Two weeks before the end of our 1990 season Ed was seen coming out of a bar in Lyons, Kansas eight miles north of Sterling. He admitted he had been with some buddies and had only "a few" beers. I took Ed into Coach Kruse's office to tell Ed he was being dismissed from the team. Ed pleaded his case saying he would not do it again and he would tell the team he was sorry he had let them down.

So You Wanna Be a Legend. So Did I.

Ed let the team down big time. He might have won a game or two more for us during the season. We might have won the Championship had Ed been with us at the end. He never pitched for Sterling College again.

With a second place finish in the KCAC Sterling College garnered a lot of respect throughout Central Kansas. At the KCAC coaches' meeting at the end of the season Roman Guerra was selected All KCAC First Team second baseman, Jay Hollis was selected All KCAC First Team Outfielder, Gustavo "Chuy" Dorado was selected First Team All KCAC shortstop and Mark Dominguez was selected All KCAC First Team Catcher. The KCAC coaches thought Ed Smith was the best pitcher in the KCAC.

Ed was selected First Team Pitcher even though I had dismissed him from the team. The coaches felt that since a coach could not vote for his own players they could vote for Ed Smith. I had no say in the matter.

Gustavo "Chuy" Dorado was named to the All District 10 First Team as Utility Infielder. This Honorary Team was comprised of all the teams in District 10. Much bigger teams such as Emporia State and Fort Hayes State were included in District 10. This was truly an honor for Sterling College to be represented by Chuy, one of SC's most outstanding baseball players.

Jay Hollis had another stellar year in 1990. Jay continued his powerful hitting and pitching; Jay had one more year of eligibility. I expected even greater things from Jay in 1991. Jay never returned to Sterling College after the 1990 season. As mentioned earlier he had his heart set on playing football for the great George Allen at Cal Poly University in Jay's home state, California. Sadly Coach Allen died before Jay had a chance to play for him.

THE REIGN OF DR. ROGER PARROTT

Dr. Roger Parrott was chosen by the Sterling College Board of Trustees to replace Dr. Veitch in the spring of 1989. Roger Parrott served as SC President until 1995; six years which began on a high, positive note and ended on a low, sour note.

Roger Parrott came to Sterling College as one of the nation's youngest college presidents. He was 34 years old. It soon became obvious that Roger Parrott knew some big names. He was personal friends with Billy Graham and had a picture of Billy Graham shaking hands wih him; you couldn't miss the picture if you went into Roger's office. Franklin Graham, Billy's son, was a chapel speaker at Sterling College Roger's first year at SC. Michael Medved well-known Jewish movie critic and outspoken conservative, was a chapel speaker. Roger Parrott was chairman of the Board for Leighton Ford Ministries. He had pull with a lot of important people which would literally pay dividends over a few years time.

Chapel Services every Wednesday mornings were anxiously looked forward to by SC students, faculty and staff. Roger provided some wonderful Christian speakers for us. Chapels and convocations had never been so well attended until Roger Parrott came to campus. Roger Parrott was a wheeler-and-dealer in Evangelical Christian circles. Soon after he took over, Sterling College saw some breathing room financially. Roger was able to get some hefty donations from some of his friends which were a welcome addition to Business Manager Bill Edwards' books.

Roger Parrott proved his worth as an effective leader of Sterling College. He had a way about him that indicated he knew what he wanted to get done and it usually got done. Roger was a "hands-on" type of guy. When something needed to be handled, he would handle it himself if at all convenient and possible. He wouldn't automatically pass off the chore to one of his assistants.

When I told Athletic Director Lonnie Kruse that I was resigning as Head Football Coach as of the end of the 1990 season Roger Parrott wasted no time coming to the football coaches' locker room to talk to me after practice. We sat in his car outside Smisor Stadium and discussed my reasons for resigning. I told him all my reasons, not just my miserable won-loss record. Roger completely understood. He understood Dr. Veitch needing an interim football coach; he understood the need for me to continue after one year; he understood my love for baseball and my desire to keep that position.

Roger had a way about him that could make one feel needed and appreciated. He said some things to me as we sat in his car that made me feel good about my decision to quit football. Roger told me that I was the kind of man that Sterling College needed.

For the past year I had been working in the Student Life Office as an assistant to Al Cureton, Student Life Director. Dr. Parrott was completely rearranging the Student Life Office. Roger told me he had other plans for me. He was working out the details and would get back with me later that week. I saw Roger in the cafeteria a few days later. He asked me to come to his office that afternoon to discuss some matters.

I did and he informed me that he was going to use me as Assistant to the President in Church Relations. I would have an office with Don Reed's Advancement Department. I would be working with Don Reed which excited me greatly. Don Reed in my opinion was a invaluable cog in the success of Sterling College. My respect for Don would only grow as the years went by.

One of my first assignments as Assistant to the President was to represent Dr. Roger Parrott at the inauguration of a new president at Central Christian College in nearby McPherson, Kansas. You talk about "putting on the dog"! Wow! I was impressed with myself. Dr. Parrott said I had to take his Doctorate ceremonial robe complete with the fancy colored shash which designated Roger's doctorate degree. He even let me wear his cap which was trimmed in fur and had a colorful red tassel. He said I had to look the part of an Assistant to the President. I had to look doctoral.

It was fun. When I arrived at Central Christian College I was ushered into a dressing room where the numerous other college representatives were gathered. When I introduced myself, I did so as "Hadley Hicks. Sterling College." I was usually greeted with, "So nice to meet you, Doctor Hicks." Walking slowly down the aisle was a real hoot. I supressed a chuckle all the way down. What was I doing here? If these intellectuals knew the truth. The guy from Sterling College was a fake, a mere Masters Degree from Northern Arizona University! A jock! Coach Hicks, not Doctor Hicks, PhD. I pulled it off though. Nobody knew the difference.

So You Wanna Be a Legend. So Did I.

THE CONVOCATION CONTROVERSY
Dr. Roger Parrott's Defining Moment

Wednesday, November 4, 1992 was a defining moment in the tenure of Roger Parrott at Sterling College. I believe strongly that the aftermath of the convocation speech by Dr. David Breese to the students and faculty of SC was the downfall of all the good will Roger Parrott infused in the faculty while President of Sterling College, the building of the beautiful new Mabee Library not withstanding.

The date of the convocation was significant. It was the day after Bill Clinton was elected President of The United States. The opening prayer for the Convocation was also significant. It was given by the wife of one of Sterling College's most outspoken liberal professors. The opening words in her prayer identified her political liberal leanings, "Dear God. Thank you for victory!" Her closing was significant as well, "God bless President Bill Clinton and Vice-President Al Gore." No request for God's blessings on President George H. Bush and Vice-President Dan Quayle.

Campus Pastor Dave Cornett worked for months to book noted evangelical Christian preacher, author, and speaker Dr. David Breese. Pastor Cornett was able to book him and speak he did. There was an air of expectancy as Dr. Breese approached the speaker's stand. I for one was well aware of Dr. Breese's conservative Christian world view. After the opening partisan libral prayer I wondered how Dr. Breese would react. I thought I knew how he would react because I had heard him many times on the radio.

Dr. Breese's opening remarks were almost as though he mentally tore up the notes of his prepared speech and answered the opening prayer extemporaneously. I know he didn't as I wrote Dr. Breese at his Hillsboro, Kansas address and received a typed text of his entire speech.

These were Dr. Breese's prophetic opening words the day after Bill Clinton's election to the Presidency of The United States:

"Now I'm quite aware that, in all probability, unless you attended some kind of service at 6:45 this morning, I may well be the first speaker that has had the opportunity for us to confront one another subsequent to the national election of yesterday. We won't take a poll as to whether you are happy or sad as to the outcome. But would, perhaps, throw in the thought, because this is going to be a time from now on in which a very provocative era will settle upon America. The day of the coup in the Soviet Union, I got 11 telephone calls for interviews on radio and television via the telephone to many places, and so there is an innate curiosity on the part of the Christians in America, especially in terms of today's events, this is very a eventful time in the midst of which we live, to ask, 'What does it mean?' and 'What are the implications of those things for us?' And I don't intend to take but a moment of the brief two hours and 12 minutes given for me to speak to you this morning (said in jest, I believe. h.h.) to comment on that. But I perhaps would say three things that it might be well to keep in mind."

I will briefly summarize his three points:

> #1 ".... the past political campaign indicates we may be entering a time in which some adverse attention will be paid to the Christian community. Both candidates spoke of a certain group that is a little cryptic (mysterious. hh) to us....they call

themselves 'the radical religious right' i.e. those who believe the Gospel and who believe God presides above the destinies of nations....if you speak with some kind of conviction, you may be accused of being one of those fanatics who believe that we have certain spiritual responsibilities in a world like this. Watch out for possible adverse attention to the Christian community."

#2 ".....we will see a reduction in discretionary income and economic capability because, let's face it, promises have been made that cost more billions of dollars than exist in the world today, much less in the United States....."

#3 "....it is therefore going to take a higher degree of discernment on the part of young Christians now than to my knowledge has ever been the case in the history of America. You are moving into a very provocative era. I call this 'the age of diffusion.' Christians used to know what they believed....we knew the answer to the questions, 'Why did Christ come into the world?'...'What must I do to be saved?'...'What is the mission of the church in the world today?'...the answers are being lost....a new age of diffusion is come upon the church and the world of our time....I pray that God will give us a generation of Christian young people who are far more perceptive, yes, filled with questions, but have real answers for a world that has lost the Christian construct."

Dr. Breese spoke convincingly that compared to the Gospel of Christ liberalism, existentialism, Darwinism, and all the other isms are foolishness. Dr. Breese did not have a title to his speech that I am aware of. He did enclose with his speech sent to me, a poem titled, *"THE LIBERAL MIND."* My guess is that was the title of his Convocation speech to Sterling College. Here are the opening lines to that poem:

THE LIBERAL MIND
There's a land where the sun never rises,
Where the dark is as sackcloth of hair,
Where the fog is so thick it surprises
And voices are lost in the air,
Where the fever swamps bubble and bubble,
Along which the blind lead the blind,
Where thinking is just too much trouble--
It's the Land of the Liberal Mind.

Dr. Breese concluded his speech to a rousing standing ovation by the students of Sterling College. Some of our liberal professors left and made a beeline to Dr. Roger Parrott's office. Dr. Parrott totally caved to the liberal professors who were unhappy with Dr. Breese's speech. The next day after the speech Dr. Parrott distributed a long email to all faculty of Sterling College. In summary this is what Roger said:

We need to take "aggressive action to make sure we don't let our chapel program waver from the core issues of the Gospel and a clear presentation of our faith....anti-intellectualism and narrow viewpoints are not what Sterling is all about…I am not about to allow the chapel program to run contrary to our educational objectives."

Dr. Parrott went on to say that Dave Cornett, Campus Pastor, concurs with me that we need to take the following action:

The "following action" was to form several committees to screen chapel speakers to get a balanced agenda that chapel speakers must follow. I know that Dave Cornett did not agree with Roger Parrott. Dave knew Dr. Breese well and knew basically what the theme of his speech entailed. Dave was obviously not aware in advance of the outcome of the National Presidential Election nor was he aware of the liberal lady's blatant partisan prayer.

Dr. Parrott further stated, "My concern is that we not get a steady diet of any specific agenda, except the clear message of Godly living and the central issues of faith. This will be difficult to accomplish for had we known the direction our last two speakers were headed, Dave and I would not have invited them…."

I find Dr. Parrott's response to Dr. Breese's speech interesting in light of the Sterling College Mission Statement which Dr. Parrott authored: "The Sterling College Mission: To develop creative and thoughtful leaders who are Academically Challenging, Enthusiastically Christian and who understand a maturing Christian Faith."

I have not found anyone who remembers the speaker who spoke in chapel before Dr. Breese. I certainly don't recall any chapel speaker who spoke out of line with our Mission Statement. David Breese certainly was "Enthusiastically Christian" and he definitely advanced an "Academically Challenging" agenda for Sterling College faculty and students.

President Roger Parrott was well in touch with who spoke in chapel. Certainly he approved of David Breese in advance of November 4. I can't believe Roger Parrott would not be on top of our speaker's philosophies. He and David Cornett were in daily dialogue about spiritual matters regarding Sterling College. It is my opinion that President Roger Parrott compromised his own stated beliefs articulated in the Sterling College Mission Statement.

Dr. Parrott compromised a month earlier on another issue involving the revision of the Faculty Handbook. Music Professor Phil Norris proposed that the following paragraph be included in the "academic freedom" section of the Handbook:

"At Sterling College, all that is truthful is freely open for investigation and discovery since all truth is God's truth. With this freedom comes the responsibility of the Christian scholar to explore all truth in light of God's Word (i.e. the written Word, the Bible; the Word manifest in creation; and the Incarnate Word, Jesus Christ)."

When the faculty discussed the Handbook and the wording of Phil Norris' proposed paragraph some of the wording was changed and the paragraph was watered down. The part in brackets was left out all together. When the faculty which were present voted on the wording they tied, eight faculty were for including Norris' paragraph, eight were against. As chairman of the oversight committee Roger Parrott cast the deciding vote. He voted against including that paragraph. In fact he led a discussion to leave out all of the paragraph except the first sentence. The result was a much weakened statement which was accepted by a majority of those voting.

Sometime after Dr. Breese's speech Sterling College students heard a speech at Chapel by Religion Professor Dr. Tom Keith which clearly reflected Dr. Keith's liberal intellectualism. Dr. Keith's talk centered around one whom he called "his very dear and close friend." Keith presented a heart wrenching scenario for the students to ponder. It seems that the friend of Dr. Keith's was misunderstood; he was horribly mistreated. Dr. Keith's friend was ridiculed and beaten by those who opposed the friend's philosophy of life. The friend was a gentle person. He loved all people, including his enemies. Halfway through Dr. Keith's talk the audience was well aware that Keith's friend was Jesus Christ. Dr. Keith described an unjust, trumped up charge against his friend for the crime of speaking blasphemy against the religion of the society the friend lived in.

The whole point of Dr. Keith's talk seemed to glorify the virtues of Amnesty International a liberal organization dedicated to "protecting Human Rights worldwide."

Dr. Keith concluded his talk by passionately telling his audience that had Amnesty International been around when Jesus was crucified He would have been saved from the cross. Jesus wouldn't have died if Amnesty International had been available to defend him. Keith's friend would not have had to endure all that horrible torture.

I don't believe Dr. Keith understood The Gospel. Jesus died willingly for the sins of the world. It was His Father's will that He died so brutally. Jesus' death was just punishment that fulfilled the Law. Jesus' blood was redemption for all who believed.

Tom Keith's talk was not enthusiasticlly Christian; nor did he exhibit a maturing Christian faith.

All of this upset me greatly. I had grown to love Sterling College. My two sons and their wives had each had spiritually uplifting experiences at Sterling College.

Sterling College had been very good to my family. I hated to think that we were going the way of several other KCAC colleges; Christian in name only.

I was saddened and concerned that President Roger Parrott was falling into the liberal mindset which too many of our faculty had. He had come to Sterling College with a wealth of leadership experience in the Christian educational world. He came from a family of Christian college presidents. Now I feared that Roger was being intimidated by the liberals on campus.

I had to let Roger know how I felt. I remeberd my time in Prescott High School when I had been a very poor example of an assistant coach. I was not supportive of Head Coach Roger Hightower my immediate authority in the football program. I would not fall into that less than Christian mode again. I confronted Roger about my concerns. First I wrote him a letter, then followed the letter up with a personal visit. Roger and I always were able to express our views openly with one another. I had no qualms about meeting with him concerning what had become an explosive issue on campus between the conservative faculty and the liberal faculty. As we talked I was honest with Roger. I named names of the professors whom I felt were a hinderance to the enthusiastically Christian environment we were striving to attain on campus. In my association with Sterling College students as a football and baseball coach, my work in the Student Life Office, my involvement with student Bible studies I was in tune with the students' lives on campus. I heard their gripes as well as many positive issues they brought up. I told Roger of concerns students had regarding some of the professors. A number of students were concerned that one professor was outspoken in class about not believing in demons as spoken of in the Bible nor did he believe in the spirit world as spoken of in the Bible. One of the professors was openly supportive of homosexuality as an alternative lifestyle. A few professors openly discussed their belief that abortion was a woman's right. They were pro-abortion. One felt that condoms should be made available in schools including Sterling College.

I believed Roger listened to me with an open mind. He advised me to go to two of the professors I mentioned. I said I would but I did not believe any good would come of doing so.

As I left Roger advised me "not to go to war with...", one of the professors. He said, "If, you go to war with him you can't win." I've often wondered what Roger meant by that. I wondered if Roger had once gone to war with him and lost.

Due to all this controversy Dr. Roger Parrott never quite regained the full support of the faculty that he had initially. I liked him personally. He always treated me well. I disagreed strongly with the liberal intellectualism he was floundering in.

Roger Parrott left Sterling College in 1995 to become President of Bellhaven College in Bellhaven, Mississippi.

The Bellhaven website suggests that Roger's 14 year Presidency has been successful. I was glad to read a quote by Roger which he said, "Bellhaven is the only school in America that requires all students to take a course in Biblical principles of marriage."

I was disappointed to read a newspaper quote from Roger which he said, "I remember my kids at ages one and three holding hands as we walked through a not-yet-opened library <u>I built</u> as we were leaving Sterling College where <u>I</u> had been President...." (emphasis mine. hh).

I couldn't help but be reminded of King Nebuchadnezzar's comment that raised God's ire in the *Book of Daniel* chapter 4:30: *"The King spoke saying, 'Is not this great Babylon, that <u>I</u> have built for a royal dwelling by <u>my</u> mighty power and for the honor of <u>my</u> majesty?'"* (emphasis mine. hh)

Shortly after the Convocation controversy Sterling College lost two fine and dedicated Christians from the spin-off. It was widely believed that Campus Pastor Dave Cornett and Music Director Phil Norris were forced to leave due to their conservative Christian views. They may have been too enthusiastically Christian. Sterling College was the loser.

First Gulf War.

A Personal Interest

1991 *Warriors*

One day in early February of 1991 as the Sterling College *Warriors* gathered to pray before start of our practice I asked if anyone had a prayer request. Our manager, Roger Reeve raised his hand.

Roger was a soft spoken young man. He told us rather haltingly that his brother who was an Army Tank Commander had been moved up to the front lines in Kuwait.

His tank battalion was to be the first battalion to move into Iraq when they got the word that the invasion was to begin; it was imminent.

Roger's brother asked Roger to pray for him and his men. Roger asked us to pray as well. Modern technology allowed Roger's family to communicate with his brother on a daily basis. Roger gave us daily updates as we began practice with prayer. His brother's tank was deployed on the border of Iraq waiting for orders. It seemed like an eternity for Roger as he waited knowing that his brother was soon to be in harm's way fighting for freedom for the Kuwaiti people. Roger came to us one day almost in tears. The invasion had begun. His brother's tank was to be among the first to cross into Iraq. The Sterling College *Warriors* prayed extra feverently that day. We felt as though a part of us was over there fighting.

As the days went by and no word from Roger's brother we were all expecting the worst. The news reports however began reporting much success with few casualties. Our hopes were bolstered. We all knew that God was in control and we knew too that He heard our prayers.

I recall vividly the day Roger came to practice all smiles. His family heard from his brother. He was safe. He had a story to tell. Roger told the story as his brother had relayed the details to him:

Roger's brother's tank was the first one to cross the border so he liked to think. The first one across got bragging rights in the battalion. The tank went into Iraq several miles before they engaged the enemy. When they did, Roger's brother said the enemy fire was intense. The tank took many hits from Iraqi small arms fire but not enough to slow the tank down. The tank in turn was inflicting heavy damage to Iraqi gun implacements.

Suddenly, Roger's brother said, the tank's guidance system went haywire. They couldn't see where they were going nor where the enemy was. The only thing to do was to do as they had been trained. As commander of the tank, Roger's brother had to be the tank's "eyes." He climbed the ladder to the door of the turret and exposed himself to the enemy. Roger's brother told his family that when he stuck his head outside there were times when he could feel the heat from the shells whizzing by his head. He was never hit. Roger's brother and his family praised God for answering prayers for his safety. We knew that the Sterling College *Warriors'* prayers had much to do with the Iraqi shells flying harmlessly by Roger's brother. God is good.

"Ump...you're outta here!"

Most college and professional baseball coaches or managers may hear an umpire tell them that they are "outta here"; meaning of course, that the coach or manager has been kicked out of a game. I never had that honor. I believe though I may have set a record of sorts by being the only college coach to actually kick an umpire out of a game.

We were playing Bethany on our home field. The home plate umpire was a guy Sterling College always had problems with. He was assigned a number of our games each season.

He did not like me or the *Warriors*. I never knew why. Sterling College always treated the umpires well. We had the cafeteria fix three sack lunches for the three umpires to eat between games of our home double-headers. We had cold drinks for them as well. On hot days I made sure the managers offered the umpires Gator Aid between innings. Most umpires liked us. This particular umpire did not like us. One game he was particularly horrible at calling balls and strikes.

Usually our players were good about not arguing with the umpires. The same can not be said about our fan support. Our students and some parents could get vocal and rowdy. Our fans got on this guy pretty good for his obvious bad calls against the *Warriors*. About the fourth inning of our seven inning first game the umpire started yelling back at our fans. This is definitely a no-no. An umpire should never let the fans know he hears them. This guy let them know he heard them. He stopped in the middle of an inning, took his mask off and threaten to kick the one yelling out of the game. Of course, he could not tell who the one was doing all the yelling as all the fans were yelling.

The first game ended. As the umpires were leaving the field to go to their dressing room in our stadium a couple of our students got rather personal with the rabbit-eared umpire. The umpire lost it. He started yelling and cussing at the students. He threatened to get them after the game. Of course, our students were loving the confrontation. They said they would wait for him.

While this was happening outside I had gone into my dressing room to prepare the lineup for the second game. Suddenly Roman Guerra who was helping me coach that year came in my room, "Coach Hicks you'd better come our here. That umpire is in our locker room cussing at our players!" Sure enough that umpire was standing at the top of the steps that led into the upstairs dressing room. He was directing foul four letter cuss words at our players. That was when I lost it! I got up those steps to the umpire as quick as I could. Mike Hubenett, one of our outfielders, said I sprinted up. I grabbed the ump by his arm, pulled him into the umpires' locker room and shoved him onto a couch. I had a hard time controlling myself. I told the other two umpires in no uncertain terms that this guy was not working the second game. If they did not pull him, I was calling the second game off and I would report the guy's conduct to the KCAC Commissioner and I would also report that the other two umpires did nothing to control the guy. The umpire did not work the second game. I don't recall him ever working another Sterling College game while I was coaching.

1991-1997 Memoir

A memoir is "an account of something noteworthy" according to The Merriam-Webster Dictionary. Every team I coached during my ten year tenure was noteworthy. I was blessed and honored to be associated with over 300 young men and women who were "planted by God" at Sterling College, who were there under my tutelage for God's purposes.

As I write this memoir I am taxed to recall each individual. The faces in the pictures are all familiar. Many of the names escape me. Many of the faces and names were at Sterling College for only one year, some two years. I obviously forget those more readily than I do those who were with us until they graduated.

Those who did not graduate left Sterling College for a variety of reasons; money was the main reason. Kansas weather was what got to many of our Arizona and New Mexico recruits. There were those who felt they could play at a bigger and more prestigious school. Only one did that I know of: Johnny Baca from the 1990 team went home to Albuquerque and later pitched for New Mexico State University, a NCAA Division I team.

Of the many who stayed at SC until they graduated, not one ever said he did not enjoy his years at Sterling College. Those who are the ones I recall vividly, the ones I grew close to, the ones whom God used to touch me so profoundly.

Hermie Padilla was here for four years but did not graduate. I have thought of Hermie over the years. He left Sterling College during his senior year needing only six hours for his degree. The mistake that Hermie made was talking the Head Resident at Kilbourne Hall into letting him have a basement room to himself for his senior year. Because Hermie was alone he had no accountabilty. He had a hard time getting up for his first hour class. He flunked that class and others as well.

Hermie was an outstanding third baseman. He was like a vacuum-nothing got by him. He was the best bunter I ever coached. We had great plans for Hermie his senior year. Sadly he was not with us.

Several times when I was in Albuquerque, Hermie's home, visiting my wife's family I tried to call him. I was not able to get in touch with him. I often wondered and prayed that he went back to school somewhere and got his degree.

Eric Hubenett was almost a permanent fixture at Sterling College for 12 years. Eric was a baseball player. He was on my first team in 1988 as a freshman; then he was on my second team in 1989, my third team in 1990 and my fourth team in 1991. Eric did not have enough hours to graduate so he took several years off. During his off years Eric worked for the Sterling College Maintenance Department as a grounds keeper. Eric could be spotted year around mowing lawns all over campus. If he wasn't mowing lawns he was putting pipes together for the movable sprinkling system.

Eric spent many hours working on our pitiful baseball field; his heart was in his work as Eric loved baseball. He did all he could to make improvements on the field.

Eric hung in there. He never gave up. He was determined to graduate and after many hours of a class here and a class there he finally graduated in 2001. I had the privilege of attending his graduation. I was proud of Eric and I hung around after the graduation ceremony to congratulate him. Most of Eric's family were proudly in attendance at his graduation; his father and mother and brothers Mike, a good speedy outfielder for the Warriors, Kirt and Phillip, both SC footballl players. I know that Mr. and Mrs. Hubenette worked and sacrificed to see their four sons graduate from Sterling College. The Hubenettes are the salt of the earth.

Eric was never a starter for the *Warriors*. He won games for us by the encouragement he gave to all of us. Eric Hubenett was a true team player. Incidentally, Eric was the only Sterling College baseball player to make it to the Major Leagues.

He was with the Kansas City *Royals* for a number of years on their grounds crew. Eric could often be seen on TV when rain caused the tarp to be rolled onto the infield. Eric was in there rolling.

Ted Webster was a renegade. He came to Sterling College to play basketball. He and Basketball Coach Jim Woudstra just did not see eye to eye on a number of issues. The main issue was doing what the coach said. Coach Woudstra dismissed Ted from the basketball team half way through the 1991 season.

So You Wanna Be a Legend. So Did I.

We had been practicing baseball for several weeks at the time Ted was dismissed. He came to me and told me that he was coming out for baseball anyway when basketball season was over and since it was over for him sooner than expected, he wanted to come out then. I talked to Coach Woudstra to find out what the problems with Ted Webster were. Basically the problem was Ted's lack of self discipline. He wanted to fight any opponent who banged him around a little too much, including his teammates.

Baseball isn't much of a contact sport so Ted had few problems getting banged around. He behaved himself pretty well. He talked back to a pitcher who threw too close to his head but nothing to cause a ruckus. In fact Ted showed much restraint in a crucial game with Tabor College. Tabor was tied for first place in the KCAC with Ottawa University at the time we played them. SC was tied with Friends for second. Tabor had to sweep us to win the championship outright. They won the first game 3-2. If they could win the second game they were KCAC Champs. In the bottom of the seventh inning Tabor was ahead of the *Warriors* 3-1. We had the bases loaded, two outs and Ted Webster coming to bat. On the second pitch to Ted he hit a blast over the right center field fence. A grand-slam home run! Game over. *Warriors* win 5-3; Tabor has to settle for a second place.

The Tabor *Blue Jays* were in shock. They made no moves to leave the field. Some just knelt in place, hands over their faces. Others just stood with heads down. One of those who just stood with head down was Tabor's All Conference third baseman, Lane Lord. As Ted Webster rounded second on his way to third he had a huge smile on his face. I was coaching in the third base coaches' box waiting to high-five Ted when he got to third. Before I could do so Tabor third baseman Lane Lord looked up at Ted as he got to third; Lord delivered a vicious forearm blow to Ted's chest. Ted staggered, regained his stride and his composure and continued to home without so much as a word to Lord. The entire team was there to greet Ted Webster as he jumped in the middle of home plate. Before the *Warriors* could grab Webster to congratulate him Ted made sure he touched home plate and quickly turned and sprinted back towards Lane Lord. Ted had mayhem in his eyes. I was in the right place at the right time. I grabbed Ted and held him just long enough for several of his teammates to come help me. Tabor Coach Gary Meyers had by that time gotten to Lane Lord. I was proud that Ted Webster kept his composure at least until he touched home plate to make sure his run counted before making a dash for Lane Lord.

The *Warriors* went on to sweep Friends University the last week of the season, 7-1 and 3-2. SC ended the 1992 season tied with Tabor for second place.

I was very proud of that '92 team. We had a fine 16-21 record; I say fine because we played a very difficult non-conference schedule: we lost to the NCAA Kansas University Jayhawks 0-28; NAIA Kansas Newman swept us; we beat NAIA Baker University 7-6 but lost the second game 0-7. NAIA Emporia State University swept us. We didn't play any weak teams.

The *Warriors* did well when the All KCAC Team was selected; James Cowan, pitcher, Greg Stewart Outfielder, and Dennis Toia second base were all selected First Team All KCAC. Honorable Mention All KCAC went to Shawn Carey, pitcher and Ted Webster, outfielder. Pitcher James Cowan was selected on the All District 10 Honorable Mention Team. It was a good year.

Great Recruiting Venue
1992 Olympics

The furthest thought from my mind as I got on the American Airlines' flight to Barcelona, Spain for the 1992 Olympics was to recruit for Sterling College baseball, yet that is exactly what happened. It proved to be the most beneficial recruiting trip I ever took.

Nancy, our two kids Kristin and Anthony and I were blessed to have been given the opportunity to accompany Nancy's mother and stepdad, Dean Thornborough for a week in Barcelona, Spain. We didn't go to see the Olympics, we went to experience the Olympics. In order to see the Olympics one must sit at home and watch them on TV. One can only experience the Olympics by actually being there. It was a once in a lifetime thrill for my family and me to experience the grandeur only the Olympic Games can provide.

In retrospect the most meaningful event for me, and I might add, for Sterling College as well, was the God ordained bus trip one evening back to our hotel room some 80 miles outside of Barcelona. Seated directly across the aisle from where Nancy and I were seated were Bill and Barbara Hamilton from Cypress, Texas and their high school sophomore son, Jared. We had much to talk about on the long trip to the motel. Nancy and I soon found out the Hamiltons were Christians and they were very interested to find out I was the baseball coach at a Christian college. Bill Hamilton told me that they would soon be looking for a Christian College for their son, Jared. Bill informed me that Jared was a pretty good pitcher at the Babe Ruth League level.

Before we parted that evening we exchanged addresses. I gave Bill Hamilton my Sterling College business card and said I would have Dennis Dutton, Director of our Admissions Office, send the Hamiltons information about SC.

I never cease to be amazed at how God works. One visit to Sterling College in the spring of 1993 convinced the Hamiltons that SC was the place for Jared. He enrolled as a freshman in 1994. The rest is history! In just a few months Jared Hamilton became one of the most popular and active students at Sterling College. Jared was God's gift to SC. He would use Jared mightily in the future at Sterling College.

1993 Season
SC's "High Water Mark"

The 1993 season was like no other in Sterling College Baseball history, nor will there ever be one like it again! I had an excellent coaching staff; *Cy Young Award* winner John Denny was back, former All KCAC outfielder Greg Stewart was coaching with us, Ryan Wills former Bethany College player was John Denny's assistant pitching coach. We worked well together. We set two Sterling College records that will never be broken. We had a 7-4 season record, the fewest games played by an SC baseball team in modern times-record # 1. We had 32 games rained out! Doing the math we made up 11 games and we won 7 and lost 4 of those. We did not play 21 of the 32 rained out-record # 2.

We did well in the All KCAC selections again. James Cowan, pitcher repeated from the '92 season, Ray Santin was selected as Utility Player All KCAC, Todd Melton was

First Team All KCAC third baseman, Dennis Toia was Unanamous First Team second baseman. Dennis Toia was also selected first team All NAIA District 10.

The following season the *Warriors* purchased "Rollie Fingers." Rollie was our game saver.

The original Rollie Fingers was a great relief pitcher for the Oakland *A's*. He is a Baseball Hall of Fame pitcher who appeared in many games in the last few innings to protect a slim lead for the Oklland *A's*. Rollie Fingers was a game saver for the *A's*. After our disastrous 1993 season I knew we needed a game saver like Rollie Fingers.

We worked hard during the 1993 fall and into the winter of 1994 to earn money to purchase a full infield-sized tarp for protection against rain outs. We were the only team in the KCAC who had a tarp. We had a game saver. We had teams wanting to use our field after heavy rains, providing of course that we weren't playing on the field that day.

We called our tarp "Rollie." He saved us many games

Our Maintenance Department welded together five 55 gallon oil barrels to roll Rollie on; we called that "Rollie's Finger". Rollie was a great investment. He saved us games for many seasons.

At the plate, Butler holds the bat with his left hand while supporting it with his right arm. He is batting .219 this season.

Meet Zach Butler

To introduce you to Zach Butler let me quote excerpts from an article which appeared in the Wichita *Eagle* newspaper April 30, 1995: "A chance to play college baseball wasn't what Peggy and Gary Butler foresaw for their middle child...as they studied him in a Phoenix hospital room more than 19 years ago.

'I just kind of wondered if he'd ever learn to tie his shoes,' Peggy Butler said of the child she would name Zachary. 'What I worried about was whether people would accept him and like him. Mostly I wanted people to like him..

'When he was born, of course, we didn't think about baseball.'

To continue the Wichita *Eagle* article:

"A week ago in a doubleheader split with Friends, Butler made two diving catches to snuff potential rallies as Sterling won the opening game 8-1. He also singled, walked, stole a base and scored a run. And while Sterling lost the second game 5-4 in 11 innings, Butler awed everyone when he crashed into the outfield fence to snare a 360-foot fly ball.

One thing hasn't changed since the day he was born; he remains without a right hand."

For approximately 39 years God had been putting the pieces together to bless Sterling College with Zach Butler. I first heard about Zach Butler from Joe Nix, Jr., the son of my Fort Ord *Warrior* football teammate, Joe Nix. Remember, Joe Nix and I went on a boat tour of San Diego Bay when we were in San Diego preparing for the United States Military National Football Championship. It was while on that tour of the San Diego Bay that Joe firmly planted in my heart a desire to coach kids with the love the kids' parents would expect. I vowed at that time I would do so.

Joe Nix, Jr., was the baseball coach of Casa Grande High School in Casa Grande, Arizona who first introduced me to Zach Butler. Coach Nix called me completely out of the blue one night at my home in Sterling. I had not seen Joe, Jr. since I babysat him for his dad, Joe, and his mom, Lora way back in 1955.

I mailed a recruiting brochure to Casa Grande High School in care of "Baseball Coach" not knowing Joe Nix, Jr., was the coach. God knew. See how God works!

Joe Nix, Jr., convinced me that Zach Butler, dispite his lack of a right hand could play college baseball at our level. He said I would have to see him to believe it.

Several months later Zach and his father Gary Butler visited Sterling College. I was impressed with Mr. Butler and Zach as we visited in the guest room of Campbell Hall, one of the men's dormitories. Gary Butler owned and farmed a 500 acre farm outside of Casa Grande, Arizona. He grew cotton, pistachios and wheat. Zach grew up working on the family farm when he wasn't excelling in football, soccer, and baseball at Casa Grande High School. At that time Zach held the Casa Grande High School record for career stolen bases with 60. He kicked field goals for the football team. He was a forward on the soccer team.

I will never forget Zach's tryout with the baseball team the day after he and his dad arrived. Coach Joe Nix, Jr., was correct. I saw him and I believed it! The first thing we did was warm up going through the John Denny Chinese torture. Zach participated right along with all the others. John Denny who was leading the warm up session told me later that he was concerned when he took them through the push ups that maybe Zach could not do push ups with only one hand. Zach's stump, where his right hand should have been, was tough. Zach was tough. He got through the rugged session as well as most of the other players.

We were all amazed at Zach's ability to catch and throw. His routine went something like this:

Zach would catch the ball in the glove on his left hand

He would quickly transfer the glove to the crook of his right arm as he removed the ball with his left hand.

Pressing the glove to his chest he threw the ball back.

So You Wanna Be a Legend. So Did I.

He then slipped the glove back onto his left hand in time to receive the next toss back to him.

And so it went. Zach did it time after time without dropping the ball. He got rid of the ball as quickly as any of the others. We were all in awe. I had to whistle the rest of the team to keep warming up and not gawk at Zach. When Zach took batting practice I got tingles just watching this remarkable young man. He held the bat with his left hand while supporting it with his right wrist which was minus a hand. Zach hit line drive after line drive as pitcher Matt Roberts threw hard fast balls. Matt did not ease up on Zach. After the workout I was convinced. Zach Butler could play at the NAIA college level. Play he did. Zach was our starting centerfielder for four years. At first the other teams thought Zach was a novelty. Most teams played their outfielders in close when Zach was batting. The first time Tabor played against Zach the outfield came way in his first at bat. Zach hit a scorching line drive for a triple over the Tabor centerfielder's head. Tabor must have been slow learners because Zach did exactly the same thing the following season when we played them, a shot over the centerfielder's head for a triple.

I wondered if it was the same kid playing centerfield as they had the season before.

Here is what Friends University Coach Derek Dukes said about Zach's defensive play in that double header with Friends previously mentioned. It was played at Friends' Wichita home field:

"Over-the-head Willie Mays catch; nothing but leather. He almost ran through the fence. That was the best catch I've seen all year. And that's the one I remember most, even though he just killed us in the first game with his glove."

SC won the first game of the double header as mentioned 8-1 as Zach made two diving catches. Zach singled, walked, stole a base and scored a run in our blowout of Friends. In the second game we lost 5-4 in 11 innings. Butler awed everyone when he made that catch Coach Dukes earlier alluded to. It has to be the best catch I have ever seen a college player make. The fence Zach crashed into was a makeshift temporary portion of the centerfield fence. Zach hit the fence going full speed; he caught the ball *after* he had run into the fence, almost as he was going down. How he ever caught the ball I'll never know.

Zach hit .289 his freshman year and flirted with .300 each of his other three years. He hit several doubles each year as any ball in the gap was a double regardless how fast the outfielders got to the ball. Zach had good speed.

Mrs. Peggy Butler pretty much summed up her family's trust in God when she was quoted by the Wichita *Eagle* newspaper as saying:

"I remember one time Zach said, 'Why?' And I said, 'I don't know. It is as if God said to you, *'You don't have a hand, but I am going to give you other abilities.'* We talked about that a lot."

Zach Butler
SC Teammates, l-r, Brett Brown, Luis Salazar, Zach, Jeremy Fredricks

"ACCIDENT HAS LARGE IMPACT ON SC"
10 March, 1995

That was the headline for an article *Warrior* outfielder Curtis Brown wrote for the March 10, 1995 edition of the *Sterling Stir* the SC weekly newspaper. I will quote a portion of the article Curtis wrote:

"It is with some hesitation that I write this, not because I feel I shouldn't write the story, but because I realize that the pain and the impact of Ray Santin and Clint McGuire's accident is still fresh in the hearts of many on this campus, including myself.

In my entire journalistic experience, I have never felt a greater need for sensitivity and understanding than I do with this article. Nor have I ever felt so inadequate and unworthy to write on a topic such as this, which truly cannot be explained or comprehended, other than through the Lord's power. I also want to do justice to a friend and a teammate who was recently taken from our team for a reason none of us understand. Yet deep within us all, we know there is a reason, so here is my story:

'Only two days before, Ray Santin pitched three incredible shutout innings in a victory over Hutchinson Junior College. His fast ball was quick and his curve was breaking well, as usual. He was so confident out on the mound. He belonged out there. But just days later, he was in the Wesley Hospital in Wichita, no longer moving, confined to a hospital bed in the intensive care unit with a broken neck. Yes, a broken neck--something that happens in the movies or to someone else's friend, but it would never happen to someone close to us would it? But now it has happened. What do we do now?

'Why did it happen to Ray? Ray Santin personifies activity and cheerfulness. His character represents vigor, enthusiasm, and competitiveness like no one else. It seems almost paradoxical. He is still now, from the neck down, possibly for life, barring God's intervention, in which we believe, and for which we pray.

We were all shocked, the entire team, and because we could not understand, Coach took us to the only One Who does understand. As we sat on the blue carpet of the dressing room that has been Ray's football and baseball home for the past four years, we held hands and prayed together. And among the prayers, tears and words of encouragement, I realized a vulnerability I had never felt before. Even a group of strong, young, confident ball players is never immune to trials and difficulties. One doesn't get special treatment for playing a game well.'

Curtis continued with his words of wisdom. Curtis Brown was one who understands a maturing Christian faith.

"Within this entire scenario are some things we can learn as Christians. We can learn the importance of being at peace with God at all times because life is unpredictable. We can learn that when we have nothing else in life to cling to, we have God. He is hope. He is peace. He is healing. He is love. In Him we need not fear anything. We can also learn to not take life, health, family, friends, or any other of God's blessings for granted."

Curtis Brown ended his heart felt article by quoting from God's Word:

> "For my thoughts are not your thoughts, neither are your ways my ways", declares the Lord. "As the heavens are higher than the earth, so are my ways higher than your ways and my thoughts than your thoughts." Isaiah 55:8,9.

All I could add to Curtis' sentiments is "Amen."

I received the phone call notifying me of Ray's accident early one morning. I hurriedly got dressed and drove to the Wesley Hospital in Wichita.

There were possibly a dozen of Ray's student friends gathered around the waiting room next to the Intensive Care Unit. All were either weeping or had been, men and ladies alike. Soon after I got there Ray's mother came in to tell the group of students that Ray was awake and aware of what was going on. When Mrs. Santin saw me she asked me to come in to see Ray. When I walked into the room and Ray saw me, he reached for my hand and whispered, "Coach, I really screwed up." I squeezed Ray's hand and told him I loved him. That was all I could think to say. I was very emotional. Had I been more rational I would have prayed with Ray. I didn't think about that until I was driving home.

Ray and several of his buddies had several beers before getting in a car and driving back to campus from Lyons. They were horsing around when the car went off the dirt road and turned over. Ray was thrown out of the car. Ray knew all too well that he had indeed "screwed up." His friend Clint McGuire was not seriously injured.

Several days after Ray was taken out of the Intensive Care Unit a potentially serious incident happened in Ray's hospital room. It was humorous but dangerous! Ray was able to have visitors as he was progressing well.

The particular day this happened one of Ray's good friends, Eddie Padron was in the room with several other Sterling College students, guys and girls. To get the full impact of the humor of a potentially very dangerous accident you have to know Eddie Padron. Eddie was a teammate of Ray's on the SC baseball team. Eddie was popular. He was a natural comedian. He had a way about him that just brought forth laughter. As Eddie and the others were talking about campus happenings to get Ray up to date, Eddie noticed a key chain on one of the girl's purse. The key chain was attached to what Eddie thought was a breath freshner to be squirted in the mouth. Being impulsive, Eddie grabbed the key chain with the "breath freshner" and squirted it into his mouth. It was not breath freshner, it was pepper spray! Eddie let out a loud howl and ran to the bathroom. The quick squirt into Eddie's mouth had produced a cloud of pepper spray which was headed towards Ray's bed. Had the cloud of pepper spray reached Ray it could have killed him. Ray was still hooked up to oxygen with various tubes in his nose, mouth and hooked into his arm. If the cloud of pepper spray reached Ray and he inhaled it a tragedy could have taken place.

Mrs. Santin's quick reactions probably saved Ray from possible serious harm if not death. An electric fan was on Ray's bedside table. Mrs. Santin quickly grabbed the fan which was turned on; she turned it toward the pepper spray cloud which was near Ray. The fan blew the cloud out the door into the hallway. That was when the Security Police got involved! In one of the adjacent rooms to Ray's was a wounded criminal who was under police surveillance. One of the policeman standing guard outside the criminal's room got a quick sniff of the pepper spray and between gasps called for reinforcements. He heard Eddie's howl and along with the pepper spray assumed that some of the criminal's buddies were trying to get to him.

The reinforcements responded quickly; one of the first things they did was put handcuffs on Eddie Padron who was gasping for breath in the hallway. Again, Mrs. Santin came to the rescue. She explained to the policemen what had happened. Despite a stern lecture on safety from the policemen Eddie was not hauled off to jail. Needless to say Eddie Padron drew a large crowd of SC students in the college cafeteria the next day. He took a lot of razzing from his buddies.

According to John Denny, Sterling College pitching coach at the time of the accident, Ray Santin was professional baseball material. John believed that Ray had the skills and the work ethic to possibly get drafted in the Major League Baseball Draft. If nothing else John was confident he could get Ray a tryout with a professional team. Ray Santin was the best left handed pitcher to wear a Sterling College baseball uniform during the ten years I coached at SC.

Approximately six months after the accident the Sterling College baseball team hosted a "Ray Santin Baseball Clinic." We hoped to raise money to help Ray's family with the many medical expenses they incurred. We had two nationally known college baseball coaches as the featured clinic speakers: Wichita State *Shockers'* Gene Stephenson and Jerry Kindall of the nationally ranked University of Arizona *Wildcats*.

So You Wanna Be a Legend. So Did I.

Ray Santin
"Ain't no wheelchairs in Heaven"
(L-R) John Denny, SC pitching coach; Wichita State Coach Gene Stephenson; Hadley Hicks, SC Coach.

Coach Jerry Kindall who is now a TV commentator for ESPN, told me when I called his Tucson office to invite him to speak that he had a National Baseball Coaches Association Clinic in Anaheim, California booked for the weekend of our clinic. He said, however, that he had been to Anaheim, California numerous times and had never been to Sterling, Kansas. He would cancel his speaking engagement in Anaheim and come to ours. Coach Jerry Kindall has class!

Coach Stephenson said he would gladly speak providing all the money went to Ray's family. He was adamant that the Sterling College baseball program not get any of the proceeds. Coach Stephenson said he had spoken at one charity clinic where the charity which was to be the beneficiary received less than 50% of the money raised. I assured Coach Stephenson Sterling College would not get a dime from the clinic.

Other speakers in addition to Coach Stephenson and Coach Kindall included *Cy Young Award* winner, John Denny always was a popular attraction to local high school coaches, and Kansas Newman University Coach Paul Sanagrski who built a strong baseball program at Kansas Newman University. Paul's talk was well received by the coaches.

I was disappointed in the turnout for the clinic. I was hoping we'd have over 200 coaches in attendance. We publicized the clinic in most of the major newspapers in Kansas. We drew less than 100.

Several of the high school coaches told me how much they enjoyed the clinic and expressed dismay that not more coaches attended. They felt that baseball in Kansas played second fiddle to Kansas basketball and football.

Ray attended and spoke to the audience from his wheel chair. That was an emotional moment for all the Sterling *Warriors* in attendance as well as the coaches.

I am certain that I will see Ray Santin walking again. His personal relationship with his Lord and Savior Jesus Christ has assured me of that. As someone once said, "There ain't no wheelchairs in Heaven."

THE RED STITCHES OF REDEMPTION

Coach Jerry Kindall coached the University of Arizona *Wildcats* baseball teams since Frank Sancet retired in 1972. In his 24 years at the U.of A. Jerry Kindall won three College Baseball World Series Championships.

I first met Coach Kindall at a Fellowship of Christian Athletes State Conference in Prescott, Arizona in the early 1980's. He is a Christian and a much sought after speaker at FCA Conferences.

The Saturday evening after the Ray Santin Baseball Clinic I had dinner with Coach Kindall before I took him to Wichita to catch a plane back to Tucson, Arizona. As we talked Coach Kindall asked me if I was going to the annual American Baseball Coaches Association Convention in Chicago later that summer. I told him I hoped to attend as I looked forward to the ABCA Conventions each year. Coach Kindall told me that at the Convention that year (1995) his good friend Carl Erskine was one of the keynote speakers. Carl Erskine was a great pitcher for the Brooklyn *Dodgers* in the 1950's. Erskin is a potential Baseball Hall of Fame inductee. Coach Kindall told me that besides Erskine's convention talk, a Fellowship of Christian Athletes banquet was going to feature Erskine. Kindall said Carl Erskine spoke at numerous FCA Conventions around the country. He said Erskin's talk in Chicago would be well worth hearing.

What a blessing that ABCA Convention was! For me the highlight was the FCA Banquet at which Carl Erskine was the main speaker. His talk centered around how Jesus Christ had been his focus throughout his Major League baseball career. Carl Erskine's talk was titled "The Red Stitches of Redemption." For his Christ centered focus Erskine used the red stitches on a baseball to show how Jesus Christ is featured on every page in Scripture. Those red stitches on a baseball are vital elements in holding the shape of the baseball. Without the red stitches to hold the baseball together it would be a lopsided mess, totally unusable for the rigors demanded of the ball in a game. In that same way Jesus Christ's redemption and atonement satisfies and holds together God's demands of the Law for our sinful nature. The blood sacrifice of Christ on the cross is pictured in the red color of the stitches. The blood of Christ is the ransom paid for our deliverance. A baseball cannot be "delivered" without the red stitches to grip. Likewise our deliverance cannot be accepted by God without our grip on the ransom of Christ.

Carl Erskine pointed out the three-fold redemptive work we have to have a grip on:

First, we must receive the forgiveness God offers through Christ's death on the cross. That is the payment of the debt sinners owe to God. Christ's death is the full payment for sinful man's deliverance.

Second, when we receive that forgiveness we are justified before God.

Third, we are then delivered from the power of sin at the coming of the Lord.

So You Wanna Be a Legend. So Did I.

Carl Erskine took us through a mini-Bible study showing how the Red Stitches of Redemption are depicted throughout the Bible. He started by showing how the first sacrifice was made by God to cover the sinful nature of Adam and Eve. Erskine then took us from the Garden of Eden to the call of Abraham, through the times of the Judges, to the Prophets, to the founding of the Kingdoms of Israel and Judah, through the dark years of the Babylonian Captivity, to the Coming of Christ, His death, the preaching of Paul, up to the Apocalypse and the End of the Age. Through these many pages in God's Word one can find the Red Stitches of Redemption clearly revealed.

Carl Erskine encouraged the coaches at the FCA Banquet to have our pitchers focus on those red threads. The baseball in their hand is a reminder of Jesus Christ and what He can do for us if our grip on Him is firm.

IT WAS TIME FOR NEW BLOOD

I was diligently working on the infield playing area one day in June of 1997 when I received some great news! Jim Woudstra, our men's basketball coach, rode up in the Maintenance Department's golf cart.

Jim was working for the college Maintenance Department that summer. He had been sitting in with some of the college administrators as they prioritized campus summer work projects. Jim went to bat for our baseball team and he told the administrators how vital a fence was to having a first class baseball program. Surprisingly, the administrators agreed with him. They told Jim to get prices and, "Let's see what we can do." Jim was excited. He said he was pretty certain that the project would fly. I wasn't. After ten years of battling tooth and toenail with no results, I told Jim I would be surprised if the fence became a reality. I even bet Jim a steak dinner we would go another year without an outfield fence. I had a gut feeling the administration would come up with the same old song and dance, "Sorry, no money. "

I made certain I saw Jim weekly from that point on. Each time he told me that things were still looking good. He and I got prices and submitted them to the administration. One day in late July, several weeks after submitting the prices, Jim sped down to the field. He yelled, "Hicks! You owe me a steak dinner!" He proceeded to tell me that the administration approved the fence price and that it would be here before next football season was over. We would finally have a quality portable fence! GOOD BYE, SLATS ROEBUCK! "Jim", I said, "when that fence gets here, we are going out for a steak dinner!" Needless to say, I was pumped! I emailed all my returning players, the new players who had recently signed with us, and those recruits still on the hook.

I excitedly told them the good news. They would be the first Sterling College *Warrior* baseball team to play on its home field enclosed by a fence we could be proud of. I even emailed many of our alumni and told them to be thinking about an Alumni Game to dedicate the new fence. We would begin the 1998 season in grand style. I had been in the teaching-coaching profession for over 30 years. I was feeling like a young rookie again! I was given a new lease on my coaching career. I would, at last, be able to recruit to a quality baseball facility.

1998 had all the earmarks of a banner year for the *Warriors*. The previous year, 1997, we had the best Sterling College hitting team in recent history. Pat Williams, our All-KCAC short stop, led the nation with a batting average of over .500. Jamie Fowler, our All-KCAC second baseman, was one of the top five doubles hitters in the nation. As a team we were one of the best NAIA hitting teams, average wise. A number of those players were coming back for the 1998 season, including Williams and Fowler. Things were indeed looking up.

One and a half weeks after sending the good news out, I received a devastating blow! I was walking out of the Administration Building that fateful day when I ran into Bill Edwards, Sterling College Business Manager. I asked Bill when we could expect to get the portable fence ordered. Bill looked rather blank and said, "Hasn't anyone told you? *We just don't have the money right now.*" I don't remember what I said to Bill. I hope it was respectful. Bill is a wonderful man. I knew it wasn't his fault that I didn't get the word that we wouldn't get the fence. I walked away heartbroken. If anyone was watching me, they saw a 64 year old coach with tears in his eyes. Somewhere along the line, someone dropped the ball. Someone neglected to show enough respect for our Sterling College players, our coaches and our program, to at least tell us they were sorry but no fence. Jim Woudstra was as much in the dark as I was. He was not told either. He was still expecting his steak dinner.

I pulled myself together as best I could. I emailed all the players that the fence was a no-go. That was a difficult letter to write. I had to swallow a lot of pride. My wife, Nancy and I prayed about the situation and decided that this was God's way of telling us that, after ten years, it was time for new blood to take over the reins of the Sterling College baseball program. I wrote a letter of resignation and turned it in to Lonnie Kruse, Sterling College Athletic Director.

Soon after turning in my resignation I met the new President of Sterling College, Dr. Ed Johnson. I hoped to meet him so I could explain the reasons for my resignation. I made an appointment with Dr. Johnson and met with him one afternoon. I liked Dr. Johnson immediately. He was from Phoenix, Arizona and was an Arizona *Diamond Backs* fan. Dr. Johnson listened to me for an hour detailing how for the past ten years each team worked extra hours after practices and on weekends making much needed improvements on the field. Dr. Johnson understood the need for a quality baseball field for the critical job of recruiting players to our campus. I told him about Slats Roebuck; how Slats had been replaced by the ugly plastic orange construction site fence we were currently using. I explained how the football team was using our outfield area for their practice field. It was their only place to practice since both Sterling High School and Sterling College football teams used the Smisor Stadium field for their home games. Through it all Dr. Johnson listened attentively. He said he could not promise anything since he "was the new kid on the block" but that he would certainly do what he could. Dr. Johnson was able to find the funds to purchase a quality portable fence for the 1998 season. The fence was taken down for the duration of the football season and put back up for the beginning of baseball season. It was a great improvement.

It was not until several years later when Andy Lambert became Head SC Football Coach that the football team had its own practice field. One of Andy's first tasks was to use his assistant coaches and our Sterling College Mainenance Department to construct a practice field behind Kilbourne Hall, well beyond the baseball field. The deed to the baseball field was at long last turned over to the baseball team!

Sterling College Football Coach Andy Lambert has a world of class and Christian servant leadership qualities.

One month after I resigned and met with Dr. Johnson, Nancy and I sold our house. We loaded a U-Haul truck with our belongings and headed for another mountain to climb. We were going to Phoenix, Arizona to attend the Victorious Christian Living, International Discipling Center (VCL). We were obeying God's call. We were going to be Bible Counselors-Disciplers.

STILL SEARCHING

It was difficult to leave Sterling, KS. We were leaving behind our daughter Kristin, her husband Scott and two precious grandchildren, Harrison and Addie. Our son, Anthony moved to Washington State where he worked as an engineer for Boeing Aircraft Company. Our oldest son, Mike, his wife Jean and sons, Michael and Taylor lived only 30 miles away in Inman, Kansas. Our daughter, Susie and family lived in Camp Verde, Arizona 60 miles from Phoenix. We would get to visit them frequently. Our son Steve, Lori his wife, and three kids were still serving God in Venezuela.

We were never returning to Sterling, Kansas. We were leaving behind ten wonderful years serving God at Sterling College. We were saying goodby to a great community and good friends. We took with us countless rich memories. I should someday learn never to say "never."

I could say that my final season at Sterling College was both rewarding and disappointing.

I coached arguably the best hitting team in Sterling College history, the best hitting team in the Kansas Collegiate Athletic Conference for 1997 and one of the best hitting NAIA teams in the country. That was most rewarding.

However, that great hitting team finished dead last in the KCAC final standings! After 37 years of teaching and coaching, I was still searching for significance. That had been the story of most of my adult life. I had a difficult time seeing my teaching and coaching career as being successful. Most of my goals and aspirations had not been achieved. It was obvious that at my age, 64, my teaching and coaching career was behind me.

I started my career in the 1950's with an abundance of promise; so many dreams of worthy accomplishments and personal gratification. The resume I was leaving behind was much less than illustrious: no teacher or coach of the year awards and no state or official conference championships. For those who knew me, I was remembered as a fair teacher, a decent coach, a nice guy. Nothing more. Nothing that legends were remembered for.

However, after 23 years as a Christian, God was not finished with me. I had so much more to learn about the ways of God.

As The Bible says, *"...being confident of this very thing, that He who began a good work in you will complete it until the day of Jesus Christ;" Philippians 1:6*

CHAPTER SEVEN

Significance Found
Victorious Christian Living International, Inc.
Phoenix, Arizona
1997-1999

Let us hear the conclusion of the whole matter: Fear God and keep His commandments, For this is man's all.
Ecclesiastes 12:13

I was pretty much in control of my emotions as Nancy and I left Sterling, Kansas and headed for Phoenix, Arizona. It wasn't until we had left Flagstaff, Arizona and headed down the long decline to Phoenix and "The Valley of the Sun" that I got a lump in my throat. I was returning to my beloved Arizona. Phoenix, Arizona was to be our home for at least a year and a half, perhaps permanently.

Nancy and I visited the school we were to attend a month before we actually felt peace about our move. The training we would receive was exactly what we felt God calling us to.

Victorious Christian Living International, VCL for short, was a very successful counseling-discipleship ministry with a long line of hurting people who could testify to Christ's healing power.

Nancy was involved with some small aspects of VCL for several years with young women from Sterling College. Mary Ver Steeg SC Volleyball Coach and a close friend had first gotten Nancy interested in the VCL discipleship program. Mary's brother-in-law Steve Phinney was one of VCL's counselor-trainers for a number of years. At Steve's urging Mary attended several VCL Weekend Conferences. Mary in turn schooled Nancy in portions of the discipling process.

Nancy proved to be an eager learner with God given gifting for the discipling process. She had a high degree of success discipling the few lady SC students Mary referred to her.

Nancy was hooked on the VCL disciplining she was learning. She wanted much more. She wanted it for me as well; Nancy's dream was for both of us to be serving God as Bible counselors.

One weekend Nancy and SC students Nicole Williams and Kathy Ethridge, drove to Phoenix to attend a VCL Conference. That Conference was the start of Nancy's deep desire to someday attend the VCL year long discipling training.

So You Wanna Be a Legend. So Did I.

I was too involved at that time in Sterling College baseball to be as enthused about VCL as Nancy. I put Nancy's excitement about VCL on the back burner of my brain until the Sterling College Administration nixed the possibility of a fence for our baseball field. God then used the SC Administration's negative response to begin to put the finishing touches that would end my deep seeded desire to find my significance in man's approval and acceptance. God was getting my attention big time!

My dear friend and Bisbee High School classmate, Chloe Kavanaugh was kind enough to let Nancy and me stay with her for a week until we could find an apartment near VCL. Nancy and I soon found a nice small apartment in a motel complex complete with swimming pool, laundry facilities and friendly neighbors.

One of those neighbors was directly across the hall from our apartment. As we were moving into our apartment I noticed a sign on their door which read, *"Jesus is the Master of this Home"*. Christian neighbors! Again God was at work.

One day when Nancy was doing the laundry in the common laundry room she met our Christian neighbor. His name was David and when he found out we were taking Bible counseling classes he was anxious to visit with us.

Over coffee one evening David confided in us that his wife of many years had left him and gone back to Indiana. One day while David was at work she just packed her things and left with a relative who was visiting. She didn't even leave a note. She just left.

David was a former missionary; his marital problems forced him and his wife to come off the mission field. His mental state was such that he felt he would never be of any use to God again.

David would prove to be a huge asset to me as I began taking VCL discipling lessons. God certainly planted David in my life at a time which would be beneficial to both of us.

Our first week at VCL was go, go, go, go! Hardly a minute to catch our breath. Nancy and I were in a class of 15 who were training in the Biblical counseling techniques of VCL. The training we were just beginning would prove to be life changing for each of us.

Our class of 15 trainees was comprised of a diverse group of men and women each seeking basically the same thing; a closer obedient walk with our Lord Jesus Christ. Nancy and I were seeking to do so via some form of full time Christian ministry. Another couple, Marsh and Joy, were already in full time ministry. They were missionaries serving in a remote mountainous area of central Mexico. Their year's furlough was being spent learning the VCL method of counseling to open a new avenue to reach the Mexican natives.

Marsh, a recent high school graduate, and I were the only men in the class. Eleven of the twelve ladies were married women living in the Phoenix area who were introduced to VCL for marital counseling. Having successfully reordered their marriages they wanted to learn more of the counseling process to help other hurting women.

Sally Childs was the exception. Sally was the wife of Bill Childs the President of VCL International. Bill and Sally would become close friends with Nancy and me during our year at VCL.

Our VCL staff trainers were just as varied. They were men and women who obeyed God's call on their lives and were full time VCL teachers-counselors who gave of their time to help train others to counsel. One of the trainers, Ted Sellers, was an associate pastor in a local church. Another, Jack Tesch, was a former Catholic priest whom God called to leave Catholicism to become a Christian Biblical counselor. Steve Phinney, Mary Ver Steg's brother-in-law, has a PhD in theology from Cambridge University in England. Each of these men were outstanding teachers. They and the other men and women who taught and trained us were used by the Holy Spirit to make God's Word come alive.

None of these VCL staff trainers were salaried by VCL but they raised their individual support. The trainers had a rigorous schedule in that they were at times required to be at the training center nine to ten hours per day. Besides their hours working with the new trainees, they all spent time several days per week discipling counselees from the outside. Nancy and I soon found out that the VCL switchboard phone rang many times day and night with hurting people wanting someone to talk to. We ourselves would be involved with some of those hurting people. First we had to be trained.

Our first several days were involved in becoming familiar with our <u>Victorious Christian Living Workbook.</u> The workbook and our Bible were our daily companions as we studied.

Each of the 12 lessons in the Workbook were solidly based on the Word of God. Our trainers told us story after story of how God spoke to hurting people through His word as illustrated in our VCL workbook. Toward the end of the first week we began an indepth study of the first lesson in the work book: **GODSHIP.**

The lesson begins with this introduction: ....*your eyes will be opened, and you will be like God.... Genesis 3:5*

"This lesson pinpoints the beginning of man's original rebellion against God and the results. Ever since Eve's conversation with Satan, man has sought to be like God. We coined the term 'godship' for this basic problem of mankind. <u>Godship</u> (sin) is the term used to identify: **(1) an individual functioning as his or her own god, (2) the self-life or walking after the flesh, (3) an individual living without considering what God has to say or (4) allowing circumstances or feeling to rule instead of God.**"

Before beginning the counseling process the counselee is first asked to take a simple, brief quiz which will reveal which of those four sin patterns is prominent. From there the counselee is taken through the first several pages of the study guides for the <u>Godship</u> lesson. This could sometimes take many sessions with the counselee before he/she recognizes the sin in their life. Until the counselee is willing to recognize and admit the sin patterns they struggle with they will continue to struggle.

Usually however the counselee recognizes and admits to the sin pattern; the sin patterns are usually very obvious traits in the counselee. Depending on the individual's sin patterns and the severity of those sins we were taught to possibly go from <u>Godship</u> to one of the other eleven lessons.

The twelve lessons we learned thoroughly were:

1. GODSHIP
2. REJECTION
3. EXTERNAL/INTERNAL
4. PROBLEMS, PROBLEMS, WHY PROBLEMS?
5. MY FLESH--GOD'S ENEMY
6. REPENTANCE

7. WHAT'S NEW ABOUT YOU?
8. ACCEPTING YOUR RIGHTEOUSNESS
9. EXTENDING FORGIVENESS
10. SEEKING FORGIVENESS
11. REST, ABIDE, WALK
12. LOVE

Our neighbor, David, agreed to let me review each day's lessons with him in the evenings. This was valuable on-the-job training for me, David too benefited from the teachings. He was quick to recognize the sin patterns which he developed over many years. As a Bible school trained missionary David had become very independent; he would not seek help or guidance from anyone, not even God. He was a "know it all." He went to Bible school. David's wife was a Bible school trained missionary. They soon became rivals instead of partners. David determined standards of conduct for not only himself but others. He expected God to abide by his same standards. David became a controller. He selfishly tried to control circumstances and people to fit his agenda.

David could see easily that he had been "playing god" in his own life and in the life of others, including most notably his wife. Often as David recognized his sins he weept over them. He believed more than ever that he was not worthy to be called a "child of God." God soon was able to convince David that he was a much loved child of His. That brought even more tears to David's eyes.

Not so strangely God used the Godship lesson in my life as well as David's. Could I ever see my godship at work as I lived my life as a legend! My whole life had been centered around seeking praise, approval and acceptance from others and not from God. When I didn't get the praise and acceptance from others that I thought I should have I felt like a failure. My athletic career did not meet the standards I set; I failed in my first marriage; my coaching career was less than noteworthy according to the standards I set for myself. However, God was not through with me.

The Godship lesson was comprised of seven pages front and back with study guides and diagrams. It took David and me several weeks to get through the entire Godship teaching.

When we finished, David was like a kid with a new toy. He could hardly wait to study the next lesson, **REJECTION** which had this introduction: *There is therefore now no condemnation for those who are in Christ Jesus. Romans 8:1*

"....Rejection is common to all of us. Those who feel Rejection tend to reject the 'rejecter' setting up a cycle of hurt and retaliation....this lesson will show how the Rejection cycle can be broken. We believe that Rejection is a consequence of man playing god in his own life or the lives of others...what we call godship."

Again as David and I went through the lesson on Rejection we both could see where we had fallen well short of God's standards. David and I worked together for most of a year and a half and we went through all twelve lessons. I had other counselees during that time but David was always just a few steps away across the hall. We got to know each other very well.

The VCL lesson God used to bring me closer to reality in my ongoing search for significance was **WHAT'S NEW ABOUT YOU?**

> *If any man is in Christ*
> *he is a <u>new</u> creature...*
> *2 Corinthians 5:17*

"......God gave you the ability to think in terms of your own personal identity as related to Him. You have a built-in need to view life in terms of meaning and purpose. Meaning and purpose in life flow from identity. <u>Personal significance is a driving objective. The constant search for meaning has always motivated man</u> (Psalm 8:3-4).

This need is only met when a person (me!) experiences Christ as his/her very life and <u>identity</u> (Philippians 1:21; Colossians 3:3-4)....."

That lesson was a true wake up call for me!

I had been saved since 1974. Yet it wasn't until that lesson in 1998 when I learned the truth that my identity and my significance was in Jesus Christ; not in my coaching record, not in my identity as assistant coach, or head coach, or even assistant to the president.

It took me 24 years before God showed me through His Word in the <u>Victorious Christian Living Work Book</u> that my real identity was in Jesus Christ. I am a slow learner.

Below are a few key diagrams in the <u>What's New About You?</u> lesson. Look them over. Look up the Scriptures. They are self-explanatory:

VCL TEACHING "WHAT'S NEW ABOUT YOU"

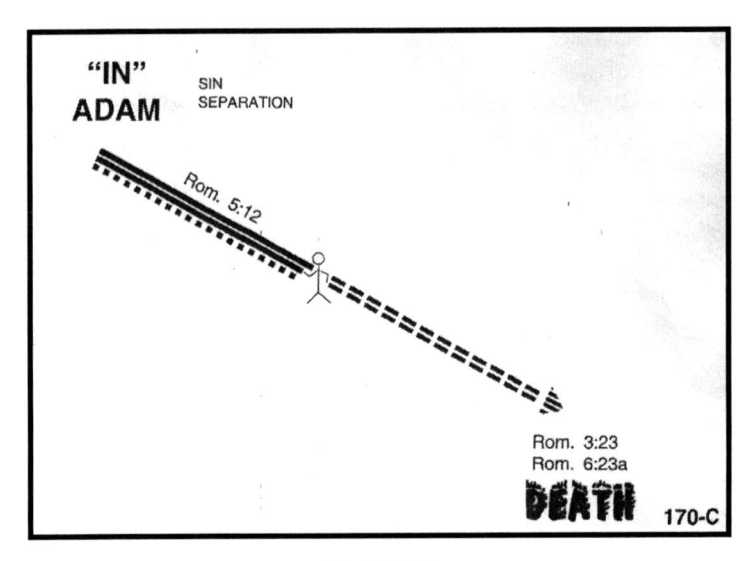

"IN" ADAM — SIN SEPARATION

Rom. 5:12

Rom. 3:23
Rom. 6:23a
DEATH

170-C

IN ADAM

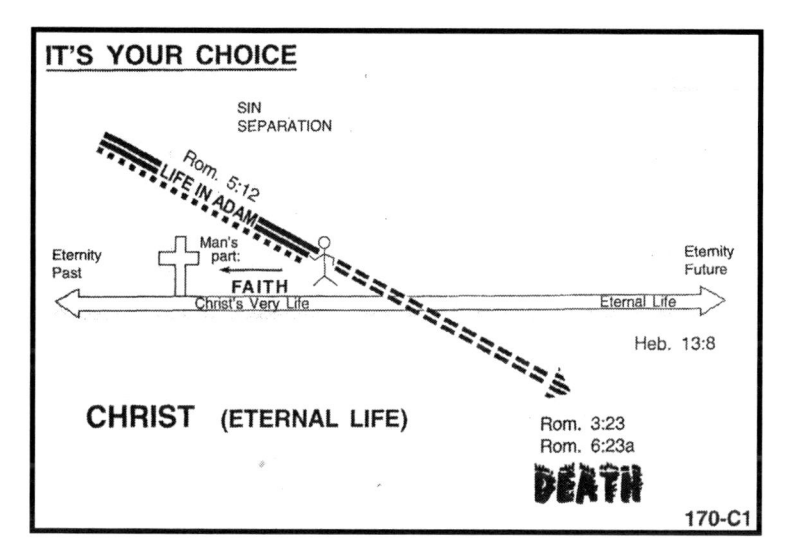

YOUR CHOICE

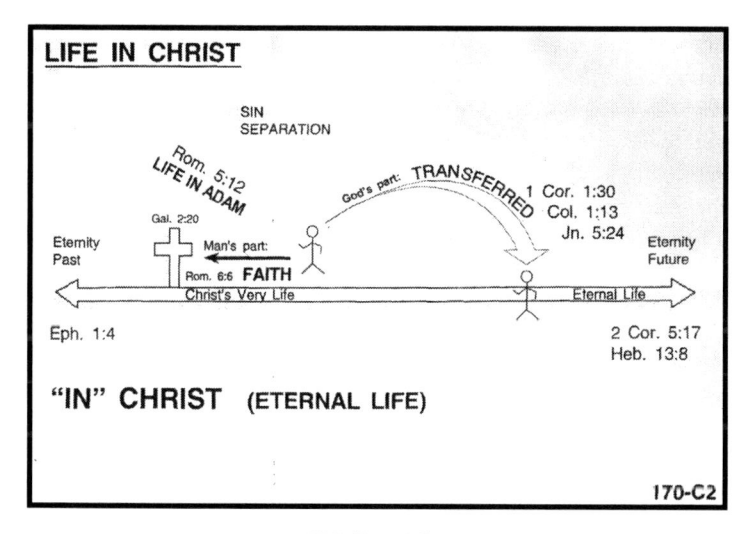

IN CHRIST

As I studied the lesson on What's New About You? which was taught daily over several weeks it became clear to me that "Whose I was" was much more important than "what I was." That was such a profound revelation to me that it took me weeks to grasp just the basics of it. I don't believe I will ever fully comprehend. It is a truth of the sanctification process that will be fully revealed only at my death.

Hadley Hicks

All of us trainees had opportunities to teach VCL Lessons to various churches around "The Valley of the Sun." I always asked if I could teach the <u>What's New About You</u> lesson. It is my favorite because it is so meaningful to me. Thank you, God.

It was in our second week of training that all the new trainees were assigned a discipler who would work closely with us for the remaining time we were at VCL. I was assigned the former Catholic priest, Jack Tesch. Nancy was assigned Diane Kazanski who was a full time VCL Administrator.

Jack's unique method of discipling was to go for a walk. Jack and I must have walked 100 miles in the months we spent together! We'd walk and talk. Jack was such a gentle soul and a yet a probing conversationalist. I enjoyed our times together, even those times he nailed me on godship issues.

Jack and I met on a regular basis weekly for our hour and a half walk. We'd always begin by just talking. On Mondays we discussed the Sunday professional football results. Jack was an avid Green Bay *Packer* fan. I let Jack know that I was chosen on a high school All America team with Green Bay quarterback Bart Starr. That gave me some credence with Jack. Then invariably Jack would dig out bits of godship I exibited. He was adept at reading "between the lines" in my conversations and opinions. Jack subtly let me know when my focus was too centered on me.

A weekly event at VCL was our joint get together with all disciplers and trainees. These meetings were when all the disciplers got a chance to publically evaluate how the individual trainees were progressing in spiritual growth. A discipler picked out a godship issue with a trainee and got feedback from any other discipler who wanted to comment. Sometimes the disciplers could be pretty blunt.

I told Jack about my divorce from Joan on one of our walks when were were discussing the issue of how to reconcile with one we had offended. I told Jack that I wanted to be reconciled with my ex-wife. Joan and her husband Wil, lived in Camp Verde, Arizona only a mile or so from my daughter Susie and her family.

Susie commented to me a time or two that her children, Jason and Megan, said they wished "Grandpa Hicks and Grandma Nancy would eat dinner with them when Grandma Joan and Grandpa Wil were here."

I told Jack I thought a family get together would please God. I would admit my sin and ask Joan to forgive me. The grandkids would love to see Grandma Joan and Grandpa Hicks speaking to each other again. The tension would be greatly reduced. It was the Christian thing to do.

These sessions with the disciplers and the trainees were valuable if the trainee was willing to accept spiritual criticism. My time to face the music came one day during one of these joint sessions.

Jack confronted me and said, "Hadley, tell us about your thoughts on reconciling with your ex-wife."

I really hadn't expected that question. I thought Jack and I had fully discussed the issue. Not so.

Jack saw a chance to really pound his point home by confronting me in front of the whole gang. I was open and honest. I told them how God was dealing with me about reconciling with Joan. I told them how our two grandchildren in Camp Verde had wanted Grandma Nancy and Grandpa Hicks to be able to come to dinner when

Grandma Joan and Grandpa Wil were there. I said I wanted to ask Joan to forgive me in front of the whole family; I thought that would be good for the family to see Joan and me reconcile.

Jack said, "Why?"

I said, "Well, the kids could see me ask Joan for forgiveness."

Jack said, "Why?"

Long pause......

I said, "Well...I just think it would be good for the family to see me humble myself and ask Joan to forgive me."

Jack said, "Why?"

Another long pause....

Jack broke the silence, "So you could look like a spiritual giant to the whole family? So you would be the spiritual one to make everything o.k. again?"

Jack then said, "Hadley, your pride is showing."

Needless to say, Jack made his point.

An indepth discussion followed. I could readily see how I had indeed wanted to look like the spiritual one in the familiy. All of the disciplers thought it would be good for Joan and I to reconcile; but not at a family gathering. I should seek out Joan privately; either in person with her husband there or on the phone. I chose to call Joan on the phone and we had a calm discussion. Joan accepted my plea for forgiveness. She admitted that she was as much to blame for the divorce as I. She saw my point however when I said that God holds the husband responsible and therefore I asked for her forgiveness. She gently said she forgave me.

Joan and I met several times in person over the years and the tension was much reduced. Joan and Nancy talked together at length at a granddaughter's wedding.

After our first year of VCL Training, Nancy and I had a firm grasp on what God was leading us toward for our future. The VCL Training merely laid the groundwork for our next step: The Training in Discipleship or TID as it was labeled.

GETTING DOWN TO THE NITTY-GRITTY (TID)
Advanced Training

I have already mentioned one of the couples Nancy and I became well acquainted with while we were in our initial VCL training, Bill and Sally Childs. Bill was a very successful businessman and the President of VCL International. Sally was going through VCL training with Nancy and me.

The Childs owned a beautiful ranch in Evergreen, Colorado. Nancy and I had the opportunity to visit the Childs' ranch two times during our 18 months training; once after our VCL Training for a week long TID training session with all the trainees and trainers. The second time we spent a four day vacation alone with Bill and Sally at the ranch.

Bill presented an opportunity for Nancy and me when we graduated from TID Training, the possibility of working in one of the churches in Evergreen, Colorado as a VCL Counseling Center Director. As an added bonus we could live in one of Bill and

Hadley Hicks

Sally's ranch guest houses and be the grounds keeper for the ranch. Bill and Sally were gone much of the year on Bill's business ventures. They wanted someone on the premise while they were gone. That sounded too good to be true But first we had TID Training to tackle. It was much more rigorous than our VCL Training had been. The TID Training was to prepare the trainee for various Church Ministry opportunities.

The first day of TID Training was a real eye opener. We had no idea it would be so demanding. We were given a TID-Checklist that seemed overwhelming:

1. We had to listen to and write reports on 26 taped teachings on such subjects as:
    - Financial management; six total tapes
    - What God Says About Men
    - Counseling
    - Raising Children; two tapes
    - Basic Principles of Marriage
    - My True Identity (I really got into that one!)
    - Liberated through Submission

Many other instructional tapes were listened to and studied. Nancy and I listened to them in our aprtment, discussed them and wrote reports. Our reports were read and evaluated in joint meetings with the trainers.

2. We had seven excellent books to read. Our written reports on each book were evaluated in joint meetings with the trainers:
    - Grace Walk by Steve McVay
    - Fearfully and Wonderfully Made by Philip Yancy
    - How to Counsel from Scripture by Martin Bobgan
    - How to Keep Your Kids on Your Team by Charles Stanley
    - Love, Acceptance and Forgiveness by Jerry Cook
    - Master Your Money by Ron Blue (Nancy and I had read this one while in Sioux Falls, South Dakota.)
    - Love Life for Every Married Couple by Ed Wheat, MD

3. Next was a fun assignment (?); we had to role play in sixteen areas:
    - All the VCL Lessons: such as Godship, What's New About You, etc.
    - Financial
    - The Natural/Spiritual Man which was a teaching we got in TID
    - External/Internal Man; a VCL teaching
    - Biblical Love
    - and other fun topics. I found I could ham it up just as well as all the other trainees.
    -

4. Next was my hardest task; memorizing 35 selected Scripture verses. John 3:16 did not count.

5. I won't list all of the 32 different teachings we had to attend and write reports on. Here are just a few:

- Abortion
- Authority
- Divorce and Remarriage (that was tough to sit through for Nancy and me)
- Eating Disorders
- Grief
- Sexual Problems
- Spiritual Gifts
- Substance Abuse
- Suicide
- Time With God
- Uncovering Trauma

These 32 TID Teachings ran a gambit of issues a Biblical counselor may encounter. These teachings would prove to be invaluable to Nancy and me in the years to come.

In addition to all of the above each disciplee was assigned a counseling responsibility; we each were given a counselee who had come to VCL with some deep seeded issue. We spent an hour and a half per week with the counselee using the counseling techniques we learned in our VCL training.

For the first several sessions we met our counselee accompanied by our own trainer just to make sure we were ready to go one-on-one with a counselee.

The counseling at VCL was free to the counselee. The philosophy of VCL International is that God's Word is free to anyone who seeks it.

Philosophy of VCL International
Training in Discipleship (TID)

In just a few weeks of indepth training in the TID material it was obvious to Nancy and me that the basic VCL training we recently finished was merely the tip of the iceburg. What we were taught theoretically in VCL was observed in real life situations and actually practiced in our TID training. To quote the TID workbook:

"The reality of Christ-as-life within the trainee is proven out as he/she learns to empathize, relate compassionately, lead with understanding, confront lovingly but firmly, and guide the counselee in the application of God's truth to daily living. TID is a hands-on learning of what it means to 'lay one's life down' for another."

We learned quickly that the basis of Jesus' Great Commission was to be our goal within the VCL outreach ministry. VCL International had a three-fold vision based on the Great Commission given to us in Matthew 28:18-20:
1. providing Biblical discipleship counseling
2. training Biblical counselors, and
3. establishing Biblical counseling centers

This last one, establishing Biblical counseling centers, really got my attention. How great it would be to establish a counseling center in a church in Evergreen, Colorado near Bill and Sally Childs' ranch!

I also learned a surprising fact about the Great Commission: Jesus said in *Matthew 28:19-20, ...go therefore and make disciples of all the nations, baptizing them in the name of the Father and of the Son and of the Holy Spirit, teaching them to observe all things that I have commanded you; and lo, I am with you always, even to the end of the age.*

Jesus was not applying an *addition* concept where one disciple leads one other person to Christ; He was applying a *multiplication* concept: we lead one person to Christ each year and then we disciple that one to win and disciple another one each year.

The chart below shows the results of this:

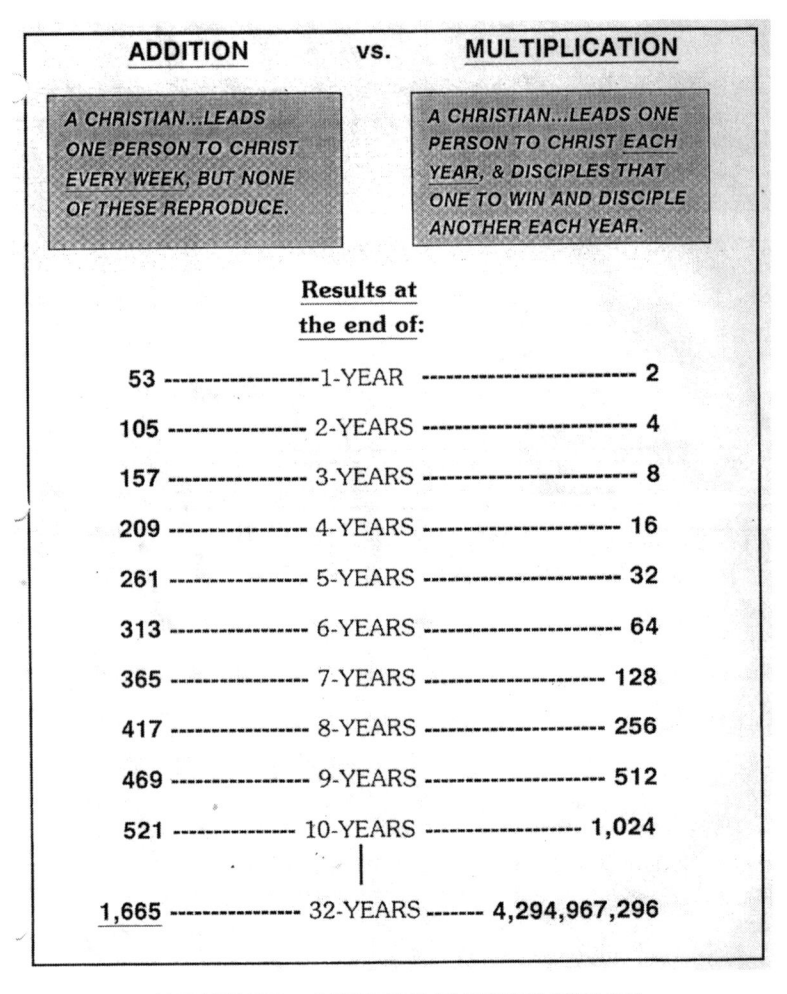

ADDITION vs. MULTIPLICATION

ADDITION	MULTIPLICATION
A CHRISTIAN...LEADS ONE PERSON TO CHRIST EVERY WEEK, BUT NONE OF THESE REPRODUCE.	A CHRISTIAN...LEADS ONE PERSON TO CHRIST EACH YEAR, & DISCIPLES THAT ONE TO WIN AND DISCIPLE ANOTHER EACH YEAR.

Results at the end of:

Addition	Years	Multiplication
53	1-YEAR	2
105	2-YEARS	4
157	3-YEARS	8
209	4-YEARS	16
261	5-YEARS	32
313	6-YEARS	64
365	7-YEARS	128
417	8-YEARS	256
469	9-YEARS	512
521	10-YEARS	1,024
1,665	32-YEARS	4,294,967,296

ADDITION vs MULTIPLICATION CHART

So You Wanna Be a Legend. So Did I.

To again quote from the TID Workbook in reference to this chart:

"We mention all this to encourage you as a TID trainee to keep <u>discipling</u> as a key part of our vision for counseling. We are not, and hope that you will not be, committed simply to 'helping hurting people' noble as that might be. Ask God for a greater, more far reaching vision; one that sees renewed men and women reproducing themselves spiritually in the lives of others, who in turn do the same to others, ad infinitum. This is the tone of the New Testament and the KEY ELEMENT in the Great Commission."

That theme, "...renewed men and women reproducing themselves spiritually in the lives of others, who in turn do the same to others, ad infinitum" was the focus of every aspect of the TID training. We heard it every day in every teaching for eight months. I could look back on my life and see this theme manifested a number of times, first by my Flagstaff, Arizona mentor, Gary Milton. Gary invested himself in my life for a number of difficult years which impacted me spiritually. Gary's love for the Lord was an attribute that I unknowingly copied. When Jesus became real to me I did my best to pass on that relationship to others, my family first, then the students God planted around me, ad infinitum.

My son Steve was a Christian missionary for seventeen years in Venezuela. Only God knows how many lives Steve impacted. I have no doubts that some of Steve's spiritual reproductions are in turn reproducing themselves in Venezuela today.

My cousin Paul Hicks, a dentist in Prescott, Arizona was touched by God at a Fellowship of Christian Athletes Conference in Prescott. Paul attended only because I invited him. Paul was "doing me a favor." Paul trusted in Jesus and passed on that relationship to any number of his dental patients as well as some in his family.

Jared Hamilton, the former Sterling College baseball player whom, I recruited in Barcelona, Spain during the 1992 Olympics had an opportunity to introduce Luis Salazar, an SC teammate to his Lord and Savior Jesus Christ.

As I write, Jared is the Head Baseball Coach at Sterling College. I know he is reproducing himself spiritually in some of his baseball players. And on it goes. Ad infinitum.

Nancy and I both needed the training in the TID discipleship area of emphasis. We felt we had a pretty good handle on the area of counseling; discipleship was a whole new ball game. Discipleship requires we have our own personal priorities in scriptual order. We needed much help in doing so. TID was geared to show us where we could get that help.

The TID training methodically drilled into us the understanding that doing the work of God apart from the enabling power of the Spirit of God was asking the impossible. We were constantly encouraged to seek the Holy Spirit's help through a disciplined prayer life which was necessary to stay in communication with God.

Just as it was necessary for us to have a mentor during our initial VCL training, our TID training was even more demanding and a mentor was invaluable to help provide accountability for the difficult tasks we were asked to undertake.

I was provided with two mentors. My old buddy Jack Tesch was still around to work me over. To keep Jack and me in line I was given Howard King. Both Jack and Howard were mature Christians who "gave their lives away" by serving others. The three of us developed a close relationship during our time together.

Nancy and Diane Kazenski continued their close relationship which began in VCL.

In April of 1999 Nancy and I finished our TID training. We were both chomping at the bit, anxious to get to Evergreen, Colorado to find a church and start a Counseling Center. At least I was chomping at the bit.

Nancy, always the cautious one, was not so sure that Evergreen was where we should focus all our efforts. Evergreen, Colorado was an up-scale community; it was expensive to live there. Nancy knew we would need to raise quite a bit more support as most of our ready cash had dwindled. Nancy told me in no uncertain terms that we could not afford to live in Evergreen, Colorado. We would need a steady income. I did not have any good arguments to debate her.

But, where could we go? We knew of several churches in the Phoenix area who were interested in establishing Counseling Centers. A few even had openings for assistant pastors but a seminary degree was needed. That let me out.

For some reason God just did not open any of those doors. There was one door which had been open since we left Sterling, Kansas. It had remained open for the past one and a half years. God was leading Nancy and me back to Sterling, Kansas.

We came back to Sterling in May of 1999. God richly blessed Nancy and me in our time back. I taught the basic Victorious Christian Living lessons in two different churches. I had the privilege of counseling/discipling a number of young Sterling College men. Several of these young men were struggling with paying homage to the same worldly gods that I struggled with for most of my life. I pray that I was able to give them a glimpse of what true significance is.

I currently work as a para-educator at our Sterling Public Grade School. I work with kindergarten through sixth grade "special needs" children. It is a job I sincerely love; especially the kindergarten children. Their daily hugs serve to remind me of Christ's unconditional love for His children. In addition to working with special needs kids, I work part time for Sterling College observing and critiquing student teachers in their various schools.

For the past six years Nancy has worked for Sterling College. She is Assistant to The Dean of The Education Department. She also teaches classes in "Field Experience" to freshman Education students. Her work with college ladies gives her opportunities to continue her counseling ministry.

Even though I did not get my Counseling Center in Evergreen, Colorado I am fully aware that God continues His work in me. He has made me realize the significance found in Him is an eternal significance. I have truely found *"..the Peace of God which passes all understanding." Philippians 4:7.*

It Has Been a Great Ride
Legend or Legacy?

My purpose in writing this book is to teach my children, my grandchildren, and others who read this book how gracious God is to those who recognize and acknowledge His sovereignty in their lives. God loves us all so much that He will use His mighty power to reach us in some strange ways. May this book be one of those ways.

I thought that by being good most of the time that I was o.k. That I someday would go to be with God based on my self-righteousness. That's not the way it works. God tells us the only way to get to Him is through a relationship with Jesus Christ.

Even after my salvation in 1974, it took me years to understand the magnitude of God's grace. It was not until Nancy and I attended Victorious Christian Living International from 1997 to 1999 that it all came together for me. I began to understand how God used people and circumstances in my life for His good. He has always been in control. I praise Him for that.

My VCL counselor, Jack Tesch, pointed out to me that God says in *Jeremiah 28:11-14* that He planned good things for my future, that His plans would someday bring me joy and peace. They have.

Jack, being a former Catholic priest, reminded me of my youthful study of Catholic catechism while I attended St. Patrick's Grade School in Bisbee, Arizona. Those nuns and priests planted seeds of respect and awe for God that would blossom someday into the knowledge that I could not get to God except through a trust in Jesus Christ.

As I mulled over my conversations with Jack, I recalled many more seeds planted by God: my high school football buddy, Bill Monahan on his knees praying, the car radio announcer suddenly mentioning Tucson High School football coach Jason "Red" Greer in a Christian context, my Carmel High School coaching partner Jason Harbert talking about God while on a church youth group ski trip, former UCLA All America Don Moomaw telling about his work with the Fellowship of Christian Athletes and his commitment to Jesus Christ, my dear friend Gary Milton leading Flagstaff High FCA Bible studies and being there when I needed him.

The VCL teaching that "the truest things about me are what God says about me" (1 Cor. 4:3-4) had a huge impact on my understanding of my self concept. A pastor I sat under for several years kept pounding home to his congregation that we were all "sinners." While that is true, VCL taught me that "we are saints who sometimes sin"; in God's eyes I am a saint! Wow! "Saint Hadley"! That has a much better ring to it than "Hadley Hicks...legend"!

As we studied these truths from God's Word at VCL it became clear to me that I want to be remembered by my family as more than a "Bisbee High School legend, a great college athlete or a great coach." I want my family to remember me as God sees me. I want my family to understand how He used people and evants all throughout my life to show me His love. I want my family to understand that what God did for me, He can do for them and more.

I want my family to understand what I learned from one of Dr. David Jeremiah's teachings:

> Psalm 90:17. *And let the beauty of the Lord our God be upon us, And establish the work of our hands for us; Yes, establish the work of our hands.*

Dr. Jeremiah taught that this verse implies God's <u>delight</u>, <u>approval,</u> and <u>favor</u> is seen in the phrase *the beauty of the Lord;* he taught that the phrase, *establish the work of our hands* implies that <u>by God's grace</u> one's life can have <u>value</u>, <u>significance</u>, and <u>meaning</u>. (see Preface)

I want my family and other readers to understand that they don't have to strive for significance in worldly pursuits as I did. A simple, yet profound relationship with Jesus Christ is all one needs.

Recently I read a book by Chuck Stecker, **Men of HONOR; Women of VIRTUE.** In this book Chuck Stecker wrote a chapter which spoke volumes to me. The chapter was titled *Legacy or Just Another Legend?* Stecker said what I want to say so much better than I ever could, "We live in a world that talks all the time about legacies but in reality focuses on legends. <u>Legends are made by the things people do and the stories that are told about them. A legacy, however, is established by **who we are**--the fiber and fabric that's passed on to future generations.</u> (emphasis mine.hh)

Chuck Stecker said that Psalm 78:5-7 are his "Legacy Verses." I don't think he would mind if I claim these verses as mine also:

Psalm 78:5-7
For He established a testimony in Jacob, and appointed a law in Israel which He commanded our fathers, that they should make them known to their children; That the generations to come might know them; The children who would be born, that they may arise and declare them to their children, that they may set their hope in God, and not forget the works of God, but keep his commandments.

The MacArthur Study Bible comments on these verses saying, "This psalm was written to teach the children how gracious God has been in the past <u>in spite of their ancestors' rebellion and ingratitude....</u>" (emphasis mine.hh).

As Chuck Stecker said, "This is what it means to leave a godly legacy!"

My prayer for my family and future generations of my family is that they will trust, remember and obey the living God; that they will understand and believe that a meaningful, eternal significance is only found through a personal relationship with Jesus Christ. That is <u>The Godly Legacy</u> I hope I will have left for them.

Epilogue

The following are some thoughts I had as I wrote various sections of this book. At the time I did not feel comfortable adding these thoughts as the flow of the particular sections was not conducive to writing the following:

My Son Mike

My Hero

Mike was born in Carmel, California on November 19, 1959.

He was a diabetic from his freshman year 1974 at Flagstaff High School until his death December 10, 2006 at his home in Inman, Kansas.

I praise God that He allowed Nancy and our family get to know and love Mike and his family. God brought us to Sterling from Sioux Falls, South Dakota for perhaps Mike's most difficult years; difficult only because the diabetes was beginning to take a horrible toll on his life.

In retrospect I can see how God's timing was once again for the best. We were here along with Jean, Michael and Taylor, Mike's immediate family. We could be close when we were needed the most.

Over the years Mike went from an athletic young man of 180 pounds to a very heavy man of at times close to 300 pounds. Diabetes and the steroids he had to take after his kidney transplant completely tore his body apart. As one of Mike's former Sterling College football teammates said, "Mike is a wonderful person in a horrible body."

Only God knows the many prayers I offered on Mike's behalf. I went to as many of his Inman High School games as I possibly could. At these games I prayed the most fervently. It was especially hard for me to see Mike labor to walk, sometimes jog, from the Inman High dugout to the third base coaches' box. How I hurt for him. The effort to just walk was taxing and painful to him.

I prayed that Mike would not have a diabetic seizure during a ball game.

He did have a seizure one time just before a baseball game started. Sadly it happened in sight of Mike's son, Michael as Michael was warming up to pitch.

An ambulance was called, paramedics ministered to Mike and he returned for the last several innings of the game.

God only knows the trauma that caused young Michael, not to mention the embarrassment it caused Mike.

I was not surprised when Jean called our home that Sunday evening December 10, 2006 to tell us Mike was taken to Hutchinson Hospital and he died in the ambulance on the way to the hospital. I was shocked, yes, but not surprised. We all knew, including Mike, that he could go to be with the Lord at any time.

I praised God that He took Mike the way He did. He was home with those he loved the most. Mike, Jean, Michael and Taylor had just watched their favorite team, the Denver *Broncos* play on TV. After the game Taylor went outside to play basketball with some buddies. Michael noticed Mike displaying familiar symptoms of a seizure and called his mother's attention to Mike. Jean called the paramedics as she had done too many times in the past. His heart gave out shortly after being placed in the ambulance.

There are a few days each school year when I don't feel well, when I'd rather just stay home and not got to school. Mike felt that way every day. I can only imagine how difficult it was for him to get his ponderous body out of bed, shower and dress for school, day after day after day. Three times per week, four hours each time, Jean had to hook him to a home dialysis machine. Often this occured late evenings, early mornings depending on Mike's athletic schedule.

Yet, those who worked with Mike at school, the students he mingled among all gave testimony to Mike's humor and his loving attitude. He was one who always offered encouragement when someone was discouraged.

Inman businessman, Bill Maurer called Mike "a special guy, caring, upbeat, a positive person, always there when someone needed help. We were good friends. Those who knew Mike were very lucky."

Steve Sell, Sports Editor for The McPherson, Kansas *Sentinel* Newspaper had these comments to make about Mike:

"...having been on the scene in this area for 28 years, we can unabashedly say that Inman's Mike Hicks was one of our all-time favorites....he never had a bad word to say about his team after a loss. He more often than not gave all the praise to the opposition for being the better team that particular game...we also had the opportunity to talk with him in the summer when his son, Michael, played for the McPherson American Legion baseball team. He never came out and said it but coaching his son in baseball during his son's high school days was one of Mike's greatest thrills."

Sell quoted long time Inman Athletic Director and coach Russ Goering saying, "The thing about Mike was he always had everything in the right perspective. Winning was important, but losing wasn't a tragedy. It was always about the kids, and that's a lesson that all of us that teach or coach can learn. Our main responsibility is to the kids."

Sports Editor Sill quoted Mike's assistant baseball coach and long time friend, Joe Pfannenstiel as saying that he remembered Mike for his sense of humor. "Mike could cut the tension in the room," Pfannenstiel said. "No matter the situation, he could always make people laugh."

Joe Pfannenstiel also said of Mike that he continued to coach and teach for many years despite his health problems. "He could have complained," Pfannenstiel said, "He certainly could have, but he didn't."

Fittingly the Memorial Service for Mike was held in the Inman High School Gymnasium. Both sides of the gym were packed with students, former students, teachers and friends, all to honor a man who was loved and respected for his 23 years of commitment to the kids of Inman, Kansas.

Nobody respected Mike Hicks for his courage in the face of such odds any more than I did. Mike was my hero.

Danny Holman

In July of 1996 my good friend and former co-football coach at Carmel High School in Carmel, California, Dick Lawitzke sent me newspaper articles on the death of Danny Holman. They saddened me greatly; not so much because Danny had died at the early age of 51 but because of Danny's life during his last years.

I can't speculate on the spiritual condition of Danny Holman's heart at the time of his death. That is strictly between between Danny and God. What brings me much sadness is what some of Danny's friends are quoted as saying at the time.

Newspaper articles say Danny was alone when he died.

His second wife of just a short two years died in 1994. His mother died in 1995. A few articles said that Danny had a daughter, Dina Lori Holman of Monterey, California; no age was given. Danny's brother Jamie lived in Sparks, Nevada at the time. His sister Victoria Holman lived in Carmel.

The Monterey Peninsula *Herald* columnist Scott A. Brown wrote a tribute to Danny under the headline, *Friends remember former CHS grid star as "Prince of Carmel."*

Here is what part of the tribute said:

"According to friends, Mr. Holman lived by the philosophy, 'If it ain't fun, don't do it.' In keeping with that theme, an announcement at the front door of Carmel's *Chez Christian* Restaurant did not read 'Closed for Wake', but exclaimed, 'In memory of Danny Holman--Party Tonight!' "

Continuing, the article stated, "A man drank from a carafe labeled *'In memory of Danny. A glass of Wine,'* and raised it heavenward saying, 'The Prince of Carmel has died. He owned this town."

All the articles I read made mention to Danny's last years. He made his career as a bartender in taverns in and around Carmel; he caddied for his friends at Pebble Beach Golf Links; he made annual trips to Wales and Scotland to play famous golf courses; Danny met his second wife Carmen on one of his trips to Zurich, Switzerland.

As Danny's friends exited *Chez Christian* Restaurant on the Monday night of their party honoring Danny, they signed a label of a wine bottle in tribute to him. One man reflected for a moment before writing, "Bet on No. 2 in the sixth at Pearly Gates Fields for me, Danny." No mention of God. No mention of prayer for Danny's daughter. No church memorial service mentioned. No buriel service mentioned. Just friends drinking to his memory. I was so grieved to read those articles. Danny Holman died alone.

Marital Priorities A Must

A VCL teaching that I should mention is the God designed order for successful Godly families. God's order of priorities is a must for the family. That was where I messed up in my marriage with Joan. Because I had God's priority out of order we went through the sin of divorce.

This is God's Priority : This Was My Priority:

1. God
2. Spouse
3. Children
4. Occupation

1. Children
2. God
3. Coaching
4. Joan

Even after I was saved in 1974 the only change I made, or tried to make, was to move God up to number one tied with Children; Coaching ran a close number two; Joan was third.

VCL and most notably my trainer Jack Tesch showed me how having an order other than God's order threw families out of whack; that is why divorce is so prevalent today. This is a simple truth; it is found throughout Scripture: If anything replaces God as number one in our lives it is idolatry, even in marriage.

The "Marriage Pyramid" is also a simple truth that if left out of a marriage can cause a marriage to flounder.

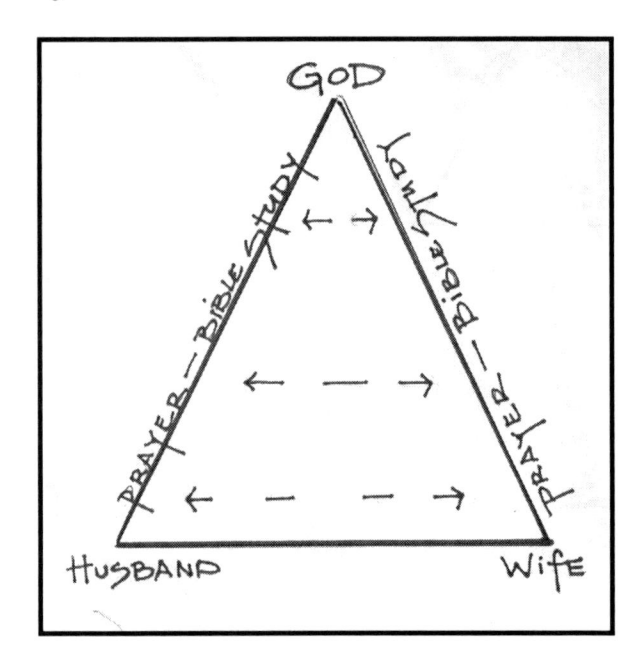

As this pyramid shows, the closer we get to God through Bible study and prayer, the closer we draw to each other.

Who I Am in Christ

VCL calls these 100 Biblical truths "1-a-day vitamins". Take one per day and meditate on it all day. They are great for one's spiritual health.

WHO I AM as a New Creation IN CHRIST

1. I am the salt of the earth (Matthew 5:13).
2. I am the light of the world (Matthew 5:14).
3. I am a child of God (John 1:12).
4. I am not coming into judgment, but have passed out of death into life (John 5:24).
5. I am secure in Christ (John 10:27-29).
6. I am given peace (John 14:27).
7. I am a branch in Christ the Vine (John 15:5).
8. I am Christ's friend (John 15:15).
9. I am chosen and appointed by Christ to bear His fruit (John 15:16).
10. I am kept from the evil one (John 17:15).
11. I am in God the Father and Jesus the Son (John 17:21).
12. I am loved by the Father as much as He loves Jesus (John 17:23).
13. I am God's gift to Christ (John 17:24).
14. I am justified by faith and at peace with God (Romans 5:1).
15. I am a recipient of God's grace (Romans 5:2).
16. I am reconciled to God through the death of Jesus (Romans 5:10).
17. I am being saved by the life of Jesus (Romans 5:10).
18. I am reigning in life through Jesus Christ (Romans 5:17).
19. I am baptized into Christ's death (Romans 6:3).
20. I am raised to walk in newness of life (Romans 6:4).
21. I am united with Christ in His death and resurrection (Romans 6:5).
22. I am freed from sin (Romans 6:7).
23. I am dead to sin, but alive to God in Christ Jesus (Romans 6:11).
24. I am not under the law, but under grace (Romans 6:14).
25. I am a slave of righteousness, having been freed from sin (Romans 6:18).
26. I am enslaved to God (Romans 6:22).
27. I am given eternal life (Romans 6:23).
28. I am free from condemnation (Romans 8:1).
29. I am free from the law of sin and death (Romans 8:2).
30. I am in the Spirit, not in the flesh (Romans 8:9).
31. I am indwelt by the Holy Spirit (Romans 8:11).
32. I am not obligated to live according to the flesh (Romans 8:12).
33. I am an heir with Christ (Romans 8:17).
34. I am a saint (Romans 8:27).
35. I am certain that God causes all things to work together for good (Romans 8:28).
36. I am being conformed to the image of Christ (Romans 8:29).
37. I am called, justified, and glorified (Romans 8:30).
38. I am more than a conqueror through Christ (Romans 8:37).
39. I am inseparable from the love of Christ (Romans 8:38-39).
40. I am accepted by Christ to the glory of God (Romans 15:7).
41. I am in Christ Jesus (1 Corinthians 1:30).
42. I am the recipient of God's Spirit (1 Corinthians 2:12).
43. I am a possessor of the mind of Christ (1 Corinthians 2:16).
44. I am washed and sanctified (1 Corinthians 6:11).
45. I am joined (united) to the Lord and am one spirit with Him (1 Corinthians 6:17).
46. I am God's temple (1 Corinthians 6:19).
47. I am bought with a price (1 Corinthians 6:20).
48. I am always provided with a way of escape from temptation (1 Corinthians 10:13).
49. I am a member of the body of Christ (1 Corinthians 12:27).
50. I am triumphant in Christ (2 Corinthians 2:14).

51. I am a sweet aroma manifesting the knowledge of Him (2 Corinthians 2:14).
52. I am adequate in Christ (2 Corinthians 3:5).
53. I am being renewed day by day (2 Corinthians 4:16).
54. I am a new creation in Christ (2 Corinthians 5:17).
55. I am reconciled to God and given the ministry of reconciliation (2 Corinthians 5:18).
56. I am an ambassador for Christ (2 Corinthians 5:20).
57. I am righteous (2 Corinthians 5:21).
58. I am a son or daughter of God (2 Corinthians 6:18).
59. I am strongest when I am weakest (2 Corinthians 12:10).
60. I am crucified with Christ and Christ lives in me (Galatians 2:20).
61. I am redeemed from the curse of the Law (Galatians 3:13).
62. I am blessed with every spiritual blessing in Christ (Ephesians 1:3).
63. I am chosen in Christ and holy and blameless before Him (Ephesians 1:4).
64. I am adopted as God's child (Ephesians 1:5).
65. I am redeemed (Ephesians 1:7).
66. I am forgiven of all my sins (Ephesians 1:7).
67. I am sealed with the Holy Spirit of promise (Eph. 1:13).
68. I am made alive with Christ (Ephesians 2:5).
69. I am raised up and seated in heavenly places with Christ (Ephesians 2:6).
70. I am God's workmanship, created in Christ Jesus for good works (Ephesians 2:10).
71. I am brought to God through the blood of Christ (Ephesians 2:13).
72. I am a fellow citizen with the saints in God's household (Ephesians 2:19).
73. I am built upon the foundation of the apostles and Christ the cornerstone (Ephesians 2:20).
74. I am light in the Lord (Ephesians 5:8).
75. I am confident that He will perfect His work in me (Philippians 1:6).
76. I am a citizen of Heaven (Philippians 3:20).
77. I am eagerly awaiting the return of my Savior (Philippians 3:20).
78. I am able to do all things through Christ who strengthens me (Philippians 4:13).
79. I am delivered from the domain of darkness (Colossians 1:13).
80. I am transferred to the kingdom of Christ (Colossians 1:13).
81. I am firmly rooted in Christ (Colossians 2:7).
82. I am complete in Christ (Colossians 2:10).
83. I am hidden with Christ in God (Colossians 3:3).
84. I am to be revealed in glory with Christ, who is my life (Colossians 3:4).
85. I am chosen by God (1 Thessalonians 1:4).
86. I am delivered from the wrath to come (1 Thessalonians 1:10).
87. I am a child of light and of the day (1 Thessalonians 5:5).
88. I am given eternal comfort and good hope (2 Thessalonians 2:16).
89. I am strengthened and protected from the evil one (2 Thessalonians 3:3).
90. I am richly supplied with all things to enjoy (1 Timothy 6:17).
91. I am given a spirit of power and love and discipline (2 Timothy 1:7).
92. I am saved by His mercy (Titus 3:5).
93. I am holy and a partaker of a heavenly calling (Hebrews 3:1).
94. I am forever able to draw near to God (Hebrews 7:25).
95. I am born again (1 Peter 1:23).
96. I am a royal priest, God's own possession (1 Peter 2:9).
97. I am an alien and stranger in the world (1 Peter 2:11).
98. I am a partaker of God's divine nature (2 Peter 1:4).
99. I am granted everything pertaining to life and godliness (2 Peter 1:3).
100. I am cleansed from all sin by the blood of Jesus (1 John 1:7).

Copyright © 1994 Victorious Christian Living International, Inc. All Rights Reserved.

My Thanks To......

The many, many students whom God planted with me throughout my teaching-coaching career. You have given me many rich memories. I wish I could mention all of you.

To the parents who loaned me their kids for a time, I thank you and appreciate your trust. God blessed me through you.

The teachers and coaches I was associated with who were instrumental in helping to shape my life. I appreciate every one of you.

Jim Brink, Arizona State Baseball Historian and John Jacobs, my ASU Baseball teammate for help with almost lost memories.

My Bisbee friend Perry Watkins for his expertise with restoring old photographs.

My cousin Taylor Hicks and his wife Marsha for the picture of the Prescott, Arizona "Thumb Butte."

My dear friend Lois Harbert for providing needed encouragement.

All the Carmel High School Alumni led by my teaching partner, Pat Sipple. Your emails and phone calls were welcome and helpful. Former CHS student and current CHS *Padre* Coach Jeff Wright who did research including getting permission for the use of "The Lone Cypress", and one of the best *Padres* of them all, Bill Stowers who has been great encouragement to me through all the years of writing this book. I am so grateful to all of you.

Dick Lawitzke, former Carmel High School line coach, who helped me remember so much. Dick, you made your point!

To my Prescott High School connection: Les Fenderson, Eddie Villiborghi, and Kelly Cordes. Thanks, guys!

Vince Lopez, former Flagstaff High School outstanding center on my first FHS team, for the research he provided; likewise Nick Lynn, former FHS quarterback who was valuable in getting the FHS football program back on the winning track. His research is appreciated.

Larry Gray, my Flagstaff High co-coach. Larry epitomizes what an assistant coach should have: Loyalty

Bob and Diane Young, whose Godly friendship for many years has been encouraging to Nancy and me. Thank you, Diane, for answering my many questions.

Our friend, Pauline May, for her continued encouragement to "finish the book".

Terry Robson, Sterling Public Schools' computer technician. Terry has put up with my many questions for years. Thanks for your time, expertise and patience, Terry.

Professor Judith Best, Sterling College Education Department, for her painstaking, time consuming, proofreading and encouragement.

Dr. David Jeremiah for his solid Biblical teaching on Christian Radio. His teachings have encouraged me.

Sterling College art student Taren Morse for the cover design.

My wife, Nancy for financial advice and administrative assistance.

West Bow Press Publishing Consultants. True professionals. Thank you.

For Information:

VCL International,
14900 W. Van Buren
Building G
Goodyear, Arizona
Phone: 602-428-2164

Fellowship of Christian Athletes
World Headquarters
8701 Leeds Road
Kansas City, MO 64129
(816)-921-0909
fca@fca.org

Hadley Hicks
808 N. Sherwood
Sterling, KS 67579
hadley2@embarqmail.com